Random House
Webster's

# Rhyming Dictionary

# Random House Webster's Rhyming Dictionary

Random House Reference
New York Toronto London Sydney Auckland

 Published in the United States by Random House Reference, an imprint of The Random House Information Group, a division of Random House, Inc., New York, and simultaneously in Canada by Random House of Canada Limited, Toronto.



An earlier edition of this work was published in 1999 as *The Random House Webster's Pocket Rhyming Dictionary* by Random House Reference, an imprint of The Random House Information Group, a division of Random House, Inc.

Please address inquiries about electronic licensing of any products for use on a network, in software, or on CD-ROM to the Subsidiary Rights Department, Random House Information Group, fax 212-572-6003.

This book is available at special discounts for bulk purchases for sales promotions or premiums. Special editions, including personalized covers, excerpts of existing books, and corporate imprints, can be created in large quantities for special needs. For more information, write to Random House, Inc., Special Markets/Premium Sales, 1745 Broadway, MD 6-2, New York, NY 10019 or e-mail *specialmarkets@randomhouse.com*

Visit the Random House Reference Web site: *www.randomwords.com*

Printed in the United States of America

10 9 8 7 6 5 4 3 2 1

Library of Congress Cataloging in Publication Data is available.

ISBN: 978-1-4000-0716-5

2008 Random House, Inc. Edition

# Contents

# Preface

The *Random House Webster's Rhyming Dictionary* helps you find the perfect rhyme every time. It offers more than 60,000 words in an easy-to-use format. The rhyming words incorporate common vocabulary, phrases, and proper names including people and places, both real and fictional.

This dictionary has three sections. Rhyming words for the final syllable are given in one section, rhymes for the final two syllables in a second section, and rhymes for the final three syllables in the last section. These rhyming words have been placed under the most common spelling for a particular sound, and within each entry the words are listed in alphabetical order and grouped according to length, from least to greatest number of syllables. Abundant cross references will help you find rhymes for different spellings of the same sound. Pronunciations are given for syllables that can be pronounced in more than one way.

In the back of the dictionary you'll find a glossary of poetic terms that serves as a handy guide to rhyming patterns.

Whenever the muse strikes, be sure to pick up *Random House Webster's Rhyming Dictionary!*

# Pronunciation Key

**a** act, bat
**ā** able, cape
**â** air, dare
**ä** art, calm

**b** back, rub
**ch** chief, beach
**d** do, bed

**e** ebb, set
**ē** equal, bee

**f** fit, puff
**g** give, beg
**h** hit, hear

**i** if, big
**ī** ice, bite

**j** just, edge
**k** kept, make
**l** low, all

**m** my, him
**n** now, on
**N** as in French **bon** (bôN) [used to indicate that the preceding vowel is nasalized. Four such vowels are found in French: **un bon vin blanc** (œn bôn van blän)]
**ng** sing, England

**o** box, hot
**ō** over, no
**ô** order, ball
**oi** oil, joy

**o͝o** book, put
**o͞o** ooze, rule
**ou** out, loud
**p** page, stop
**r** read, cry
**s** see, miss
**sh** shoe, push
**t** ten, bit
**th** thin, path
**t͟h** that, other

**u** up, love
**yo͞o** use, cute
**û** urge, burn

**v** voice, live
**w** west, away
**y** yes, young
**z** zeal, lazy, those
**zh** vision, measure

**ə** occurs only in unaccented syllables and indicates the sound of
a *in* along
e *in* system
i *in* easily
o *in* gallop
u *in* circus

$^{ə}$ used between *i* and *r* and between *ou* and *r* to show triphthongal quality, as in *fire* (fī$^{ə}$r), *hour* (ou$^{ə}$r)

# One-Syllable Rhymes

**-a** (-ä), aah, ah, baa, bah, blah, bra, dah, droit, fa, froid, ha, ja, Kwa, la, ma, nah, pa, pah, pas, qua, Ra, schwa, shah, ska, spa, yah; à bas, Accra, aha, Allah, blah-blah, bourgeois, brava, Casbah, chamois, Chechnya, chutzpah, Degas, dolma, Dumas, éclat, état, faux pas, fella, Fermat, feta, foie gras, gaga, Galois, goombah, grandma, grandpa, ha-ha, halvah, hoo-ha, hoopla, hurrah, huzza, izba, mama, Marat, markka, Maurois, mirepoix, mudra, oompah, orgeat, quinoa, paisa, papa, pasha, pasta, patois, Poo Bah, prutah, pya, rah-rah, sang-froid, Seurat, Shema, Shoah, sola, sol-fa, supra, ta-ta, tra-la, Utah, Valois, viva, voilà, wah-wah; abaca, Abdullah, agora, ahimsa, Akita, Al Fatah, aliyah, aloha, assignat, baccarat, baklavah, blah-blah-blah, Bogotá, brouhaha, cha cha cha, Chippewa, coup d'état, Delacroix, Directoire, entrechat, feria, grandmamma, guarana, Haftarah, haniwa, Havdalah, koruna, la-di-da, Mardi Gras, Modena, moussaka, Omaha, oompah-pah, Ottawa, padishah, panama, Panama, Parashah, pas de chat, pas de trois, peau de soie, petit pois, Pietà, podesta, port de bras, Québecois, Shangri-la, tra-la-la, ulama, usquebaugh; Ali Baba, ayatollah, Caligula, cucaracha, hors de combat, je ne sais quoi, ménage à trois, res publica, utopia; exempli causa, pâté de foie gras, Tegucigalpa; exempli gratia, funiculi-funicula.

**-a** (-ā). See **-ay.**

**-aa.** See **-a.**
**-ab,** ab, bab, blab, cab, crab, dab, drab, fab, flab, gab, grab, jab, lab, Lab, Mab, nab, scab, slab, stab, tab; Ahab, backstab, bedab, confab, Joab, Moab, prefab, Punjab, Queen Mab, rehab, she-crab, Skylab, smack-dab; bafflegab, baobab, minilab, pedicab, taxicab.
**-abe,** Abe, babe, nabe; astrolabe.
**-ac.** See **-ack.**
**-ace,** ace, base, bass, brace, case, chase, dace, face, grace, Grace, lace, mace, Mace, pace, place, plaice, race, space, Thrace, trace, vase; abase, air space, Alsace, apace, backspace, best-case, birthplace, blackface, boldface, bookcase, bootlace, braincase, briefcase, crankcase, cyclase, debase, deface, disgrace, displace, dogface, doughface, efface, embrace, emplace, encase, enchase, enlace, erase, footpace, footrace, freebase, grimace, gyrase, hard case, hard-case, headspace, horse race, hydrase, kinase, lactase, lightface, lipase, lyase, maltase, millrace, milreis, misplace, notecase, null-space, nutcase, outface, outpace, outrace, paleface, rat race, reface, replace, retrace, scapegrace, shoelace, showcase, showplace, slipcase, smearcase, someplace, staircase, suitcase, test case, typeface, ukase, unbrace, uncase, unlace, watchcase, wheelbase, wheyface, whiteface, workplace, worst-case; about-face, aerospace, anelace, anyplace, basket case, boniface, bouillabaisse, breathing space, carapace, commonplace, contrabass, cyberspace, database, double bass, everyplace, figured bass, firebase, fireplace, funnyface, hiding place, hydrolase, idocrase, inner space, interface, interlace, interspace, invertase, lowercase, marketplace, outer space, oxidase, pillowcase, reductase, resting place, Samothrace, single-space,

steeplechase, thorough bass, thorough brace, trysting place; attaché case, chariot race; in medias res.

**-aced.** See **-aste.**

**-ach** (-ak). See **-ack.**

**-ach** (-ach). See **-atch.**

**-ache** (-āk). See **-ake.**

**-ache** (-ash). See **-ash.**

**-acht** (-ät). See **-ot.**

**-ack,** back, black, cack, clack, claque, crack, hack, flack, flak, hack, jack, Jack, knack, lac, lack, lakh, mac, Mac, pack, plack, plaque, quack, rack, sac, sack, sacque, shack, slack, smack, snack, stack, tach, tack, thwack, track, Wac, wack, whack, wrack, yak; aback, ack-ack, alack, amtrac, Anzac, Arak, arrack, attack, backpack, backtrack, bareback, bivouac, blackjack, blue-black, bookrack, bootblack, bootjack, bushwhack, buyback, callback, calpac, carjack, champak, cheap-jack, coatrack, cognac, comeback, Cossack, cutback, crookback, drawback, fallback, fastback, fast track, fatback, feedback, flapjack, flashback, fullback, gimcrack, giveback, gopak, greywacke, greenback, gripsack, halfback, half-track, hardback, hardtack, hatchback, haystack, hijack, hogback, hopsack, horseback, humpback, hunchback, Iraq, jam-pack, jet-black, jimcrack, kayak, Kazakh, kickback, knapsack, knickknack, Kodak, kulak, laidback, lampblack, leaseback, linac, macaque, Meshach, Micmac, mossback, muntjac, Muzak, notchback, offtrack, one-track, outback, payback, pitch-black, playback, Prozac, pullback, racetrack, ransack, repack, restack, rollback, roorback, rucksack, sad sack, sérac, setback, Shadrach, shellac, shoeblack, shoepac, sidetrack, six-pack, skipjack, skyjack, slapjack, Slovak, softback, smokestack, snapback, sumac, swayback, switchback, tarmac, throwback, thumbtack, ticktack, tieback, tie tack, unpack, wetback, wet pack, wingback, wisecrack, wolf pack, woolpack, woolsack, yashmak, zweiback; almanac, amberjack, amphibrach, anorak, antiblack, applejack, Arawak, Armagnac, back-to-back, bivouac, black-on-black, brainiac, bric-a-brac, Cadillac, camelback, canvasback, cardiac, carryback, celiac, crackerjack, cul-de-sac, daddy track, diamondback, Fond du Lac, Frontenac, gunnysack, Hackensack, hackmatack, haversack, huckaback, Kodiac, iliac, ipecac, leatherback, leather jack, lumberjack, maniac, medevac, Merrimack, mommy track, multipack, multitrack, natterjack, off-the-rack, paperback, Pasternak, pickaback, piggyback, Pontiac, postattack, quarterback, razorback, retropack, running back, Sarawak, silverback, single-track, steeplejack, stickleback, Syriac, tamarack, tenure-track, umiak, Union Jack, yellow jack, zodiac; Adirondack, ammoniac, amnesiac, biofeedback, celeriac, counterattack, demoniac, elegiac, insomniac, Monterey Jack, paranoiac, simoniac, symposiac; aphrodisiac, dipsomaniac, egomaniac, hemophiliac, hypochondriac, kleptomaniac, monomaniac, necrophiliac, nymphomaniac, pyromaniac, sacroiliac, sal ammoniac; megalomaniac.

**-acked.** See **-act.**

**-acks.** See **-ax.**

**-act,** act, bract, fact, pact, tact, tract; abstract, attract, class act, compact, contact, contract, coact, crookbacked, detract, didact, diffract, distract, enact, entr'acte, epact, exact, extract, humpbacked, hunchbacked, impact, infract, intact, misact, mossbacked, one-act, outact, playact, protract, react, redact, refract, retract, subtract, swaybacked, transact, unbacked, untracked; abreact, artifact, bicompact, cataract, census tract, chain-react, counteract, counterfact, cross-react, eye contact, inexact, interact, nonabstract, noncontact, nonimpact, overact, precontact, razor-backed, re-enact, retroact, riot act, saddle-backed, special act, subcompact, tesseract, underact, vacuum-packed, ventifact; autodidact, breach of contract, matter-of-fact, overreact, question of fact, semiabstract, social compact, social contract, suicide pact, sweetheart contract, underreact, ultracompact; attorney-in-fact.

Also: **-ack** + **-ed** (as in *packed, attacked,* etc.)

**-ad** (-ad), ad, add, bad, bade, brad, cad, chad, Chad, clad, dad, fad, gad, glad, grad, had, lad, mad, pad, plaid, rad, sad, scad, shad, tad; aubade, Baghdad, Belgrade, Carlsbad, caudad, comrade, Conrad, crash pad, doodad, dryad, dyad, egad, farad, footpad, forbade, gonad, granddad, heptad, hexad, keypad, launchpad, maenad, monad, mouse pad, naiad, nomad, NORAD, notepad, Pleiad, postgrad, reclad, scratch pad, Sinbad, tetrad, touchpad, trackpad, triad, unclad, yclad; aoudad, armor-clad, chiliad, deadbeat dad, Dunciad, ennead, Galahad, hebdomad, helipad, Iliad, ironclad, legal pad, Leningrad, lily pad, mediad, oread, Petrograd, Stalingrad, Trinidad, undergrad, Volgograd; olympiad, Upanishad.

**-ad** (-od). See **-od.**

**-ade,** aid, aide, bade, blade, braid, cade, clade, fade, glade, grade, hade, jade, lade, laid, made, maid, neighed, paid, raid, rayed, shade, spade, stade, staid, suede, they'd, trade, wade; abrade, afraid, aggrade, air raid, arcade, Band-Aid, barmaid, Belgrade, blockade, block trade, brake fade, bridesmaid, brigade, brocade, cascade, charade, clichéd, cockade, corrade, cross-fade, cross-trade, croupade, crusade, day-trade, degrade, dissuade, downgrade, evade, eyeshade, fair-trade, field grade, first aid, forebade, free trade, gainsaid, gambade, gem jade, glissade, grenade, handmade, handmaid, high-grade, homemade, horse-trade, housemaid, inlaid, invade, limeade, low-grade, man-made, mermaid, milkmaid, misgrade, navaid, nightshade, nonpaid, nursemaid, old maid, outlaid, parade, parkade, passade, pay grade, persuade, pervade, pesade, pomade, postpaid, prefade, prepaid, rag trade, repaid, scalade, self-made, slave trade, sleep shade, stockade, sunshade, switchblade, tirade, toadshade, tongue blade, torsade, twayblade, twice-laid, unbraid, unlade, unmade, unpaid, upbraid, upgrade, waylaid, well-made, well-paid; accolade, Adelaide, ambuscade, aquacade, autocade, balustrade, barricade, bastinade, bench-made, bigarade, Burma jade, cablelaid, camisade, cannonade, carbonnade, carriage trade, cavalcade, Centigrade, chambermaid, chiffonade, colonnade, cottonade, custom-made, dragonnade, enfilade, escalade, escapade, esplanade, everglade, foreign aid, fusillade, gallopade, gasconade, grant-in-aid, half-afraid, hearing aid, hit parade, intergrade, interstade, kitchen maid, lady's maid, legal aid, lemonade, marinade, marmalade, masquerade, mauve decade, Medicaid, meter maid, microblade, motorcade, multiblade, multigrade, oil of cade, orangeade, overlaid, palisade, panty raid, parlormaid, pasquinade, phylloclade, pilastrade, pinnigrade, plantigrade, promenade, ready-made, renegade, retrograde, Rollerblade, Roman shade, rotor blade, saltigrade, serenade, shoulder blade, stock in trade, tailor-made, taligrade, tamponade, tardigrade, teaching aid, underpaid, undismayed, union-made; biodegrade, Damascus blade, digitigrade, fanfaronade, fire brigade, harlequinade, penny arcade, rodomontade.

Also: **-ay** + **-ed** (as in *played*, etc.)

Also: **-eigh** + **-ed** (as in *weighed*, etc.)

Also: **-ey** + **-ed** (as in *preyed*, etc.)

**-ade** (-ad). See **-ad.**

**-ade** (-od). See **-od.**

**-adge,** badge, cadge, hajj, Madge.

**-afe,** chafe, safe, skeif, strafe, waif; fail-safe, unsafe, vouchsafe; bathyscaphe.

**-aff,** baff, caff, calf, chaff, daff, draff, gaff, gaffe, graph, half, laugh, quaff, raff, sclaff, staff, staph, yaff; agraffe, bar graph, behalf, carafe, chiffchaff, cross-staff, digraph, distaff, Falstaff, flagstaff, giraffe, half-staff, horselaugh, kenaf, line graph, mooncalf, outquaff, pikestaff, riffraff, tipstaff; allograph, autograph, bathyscaphe, belly laugh, better half, cenotaph, chronograph, cryptograph, epigraph, epitaph, half-and-half, homograph, lithograph, monograph, overstaff, paragraph, phonograph, photograph, pictograph, polygraph, quarterstaff, seismograph, serigraph, shandygaff, spectrograph, telegraph, understaff; actinograph, cardiograph, choreograph, ideograph, mimeograph; electrocardiograph. See also **-off.**

**-affed.** See **-aft.**

**-aft,** aft, craft, daft, draft, draught, graft, haft, kraft, laughed, raft, shaft, Taft, waft; abaft, aircraft, camshaft, crankshaft, downdraft, driveshaft, handcraft, ingraft, life raft, redraft, seacraft, skin graft, spacecraft, stagecraft, statecraft, swordcraft, updraft, witchcraft, woodcraft; allograft, fore-and-aft, handicraft, hovercraft, landing craft, needlecraft, overdraft, rivercraft, watercraft, xenograft; antiaircraft.

Also: **-aff** + **-ed** (as in *staffed*, etc.)

Also: **-aph** + **-ed** (as in *autographed*, etc.)

**-ag,** ag, bag, brag, crag, dag, drag, fag, flag, gag, hag, jag, lag, mag, nag, quag, rag, sag, scrag, shag, slag, snag, stag, swag, tag, wag, zag; airbag, barf bag, beachbag, beanbag, belt bag, brainfag, brown-bag, chinwag, dime-bag, dirtbag, dishrag, dog tag, do-rag, douche bag, fag hag, feedbag, fleabag, flight bag, grab bag, graylag, handbag, hangtag, ice bag, jet lag, kitbag, mailbag, main drag, mixed bag, name tag, oaktag, outbrag, phone tag, price tag, ragbag, ragtag, red flag, sandbag, schoolbag, scumbag, sight gag, sleazebag, sweet flag, tea bag, tote bag, washrag, wigwag, windbag, zigzag; battle flag, body bag, boil-in-bag, Brobdingnag, bullyrag, carpetbag, chew the rag, Chinese tag, ditty bag, doggy bag, dufflebag, garment bag, isopag, lally-gag, punching bag, saddle-bag, scalawag, shopping bag, shoulder bag, sleeping bag; cultural lag, overnight bag, telephone tag.

**-age** (-āj), age, cage, gage, gauge, mage, page, phage, rage, sage, stage, swage, wage; assuage, backstage, birdcage, broad-gauge, coon's age, dark age, down-stage, end stage, engage, enrage, front page, green-gage, ice age, New Age, offstage, old age, onstage, Osage, outrage, presage, rampage, restage, rib cage, road rage, roll cage, school-age, space age, Stone Age, teenage, uncage, upstage; batting cage, center stage, disengage, golden age, Iron Age, legal age, mental age, middle age, multistage, saxifrage, overage, under-age; atomic age, minimum wage.

**-age** (-ij), bridge, fridge, midge, ridge; abridge, Cambridge, drawbridge, footbridge, gall midge, pillage, presage, ullage, village; acreage, alienage, anchorage, appanage, arbi-trage, auction bridge, aver-age, beverage, biting midge, brigandage, brokerage, car-tilage, contract bridge, cov-ered bridge, flying bridge, cozenage, equipage, factorage, foliage, fuselage, harborage, hemorrhage, heritage, hermitage, leverage, lineage, mucilage, overage, parentage, parsonage, pasturage, patronage, personage, pilgrimage, porterage, privilege, pupilage, quarterage, reportage, sacrilege, sortilege, tutelage, vassalage, verbiage, vicarage; chaperonage, concubinage, suspension bridge.

**-age** (-äzh), plage; barrage, chantage, collage, corsage, dressage, fromage, frottage, garage, gavage, lavage, massage, ménage, mirage, montage, moulage, portage, potage, treillage, triage; abattage, arbitrage, badinage, balisage, bon voyage, bricolage, burelage, cabotage, camouflage, colportage, coquillage, curettage, decoupage, effleurage, empennage, enfleurage, entourage, fuselage, Hermitage, maquillage, moyenâge, persiflage, racinage, repechage, reportage, repoussage, sabotage; décolletage, espionage, photomontage; counterespionage.

**-agm.** See **-am.**

**-agne.** See **-ain.**

**-ague,** Craig, Hague, plague, vague; fainaigue, stravage; gyrovague; Bubonic plague.

**-ah.** See **-a.**

**-aid** (-ād). See **-ade.**

**-aid** (-ed). See **-ed.**

**-aif.** See **-afe.**

**-aight.** See **-ate.**

**-aign.** See **-ain.**

**-ail,** ail, ale, Baal, bael, bail, bale, brail, Braille, dale, Dale, fail, flail, frail, Gael, Gail, Gale, gale, gaol, Gayle, grail, hail, hale, jail, kale, mail, male, nail, pail, pale, quail, Quayle, rail, sail, sale, scale, shale, snail, stale, swale, tael, tail, taille, tale, they'll, trail, vail, vale, veil, wail, wale, whale, Yale; abseil, Airedale, airmail, all hail, assail, avail, bake sale, bewail, blackmail, blue whale, bobtail, broad-scale, broadtail, camail, canaille, cocktail, contrail, curtail, death-pale, derail, detail, doornail, dovetail, downscale, ducktail, e-mail, entail, exhale, fan mail, fantail, female, fishtail, folktale, foresail, foxtail, fresh gale, full-scale, gray scale, greenmail, grisaille, guardrail, Hallel, handrail, hangnail, headsail, hightail, hobnail, horsetail, impale, inhale, inwale, junk mail, keel hale, light rail, lugsail, mainsail, Mach scale, mare's tail, moon snail, oxtail, pass-fail, percale, pigtail, pintail, pinwale, presale, prevail, rattail, regale, resale, retail, ringtail, sea kale, sei whale, shirttail, slop pail, small-scale, snail mail, sperm whale, split rail, spritsail, square sail, staysail, surveil, taffrail, tag sale, telltale, third rail, thumbnail, toenail, topsail, travail, unveil, upscale, voice mail, wage scale, wash sale, wassail, whiptail, white sale, wholesale, yard sale; abigail, Abigail, altar rail, audit trail, aventail, Beaufort scale, bill of sale, Bloomingdale, bristletail, cakes and ale, Chippendale, Chisholm Trail, coffin nail, cottontail, countervail, direct mail, express mail, fairytale, farthingale, fingernail, fire sale, galingale, garage sale, ginger ale, Holy Grail, humpback whale, intervale, killer whale, martingale, monorail, montadale, nanoscale, nightingale, old wives' tale, paper trail, point-of-sale, ponytail, Richter scale, rummage sale, sliding scale, solar sail, supermale, swallowtail, tattletale, tooth and nail, triticale, union scale, vapor trail, yellowtail.

**-ails.** See **-ales.**

**-aim.** See **-ame.**

**-ain** (-ān), ain, Aisne, ane, bane, blain, brain, Cain, cane, chain, crane, Dane, deign, drain, fain, fane, feign, gain, grain, Jane, lain, lane, main, Maine, mane, pain, pane, plain, plane, rain, reign, rein, sane, seine, Shane, skein, slain, Spain, sprain, stain, strain, swain, ta'en, tain, thane, thegn, train, twain, Twain, vain, vane, vein, wain, wane, Wayne, Zane; abstain, again, air lane, airplane, amain, arcane, arraign, attain, Bahrain, biplane, birdbrain, bloodstain, brain drain, brain gain, bugbane, campaign, champagne, Champlain, checkrein, chicane, chilblain, chow mein, cinquain, cocaine, complain, constrain, contain, coxswain, cowbane, crackbrain, cross-train, demesne, deplane, detain, devein, disdain, distrain, dizain, dogbane, domain, drive train, dumb cane, Duquesne, durain, Elaine, enchain, enplane, enchain, entrain, ethane, explain, eye strain, fast lane, fleabane, floodplain, food chain, forebrain, freight train, fusain, gas main Gawain, germane, Great Dane, grosgrain, henbane, hindbrain, house-train, humane, Hussein, inane, ingrain, insane, lamebrain, left brain, lo mein, Lorraine, maintain, marchpane, membrane, methane, midbrain, migraine, montane, moraine, mortmain, mundane, murrain, obtain, octane, ordain, pertain, plain Jane, plantain, procaine, profane, propane, ptomaine, purslane, quatrain, quintain, raise Cain, refrain, regain, remain, restrain, retain, retrain, right brain, romaine, sea lane, seaplane, Sinn Fein, split-brain, sustain, tearstain, terrain, terrane, Ukraine, unchain, urbane, vervain, vicereine, villain, warplane, wave train, wolfsbane; acid rain, aeroplane, appertain, aquaplane, ascertain, ball and chain, bullet train, cell membrane, cellophane, chamberlain, Charlemagne, chatelain, chatelaine, chevrotain, counterpane, daisy chain, down the drain, entertain, featherbrain, focal plane, foreordain, frangipane, gravy train, gyroplane, high-octane, hurricane, hydroplane, inclined plane, inhumane, La Fontaine, marocain, Mary Jane, monoplane, multigrain, multilane, neutercane, Novocain, overtrain, paravane, peneplain, pollen grain, porcelain, port-wine stain, power train, preordain, rocket plane, sandhill crane, scatterbrain, souterrain, Spanish Main, sugarcane, superbrain, suzerain, take in vain, Tamerlane, terreplein, toilet-train, tramontane, urethane, wagon train, water main, weather vane, whooping crane, windowpane, yellow rain; balletomane, capital gain, Cartesian plane, castle in Spain, demimondaine, legerdemain, memory lane, public domain; Andromeda strain.

**-ain** (-en). See **-en.**

**-ainst,** 'gainst; against.

Also: **-ence** + **-ed** (as in *fenced,* etc.)

Also: **-ense** + **-ed** (as in *condensed,* etc.)

**-aint,** ain't, faint, feint, mayn't, paint, plaint, quaint, saint, taint, 'taint; acquaint, attaint, complaint, constraint, distraint, Geraint, greasepaint, inpaint, oil paint, repaint, restraint, spray paint, war paint; finger paint, head restraint, latex paint, patron saint, poster paint, self-restraint; Latter-day Saint, passive restraint, prior restraint, water-base paint.

**-aipse,** traipse; jackanapes.

Also: **-ape** + **-s** (as in *grapes,* etc.)

**-air.** See **-are.**

**-aire.** See **-are.**

**-aired,** aired, haired, laird, merde; fair-haired, impaired, long-haired, prepared, short-haired, unpaired, unshared; golden-haired, silver-haired, unimpaired, unprepared, wire-haired.

**-airn,** bairn, cairn.

**-airs.** See **-ares.**

**-aise** (-āz). See **-aze.**

**-aise** (-ez). See **-ez.**

**-ait.** See **-ate.**

**-aith,** eighth, faith, Faith, wraith; bad faith, good faith; breach of faith, interfaith.

**-aize.** See **-aze.**

**-ak.** See **-ack.**

**-ake,** ache, bake, Blake, brake, break, cake, crake, drake, Drake, fake, flake, hake, jake, Jake, lake, make, quake, rake, sake, shake, sheik, slake, snake, spake, stake, steak, strake, take, wake; air brake, awake, backache, bespake, beefcake, beefsteak, betake, canebrake, cheesecake, cheesesteak, clambake, club steak, corn crake, cornflake, cube steak, cupcake, daybreak, disc brake, drum brake, earache, earthquake, fair shake, fernbrake, fish cake, forsake, fruitcake, grubstake, hand brake, handshake, headache, heartache, heartbreak, hoecake, hotcake, housebreak, intake, jailbreak, keepsake, mandrake, milk snake, milkshake, mistake, moonquake, muckrake, namesake, newsbreak, oatcake, opaque, outbreak, outtake, pancake, partake, pound cake, prebake, remake, retake, sea quake, seedcake, Sheldrake, shortcake, snowflake, sponge cake, sweepstake, Swiss steak, teacake, toothache, uptake, windbreak, yeast cake; bellyache, coffee break, coffee cake, coral snake, double take, firebreak, garter snake, give-and-take, griddle cake, icebox cake, johnnycake, kittiwake, layer cake, make-or-break, marble cake, minute steak, overtake, parking brake, patty-cake, piece of cake, rattlesnake, station break, stomachache, undertake, wapentake, wedding cake, wide-awake; angel food cake, devil's food cake, golden handshake, radiopaque, tension headache, upside-down cake; Delmonico steak, emergency brake, potato pancake.

**-al,** Al, gal, Hal, pal, sal, shall; banal, cabal, canal, chorale, copal, corral, decal, grand-mal, joual, locale, mescal, morale, Natal, Pascal, quetzal, salal, serval, timbale; bacchanal, caracal, chapparal, falderal, femme fatale, musicale, pastorale, rationale; Guadalcanal.

**-ald,** bald, scald, skald; appalled, blackballed, piebald, skewbald, so-called; Archibald, Buchenwald.
Also: **-all** + **-ed** (as in *stalled*, etc.)
Also: **-aul** + **-ed** (as in *hauled*, etc.)
Also: **-awl** + **-ed** (as in *crawled*, etc.)

**-ale** (-āl). See **-ail.**

**-ale** (-al). See **-al.**

**-ales,** Wales; entrails, marseilles, Marseilles; bed of nails, heads or tails, Prince of Wales; cat-o'-nine-tails.
Also: **-ail** + **-s** (as in *fails*, etc.)
Also: **-ale** + **-s** (as in *scales*, etc.)

**-alf.** See **-aff.**

**-alk,** auk, balk, calk, chalk, gawk, hawk, squawk, stalk, talk, walk; backtalk, Bartók, boardwalk, cakewalk, catwalk, cornstalk, crosstalk, crosswalk, fast-talk, goshawk, jaywalk, leafstalk, langue d'oc, Mohawk, moonwalk, nighthawk, pep talk, racewalk, shop talk, sidewalk, skywalk, sleepwalk, small talk, space walk, sweet-talk, trash talk, war hawk; baby talk, belle époque, catafalque, chicken hawk, double talk, Kitty Hawk, pillow talk, power walk, tomahawk, widow's walk; Manitowoc; Oconomowoc.

**-all** (-al). See **-al.**

**-all** (-ôl). See **-awl.**

**-alled.** See **-ald.**

**-alm,** alm, balm, calm, gaum, Guam, malm, palm, psalm, qualm; becalm, bee balm, embalm, imam, Islam, madame, napalm, nizam, salaam.

**-alp,** alp, Alp, palp, scalp.

**-alt** (-ôlt), fault, gault, halt, malt, salt, smalt, vault, Walt; asphalt, assault, basalt, cobalt, default, desalt, exalt, foot fault, gestalt, no-fault, pole vault, rock salt, stringhalt; double fault, garlic salt, single-malt, sour salt, somersault, table salt; pepper-and-salt; San Andreas Fault.

**-alt** (-alt), alt, shalt.

**-alts.** See **-altz.**

**-altz,** schmaltz, waltz.
Also: **-alt** + **-s** (as in *salts,* etc.)
Also: **-ault** + **-s** (as in *faults,* etc.)

**-alve** (-av), calve, halve, have, lav, salve, Slav; Yugoslav.

**-alve** (-äv), Av, calve, grave, Graves, halve, salve, schav, Slav, suave, tav, vav; lulav, moshav, Zouave; Yugoslav.

**-alve** (-alv), salve, valve; bivalve; multivalve, safety valve, univalve.

**-am,** am, bam, cam, cham, clam, cram, dam, damn, drachm, dram, DRAM, gam, glam, gram, ham, jam, jamb, lam, lamb, ma'am, pam, Pam, pram, ram, RAM, Sam, scam, scram, sham, slam, spam, swam, tam, tram, wham, yam; ashram, Assam, dirham, Edam, exam, flimflam, Graham, goddamn, granddam, grand slam, iamb, imam, logjam, madame, Mailgram, milldam, pangram, Priam, pro-am, program, quondam, ramstam, tam-tam, Siam, webcam, ziram; Abraham, aerogram, Alabam, Amsterdam, anagram, bar exam, Birmingham, cablegram, Candygram, centigram, chronogram, cofferdam, cryptogram, decagram, diagram, diaphragm, dithyramb, epigram, fluid dram, hexagram, histogram, hologram, kilogram, mammogram, marjoram, milligram, minicam, monogram, nomogram, oriflamme, pentagram, petersham, picnic ham, pictogram, pillow sham, risurgam, Rotterdam, scattergram, skiagram, soft-shell clam, sonogram, Suriname, telegram, thank-you-ma'am, tinker's damn, Uncle Sam, Vietnam; ad nauseam, angiogram, audiogram, battering ram, cardiogram, ideogram, in personam, lorazepam, per curiam, radiogram, Virginia ham; parallelogram; echocardiogram; electrocardiogram.

**-amb.** See **-am.**

**-ame,** aim, blame, came, claim, dame, fame, flame,

frame, game, kame, lame, maim, Mame, name, same, shame, tame; acclaim, aflame, A-frame, ballgame, became, bedframe, beldame, big game, big name, birth name, board game, brand name, by-name, code name, con game, cross-claim, day name, declaim, defame, disclaim, endgame, exclaim, fair game, filename, first name, freeze frame, grandame, inflame, last name, mainframe, mind game, misaim, misclaim, misname, nickname, no-name, pen name, pet name, placename, postgame, pregame, proclaim, quitclaim, reclaim, reframe, rename, self-blame, selfsame, shell game, street name, surname, time frame, trade name, war game, word game; all the same, aspartame, counterclaim, domain name, given name, Hall of Fame, maiden name, numbers game, overcame, proper name, spinning frame, waiting game; family name, name of the game, video game.

**-amp** (-amp), amp, camp, champ, clamp, cramp, damp, guimpe, lamp, ramp, samp, scamp, stamp, tamp, tramp, vamp; base camp, bedlamp, boot camp, day camp, death camp, decamp, encamp, firedamp, flood lamp, floor lamp, food stamp, headlamp, heat lamp, off-ramp, on-ramp, revamp, sun lamp, time-stamp, unclamp, work camp; afterdamp, aide-de-camp, boarding ramp, gooseneck lamp, labor camp, postage stamp, prison camp, rubber stamp, trading stamp, writer's cramp; concentration camp.

**-amp** (-omp). See **-omp.**

**-an** (-an), an, Ann, Anne, ban, bran, can, clan, Dan, fan, flan, Fran, Jan, Klan, man, Nan, pan, Pan, plan, ran, scan, span, tan, than, van; adman, afghan, Afghan, ashcan, badman, bagman, bedpan, began, best man, birdman, bookman, bossman, brainpan, brain scan, caftan, caiman, cancan, capstan, CAT scan, cave man, chessman, Cheyenne, con man, corban, cyan, deadman, deadpan, Diane, dishpan, divan, doorman, dustpan, end man, fan-tan, flight plan, foreran, FORTRAN, frogman, frontman, gagman, game plan, gasman, G-man, hardpan, heman, iceman, Iran, japan, Japan, jazzman, Joanne, keyman, Koran, lawman, leadman, life span, loafpan, loran, madman, main man, man's man, mailman, merman, Milan, milkman, newsman, oat bran, oilcan, oil pan, old man, outran, pavane, pecan, PET scan, pikeman, plowman, point man, postman, pressman, Queen Anne, Qur'an, ragman, rattan, reedman, sampan, sandman, saucepan, sedan, snowman, soundman, soutane, spaceman, spray can, straight man, straw man, strongman, stunt man, suntan, taipan, tarpan, Tarzan, test ban, tin can, tisane, toucan, trepan, Tristan, tube pan, unman, Walkman, wingspan, wise man, yes-man, young man; advance man, Alcoran, also-ran, Ameslan, anchorman, astrakhan, Astrakhan, ataman, billycan, body plan, bogeyman, businessman, caravan, catalan, cattleman, counterman, countryman, courtesan, detail man, engineman, everyman, fancy-dan, fellow man, frying pan, funnyman, garbage can, garbageman, grand old man, handyman, harmattan, hatchet man, Hindustan, in the can, iron man, Isle of Man, Java man, jerry can, Kazakhstan, Ku Klux Klan, Kurdistan, Kyrgyzstan, ladies' man, leading man, little man, man-forman, master plan, mercaptan, middleman, minivan, minuteman, moneyman, mountain man, moving van, muscleman, ombudsman, other man, outdoorsman, overran, Pakistan, Parmesan, partisan, party man, pattypan, Peking man, Peter Pan, pivotman, plainclothesman, repairman, rewriteman, right-hand man, service man, spick-and-span, superman, to a man, Taliban, turbofan, Turkestan, warming pan, weatherman, workingman, yataghan, Yucatan; Afghanistan, angry young man, arrière-ban, attention span, cameraman, catamaran, catch-as-catch-can, cavalryman, confidence man, company man, dirty old man, El Capitan, family man, flash in the pan, layaway plan, marginal man, medicine man, newspaper man, orangutan, rag-and-bone man, Renaissance man, salary man, Turkmenistan, Uzbekistan, watering can; contingency plan, delivery man, dollar-a-year man, retirement plan, second-story man.

**-an** (-on). See **-on.**

**-ance** (-ans), chance, dance, France, glance, hanse, lance, manse, pants, prance, stance, trance; advance, askance, barn dance, bechance, break dance, by chance, clog dance, enhance, entrance, expanse, finance, freelance, lap dance, line dance, main chance, mischance, Penzance, perchance, romance, round dance, side glance, snake dance, square dance, stepdance, sweatpants, tap dance, war dance; at first glance, ballroom dance, belly dance, circumstance, countredance, country-dance, fancy-pants, fighting chance, game of chance, happenchance, happenstance, in advance, Liederkranz, modern dance, morris dance, open stance, refinance, smarty-pants, song and dance, underpants, waggle dance; seat-of-the-pants; St. Vitus's dance.

Also: **-ant** + **-s** (as in *grants,* etc.)

**-ance** (-äns), brisance, faience, nuance, Provence, séance; ambience, fer-de-lance, Liederkranz, nonchalance, renaissance; insouciance, par excellence; pièce de résistance.

**-anch,** blanch, Blanche, branch, ganch, planch, ranch, stanch; carte blanche, dude ranch; avalanche, olive branch.

**-anct,** sacrosanct.

Also: **-ank** + **-ed** (as in *spanked,* etc.)

**-and** (-and), and, band, bland, brand, gland, grand, hand, land, manned, rand, sand, stand, strand, Strand; armband, at hand, backhand, badland, bandstand, barehand, bedstand, big band, bookstand, brass band, broadband, brushland, cabstand, coastland, cobrand, command, cowhand, crash-land, cropland, crown land, dab hand, deck hand, demand, disband, dockhand, dockland, dreamland, ear band, expand, farm hand, fenland, field hand, firsthand, flatland, forehand, fourhand, gangland, glad-hand, grandstand, grassland, Greenland, handstand, hatband, headband, headland, headstand, heartland, homeland, home stand, hour hand, Iceland, in hand, inkstand, inland, jack stand, jazz band, jug band, kickstand, left-hand, longhand, lowland, lymph gland, mainland, marshland, misbrand, namebrand, newsstand, nightstand, noseband, offbrand, offhand, old hand, on hand, parkland, playland, quicksand, rangeland, remand, Rhineland, ribband, right hand, scrubland, shorthand, sideband, soft-land, stagehand, steel band, Streisand, sweatband, sweat gland, tideland, unhand, unmanned, vineland, waistband, washstand, wasteland, watchband, wetland, withstand, wristband, yardland; ampersand, baby grand, beforehand, belly-land, borderland, cap in hand, close-at-hand, concert grand, contraband, countermand, dairyland, Disneyland, Dixieland, fairyland, fatherland, firebrand, forestland, four-in-hand, hand in hand, helping hand, high command, hinterland, hired hand, Holy Land, honorand, Houyhnhnmland, iron hand, Krugerrand, la-la land, lotusland, master hand, meadowland, minute hand, motherland, movieland, muffin stand, music stand, narrowband, no man's land, on demand, one-man band, one-night stand, operand, out of hand, overhand, overland, pastureland, promised land, reprimand, Rio Grande, rubber band, Samarkand, saraband, second hand, secondhand, self-command, shadowland, sleight of hand, tableland, taxi stand, timberland, underhand, understand, upper hand, wedding band, witness stand, wonderland; chain of command, cloud-cuckoo-land, endocrine gland, fantasyland, head-in-the-sand, lay of the land, mammary gland, misunderstand, multiplicand, overexpand, vacationland, Witwatersrand; invisible land, never-never land; Alice in Wonderland.

Also: **-an** + **-ed** (as in *banned,* etc.)

**-and** (-ond). See **-ond.**

**-ane.** See **-ain.**

**-ang,** bang, bhang, clang, dang, fang, gang, gangue, hang, pang, rang, sang, slang, spang, sprang, stang, tang, twang, vang, whang, yang; big bang, birth pang, boomslang, chain gang, cliffhang, defang, gang bang, gobang, harangue, Lapsang, lingsang, meringue, mustang, orang, parang, Penang, pinang, press gang, shebang, slambang, slap-bang, straphang, trepang, whizbang; boomerang, charabanc, overhang, parasang, rhyming slang, siamang, yin and yang; interrobang, orangutang.

**-ange,** change, grange, mange, range, strange; arrange, chump change, derange, downrange, estrange, exchange, free-range, gas range, home range, long-range, midrange, outrange, price range, sea change, sex change, short-change, shortrange, small change; base exchange, disarrange, driving range, interchange, mountain range, post exchange, prearrange, rearrange, rifle range; bill of exchange, firing range, foreign exchange, rate of exchange, visual range; cultural exchange, telephone exchange.

**-angue.** See **-ang.**

**-ank,** bank, blank, brank, clank, crank, dank, drank, flank, franc, frank, Frank, hank, Hank, lank, plank, prank, rank, sank, schrank, shank, shrank, skank, spank, stank, swank, tank, thank, trank, yank, Yank; blood bank, embank, fishtank, fog bank, food bank, foreshank, front-rank, gangplank, gas tank, hind shank, job bank, land bank, left bank, outflank, outrank, pointblank, sandbank, snowbank, think tank; antitank, central bank, data bank, draw a blank, entry blank, holding tank, interbank, mountebank, piggy bank, riverbank, savings bank, water tank, walk the plank; blankety-blank, clickety-clank, memory bank; academic rank.

**-anked.** See **-anct.**

**-anned.** See **-and.**

**-anse.** See **-ance.**

**-ant** (-ant), ant, aunt, brant, can't, cant, chant, grant, Grant, Kant, pant, plant, rant, scant, shan't, slant; askant, aslant, bacchant, bezant, decant, descant, displant, eggplant, enchant, extant, gallant, grandaunt, implant, jade plant, land grant, Levant, pissant, recant, replant, supplant, transplant; adamant, commandant, complaisant, confidant, confidente, debutante, disenchant, fire ant, gallivant, hierophant, power plant, rubber plant, spider plant, sycophant; hierophant.

**-ant** (-änt), aunt, can't, taunt, vaunt; avaunt, bacchant, bouffant, brisant, courant, détente, entente, gallant, grandaunt, piquant, romaunt, savant; bon vivant, commandant, confidant, debutant, debutante, dilettante, Maupassant, nonchalant, restaurant; celebutante.

**-ant** (-äN) beurre blanc, croissant, savant; en passant, Maupassant; au courant, contretemps, dénouement, en passant, soi disant, vol-au-vent; accouchement, rapprochement; arrondissement; idiot savant.

**-ant.** (-ont). See **-aunt.**

**-ants.** See **-ance.**

**-ap,** app, cap, chap, clap, crap, dap, flap, gap, hap, Jap, lap, map, nap, nappe, pap, rap, sap, scrap, slap, snap, strap, tap, trap, wrap, yap, zap; ASAP, backslap, bad rap, bit map, bootstrap, bum rap, burlap, catnap, claptrap, cold snap, death trap, dewlap, dognap, dunce cap, earflap, entrap, enwrap, firetrap, flytrap, foolscap, gelcap, giddap, gift wrap, handclap, heeltap, hubcap, icecap, jockstrap, kidnap, kneecap, lagniappe, largecap, love tap, madcap, man-trap, mayhap, mishap, mousetrap, mud flap, nightcap, old chap, on tap, rattrap, recap, remap, road map, rootcap, sand trap, satrap, shrink-wrap, skullcap, skycap, snowcap, speed trap, star map, stopgap, uncap, unsnap, unwrap, whitecap, Winesap, word wrap; afterclap, baseball cap, beat the rap, body wrap, booby trap, bottle cap, bubble wrap, contour map, cradle cap, dollar gap, gangsta rap, giddyap, gimme cap, gingersnap, handicap, gender gap, killer app; lobster trap, overlap, plastic wrap, polar cap, power nap, rattletrap, relief map, shoulder strap, spinal tap, stocking cap, thinking cap, thunderclap, tourist trap, verbum sap, water gap, weather map, wiretap; spaghetti strap; generation gap, Venus's-flytrap.

**-ape,** ape, cape, chape, crepe, drape, gape, grape, jape, nape, rape, scape, scrape, shape, tape; agape, blank tape, broomrape, cloudscape, date rape, dreamscape, duct tape, escape, gang rape, great ape, handshape, landscape, moonscape, name tape, red tape, reshape, retape, Scotch tape, seascape, shipshape, streetscape, townscape, undrape; cassette tape, cityscape, Concord grape, masking tape, ticker tape, xeriscape; acquaintance rape, adhesive tape, anthropoid ape, audiotape, bent out of shape, fire escape, magnetic tape, videotape; statutory rape.

**-apes.** See **-aipse.**

**-aph.** See **-aff.**

**-aphed.** See **-aft.**

**-apped.** See **-apt.**

**-aps.** See **-apse.**

**-apse,** apse, chaps, craps, lapse, schnapps, taps; collapse, elapse, perhaps, prolapse, relapse, synapse, time-lapse.

Also: **-ap** + **-s** (as in *claps,* etc.)

**-apt,** apt, rapt, wrapt; adapt, inapt.

Also: **-ap** + **-ed** (as in *clapped,* etc.)

**-aque.** See **-ack.**

**-ar** (-är), Aar, are, bar, barre, car, char, czar, far, gar, guar, jar, knar, Loire, maar, mar, par, parr, Saar, scar, spar, star, tar, tahr, tsar; afar, agar, ajar, all-star, armoire, bar car, bazaar, Beaux-Arts, bête noire, bizarre, boudoir, boxcar, boyar, bulbar, bursar, cash bar, catarrh, chukar, cigar, coal tar, costar, couloir, crossbar, crowbar, Dakar, debar, devoir, dinar, disbar, durbar, feldspar, fern bar, film noir, five-star, fixed star, flatcar, four-star, gaydar, gazar, guitar, horsecar, hussar, jaguar, kantar, lascar, lekvar, lidar, lodestar, lounge car, louvar, lumbar, Magyar, memoir, Mylar, NASCAR, Navarre, nightjar, North Star, peignoir, pine tar, pourboire, pulsar, qintar, quasar, radar, rail car, raw bar, roll bar, sandbar, shikar, sidebar, sidecar, simar, sirdar, sitar, snack bar, sonar, sports bar, sports car, stock car, streetcar, taskbar, T-bar, thenar, toolbar, tow bar, town car, tramcar, trocar; abbatoir, aide-mémoire, air guitar, Alcazar, au revoir, avatar, Balthazar, blazing star, bolivar, bumper car, cable car, caviar, cinnabar, coffee bar, commissar, cultivar, deodar, dining car, double bar, escritoire, exemplar, falling star, handlebar, hospodar, insofar, isobar, jacamar, jaguar, jemadar, kilobar, mason jar, megastar, minibar, minicar, morning star, motorcar, open bar, parlor car, registrar, rent-a-car, repertoire, reservoir, rising star, salad bar, samovar, seminar, shooting star, singles bar, sleeping car, steak tartare, steel guitar, superstar, tiki bar, touring car, trolley car, VCR, wunderbar, zamindar, Zanzibar; agar-agar, budgerigar, conservatoire, proseminar, radio car.

**-ar** (-ôr). See **-or.**

**-arb,** arb, barb, carb, garb; rhubarb.

**-arce.** See **-arse.**

**-arch,** arch, larch, march, March, parch, starch; cornstarch, dead march, frogmarch, outmarch; countermarch, freedom march, Gothic arch, overarch, wedding march; triumphal arch.

**-arch.** See **-ark.**

**-ard** (-ärd), bard, card, chard, guard, hard, lard, nard, pard, sard, shard, yard; backyard, bank card, barnyard, Bernard, blackguard, blowhard, boatyard, bombard, boneyard, brassard, canard, charge card, churchyard, coast guard, courtyard, dance card, diehard, discard, dockyard, dooryard, farmyard, flash card, foulard, Gerard, graveyard, green card, ill-starred, jacquard, junkyard, lifeguard, mallard, mansard, midgard, milliard, mudguard, noseguard, off guard, old guard, on guard, petard, phone card, Picard, placard, place card, point guard, postcard, punch card, rearguard, regard, retard, safeguard, schoolyard, scorecard, shipyard, smart card, sound card, spikenard, steelyard, stock-yard, timecard, vanguard, wild card; Abelard, avant-garde, bingo card, body-guard, boulevard, business card, calling card, Christ-mas card, color guard, credit card, debit card, dis-regard, drawing card, greeting card, Hildegarde, honor guard, ID card, index card, interlard, Kierkegaard, leotard, lumberyard, navy yard, no-holds-barred, playing card, report card, Saint Bernard, Savoyard, Scotland Yard, self-regard, trading card, union card, unitard; camelopard, expansion card; affinity card, identity card.

Also: **-ar** + **-ed** (as in *starred*, etc.)

**-ard** (-ôrd). See **-ord.**

**-are,** air, Ayr, bare, bear, blare, care, chair, Claire, dare, e'er, ere, fair, fare, flair, flare, gare, glair, glare, hair, hare, heir, Herr, lair, mare, mayor, ne'er, pair, pare, pear, Pierre, prayer, rare, scare, share, snare, spare, square, stair, stare, swear, tare, tear, their, there, they're, vair, ware, wear, where, yare; affair, airfare, armchair, au pair, aware, bakeware, barware, beach-wear, bergère, beware, big hair, black bear, brood-mare, brown bear, bugbear, caneware, carfare, chi square, cochair, coheir, compare, compère, con-frere, cookware, corsair, courseware, day care, dead air, deck chair, declare, despair, dishware, éclair, elsewhere, ensnare, eye-wear, fanfare, firmware, flatware, footwear, forbear, forebear, forswear, four-square, freeware, funfair, giftware, glassware, Gruyère, hardware, health-care, hectare, high chair, horsehair, hot air, howe'er, impair, knitwear, life-care, longhair, loungewear, menswear, midair, mohair, Mynheer, neckwear, night-mare, no fair, nonglare, nowhere outstare, parterre, Pierre, playwear, plein air, plowshare, portiere, premiere, prepare, pushchair, rainwear, repair, shank's mare, shareware, shorthair, side chair, skiwear, sleepwear, software, somewhere, sportswear, stemware, stoneware, swimwear, threadbare, torchère, trouvère, unfair, Voltaire, warfare, welfare, whate'er, wheelchair, whene'er, where'er, workfare; aftercare, air-to-air, antiglare, anywhere, bêche-de-mer, Belgian hare, billionaire, bill of fare, boutonniere, bring to bear, camelhair, Camembert, captain's chair, chinaware, county fair, country fair, croix de guerre, debonair, Delaware, derrière, dinnerware, disrepair, doctrinaire, earthenware, easy chair, en plein air, étagère, everywhere, fourragère, Frigidaire, germ warfare, grizzly bear, here and there, hollowware, in the air, ironware, jardiniere, jasperware, kitchenware, lacquerware, laissez faire, legionnaire, lion's share, love affair, luminaire, magic square, maidenhair, mal de mer, managed care, market share, Medicare, metalware, millionaire, nom de guerre, open-air, outerwear, perfect square, polar bear, potty chair, porte-cochere, prickly pear, questionnaire, rivière, rocking chair, savoir faire, science fair, self-aware, silverware, snowshoe hare, solitaire, swivel chair, tableware, teddy bear, thoroughfare, trench warfare, unaware, underwear, vaporware, wash-and-wear, wear and tear, whatsoe'er, wheresoe'er, world premiere, zillionaire; chargé d'affaires, chemin de fer, concessionaire, devil-may-care, electric chair, enamelware, lighter-than-air, pied-à-terre, primary care, ready-to-wear, son et lumière, surface-to-air, up in the air, vanity fair, vin ordinaire; Adirondack chair, castle in the air, cordon sanitaire, middle of nowhere.

**-ares,** theirs; back stairs, cross hairs, downstairs, housewares, nowheres, somewheres, upstairs; unawares; foreign affairs, musical chairs, public affairs.
Also: **-air** + **-s** (as in *stairs,* etc.)
Also: **-are** + **-s** (as in *dares,* etc.)
Also: **-ear** + **-s** (as in *swears,* etc.)
Also: **-eir** + **-s** (as in *heirs,* etc.)

**-arf** (-ärf), arf, barf, scarf, zarf.

**-arf** (-ôrf). See **-orf.**

**-arge,** barge, charge, large, marge, Marge, sarge, sparge; at-large, depth charge, discharge, enlarge, late charge, recharge, surcharge, take charge, writ large; access charge, by and large, cover charge, finance charge, overcharge, service charge, supercharge, turbocharge, undercharge; carrying charge.

**-ark,** arc, ark, bark, barque, cark, Clark, dark, hark, lark, mark, Mark, marque, narc, park, quark, sark, shark, snark, spark, stark; aardvark, autarch, ballpark, benchmark, birthmark, Bismarck, bookmark, checkmark, debark, Denmark, earmark, embark, exarch, futhark, hallmark, hash mark, landmark, monarch, ostmark, Ozark, Petrarch, pitch-dark, pockmark, postmark, remark, remarque, skylark, stress mark, tanbark, tetrarch, theme park, titlark, trademark; accent mark, antiquark, Deutsche mark, disembark, double-park, easy mark, great white shark, hierarch, Joan of Arc, mako shark, matriarch, meadowlark, minipark, oligarch, patriarch, Plimsoll mark, question mark, service mark, tiger shark, toe the mark, watermark, water park; amusement park, high-water mark, shot in the dark, vest-pocket park; whistle in the dark.

**-arl,** carl, Carl, gnarl, marl, snarl.

**-arm** (-ärm), arm, barm, charm, farm, harm, marm,

smarm; alarm, disarm, fat farm, fish farm, forearm, gendarme, schoolmarm, side-arm, sidearm, stock farm, straight-arm, strong-arm, tree farm, truck farm, unarm, windfarm, work farm, yardarm; arm-in-arm, buy the farm, dairy farm, false alarm, firearm, funny farm, smoke alarm, underarm, upper arm; burglar alarm.

**-arm** (-ôrm). See **-orm.**

**-arn** (-ärn), barn, darn, Marne, tarn, yarn; carbarn, lucarne.

**-arn** (-ôrn). See **-orn.**

**-arp** (-ärp), carp, harp, scarp, sharp, tarp; cardsharp, escarp, French harp, Jew's harp, wind harp; Autoharp, counterscarp, endocarp, epicarp, exocarp, mesocarp, pericarp, supersharp, vibraharp; aeolian harp.

**-arp** (-ôrp). See **-orp.**

**-arred.** See **-ard.**

**-arse,** arse, farce, marse, parse, sparse.

**-arsh,** harsh, marsh; overharsh.

**-art** (-ärt), art, Bart, cart, chart, dart, fart, hart, heart, mart, part, smart, start, tart; apart, at heart, bar cart, bar chart, bit part, black art, blackheart, bogart, by heart, cave art, clip art, compart, depart, Descartes, dispart, dogcart, eye chart, faintheart, false start, fine art, flip chart, flowchart, folk art, found art, go-cart, golf cart, head start, impart, jump-start, junk art, kick-start, line art, mouthpart, Mozart, old fart, op art, outsmart, oxcart, pie chart, pop art, pushcart, rampart, redstart, restart, street-smart, sweetheart, take heart, take part, teacart, time chart, upstart, voice part; à la carte, applecart, bleeding heart, body art, broken heart, change of heart, concept art, Cuisinart, counterpart, flying start, from the heart, gentle art, heart-to-heart, household art, housing start, Lily Bart, martial art, minimart, multipart, open heart, poles apart, purpleheart, Purple Heart, running start, Sacred Heart, shopping start, supersmart, underpart, work of art; Banbury tart, calendar art, kinetic art, minimal art, performance art, practical art, state-of-the-art, video art; artificial heart.

**-art** (-ôrt). See **-ort.**

**-arth** (-ôrth). See **-orth.**

**-arts** (-ôrts). See **-orts.**

**-artz** (-ôrts). See **-orts.**

**-arve,** carve, starve.

**-as** (-oz), Boz, Oz, was.

**-as** (-ä). See **-a.**

**-as** (-as). See **-ass.**

**-ase** (-ās). See **-ace.**

**-ase** (-āz). See **-aze.**

**-ased.** See **-aste.**

**-ash** (-ash), ash, bash, brash, cache, cash, clash, crash, dash, flash, gash, gnash, hash, lash, mash, Nash, pash, plash, rash, sash, slash, smash, splash, thrash, trash; abash, backlash, backslash, backsplash, bone ash, calash, cold cash, eyelash, gate-crash, goulash, heat rash, hot flash, kurbash mishmash, moustache, panache, potash, rehash, slapdash, soutache, tongue-lash, Wabash, whiplash, white ash; balderdash, calabash, diaper rash, mountain ash, petty cash, photoflash, prickly ash, sabretache, sour mash, spatterdash, succotash; red flannel hash.

**-ash** (-osh), bosh, gosh, frosh, gosh, gouache, josh, nosh, mosh, posh, quash, skosh, slosh, squash, swash, tosh, wash; awash, brainwash, car wash, cohosh, eyewash, galosh, goulash, hogwash, kibosh, mouthwash, musquash, Oshkosh, prewash, whitewash; acorn squash, mackintosh, summer squash, winter squash.

**-ask,** ask, bask, Basque, cask, casque, flask, mask, masque, Pasch, task; death mask, face mask, gas mask, life mask, ski mask, uncask, unmask; multitask, photomask, powder flask, shadow mask, take to task, vacuum flask.

**-asm,** chasm, plasm, spasm; chiasm, orgasm, phantasm, sarcasm; bioplasm, bronchospasm, cataplasm, chiliasm, cytoplasm, ectoplasm, endoplasm, isochasm, metaplasm, neoplasm, pleonasm, periplasm, phytoplasm, protoplasm, sarcoplasm, teleplasm, tonic spasm; biblioclasm, enthusiasm, iconoclasm, nucleoplasm.

**-asp,** asp, clasp, gasp, grasp, hasp, rasp; beclasp, enclasp, handclasp, tie clasp, unclasp.

**-ass,** ass, bass, brass, class, crass, frass, gas, glass, grass, lass, mass, pass, sass, tass, strass, wrasse; admass, air mass, alas, Alsace, amass, art glass, badass, bagasse, band-pass, beach grass, bent grass, bird grass, black bass, Black Mass, bluegrass, bromegrass, bunch grass, bypass, case glass, cloud grass, cordgrass, crabgrass, crevasse, cuirass, cut glass, declass, drop pass, dune grass, eelgrass, en masse, eyeglass, filasse, first-class, groundmass, harass, high-class, High Mass, impasse, jackass, jump pass, landmass, low-class, Madras, milk glass, misclass, morass, outclass, paillasse, plate glass, rascasse, reclass, repass, rock bass, rubasse, sea bass, sheet glass, shot glass, smart ass, spyglass, stained glass, striped bass, subclass, surpass, tear gas, top brass, trespass, vinasse, wheatgrass, wineglass, wise-ass, world-class, zebrass; alpha brass, Amen glass, antique glass, beta brass, biomass, boarding pass, bottle glass, burning glass, business class, cabin class, camel grass, Candlemas, cocktail glass, cupping glass, demitasse, fiberglass, forward pass, galloglass, gravitas, Hallowmas, hippocras, hourglass, isinglass, laughing gas, lemongrass, looking glass, lower-class, master class, meadowgrass, middle-class, opera glass, outclass, overclass, overpass, quaking grass, ruby glass, safety glass, sassafras, second-class, social class, solar mass, tourist class, underclass, underpass, upper-class, water glass, working class; atomic mass, chattering class, critical mass, Depression glass; economy class, magnifying glass.

**-assed.** See **-ast.**

**-ast,** bast, blast, cast, caste, clast, dast, fast, hast, last, mast, past, vast; aghast, at last, avast, backcast, beech mast, Belfast, bombast, broadcast, contrast, dicast, die-cast, downcast, durmast, dynast, fantast, flycast, flypast, forecast, foremast, full blast, gymnast, half-caste, half-mast, holdfast, lambaste, mainmast, march-past, miscast, newscast, oblast, offcast, outcast, outlast, peltast, recast, repast, roughcast, sandblast, sand-cast, sportscast, steadfast, topmast, typecast, well-cast, webcast, wind blast; aftercast, after mast, at long last, cablecast, captain's mast, chiliast, chloroplast, cineaste, colorcast, colorfast, counterblast, cytoplast, flabbergast, hard-and-fast, jiggermast, main-topmast, mizzenmast, narrowcast, neuroblast, overcast, pederast, plaster cast, protoplast, rebroadcast, royal mast, scholiast, simulcast, telecast, unsurpassed, weathercast; biblioclast, ecclesiast, ecdysiast, encomiast, enthusiast, gymnasiast, iconoclast, symposiast.

Also: **-ass** + **-ed** (as in *passed*, etc.)

**-aste,** baste, chaste, haste, paste, taste, waist, waste; bald-faced, barefaced, distaste, dough-faced, foretaste, impaste, lambaste, lean-faced, light-faced, pale-faced, pie-faced, pofaced, posthaste, red-faced, shamefaced, shirtwaist, slipcased, slow-paced, snail-paced, stone-faced, straight-faced, straightlaced, toothpaste, twofaced, unchaste; aftertaste, double-faced, freckle-faced, Janus-faced, open-faced, pantywaist, poker-faced.

Also: **-ace** + **-ed** (as in *placed*, etc.)

Also: **-ase** + **-ed** (as in *chased*, etc.)

**-at** (-at), at, bat, batt, brat,

cat, chat, drat, fat, flat, frat, ghat, gnat, hat, kat, mat, Matt, matte, Nat, pat, Pat, phat, plat, prat, rat, sat, scat, sceat, skat, slat, spat, splat, sprat, stat, tat, that, vat; at bat, backchat, bathmat, begat, black hat, bobcat, brass hat, brickbat, chitchat, combat, Comsat, cravat, dingbat, doormat, expat, fat cat, fiat, format, fruit bat, hard-hat, hellcat, hepcat, hereat, high-hat, house cat, jurat, kit-kat, low-fat, meerkat, milkfat, molerat, mudcat, mud flat, Muscat, muskrat, nonfat, old hat, pack rat, place mat, polecat, rabat, rink rat, rug rat, run-flat, salt flat, snowcat, stand pat, stonecat, stonechat, strawhat, thereat, tipcat, tomcat, top hat, trans fat, whereat, whinchat, wildcat, wombat; acrobat, aerobat, aerostat, alley cat, apparat, appestat, Ararat, army brat, assignat, autocrat, Automat, bureaucrat, burning ghat, butterfat, caveat, cervelat, Cheshire cat, chew the fat, coelostat, concordat, copycat, cowboy hat, cryostat, dandiprat, democrat, desert rat, diplomat, Dixiecrat, exeat, fraidy-cat, granny flat, gyrostat, habitat, hemostat, hydrostat, Kattegat, kittycat, kleptocrat, Laundromat, monocrat, Montserrat, noncombat, off the bat, photostat, pitapat, plutocrat, pussycat, railroad flat, rat-a-tat, reformat, rheostat, scaredycat, smell a rat, technocrat, theocrat, thermostat, three-a-cat, tidal flat, tit for tat, water rat, welcome mat, ziggurat; aristocrat, calico cat, fireside chat, gerontocrat, humidostat, Jehoshaphat, Magnificat, meritocrat, nihil obstat, rat-a-tat-tat, requiescat, Siamese cat, siderostat.

**-at** (-ä). See **-a.**

**-at** (-ot). See **-ot.**

**-atch** (-ach), bach, batch, catch, hatch, klatsch, latch, match, natch, patch, scratch, slatch, snatch, thatch; armpatch, attach, cold patch, crosshatch, cross-match, detach, dispatch, fair catch, from scratch, love match, mismatch, nuthatch, oil patch, potlatch, rematch, repatch, Sasquatch, spring catch, test match, throatlatch, unlatch; bandersnatch, best-ball match, booby hatch, coffee klatsch, escape hatch, friction match, kitchen match, mix-and- match, rubber match, safety catch, safety match, shooting match, shoulder patch, shouting match.

**-atch** (-och). See **-otch.**

**-ate,** ait, ate, bait, bate, crate, date, eight, fate, fête, frate, freight, gait, gate, grate, great, hate, Kate, late, mate, Nate, pate, plait, plate, prate, rate, sate, skate, slate, spate, state, straight, strait, Tate, trait, wait, weight; abate, ablate, adnate, aerate, age-mate, agnate, airdate, airfreight, alate, await, baccate, backdate, baldpate, bandmate, baseplate, bedmate, bedplate, berate, birthdate, birthrate, bistate, biteplate, blank slate, blind date, blue plate, bookplate, breastplate, bromate, bunkmate, casemate, castrate, caudate, cerate, cheapskate, checkmate, chelate, chlorate, chordate, chromate, cirrate, citrate, classmate, clavate, cognate, collate, comate, conflate, connate, cordate, costate, create, cremate, crenate, crispate, cristate, curate, curvate, cut-rate, deadweight, death rate, debate, deflate, delate, dentate, dictate, dilate, donate, doorplate, downstate, drawplate, elate, enate, end plate, equate, estate, faceplate, falcate, filtrate, first mate, first-rate, fishplate, fixate, flatmate, floodgate, flyweight, folate, formate, frontate, frustrate, furcate, gelate, gemmate, gestate, globate, gradate, ground state, guttate, gyrate, hamate, harnate, hastate, headgate, helpmate, homeplate, hot plate, housemate, hydrate, ice-skate, inflate, ingrate, inmate, innate, instate, irate, jail-bait, jugate, khanate, Kuwait, lactate, lapse rate, larvate, legate, lichgate, ligate, lightweight, liquate, lobate, locate, lunate, lustrate, lych-gate, lyrate, magnate, makeweight, mandate, messmate, migrate, misdate, mismate, misstate, mutate, nameplate, narrate, negate, nervate, nictate, nitrate, notate, nutate, oblate, of late, orate, ornate, outdate, ovate, palmate, palpate, peltate, pennate, phonate, phosphate, picrate, pinnate, placate, play date, playmate, plicate, portrait, postdate, predate, prelate, primate, prime rate, private, probate, prolate, pronate, prorate, prostate, prostrate, pulsate, punctate, pupate, quadrate, quinate, rain date, ramate, rebate, red-bait, relate, restate, roommate, rostrate, rotate, rugate, saccate, schoolmate, seatmate, sedate, self-hate, sensate, septate, serrate, shipmate, short weight, sigmate, slave state, soleplate, soulmate, spectate, spicate, squamate, stagnate, stalemate, stannate, stearate, stellate, striate, sublate, substrate, sulcate, sufflate, sulfate, tailgate, tannate, tartrate, teammate, template, tentmate, ternate, terneplate, testate, third-rate, tin plate, to date, titrate, toeplate, tollgate, tractate, translate, tristate, truncate, update, upstate, V-8, vacate, vallate, valvate, vibrate, Vulgate, whitebait, workmate, xanthate, zonate; abdicate, ablactate, abnegate, abrogate, absorbate, acclimate, acerbate, acetate, activate, actuate, addlepate, adulate, adumbrate, advocate, aggravate, aggregate, agitate, allocate, altercate, alternate, ambulate, ampliate, amputate, angulate, animate, annotate, annulate, antedate, antiquate, apartheid, apostate, appellate, approbate, arbitrate, arnor plate, arrogate, aspirate, aureate, auscultate, auspicate, automate, aviate, bantamweight, bifurcate, Billingsgate, bilobate, bipinnate, boilerplate, brachiate, bracteate, branchiate, buffer state, cabinmate, cachinnate, caffeinate, calcarate, calculate, calibrate, caliphate, camphorate, cancellate, candidate, cannulate, cantillate, capitate, capsulate, captivate, carbonate, carbon-date, caseate, castigate, catenate, cavitate, celebrate, celibate, cellulate, cerebrate, chief of state, chloridate, chlorinate, ciliate, circinate, circulate, city-state, client state, clypeate, coarctate, cochleate, cogitate, colligate, collimate, collocate, commentate, comminate, commutate, compensate, complicate, concentrate, confiscate, conformate, conglobate, congregate, conjugate, consecrate, constipate, consulate, consummate, contemplate, copperplate, copulate, cornuate, coronate, correlate, corrugate, corticate, coruscate, counterweight, crenellate, crenulate, crepitate, criminate, cruciate, cucullate, culminate, cultivate, cumulate, cuneate, cupulate, cuspidate, cyanate, cyclamate, decimate, declinate, decollate, decorate, decussate, dedicate, defalcate, defecate, dehydrate, delectate, delegate, demarcate, demonstrate, denigrate, denudate, depilate, deprecate, depredate, derogate, desecrate, desiccate, designate, desolate, detonate, devastate, deviate, digitate, diplomate, dislocate, dissipate, distillate, divagate, dominate, double date, dunderpate, duplicate, ebriate, echinate, edentate, educate, elevate, elongate, emanate, embrocate, emigrate, emirate, emulate, enervate, eructate, escalate, estimate, estivate, excavate, exchange rate, exculpate, execrate, expiate, explanate, explicate, expurgate, extirpate, extricate, exudate, fabricate, fasciate, fascinate, fashion plate, featherweight, fecundate, federate, fenestrate, fibrillate, figure eight, filiate, fimbriate, fimbrillate, first estate, fistulate, flagellate, flocculate, floriate, fluctuate, fluoridate, fluorinate, foliate, formicate, formulate, fornicate, fructuate, fourth estate, fractionate, fragmentate, fulgurate, fulminate, fumigate, fustigate, geminate, generate, germinate, glaciate, gladiate, glomerate, glutamate, Golden Gate, graduate, granulate, gravitate, guesstimate, heavyweight, hebetate, herniate, hesitate, hibernate, hundredweight, hyphenate, ideate, illustrate, imamate, imbricate, imitate, immigrate, immolate, implicate, imprecate, impregnate, incarnate, inchoate, incrassate, incubate, inculcate, inculpate, incurvate, indagate, indicate, indurate, infiltrate, infuscate, in-line skate, innervate, innovate, inornate, insensate, insolate, inspissate, instigate, insufflate, insulate, integrate, interstate, intestate, intimate, intonate, inundate, invocate, irrigate, irritate, isolate, iterate, jubilate, jugulate, labiate, lacerate, lamellate, laminate, lancinate, lapidate, Latinate, laureate, legislate, levigate, levirate, levitate, liberate, license plate, ligulate, lineate, lingulate, liquidate, litigate, loricate, lubricate, lucubrate, lunulate, macerate, machinate, maculate, magistrate, majorate, mammillate, manducate, manganate, marginate, margravate, marinate, marquisate, masticate, masturbate, maturate, mediate, medicate, meditate, menstruate, methylate, microstate, micturate, middleweight, militate, mitigate, moderate, modulate, molybdate, mortgage rate, motivate, multistate, muriate, muricate, mutilate, nation-state, nauseate, navigate, neonate, nictitate, niobate, nominate, nucleate, numerate, obfuscate, objurgate, obligate, obovate, obsecrate, obturate, obviate, ocellate, oculate, oleate, omoplate, operate, opiate, oppilate, orchestrate, ordinate, oscillate, oscitate, osculate, out-of-date, overrate, overstate, overweight, ovulate, oxalate, paginate, palliate, palpitate, paperweight, papillate, pastorate, patellate, patinate, pectinate, peculate, pejorate, pendulate, penetrate, pennyweight, percolate, perennate, perforate, permeate, permutate, perorate, perpetrate, personate, phenolate, phosphorate, pileate, police state, pollinate, populate, postulate, potentate, predicate, principate, priorate, procreate, profligate, promulgate, propagate, propinquate, prussiate, pullulate, pulmonate, pulverate, pulvinate, punctuate, punctulate, pustulate, quantitate, quaternate, rabbinate, radiate, radicate, raffinate, rattlepate, real estate, reclinate, recreate, re-create, recurvate, registrate, regulate, reinstate, relegate, relocate, reluctate, remigrate, remonstrate, renovate, replicate, reprobate, resinate, resonate, retardate, roller-skate, roseate, rostellate, rubricate, ruminate, running mate, rusticate, sagittate, salivate, sanitate, satiate, saturate, scintillate, scutellate, second-rate, segmentate, segregate, selenate, self-portrait, separate, septenate, sequestrate, seriate, serrulate, ship of state, shogunate, sibilate, silicate, silverplate, simulate, sinuate, situate, solid-state, spatulate, speculate, spiculate, spiflicate, spoliate, sporulate, stablemate, staminate, starting gate, steady state, stearate, stellulate, stimulate, stipulate, strangulate, stridulate, stylobate, subjugate, sublimate, subrogate, subulate, succinate, suffocate, sulfurate, sultanate, supinate, supplicate, suppurate, suricate, surrogate, syncopate, syndicate, tablemate, tabulate, target date, tellurate, temperate, terminate, tessellate, titanate, titillate, titivate, tolerate, toluate, trabeate, tracheate, transmigrate, transudate, tribulate, tribunate, tridentate, trifurcate, trijugate, trilobate, tripinnate, triplicate, trisulcate, triturate, tubulate, tunicate, turbinate, ulcerate, ululate, umbellate, uncinate, underrate, understate, underweight, undulate, ungulate, urinate, urticate, ustulate, vaccinate, vacillate, vaginate, valerate, validate, valuate, vanadate, vanillate, variate, variegate, vegetate, vellicate, venerate, ventilate, vertebrate, vesicate, vicarate, vindicate, violate, viscerate, vitiate, vizierate, Watergate, welfare state, welterweight; abbreviate, abominate, absquatulate, accelerate, accentuate, accommodate, acculturate, accumulate, acidulate, acuminate, adjudicate, administrate, adulterate, affiliate, agglomerate, agglutinate, aldermanate, alienate, alleviate, alliterate, amalgamate, annihilate, annunciate, anticipate, apiculate, apostolate, appreciate, appropinquate, appropriate, approximate, areolate, articulate, asphyxiate, assassinate, asseverate, assimilate, associate, at any rate, attenuate, auriculate, authenticate, barbiturate, bicarbonate, bifoliate, calumniate, capacitate, capitulate, carboxylate, cardinalate, catholicate, centuplicate, certificate, chalybeate, circumvallate, coagulate, coelenterate, collaborate, commemorate, commiserate, communicate, compassionate, concatenate, conciliate, confabulate, confederate, conglomerate, conglutinate, congratulate, consolidate, contaminate, conterminate, continuate, cooperate, coordinate, corroborate, corymbiate, curvicaudate, curvicostate, deactivate, debilitate, debranchiate, decaffeinate, decapitate, decelerate, decemvirate, decorticate, decrepitate, deescalate, defoliate, defibrillate, degenerate, deglutinate, deliberate, delineate, demodulate, denominate, denticulate, denunciate, depopulate, depreciate, deracinate, deregulate, desalinate, desegregate, desiderate, determinate, devaluate, dictatorate, dilapidate, discriminate, disintegrate, disseminate, dissimilate, dissimulate, dissociate, divaricate, domesticate, duumvirate, ebracteate, effectuate, ejaculate, elaborate, electroplate, eliminate, elucidate, elucubrate, emaciate, emancipate, emasculate, encapsulate, enucleate, enumerate, enunciate, episcopate, equilibrate, equivocate, eradiate, eradicate, etiolate, evacuate, evaginate, evaluate, evaporate, eventuate, eviscerate, exacerbate, exaggerate, exanimate, exasperate, excited state, excogitate, excoriate, excruciate, exfoliate, exhilarate, exonerate, expatiate, expatriate, expectorate, expostulate, expropriate, exsanguinate, extenuate, exterminate, extrapolate, extravagate, exuberate, facilitate, faveolate, felicitate, foraminate, gelatinate, geniculate, gesticulate, habilitate, habituate, hallucinate, horripilate, humiliate, hydrogenate, hypothecate, illuminate, imperforate, impersonate, impropriate, improvisate, inactivate, inaugurate, incarcerate, incinerate, incorporate, incriminate, indoctrinate, inebriate, infatuate, infuriate, ingeminate, ingratiate, ingurgitate, initiate, inoculate, insatiate, inseminate, insinuate, instantiate, intercalate, interpolate, interrelate, interrogate, intimidate, intoxicate, invaginate, invalidate, invertebrate, investigate, invigilate, invigorate, inviolate, irradiate, Italianate, itinerate, laciniate, lanceolate, legitimate, licentiate, lineolate, lixiviate, luxuriate, machicolate, mandibulate, manipulate, marsupiate, matriarchate, matriculate, meliorate, miscalculate, multidentate, multilobate, multiplicate, necessitate, negotiate, nidificate, noncandidate, novitiate, nudirostrate, obliterate, officiate, operate, operculate, orbiculate, orientate, originate, oxygenate, pacificate, palatinate, paniculate, participate, particulate, patriarchate, patriciate, pediculate, perambulate, peregrinate, permanganate, perpetuate, petiolate, pontificate, precipitate, precogitate, predesignate, predestinate, predominate, prefabricate, prejudicate, premeditate, prenominate, preponderate, presbyterate, prevaricate, procrastinate, prognosticate, proliferate, propitiate, proportionate, protuberate, quadruplicate, quintuplicate, reactivate, reanimate, recalcitrate, reciprocate, recriminate, recuperate, redecorate, reduplicate, reeducate, refrigerate, regenerate, regurgitate, reincarnate, reiterate, rejuvenate, remediate, remunerate, repatriate, repopulate, repudiate, resuscitate, retaliate, reticulate, reverberate, salicylate, second estate, self-flagellate, self-pollinate, somnambulate, sophisticate, stereobate, subordinate, substantiate, syllabicate, tergiversate, testiculate, testudinate, trabeculate, transliterate, triangulate, trifoliate, triumvirate, vanadiate, variegate, vaticinate, vermiculate, vesiculate, vestibulate, vicariate, vituperate, vociferate; ameliorate, baccalaureate, canaliculate, circumambulate, circumnavigate, circumstantiate, consubstantiate, contraindicate, decontaminate, deoxygenate, deteriorate, diagnosticate, differentiate, disaffiliate, disassociate, discombobulate, disorientate, domiciliate, excommunicate, expiration date, free-associate, hyperventilate, imbecilitate, incapacitate, individuate, intermediate, interpenetrate, latifoliate, misappropriate, multivariate, overcompensate, overeducate, overestimate, overmedicate, overpopulate, overstimulate, quadrifoliate, quadrigeminate, quinquefoliate, ratiocinate, recapitulate, reconciliate, rehabilitate, reinvigorate, renegotiate, secretariate, superannuate, supererogate, supersaturate, transubstantiate, trifoliolate, underestimate, unifoliate; radioactivate.

**-ath** (-ath), bath, Bath, Gath, hath, lath, math, path, rath, snath, wrath; bike path, birdbath, bloodbath, bypath, flight path, half bath, new math, sitz bath, sponge bath, steam bath, sunbath, towpath, warpath; aftermath, allopath, bridle path, bubble bath, hydropath, isobath, master bath, metal lath, monobath, multipath, naprapath, polymath, primrose path, psychopath, stenobath, Turkish bath, water bath, whirlpool bath; homeopath, naturopath, osteopath, sociopath.

**-ath** (-ôth). See **-oth.**

**-athe,** bathe, lathe, rathe, scathe, snathe, spathe, swathe; enswathe, sunbathe, unswathe; cryolathe.

**-au** (-ou). See **-ow** (-ou).

**-au** (-ō). See **-ow** (-ō).

**-auce.** See **-oss.**

**-aud,** baud, bawd, broad, Claude, fraud, gaud, laud, Maud; abroad, applaud, belaud, defraud, maraud; eisteddfod, lantern-jawed, overawed, wire fraud.

Also: **-aw** + **-ed** (as in *clawed,* etc.)

**-augh.** See **-aff.**

**-aught.** See **-ough** or **-aft.**

**-aul.** See **-awl.**

**-auled.** See **-ald.**

**-ault.** See **-alt.**

**-aunch,** craunch, haunch, launch, paunch, raunch,

stanch, staunch; post-launch, prelaunch, relaunch.

**-aunt,** aunt, daunt, flaunt, gaunt, haunt, jaunt, taunt, vaunt, want; avaunt, grandaunt, great-aunt, romaunt; bon vivant, confidant, debutante, dilettante, restaurant.

**-aunts.** See **-ounce.**

**-ause,** cause, 'cause, clause, gauze, hawse, pause, taws, yaws; applause, because, kolkhoz, lost cause, main clause, noun clause, stop clause; diapause, escape clause, grasp at straws, menopause, Santa Claus; grandfather clause, heliopause, male menopause, principle clause, probable cause, relative clause.

Also: **-aw** + **-s** (as in *claws,* etc.)

**-aust.** See **-ost.**

**-aut.** See **-ot** and **-ought.**

**-ave** (-av). See **-alve.**

**-ave** (-āv), brave, cave, clave, crave, Dave, fave, gave, glaive, grave, knave, lave, nave, pave, rave, save, shave, slave, stave, they've, trave, waive, wave; airwave, behave, bondslave, brain wave, burgrave, close shave, cold wave, concave, conclave, deprave, enclave, engrave, enslave, exclave, forgave, heat wave, land-grave, margrave, misgave, new wave, octave, pals-grave, palstave, proslave, repave, shock wave, short-wave, sound wave, wage slave; aftershave, alpha wave, architrave, autoclave, beta wave, body wave, delta wave, galley slave, microwave, misbehave, pressure wave, standing wave, tidal wave; cradle-to-grave, photoengrave, radio wave.

**-aw,** aw, awe, caw, chaw, claw, craw, daw, draw, faugh, flaw, gnaw, haw, jaw, law, maw, paw, pshaw, raw, saw, Shaw, slaw, squaw, straw, taw, thaw, yaw; backsaw, band saw, bashaw, bear claw, bed-straw, blue law, Boyle's law, buzzsaw, bylaw, case law, cat's-claw, cat's-paw, chain saw, Choctaw, coleslaw,

Crenshaw, cumshaw, cushaw, declaw, dewclaw, forepaw, foresaw, gewgaw, guffaw, hacksaw, hawkshaw, heehaw, in-law, jackdaw, jackstraw, jigsaw, kickshaw, landau, last straw, leash law, lockjaw, lynch law, macaw, Ohm's law, outlaw, pawpaw, pilau, pre-law, quick draw, rickshaw, ripsaw, scofflaw, scrimshaw, seesaw, southpaw, Utah, Warsaw, whipsaw, withdraw; Arkansas, blue-sky law, canon law, Chickasaw, civil law, common law, court of law, foofaraw, in the raw, jinrikisha, lantern jaw, lemon law, mackinaw, martial law, miter saw, Omaha, Ottawa, overawe, overdraw, padishah, Panama, power saw, son-in-law, tragic flaw, usquebaugh, wappenshaw, wapperjaw, Wichita, williwaw; brother-in-law, criminal law, daughter-in-law, father-in-law, mother-in-law, sister-in-law; attorney-at-law, dietary law, periodic law.

**-awd.** See **-aud.**

**-awed.** See **-aud.**

**-awk.** See **-alk.**

**-awl,** all, awl, ball, bawl, brawl, call, caul, crawl, drawl, fall, gall, Gaul, hall, haul, mall, maul, pall, Paul, pawl, Saul, scrawl, shawl, small, spall, sprawl, squall, stall, tall, thrall, trawl, wall, y'all, yawl; air ball, Algol, ALGOL, appall, AWOL, baseball, beachball, beer hall, befall, Bengal, bird call, blackball, blank wall, bookstall, box stall, brick wall, catcall, catchall, cell wall, close call, COBOL, cold call, cornball, cue ball, cure-all, curve ball, deadfall, dodge ball, downfall, drywall, dust ball, eight ball, end-all, enthrall, eyeball, fair ball, fastball, flood wall, foosball, football, footfall, forestall, free-fall, glycol, golf ball, goofball, googol, guildhall, hairball, handball, hardball, hardwall, headstall, heal-all, highball, holdall, house call, install, jump ball, keelhaul, kickball, know-all, landfall, lowball, masked ball, meatball, menthol, mess hall, miscall, moonball, mothball, naphthol, nightfall, nutgall, oddball, pall-mall, pinball, pitfall, plimsoll, pool hall, pratfall, prayer shawl, pub crawl, puffball, rainfall, recall, riyal, rock wall, roll call, rootball, screwball, seawall, shortfall, short-haul, sick call, sidewall, sleazeball, snowball, snowfall, softball, speedball, spitball, stickball, stonewall, strip mall, T-ball, tea ball, tell-all, toll call, town hall, trackball, Whitehall, whitewall, will-call, windfall, withal, wolf call, you-all; aerosol, alcohol, all in all, altar call, banquet hall, basketball, Berlin Wall, billiard ball, borough hall, bowling ball, buckyball, butterball, cannonball, carryall, caterwaul, cattle call, city hall, climbing wall, coverall, crystal ball, curtain call, dining hall, ethanol, evenfall, fireball, firewall, foul ball, free-for-all, gasohol, girasol, judgment call, know-it-all, knuckleball, matzo ball, music hall, nature's call, off-the-wall, overall, overhaul, paddleball, parasol, party wall, Pentothal, pre-install, protocol, racquetball, reinstall, shopping mall, shower stall, sourball, study hall, tattersall, tennis ball, tetherball, uninstall, urban sprawl, volleyball, wake-up call, wall-to-wall, waterfall, wherewithal, wrecker's ball; cholesterol, Neanderthal, retaining wall.

**-awled.** See **-ald.**

**-awn.** See **-on** (ôn).

**-aws.** See **-ause.**

**-ax,** ax, fax, flax, lax, max, Max, pax, sax, slacks, tax, wax, zax; addax, Ajax, anthrax, beeswax, borax, broadax, climax, death tax, earwax, flat tax, gift tax, head tax, hyrax, meat ax, panchax, pickax, poleax, poll tax, pretax, relax, sales tax, sin tax, smilax, storax, surtax, syntax, Tay-Sachs, thorax; aftertax, ball of wax, battle-ax, double ax, excise tax, Halifax, income tax, Kallikaks, minimax, nanny tax, nuisance tax, overlax, overtax, parallax, payroll tax, sealing wax, single tax; Adirondacks, anticlimax, Astyanax.

Also: **-ack** + **-s** (as in *sacks,* etc.)

**-ay,** (-ā), a, aye, bay, bey, brae, bray, cay, chez, clay, day, dey, dray, ey, fay, Fay, fey, flay, fray, gay, gray, grey, hay, hey, jay, Jay, Kay, lay, lei, Mae, may, May, nay, née, neigh, pay, play, pray, prey, quay, ray, Ray, say, sei, shay, slay, sleigh, spay, splay, spray, stay, stray, sway, they, trait, tray, trey, way, weigh, whey, yea; abbé, affray, agley, airplay, airway, allay, all-day, archway, array, ashtray, assay, astray, au fait, away, aweigh, ballet, base pay, beignet, belay, beltway, beret, betray, bewray, bidet, bikeway, birthday, blasé, bobsleigh, Bombay, bomb bay, bombé, bouclé, bouquet, bourreé, breezeway, Broadway, buffet, byway, cachet, café, Calais, Cathay, causeway, chalet, chambray, chassé, child's play, cliché, cogway, convey, copay, corvée, couché, coupé, Courbet, crochet, croquet, curé, DA, daresay, D-day, death ray, decay, deejay, defray, delay, dengue, dismay, display, distrait, DJ, doomsday, doorway, dragée, downplay, driveway, duvet, Earl Grey, endplay, entrée, épée, essay, fair play, fairway, field day, filé, filet, fillet, flambé, floodway, flyway, folkway, foray, force play, foreplay, forestay, forte, Fouquet, fourchée, foyer, franglais, frappé, freeway, Friday, frisé, furnet, gainsay, gangway, gateway, gelée, glacé, gourmet, greenway, gunplay, hairspray, half-day, halfway, hallway, haole, harm's way, headway, hearsay, heyday, highway, hooray, horseplay, in play, in re, inlay, inveigh, Issei, jackstay, jeté, Jetway, Koine, lamé, leeway, lycée, maguey, mainstay, Malay, Manet, manqué, margay, match play, maté, May

Day, mayday, melee, métier, meze, midday, midway, Millet, mislay, misplay, moiré, Monday, Monet, moray, Mornay, name day, naysay, Nisei, nosegay, no way, obey, okay, olé, one-way, osprey, outlay, outré, outstay, outweigh, oyez, PA, parfait, parkway, parlay, parquet, part-way, passé, pâté, pathway, pavé, payday, per se, pince-nez, piqué, piquet, plié, Pompeii, portray, prepay, purée, purvey, Rabelais, raceway, railway, relay, repay, replay, risqué, roadway, Roget, role-play, roquet, rosé, roué, runway, sachet, sansei, sashay, sauté, screenplay, scrub jay, seaway, shar-pei, sick bay, sick day, sick pay, skyway, soigné, soiree, someday, soothsay, sorbet, soufflé, speedway, spillway, squeeze play, stageplay, stairway, stingray, subway, sundae, Sunday, survey, sweet bay, swordplay, tempeh, thruway, Thursday, today, tokay, Tokay, touché, toupée, tramway, Tuesday, two-way, valet, V-day, veejay, walkway, waylay, Wednesday, weekday, wordplay, workday, x-ray; A-OK, All Saints' Day, all the way, anyway, appliqué, atelier, attaché, bad hair day, ballonet, Bastille Day, Beaujolais, beurre manié, bird of prey, Boxing Day, breakaway, bustier, cabaret, canapé, caraway, carriageway, cassoulet, castaway, cathode ray, chansonnier, chardonnay, chevalier, Chevrolet, Chippewa, cloisonné, consommé, cosmic ray, croupier, crudités, cutaway, day-to-day, debauchee, déclassé, devotee, deMusset, disarray, disobey, distingué, divorcée, DNA, dollar day, dossier, double play, dress-down day, émigré, engagé, entranceway, entremets, entryway, espalier, étouffée, everyday, exposé, expressway, fadeaway, faraday, faraway, Father's Day, feet of clay, fiancé(e), flageolet, flyaway, foldaway, foul play, gal Friday, gamma ray, garde-manger, getaway, giveaway, gratiné, Groundhog Day, guillemet, Hemingway, hideaway, Hogmanay, holiday, holy day, interplay, IPA, IRA, judgment day, Kyrie, Labor Day, lackaday, latterday, layaway, lingerie, macramé, Mandalay, manta ray, matelassé, matinee, medal play, MIA, Milky Way, Monterey, Monterrey, Mother's Day, motorway, muscadet, negligée, New Year's Day, Nez Percé, night and day, off-Broadway, Ojibwa, on the way, out of play, overlay, overpay, overstay, passageway, passion play, pepper spray, photoplay, piolet, pis aller, play-by-play, Plug and Play, pop injay, potter's clay, pourparler, pousse-café, power play, present-day, protégé(e), rainy day, recherché, repartee, repoussé, résumé, ricochet, right away, right-of-way, rissolé, RNA, rollaway, roundelay, runaway, Saint-Tropez, Salomé, Santa Fe, Saturday, semplice, severance pay, shadow play, s'il vous plaît, sleepaway, sobriquet, sommelier, stowaway, straightaway, taboret, take-away, teleplay, Tenebrae, thataway, throwaway, triple play, underlay, underpay, underway, Uruguay, velouté, vertebrae, virelay, wedding day, waterway, workaday, yesterday; alackaday, Appian Way, April Fool's Day, Armistice Day, auto-da-fé, bank holiday, beta decay, bichon frisé, bioassay, cabriolet, café au lait, caloo-calay, cantabile, Columbus Day, communiqué, corps de ballet, couturier, décolleté, devil to pay, Dies Irae, Election Day, electric ray, felo-de-se, habitué, High Holiday, instant replay, laissez-passer, marrons glacé, mystery play, objet trouvé, off-off-Broadway, Olivier, out-of-the-way, papier collé, papier-mâché, pas de bourrée, photo essay, prêt-à-porter, Presidents' Day, roman à clef, severance pay, sine die, superhighway, Thanksgiving Day, ukiyo-e, Valentine's Day, Veterans Day, yerba maté; arrière pensée, Independence Day, lettre de cachet, Memorial Day, morality play, Mrs. Dalloway; cinéma vérité; Edna St. Vincent Millay.

**-ayed.** See **-ade.**

**-ays.** See **-aze.**

**-aze,** baize, blaze, braise, braze, chaise, craze, daze, faze, fraise, gaze, glaze, graze, haze, lase, laze, maize, maze, phase, phrase, praise, raise, raze, vase; ablaze, always, amaze, anglaise, appraise, catchphrase, crossways, deglaze, dispraise, dog days, edgeways, emblaze, folkways, foodways, fund-raise, leastways, lengthways, liaise, longways, malaise, mores, noun phrase, pj's, post chaise, rephrase, sideways, slantways, stargaze, ukase, weekdays; anyways, crème anglaise, chrysoprase, écossaise, hollandaise, lyonnaise, Marseillaise, mayonnaise, multiphrase, nowadays, overgraze, overpraise, paraphrase, polonaise, salad days, underglaze.

Also: **-ay** + **-s** (as in *days,* etc.)

Also: **-ey** + **-s** (as in *preys,* etc.)

Also: **-eigh** + **-s** (as in *weighs,* etc.)

**-azz,** as, has, jazz, razz; pizzazz, topaz, whereas; Alcatraz, razzmatazz.

**-e.** See **-ee.**

**-ea.** See **-ee.**

**-eace.** See **-ease.**

**-each,** beach, beech, bleach, breach, breech, each, leach, leech, peach, pleach, preach, reach, screech, speech, teach; beseech, free speech, hate speech, impeach, outreach, stump speech; copper beech, overreach, part of speech; figure of speech.

**-ead** (-ēd). See **-eed.**

**-ead** (-ed). See **-ed.**

**-eaf** (-ef). See **-ef.**

**-eaf** (-ēf). See **-ief.**

**-eague,** gigue, Grieg, klieg, league, peag; big-league, blitzkrieg, bush league, colleague, enleague, fatigue, intrigue, sitzkrieg; Ivy League, little league, major league, minor league, wampumpeag; battle fatigue, combat fatigue.

**-eak** (-ēk), beak, bleak, cheek, chic, clique, creak, creek, Creek, eke, freak, geek, gleek, Greek, leak, leek, meek, peak, peek, peke, phreak, pique, reek, screak, seek, sheik, shriek, Sikh, sleek, sneak, speak, squeak, streak, teak, tweak, weak, week, wreak; antique, batik, Belleek, bespeak, bezique, blue streak, boutique, cacique, caïque, chinbeak, critique, grosbeak, houseleek, midweek, misspeak, Monique, mystique, newspeak, oblique, off-peak, perique, phone phreak, physique, pipspeak, plastique, pratique, relique, silique, speed freak, technique, unique, workweek; Chesapeake, control freak, domestique, doublespeak, ecofreak, fenugreek, Frederique, hide-and-seek, Holy Week, Martinique, Mozambique, Pathétique, tongue-in-cheek, widow's peak; bubble and squeak, electroweak, radical chic, opéra comique, realpolitik.

**-eak** (-āk). See **-ake.**

**-eal,** ceil, creel, deal, eel, feel, heal, heel, he'll, keel, Kiel, kneel, leal, meal, Neal, Neil, peal, peel, real, reel, seal, seel, she'll, spiel, squeal, steal, steel, teal, tuille, veal, weal, we'll, wheel, zeal; aiguille, allele, allheal, anele, anneal, appeal, Bastille, big deal, big wheel, bonemeal, bonspiel, cartwheel, Castile, chenille, cogwheel, conceal, congeal, cornmeal, done deal, double-deal, Émile, fifth wheel, fish meal, flywheel, fourwheel, freewheel, fur seal, gearwheel, genteel, good deal, great seal, handwheel, harp seal, ideal, inchmeal, Lucille, mill wheel, misdeal, mobile, Mobile, mouthfeel, New Deal, newsreel, oatmeal, ordeal, pastille, piecemeal, pinwheel, raw deal, repeal, reveal, schlemiel, selfheal, spike heel, square meal, stabile, surreal, Tar Heel, unreal, wedge heel; balance wheel, bidonville, beau ideal, blastocoel, bloodmobile, bookmobile, camomile, campanile, carbon steel, cochineal, cockatiel, color wheel, commonweal, conger eel, curb appeal, daisy wheel, deshabille, difficile, down-at-heel, driving wheel, eye appeal, Ferris wheel, glockenspiel, goldenseal, harbor seal, machineel, matzo meal, megadeal, mercantile, moray eel, orange peel, package deal, paddlewheel, potter's wheel, privy seal, reel-to-reel, sex appeal, skimobile, snob appeal, snowmobile, spinning wheel, stainless steel, thunderpeal, tracing wheel; Achilles heel, automobile, chemical peel, Court of Appeal, Damascus steel, Virginia reel.

**-eald.** See **-ield.**

**-ealed.** See **-ield.**

**-ealm.** See **-elm.**

**-ealth,** health, stealth, wealth; bill of health, board of health, commonwealth, public health.

**-eam,** beam, bream, cream, deem, deme, dream, fleam, gleam, meme, neem, ream, scheme, scream, seam, seem, steam, stream, team, teem, theme; abeam, agleam, airstream, beseem, bireme, blaspheme, bloodstream, centime, coal seam, cold cream, crossbeam, daydream, downstream, dream team, egg cream, esteem, extreme, grapheme, Gulf Stream, hakim, headstream, high beam, hornbeam, ice cream, inseam, jet stream, kilim, lexeme, low beam, mainstream, midstream, millstream, moonbeam, morpheme, phoneme, pipe dream, redeem, regime, rhyme scheme, sidestream, slipstream, sunbeam, supreme, tag team, taxeme, trireme, upstream, wet dream; academe, balance beam, blow off steam, buttercream, clotted cream, heavy cream, monotreme, Ponzi scheme, self-esteem, sour cream; ancien régime, pyramid scheme, vanishing cream; American dream, Bavarian cream.

**-ean,** bean, been, clean, dean, Dean, e'en, gene, Gene, glean, green, jean, Jean, keen, lean, lien, mean, mesne, mien, peen, preen, quean, queen, scene, screen, seen, sheen, skean, spleen, teen, tween, wean, ween, yean; achene, arsine, baleen, beguine, benzene, benzine, between, black bean, broad bean, bromine, caffeine, canteen, careen, chlorine, chorine, chopine, Christine, citrine, Claudine, codeine, colleen, convene, cuisine, dasheen, dauphine, demean, demesne, dentine, drag queen, dry-clean, dudeen, eighteen, Eileen, Essene, Eugene, e-zine, fanzine, fifteen, flat-screen, flavine, fluorine, foreseen, fourteen, gamine, gangrene, glassine, Hellene, Holstein, houseclean, hygiene, ich dien, Irene, Kathleen, khamsin, lateen, latrine, machine, marine, Marlene, Maureen, moreen, morphine, mung bean, nankeen, naphthene, Nicene, nineteen, obscene, offscreen, on-screen, patine, Pauline, phosgene, piscine, pontine, poteen, praline, preteen, pristine, protein, purine, quinine, ravine, routine, saline, saltine, sardine, sateen, scalene, serene, shagreen, sixteen, Slovene, snapbean, sourdine, soybean, split screen, string bean, strychnine, subteen, subvene, sunscreen, taurine, terrine, thirteen, tontine, trephine, tureen, umpteen, unclean, undine, unseen, vaccine, vitrine, wax bean, widescreen, windscreen; Aberdeen, Abilene, almandine, Argentine, astatine, atabrine, atropine, aubergine, Augustine, bandoline, barkentine, Benzedrine, bombazine, bowling green, brigantine, brilliantine, Byzantine, carotene, carrageen, celandine, Constantine, galantine, contravene, crêpe de chine, crystalline, cysteine, damascene, dopamine, eglantine, Eocene, epicene, evergreen, fairy queen, fava bean, fellahin, figurine, Florentine, gabardine, gasoline, Geraldine, Ghibelline, go-between, golden mean, grenadine, guillotine, Halloween, haute cuisine, Hippocrene, histamine, Holocene, in-between, indigene, intervene, jellybean, Josephine, kerosene, kidney bean, langoustine, libertine, lima bean, limousine, lycopene, magazine, mangosteen, margravine, melamine, mezzanine, Miocene, mousseline, navy bean, Nazarene, nectarine, nicotine, olivine, opaline, overseen, overween, palanquin, Paris green, pelerine, peregrine, Philistine, pinto bean, plasticene, Pleistocene, putting green, quarantine, serpentine, seventeen, slot machine, submarine, subroutine, supergene, supervene, tambourine, tangerine, time machine, tourmaline, unforeseen, Vaseline, velveteen, wintergreen, wolverine; acetylene, alexandrine, amphetamine, aquamarine, Benedictine, elephantine, flying machine, garbanzo bean, incarnadine, internecine, labyrinthine, merchant marine, mujahideen, nouvelle cuisine, Oligocene, Paleocene, pinball machine, rowing machine, ultramarine, vending machine, voting machine, washing machine; answering machine, antihistamine, beta carotene, Mary Magdalene.

**-eaned.** See **-iend.**

**-eant.** See **-ent.**

**-eap.** See **-eep.**

**-ear.** See **-eer.**

**-earch.** See **-urch.**
**-eard** (-ird), beard, tiered, weird; afeard, Bluebeard, dog-eared, graybeard, lop-eared, sharp-eared, white-beard.
Also: **-ear** + **-ed** (as in *reared*, etc.)
Also: **-ere** + **-ed** (as in *interfered*, etc.)
Also: **-eer** + **-ed** (as in *veered*, etc.)
**-eard** (-ûrd). See **-urd.**
**-eared.** See **-eard.**
**-earl.** See **-url.**
**-earn.** See **-urn.**
**-ears.** See **-ares.**
**-earse.** See **-erse.**
**-eart.** See **-art.**
**-earth.** See **-irth.**
**-eas.** See **-ease.**
**-ease** (-ēs), cease, crease, fleece, geese, grease, Greece, lease, Nice, niece, peace, piece; apiece, at peace, Bernice, camise, caprice, cassis, cerise, Chinese, codpiece, coulisse, crosspiece, decease, decrease, degrease, earpiece, eyepiece, grandniece, hairpiece, headpiece, increase, lend-lease, Matisse, Maurice, mouthpiece, nosepiece, obese, one-piece, pastis, pelisse, police, release, set piece, showpiece, sublease, surcease, tailpiece, think piece, timepiece, three-piece, two-piece, valise; altarpiece, ambergris, Balinese, Bengalese, Brooklynese, cantatrice, Cantonese, centerpiece, chimneypiece, Congolese, diocese, directrice, ex libris, expertise, frontispiece, Golden Fleece, Japanese, journalese, Lebanese, legalese, manganese, mantelpiece, masterpiece, Pekinese, Portuguese, predecease, Siamese, Singalese, timed-release, verdigris, Viennese; archdiocese, bureaucratese, companion piece, computerese, crème de cassis, museum piece, officialese, period piece, secret police, sustained-release, telegraphese, Vietnamese; conversation piece, justice of the peace.

**-ease** (-ēz), breeze, cheese, ease, freeze, frieze, grease, he's, jeez, lees, pease, please, seize, she's, skis, sleaze, sneeze, squeeze, tease, these, wheeze; Andes, appease, Aries, at ease, bee's knees, Belize, bêtise, big cheese, blue cheese, boonies, brain freeze, Burmese, camise, cerise, chemise, Chinese, deep-freeze, disease, displease, d.t.'s, en pris, fasces, fauces, Ganges, headcheese, heartsease, Hermes, Louise, Maltese, marquise, menses, nates, Pisces, quick-freeze, reprise, sea breeze, soubise, striptease, Swiss cheese, Thales, trapeze, unease, Xerxes; ABC's, Achilles, Androcles, antifreeze, Antilles, Balinese, Bengalese, Brooklynese, BVDs, Cantonese, cheddar cheese, congeries, Congolese, cottage cheese, Damocles, diocese, expertise, fifth disease, gourmandize, Heloise, Hercules, ill at ease, Japanese, Javanese, journalese, legalese, litotes, manganese, Milanese, Nepalese, obsequies, overseas, Pekinese, Pericles, Pleiades, Portuguese, Pyrennes, shoot the breeze, Siamese, Socrates, Sophocles, Viennese; academese, anopheles, antipodes, antitheses, archdiocese, bona fides, bureaucratese, cheval-de-frise, computerese, Dutch elm disease, éminence grise, Gaucher's disease, governmentese, Hippocrates, Hodgkin's disease, hypotheses, Indo-Chinese, kissing disease, mad cow disease, officialese, parentheses, Peloponnese, social disease, soliloquies, superficies, telegraphese, Vietnamese; aborigines, Mephistopheles, Parkinson's disease, superficies, sword of Damocles.

Also: **-ea** + **-s** (as in *teas,* etc.)

Also: **-ee** + **-s** (as in *bees, frees,* etc.)

**-eased.** See **-east.**

**-east,** beast, east, feast, least, piste, priest, yeast; artiste, at least, batiste, deceased, down east, Far East, love feast, Mideast, modiste, Near East, northeast, southeast, tachiste; arriviste, brewer's yeast, hartebeest, Middle East, wedding feast, wildebeest.

Also: **-ease** + **-ed** (as in *released*, etc.)

**-eat** (-ēt), beat, beet, bleat, cheat, cleat, Crete, eat, feat, feet, fleet, greet, heat, meat, meet, mete, neat, peat, Pete, pleat, seat, sheet, skeet, sleet, street, suite, sweet, teat, treat, tweet, wheat; accrete, aesthete, afreet, athlete, backseat, backstreet, bedsheet, box pleat, box seat, broadsheet, browbeat, buckwheat, bystreet, call sheet, carseat, cheat sheet, cold feet, compete, complete, conceit, concrete, crabmeat, crib sheet, deadbeat, dead heat, dead meat, deceit, defeat, delete, deplete, discreet, discrete, downbeat, drumbeat, Dutch treat, effete, elite, en suite, entreat, escheat, esthete, excrete, fly sheet, forcemeat, foresheet, gamete, groundsheet, Grub Street, hard wheat, heartbeat, heat-treat, helpmeet, hoofbeat, hot seat, ice sheet, ill-treat, jump seat, kick pleat, love seat, mainsheet, Main Street, maltreat, mesquite, mincemeat, mistreat, offbeat, petite, preheat, rap sheet, receipt, red meat, reheat, repeat, replete, retreat, scratch sheet, secrete, side street, spreadsheet, sweetmeat, tear sheet, threepeat, through street, time sheet, unseat, upbeat, Wall Street, white heat; aquavit, balance sheet, biathlete, bittersweet, booster seat, bucket seat, catbird seat, cellulite, cookie sheet, countryseat, county seat, decathlete, driver's seat, durum wheat, Easy Street, exegete, incomplete, indiscreet, lorikeet, make ends meet, marguerite, Marguerite, meadowsweet, meet and greet, miss a beat, obsolete, overeat, overheat, parakeet, prickly heat, rumble seat, scandal sheet, self-conceit, semi-sweet, shredded wheat, spirochete, triathlete, trick or treat, two-way street, winding-sheet, window seat; ejection seat, man in the street, souvenir sheet; Nibelungenlied.

**-eat** (-āt). See **-ate.**

**-eat** (-et). See **-et.**

**-eath** (-eth), Beth, breadth, breath, death, meth, saith, Seth; bad breath, Black Death, brain death, crib death, Macbeth; Ashtoreth, baby's-breath, crystal meth, dance of death, kiss of death, life-and-death, living death, out of breath, shibboleth, sudden death, thirtieth, twentieth, wrongful death; Elizabeth.

**-eath** (-ēth), heath, Keith, 'neath, sheath, teeth, wreath; beneath, bequeath, hadith, monteith; bridal wreath, underneath.

**-eathe** (-ēt̸h), breathe, seethe, sheathe, teethe, wreathe; bequeath, ensheathe, enwreathe.

**-eau.** See **-ow.**

**-eave** (-ēv), breve, cleave, eave, eve, Eve, greave, grieve, heave, leave, lieve, peeve, reave, reeve, sleeve, Steve, thieve, weave, we've; achieve, aggrieve, believe, bereave, cap sleeve, conceive, deceive, endive, French leave, frost heave, khedive, naive, perceive, pet peeve, plain weave, qui vive, receive, relieve, reprieve, retrieve, shirtsleeve, shore leave, sick leave, unreeve; apperceive, basket weave, by-your-leave, Christmas Eve, disbelieve, dolman sleeve, Genevieve, interleave, interweave, make-believe, misconceive, New Year's Eve, preconceive, raglan sleeve, satin weave, semibreve, Tel Aviv; Adam and Eve, family leave, overachieve, recitative, underachieve; absent without leave.

**-eb,** bleb, deb, ebb, neb, pleb, reb, web; ardeb, celeb, cobweb, cubeb, food web, subdeb, zineb; mahaleb, spider web, World Wide Web.

**-eck,** beck, check, cheque, Czech, deck, dreck, fleck, heck, keck, lek, neck, pec, peck, reck, sec, spec, speck, tech, trek, wreck; Aztec, bank check, bedcheck, bedeck, blank check, boat neck, breakneck, bullneck, chebec, crew neck, cromlech, crookneck, crosscheck, cusec, ewe-neck, exec, fact-check, fennec, flight deck, flyspeck, foredeck, gooseneck, hacek, hatcheck, henpeck, high-tech, home ec, kopeck, longneck, low-tech, main deck, Mixtec, on deck, OPEC, parsec, paycheck, pinchbeck, pincheck, poop deck, Quebec, raincheck, rebec, redneck, ringneck, roll-neck, roof-deck, roughneck, sales check, scoop neck, shipwreck, spar deck, spell-check, spot-check, Star Trek, Steinbeck, sun deck, tape deck, tenrec, Toltec, V-neck, wryneck, xebec; afterdeck, à la greque, biotech, body check, bottleneck, canceled check, cashier's check, cassette deck, demi-sec, discotheque, double-check, double-deck, hunt and peck, leatherneck, limberneck, littleneck, lower deck, nanotech, neck and neck, quarterdeck, rubber check, rubberneck, triple sec, turtleneck, weather deck, Zapotec; cinematheque, hurricane deck, parity check, promenade deck, Toulouse-Lautrec, traveler's check; reality check, Tehuantepec.

**-ecked.** See **-ect.**

**-ecks.** See **-ex.**

**-ect,** lect, sect; abject, advect, affect, aspect, bedecked, bisect, collect, complect, confect, connect, convect, correct, defect, deflect, deject, detect, direct, dissect, effect, eject, elect, erect, expect, infect, inflect, inject, insect, inspect, neglect, object, obtect, pandect, perfect, porrect, prefect, prelect, project, prospect, protect, refect, reflect, reject, resect, respect, select, subject, suspect, transect, trisect; acrolect, architect, basilect, birth defect, circumspect, deselect, dialect, disaffect, disconnect, disinfect, disrespect, found object, genuflect, imperfect, incorrect, indirect, intellect, interject, intersect, introject, introspect, misconnect, misdirect, pluperfect, preselect, recollect, reconnect, redirect, reelect, reinfect, reinject, reinspect, resurrect, retrospect, self-respect, sex object, side effect, sound effect, vivisect; aftereffect, benign neglect, cause-and-effect, direct object, eye dialect, greenhouse effect, halo effect, housing project, hypercorrect, idiolect, interconnect, ratchet effect, ripple effect, sociolect, tunnel effect; domino effect; politically correct.

Also: **-eck** + **-ed** (as in *wrecked*, etc.)

**-ed,** bed, bled, bread, bred, dead, dread, Ed, fed, fled, Fred, head, Jed, lead, led, Ned, pled, read, red, redd, said, shed, shred, sled, sped, spread, stead, ted, Ted, thread, tread, wed, zed; abed, ahead, airhead, beachhead, bedspread, bedstead, behead, biped, blackhead, blockhead, blood-red, bloodshed, bobsled, bonehead, bowhead, box head, brain-dead, bridgehead, brown bread, bulkhead, childbed, Club Med, coed, conehead, cornbread, corn-fed, cowshed, crackhead, crispbread, crossbred, daybed, deadhead, deathbed, death's-head, dogsled, drop-dead, drumhead, egghead, embed, farmstead, fathead, flatbed, flatbread, forehead, French bread, godhead, half-dead, half-read, hardhead, highbred, hogshead, homebred, homestead, hophead, hotbed, hothead, ill-bred, inbred, instead, jarhead, jughead, loaf bread, lunkhead, masthead, meathead, misled, moped, nailhead, Op-Ed, outspread, phys ed, pig lead, pillhead, pinhead, point spread, pothead, premed, printhead, purebred, quick bread, railhead, redhead, retread, retread, roadbed, roadstead, rye bread, screw thread, seabed, sheet-fed, shewbread, shortbread, sickbed, skinhead, snowshed, sorehead, spearhead, spoon bread, stone-dead, subhead, sweetbread, swelled head, toolshed, towhead, trailhead, undead, unread, unsaid, unwed, warhead, well-bred, well-read, white bread, white-bread, widespread, wingspread, woodshed; acid-head, aforesaid, arrowhead, bubblehead, center spread, chapter head, chowderhead, copperhead, curlyhead, double spread, dunderhead, featherbed, fiddlehead, figurehead, fissiped, fountainhead, gingerbread, go-ahead, hammerhead, head-to-head, holy bread, infrared, interbred, knucklehead, letterhead, loggerhead, maidenhead, metalhead, muddlehead, muttonhead, newlywed, noodlehead, overhead, overspread, photo spread, pinniped, pita bread, pointy-head, quadruped, riverbed, riverhead, running head, showerhead, sleepyhead, soda bread, straight-ahead, talking head, thoroughbred, thunderhead, truckle bed, trundle bed, underfed, watershed; middle-age spread, propeller head.

**-ede.** See **-eed.**

**-edge,** dredge, edge, fledge, hedge, kedge, ledge, pledge, sedge, sledge, veg, wedge; allege, frankpledge, gilt-edge, hard-edge, straightedge, unedge; cutting edge, deckle edge, featheredge, foxtail wedge, leading edge, ragged edge.

**-ee,** be, Bea, bee, Brie, cay, Cree, fee, flea, flee, free, gee, ghee, glee, he, key, knee, lea, lee, me, mi, pea, pee, plea, quay, re, scree, sea, see, she, ski, spree, tea, tee, the, thee, three, tree, twee, we, wee, whee, ye; acme, acne, agree, agley, aiguille, akee, alee, at sea, bailee, banshee, bohea, bootee, bo tree, burgee, CD, Chablis, Chaldee, chickpea, chili, church key, Coetzee, confit, cowpea, curie, Darcy, debris, decree, deep-sea, degree, donee, draftee, drawee, Dundee, emcee, ennui, esprit, etui, farci, feoffee, foresee, Frisbee, fusee, germ-free, glacis, goatee, grandee, grand prix, grantee, greens fee, green tea, he/she, high sea, high tea, home-free, hot key, Humvee, ID, IV, Jaycee, latchkey, lemme, lessee, levee, listee, litchi, look-see, low-key, LP, lychee, mamey, maquis, Marie, marquee, marquis, MC, MD, mentee, métis, mille-feuille, muggee, must-see, Mowgli, Nancy, ngwee, OD, off-key, ogee, Parsee, passkey, Pawnee, payee, peewee, pewee, PG, pledgee, pollee, pongee, précis, pugree, puttee, raki, ranee, razee, Red Sea, rupee, rushee, RV, sati, scot-free, settee, shift key, shoetree, sightsee, signee, sirree, snap pea, snow pea, spahi, spondee, squeegee, standee, state tree, strophe, tax-free, teepee, 3-D, to-be, toll-free, topee, towhee, townee, trainee, trochee, trustee, turnkey, Tutsi, TV, vendee, vestee, whoopee, would-be; ABC, abductee, abscissae, absentee, addressee, adobe, adoptee, advisee, agony, alumnae, ambergris, amputee, anomie, apogee, appellee, appointee, après-ski, arrestee, assignee, attendee, axletree, bain-marie, baloney, batterie, bonhomie, booboisie, botany, bourgeoisie, B2B, bumblebee, BVD, calorie, calumny, camparee, canopy, cap-a-pie, causerie, Cherokee, chickadee, chimpanzee, Christmas tree, coati, C.O.D., company, conferee, consignee, context-free, cop a plea, coterie, counterplea, cruelty-free, DDT, debauchee, deportee, dernier cri, deshabille, designee, destiny, detainee, devotee, disagree, dungaree, duty-free, DVD, eau-de-vie, ebony, employee, endorsee, enlistee, enrollee, epopee, escapee, ESP, evictee, fancy-free, fantasy, felony, filigree, fleur-de-lis, fricassee, function key, garnishee, gaucherie, gelati, gluttony, guarantee, harmony, HIV, honeybee, honoree, housemaid's knee, inductee, internee, invitee, irony, jamboree, jeu d'esprit, jubilee, Judas tree, jus soli, kedgeree, killer bee, LCD, LED, legatee, licensee, Lombardy, LSD, Maccabee, maître d', manatee, master key, mortgagee, nepenthe, Niobe, nominee, Normandy, oversee, parolee, parti pris, pedigree, perigee, Pharisee, Ph.D., Picardy, piroshki, potpourri, praecipe, presentee, Ptolemy, pugaree, rapparee, recipe, referee, refugee, repartee, returnee, reveille, Sadducee, sangaree, satori, sesame, shivaree, simile, singletree, snickersnee, spelling bee, SUV, symphony, systole, syzygy, Tennessee, third degree, thirty-three, TNT, to a tee, torii, transferee, tulip tree, tyranny, undersea, user fee, verdigris, vertebrae, VIP, vis-à-vis, wannabe, warranty, whiffletree; abalone, anemone, anomaly, apostrophe, Antigone, Ariadne, ASAP, bouquet garni, caller ID, calliope, carpenter bee, casus belli, catastrophe, charcuterie, chinoiserie, digerati, distributee, Euphrosyne, evacuee, examinee, facsimile, fait accompli, family tree, fiddle-de-dee, Gethsemane, HDTV, hyperbole, interviewee, jaborandi, karaoke, macaroni, Melpomene, minutiae, omega-3, on the q.t., patisserie, Penelope, prima facie, proclivity, retiree, skeleton key, synecdoche, synonymy; aborigine, Deuteronomy, japonaiserie; amicus curiae.

**-eece.** See **-ease.**

**-eech.** See **-each.**

**-eed,** bead, Bede, bleed, breed, cede, creed, deed, feed, freed, greed, he'd, heed, keyed, knead, kneed, lead, lied, mead, Mede, meed, need, plead, read, reed, screed, seed, she'd, speed, steed, swede, Swede, tweed, we'd, weed; accede, airspeed, allseed, bindweed, birdseed, bourride, breast-feed, burreed, Candide, cheerlead, chickweed, concede, crossbreed, debride, decreed, dillweed, drip-feed, duckweed, exceed, flaxseed, force-feed, full speed, Godspeed, goateed, good speed, half-breed, hand-feed, hayseed, high-speed, impede, implead, inbreed, indeed, knock-kneed, knotweed, linseed, lip-read, milkweed, misfeed, misdeed, mislead, misread, nosebleed, pokeweed, precede, proceed, proofread, ragweed, rapeseed, recede, seaweed, secede, sight-read, speed-read, spoon-feed, stampede, stinkweed, succeed, ten-speed, warp speed, weak-kneed, wormseed; aniseed, antecede, bottle-feed, centipede, chicken feed, copyread, cottonseed, cottonweed, double-reed, fennel seed, Ganymede, half-agreed, interbreed, intercede, interplead, ironweed, jimson weed, millipede, overfeed, pedigreed, poppyseed, quitclaim deed, retrocede, Runnymede, supersede, thimbleweed, title deed, tumbleweed, underfeed, up to speed; caraway seed, velocipede, warranty deed.

Also: **-ee** + **-ed** (as in *agreed*, etc.)

**-eef.** See **-ief.**

**-eek.** See **-eak.**

**-eel.** See **-eal.**

**-eeled.** See **-ield.**

**-eem.** See **-eam.**

**-een.** See **-ean.**

**-eened.** See **-iend.**

**-eep,** beep, bleep, cheap, cheep, creep, deep, heap, Jeep, keep, leap, neap, peep, reap, seep, sheep, sleep, steep, sweep, veep, weep; asleep, barkeep, beweep, black sheep, clean sweep, dirt cheap, dustheap, housekeep, knee-deep, REM sleep, scrap heap, skin-deep, upkeep, upsweep; beauty sleep, bighorn sheep, bracket creep, cassareep, chimney sweep, lover's leap, mountain sheep, oversleep, quantum leap; Uriah Heep.

**-eer,** beer, bier, blear, cere, cheer, clear, dear, deer, drear, ear, fear, fleer, gear, hear, here, jeer, Lear, leer, mere, mir, near, peer, pier, queer, rear, schmear, sear, seer, sere, shear, sheer, smear, sneer, spear, sphere, steer, tear, tier, veer, weir, year; adhere, amir, ampere, appear, arrear, austere, brassière, Bronx cheer, by ear, career, cashier, cashmere, cohere, compeer, dog-ear, emir, endear, fakir, footgear, frontier, gambier, headgear, inhere, kefir, killdeer, leap year, life peer, light-year, man-year, menhir, midyear, mishear, mule deer, musk deer, nadir, near beer, New Year, off year, Pap smear, portiere, premier, premiere, red deer, reindeer, revere, roe deer, root beer, santir, severe, Shakespeare, sincere, spruce beer, steer clear, Tangier, tapir, tin ear, veneer, vizier, voir dire, wind shear, wood ear, worm gear, Zaire, zaire; atmosphere, auctioneer, balladeer, bandoleer, bathysphere, bayadere, belvedere, biosphere, blogosphere, bombardier, boutonniere, brigadier, buccaneer, cannoneer, carbineer, cassimere, cavalier, chandelier, chanticleer, chevalier, chiffonier, commandeer, corsetiere, crystal clear, cuirassier, disappear, domineer, ecosphere, engineer, fallow deer, financier, fiscal year, fusilier, gazeteer, ginger beer, gondolier, grand vizier, grenadier, Guinevere, halberdier, hemisphere, inner ear, insincere, interfere, jardiniere, landing gear, lavaliere, leafleteer, middle ear, mountaineer, muffineer, muleteer, musketeer, mutineer, outer ear, overhear, overseer, pamphleteer, persevere, pioneer, pistoleer, pontonier, privateer, profiteer, puppeteer, racketeer, reappear, sloganeer, sonneteer, souvenir, stratosphere, summiteer, swimmer's ear, troposphere, vintage year, volunteer, white-tailed deer, yesteryear; boulevardier, carabineer, charioteer, chocolatier, conventioneer, dollar-a-year, electioneer, harquebusier, ionosphere, orienteer; academic year, bioengineer, civil engineer, sidereal year, social engineer.

**-eered.** See **-eard.**

**-ees.** See **-ease** (-ēz).

**-eese.** See **-ease** (-ēs).

**-eet.** See **-eat.**

**-eethe.** See **-eathe.**

**-eeze.** See **-ease.**

**-ef,** chef, clef, deaf, def, Jeff, kef, lev, nef, ref, teff; aleph, bass clef, C clef, enfeoff, sous-chef, stone-deaf, tone-deaf; treble clef, UNICEF; Diaghilev, Prokofiev.

**-eft,** cleft, deft, eft, heft, left, reft, theft, weft; bereft, grand theft, New Left, stage left; identity theft.

**-eg,** beg, dreg, egg, keg, leg, meg, Meg, peg, Peg, reg, skeg, squeg, teg, yegg; blackleg, bootleg, dogleg, foreleg, gate leg, jackleg, jake leg, JPEG, MPEG, muskeg, nutmeg, pant leg, pegleg, renege, Tuareg; break a leg, filibeg, powder keg, Winnipeg; mumbletypeg.

**-ege** (-ezh), barege, cortege, manège, solfège.

**-ege** (-ij). See **-age.**

**-egm.** See **-em.**

**-eigh.** See **-ay.**

**-eighed.** See **-ade.**

**-eighs.** See **-aze.**

**-eight** (-āt). See **-ate.**

**-eight** (-īt). See **-ite.**

**-eign.** See **-ain.**

**-eil** (-āl). See **-ail.**

**-eil** (-ēl). See **-eal.**

**-ein** (-ān). See **-ain.**

**-ein** (-īn). See **-ine.**

**-eint.** See **-aint.**

**-eir.** See **-are.**

**-eird.** See **-eard.**

**-eirs.** See **-ares.**

**-eith.** See **-eath** (-ēth).

**-eive.** See **-eave.**

**-eize.** See **-ease.**

**-eke.** See **-eak.**

**-el,** bell, belle, Belle, cel, cell, dell, dwell, el, ell, fell, gel, hell, jell, kell, knell, kvell, mell, Nell, quell, sell, shell, skell, smell, snell, spell, swell, tell, they'll, well, yell; agnel, appel, artel, band shell, barbell, befell, bluebell, boatel, bombshell, Boswell, bretelle, bridewell, cadelle, cartel, chandelle, clamshell, cold spell, compel, cordelle, cormel, Cornell, cowbell, crenelle, cupel, Danielle, death knell, dentelle, dispel, doorbell, dry cell, dry spell, dumbbell, duxelles, eggshell, Estelle, excel, expel, farewell, ficelle, footwell, foretell, fresnel, fuel cell, gabelle, gazelle, germ cell, Giselle, grandrelle, groundswell, half shell, handbell, hard sell, hard-shell, harebell, hotel, impel, inkwell, jurel, lampshell, lapel, marcel, martel, maxwell, micelle, Michelle, misspell, morel, Moselle, motel, nacelle, nerve cell, Nobel, Noel, nouvelle, nutshell, oil well, outsell, outyell, pastel, pell-mell, pixel, pointelle, prequel, presell, propel, prunelle, quenelle, rakehell, rappel, rebel, repel, respell, retell, riel, rondel, rondelle, roselle, seashell, sequel, sleigh bell, soft sell, soft-shell, speedwell, spinel, stairwell, stem cell, unwell, vervelle, volvelle; aerogel, aludel, amarelle, Appenzell, aquarelle, asphodel, Astrophel, bagatelle, barbicel, béchamel, brocatel, calomel, caramel, caravel, carousel, cascabel, chanterelle, chevronel, citadel, clientele, cockerel, cockleshell, decibel, demoiselle, dinner bell, fair-thee-well, fingerspell, fontanel, hydrogel, hydromel, immortelle, infidel, isohel, Jezebel, kiss-and-tell, lenticel, mangonel, mirabelle, moschatel, muscatel, n'er-do-well, Neufchâtel, nonpareil, oenomel, organelle, parallel, pedicel, pennoncel, personnel, philomel, photocell, pimpernel, pipistrelle, plasma cell, plasmagel, radicel, rebel yell, red blood cell, Sanctus bell, show and tell, sickle cell, sentinel, solar cell, tortoiseshell, undersell, villanelle, white blood cell, wishing well, zinfandel; artesian well, au naturel, créme caramel, mademoiselle, maître d'hôtel, matériel; antipersonnel.

**-elch,** belch, squelch.

**-eld,** eld, geld, held, meld, weld; beheld, Danegeld, fjeld, handheld, unquelled, upheld, withheld; jet-propelled, self-propelled; unparalleled.

Also: **-ell** + **-ed** (as in *spelled*, etc.)

**-elf,** delf, elf, Guelph, pelf, self, shelf; bookshelf, herself, himself, ice shelf, itself, myself, oneself, ourself, thyself, top-shelf, yourself; mantelshelf, off-the-shelf, open-shelf, second self; do-it-yourself.

**-elk,** elk, whelk.

**-ell.** See **-el.**

**-elle.** See **-el.**

**-elled.** See **-eld.**

**-elm,** elm, helm, realm, whelm; overwhelm, underwhelm.

**-elp,** help, kelp, skelp, whelp, yelp; self-help.

**-elt,** belt, celt, Celt, dealt, dwelt, felt, gelt, kelt, Kelt, knelt, melt, pelt, smelt, spelt, svelte, veld, welt; black belt, borscht belt, brown belt, chainbelt, Corn Belt, Cotton Belt, farm belt, greenbelt, heartfelt, lap belt, life belt, rust belt, seatbelt snowbelt, snowmelt, Sunbelt; Bible belt, garter belt, money belt, Roosevelt, safety belt, shoulder belt.

**-elve,** delve, helve, shelve, twelve.

**-em,** crème, Dem, em, fem, femme, gem, hem, phlegm, REM, Shem, stem, them; ad quem, ad rem, ahem, AM, begem, bluestem, brainstem, condemn, contemn, dirhem, FM, golem, idem, in rem, main stem, mayhem, millieme, modem, phloem, pipestem, proem, pro tem, xylem;

ABM, ad litem, anadem, apothem, apothegm, ATM, Bethlehem, diadem, diastem, fax modem, ibidem, meristem, millirem, OEM, requiem, strategem, theorem; ad hominem, alter idem, cable modem, carpe diem, cave canem, crème de la crème, ICBM, semper idem; post meridiem, star-of-Bethlehem; ante meridiem.

**-eme.** See **-eam.**

**-emn.** See **-em.**

**-empt,** dreamt, kempt, tempt; attempt, contempt, exempt, pre-empt, ill-kempt, unkempt; nonexempt, self-contempt, tax-exempt.

**-en,** Ben, den, en, fen, glen, Gwen, hen, ken, Ken, Len, men, pen, Seine, sen, ten, then, wen, when, wren, yen, Zen; again, amen, Big Ben, bullpen, cayenne, Cheyenne, doyen, doyenne, game hen, hang ten, Karen, light pen, marsh hen, moorhen, peahen, pigpen, playpen, RN; allergen, born-again, citizen, cyclamen, five-and-ten, fountain pen, guinea hen, halogen, hydrogen, julienne, lion's den, LPN, madrilène, mise en scène, mother hen, nitrogen,
oxygen, poison pen, prairie hen, regimen, samisen, Saracen, specimen; carcinogen, comedienne, equestrienne, Parisienne, time and again, tragedienne; again and again.

**-ence,** cense, dense, fence, flense, hence, pence, sense, tense, thence, whence; commence, condense, defense, dispense, expense, horse sense, Hortense, immense, incense, intense, nonsense, offense, past tense, prepense, pretense, sequence, sixth sense, suspense; abstinence, accidence, affluence, ambience, antisense, audience, common sense, confidence, competence, consequence, continence, difference, diffidence, diligence, eloquence, eminence, evidence, excellence, frankincense, hypertense, immanence, imminence, impotence, impudence, indigence, indolence, inference, influence, innocence, multisense, nondefense, negligence, no-nonsense, opulence, penitence, preference, present tense, providence, recompense, redolence, reference, residence, reticence, reverence, sapience, self defense, subsequence, truculence, turbulence, vehemence, violence, virulence; beneficence, benevolence, circumference, coincidence, grandiloquence, inconsequence, intelligence, intransigence, magnificence, munificence, nonresidence, obedience, omnipotence, pre-eminence, self-confidence, subservience.

Also: **-ent** + **-s** (as in *tents,* etc.)

**-enced.** See **–ainst.**

**-ench,** bench, blench, clench, drench, flench, french, French, kench, mensch, plench, quench, stench, tench, trench, wench, wrench; back bench, box wrench, entrench, front bench, lug wrench, Old French, pipe wrench, retrench, unclench, workbench; Allen wrench, Anglo-French, Middle French, monkey wrench, Norman French, socket wrench.

**-end,** bend, blend, blende, end, fend, friend, lend, mend, rend, scend, send, spend, tend, trend, vend, wend; addend, amend, append, ascend, attend, backbend, bartend, befriend, bookend, boyfriend, closed-end, commend, compend, contend, dead end, defend, depend, descend, distend, downtrend, emend, expend, extend, fag end, forfend, front-end, girlfriend, godsend, high-end, hornblende, impend, intend, knee bend, loanblend, loose end, low-end, missend, misspend, offend, on end, outspend, perpend, pitchblende, portend, pretend, rear-end, resend, split end, stipend, subtend, suspend, tag end, tail end, tight end, top-end, transcend, unbend, upend, uptrend, weekend, year-end; apprehend, bitter end, carrick bend, comprehend, condescend, dividend, in the end, megatrend, minuend, misintend, on the mend, open-end, overspend, recommend, reprehend, subtrahend, vilipend; hyperextend, misapprehend, overextend, peace dividend, receiving end, superintend.

Also: **-en** + **-ed** (as in *penned,* etc.)

**-ene.** See **-ean.**

**-enge,** henge, venge; avenge, revenge, Stonehenge.

**-ength,** length, strength; arm's-length, bench strength, floor length, full-length, hiplength, wavelength; feature-length, focal length; industrial strength.

**-enned.** See **-end.**

**-ens.** See **-ense.**

**-ense** (-ens). See **-ence.**

**-ense** (-enz), ens, cleanse, gens, lens; parens, zoom lens; contact lens, persiennes; delirium tremens.

Also: **-en** + **-s** (as in *pens,* etc.)

Also: **-end** + **-s** (as in *bends,* etc.)

**-ensed.** See **-ainst.**

**-ent,** bent, blent, cent, dent, gent, Ghent, Kent, leant, lent, Lent, meant, pent, rent, scent, sent, spent, stent, tent, Trent, vent, went; absent, accent, Advent, anent, ascent, assent, augment, cement, comment, consent, content, convent, descent, detent, dissent, docent, event, extent, ferment, foment, forewent, fragment, frequent, hell-bent, indent, intent, invent, lament, loment, low-rent, misspent, outspent, percent, pigment, portent, present, prevent, pup tent, quitrent, rack-rent, relent, repent, resent, segment, torment, unbent, unspent, well-meant, well-spent; abstinent, accident, aliment, argument, armament, banishment, battlement, betterment, blandishment, chastisement, circumvent, compartment, competent, complement, compliment, condiment, confident, consequent, continent, detriment, devilment, different, diffident, diligent, discontent, dissident, document, element, eloquent, eminent, evident, excellent, exigent, filament, firmament, fraudulent, government, heaven-sent, immanent, imminent, implement, impotent, impudent, incident, increment, indigent, innocent, insolent, instrument, languishment, liniment, malcontent, management, measurement, merriment, monument, negligent, nonevent, nourishment, nutriment, occident, opulent, orient, ornament, overspent, parliament, penitent, permanent, pertinent, precedent, president, prevalent, provident, punishment, ravishment, redolent, regiment, reinvent, represent, resident, reticent, reverent, rudiment, sacrament, sediment, self-content, sentiment, settlement, subsequent, succulent, supplement, temperament, tenement, testament, underwent, vehement, violent, virulent, wonderment; accomplishment, acknowledgment, advertisement, age of consent, astonishment, belligerent, benevolent, coincident, development, disarmament, disorient, embarrassment, embodiment, enlightenment, environment, establishment, experiment, impenitent, impertinent, imprisonment, improvident, intelligent, irreverent, magnificent, magniloquent, misrepresent, nonresident, presentiment, subservient, temperament, self-confident, self-evident, vice president; accompaniment.

**-ep,** cep, hep, nep, pep, prep, rep, repp, schlep, skep, step, steppe, strep, yep; bicep, Dieppe, doorstep, footstep, goose step, half step, instep, in step, kelep, lockstep, misstep, one-step, quick-step, salep, sidestep, tricep, Twelve Step, two-step, whole step; corbie-step, demirep, out of step, overstep, quadricep, step-by-step; Amenhotep.

**-ept,** clept, crept, drept, kept, leapt, sept, slept, stepped, swept, wept; accept, adept, backswept, concept, except, incept, inept, inswept, percept, precept, recept, transept, upswept, well-kept, windswept, yclept; contracept, high concept, intercept, overslept, self-concept; biblioklept.

**-er,** birr, blur, bur, burr, chirr, cur, err, fir, fur, her, knur, murre, myrrh, per, purr, shirr, sir, skirr, slur, spur, stir, 'twere, were, whir; astir, auteur, aver, Ben Hur, bestir, Big Sur, chanteur, chasseur, chauffeur, claqueur, coiffeur, concur, confer, danseur, defer, demur, deter, diseur, douceur, farceur, frondeur, frotteur, hauteur, him/her, his/her, incur, infer, inter, jongleur, larkspur, liqueur, longueur, longspur, masseur, millefleur, monsieur, occur, poseur, prefer, recur, refer, rongeur, sandbur, sandspur, seigneur, tailleur, transfer, voyeur, white fir; accoucheur, amateur, arbiter, balsam fir, barrister, bateleur, calendar, chronicler, chorister, cocklebur, colander, comforter, connoisseur, cri de coeur, cross-refer, cylinder, de rigueur, disinter, Douglas fir, dowager, gossamer, harbinger, Jennifer, Jupiter, lavender, Lucifer, mariner, massacre, messenger, minister, officer, passenger, prisoner, prosateur, raconteur, raissoneur, rapporteur, register, régisseur, renifleur, répétiteur, saboteur, scimitar, secateurs, sepulcher, traveler, underfur, voyageur; administer, arbitrageur, astrologer, astronomer, barometer, carillonneur, entrepreneur, Excalibur, idolater, infopreneur, intrapreneur, littérateur, provocateur, restaurateur, thermometer; conglomerateur.

**-erb,** blurb, burb, curb, herb, kerb, Serb, slurb, urb, verb; acerb, adverb, disturb, exurb, perturb, potherb, proverb, reverb, suburb, superb.

**-erce.** See **-erse.**

**-erced.** See **-urst.**

**-erch.** See **-urch.**

**-erd.** See **-urd.**

**-ere** (-ār). See **-are.**

**-ere** (-ēr). See **-eer.**

**-ered.** See **-eard.**

**-erf.** See **-urf.**

**-erg,** berg, burgh; iceberg.

**-erge,** dirge, gurge, merge, purge, scourge, serge, splurge, spurge, surge, urge, verge; absterge, converge, deterge, diverge, emerge, immerge, resurge, submerge, upsurge; demiurge, dramaturge, reemerge, thaumaturge.

**-erm.** See **-irm.**

**-ern.** See **-urn.**

**-erp.** See **-urp.**

**-err.** See **-er.**

**-erred.** See **-urd.**

**-erse,** burse, curse, Erse, hearse, herse, nurse, perse, purse, terce, terse, verse, worse; accurse, adverse, amerce, asperse, averse, blank verse, coerce, commerce, converse, cutpurse, disburse, disperse, diverse, dry nurse, free verse, imburse, immerse, inverse, light verse, Nez Percé, obverse, perverse, rehearse, reverse, scrub nurse, sea purse, sesterce, submerse, transverse, traverse, wet nurse; e-commerce, intersperse, nonsense verse, privy purse, reimburse, universe; chapter and verse, heroic verse, practical nurse, registered nurse, visiting nurse.

**-ersed.** See **-urst.**

**-ert,** Bert, blurt, Burt, chert, curt, dirt, flirt, Gert, girt, hurt, Kurt, pert, quirt, shirt, skirt, spurt, squirt, vert, wert, whort, wort; advert, Albert, alert, assert, avert, bellwort, birthwort, Black Shirt, bloodwort, brownshirt, camp shirt, colewort, concert, convert, covert, desert, dessert, dissert, divert, dress shirt, drop girt, dropwort, evert, exert, expert, exsert, fanwort, figwort, filbert, fleawort, Frankfurt, glasswort, hair shirt, Herbert, honewort, hoop skirt, hornwort, inert, insert, invert, lousewort, lungwort, madwort, milkwort, mugwort, nightshirt, outskirt, overt, pay dirt, pervert, pilewort, ragwort, redshirt, revert, sandwort, seagirt, sea squirt, soapwort, sports shirt, stuffed shirt, subvert, sweatshirt, toothwort, T-shirt, unhurt; bitterwort, bladderwort, bloody shirt, butterwort, controvert, disconcert, extrovert, feverwort, hobble skirt, honeywort, hula skirt, introvert, inexpert, liverwort, maxiskirt, miniskirt, miterwort, moneywort, motherwort, muscle shirt, overshirt, pennywort, polo shirt, preconcert, reconvert, red alert, Rugby shirt, Saint-John's-wort, spiderwort, undershirt, underskirt, wing covert; animadvert, Hawaiian shirt.

**-erth.** See **-irth.**

**-erve,** curve, Irv, nerve, serve, swerve, verve; bell curve, conserve, deserve, disserve, French curve, hors d'oeuvre, incurve, innerve, observe, outcurve, preserve, reserve, S-curve, self-serve, subserve, unnerve; brown-and-serve, facial nerve, Laffer curve, learning curve, normal curve, optic nerve, spinal nerve.

**-es.** See **-ess.**

**-esce.** See **-ess.**

**-ese.** See **-ease.**

**-esh,** crèche, flèche, flesh, fresh, mesh, thresh; afresh, bobeche, calèche, crème fraîche, enmesh, gooseflesh, horseflesh, immesh, parfleche, proud flesh, refresh; Gilgamesh, intermesh, Marrakesh, pound of flesh.

**-esk.** See **-esque.**

**-esque,** desk; burlesque, Dantesque, front desk, grotesque, Moresque, newsdesk; Alhambresque, arabesque, Bunyanesque, city desk, copy desk, gigantesque, humoresque, Kafkaesque, Lincolnesque, picaresque, picturesque, plateresque, reading desk, roll-top desk, Romanesque, Rubenesque, sculpturesque, statuesque, writing desk; carnivalesque, churrigueresque.

**-ess,** Bess, bless, cess, chess, cress, dress, ess, fess, guess, jess, Jess, less, loess, mess, ness, press, stress, Tess, tress, yes; abscess, access, actress, address, aggress, assess, bench-press, caress, clothespress, coatdress, cold-press, comtesse, compress, confess, countess, cross-dress, depress, destress, digress, distress, drill press, duchesse, duress, egress, empress, excess, express, finesse, fluoresce, full-dress, handpress, headdress, housedress, idlesse, impress, ingress, largesse, Loch Ness, mattress, nightdress, noblesse, obsess, oneness, oppress, outguess, possess, princess, process, profess, progress, recess, redress, repress, shirt-dress, success, suit-dress, sundress, suppress, tent dress, topdress, transgress, tumesce, undress, unless, web press, winepress, word stress; acquiesce, air express, bitter cress, coalesce, convalesce, cookie press, crown princess, decompress, defervesce, deliquesce, dispossess, due process, effervesce, effloresce, evanesce, fancy dress, full-court press, gentilesse, granny dress, incandesce, intumesce, Inverness, letterpress, luminesce, marchioness, minidress, nonetheless, obsolesce, opalesce, overdress, pennycress, phosphoresce, PMS, politesse, prepossess, preprocess, recrudesce, repossess, retrogress, second-guess, sorceress, SOS, sweater dress, underdress, vicomtesse, watercress, wilderness, window-dress; keynote address, nevertheless, random-access.

Also: many words with the suffix **-ness** (as in *smallness,* etc.) and **-less** (as in *homeless,* etc.)

**-esse.** See **-ess.**

**-essed.** See **-est.**

**-est,** best, blest, breast, Brest, chest, crest, fest, gest, geste, guest, jest, lest, nest, pest, quest, rest, test, vest, west, wrest, zest; abreast, armrest, arrest, at best, at rest, attest, backrest, beau geste, bed rest, behest, bequest, bird's-nest, blood test, Celeste, congest, conquest, contest, crow's nest, depressed, detest, devest, digest, distressed, divest, egest, field-test, flight-test, footrest, funfest, gabfest, hard-pressed, headrest, high-test, hillcrest, hope chest, houseguest, imprest, incest, infest, inquest, invest, Key West, lovefest, love nest, mare's nest, means test, Midwest, molest, northwest, obtest, patch test, pretest, protest, redbreast, repressed, request, retest, revest, road test, scratch test, screen test, slugfest, songfest, southwest, spot test, stress test, suggest, talkfest, unblest, unrest, unstressed, war chest, whole rest, Wild West; acid test, alkahest, Almagest, anapest, beta test, Budapest, disinvest, empty-nest, Everest, false arrest, hornet's nest, house arrest, inkblot test, manifest, palimpsest, placement test, predigest, reinvest, rinderpest, Rorschach test, second-best, self-addressed, self-possessed, sweatervest, vision quest; aptitude test, auto-suggest, beauty contest, chanson de geste, robin redbreast.

Also: **-ess** + **-ed** (as in *pressed,* etc.)

Also: many superlative forms ending in **-est** (as in *happiest,* etc.)

**-et,** bet, debt, fete, fret, get, jet, let, Lett, met, net, pet, ret, Rhett, set, sett, stet, sweat, threat, tret, vet, wet, whet, yet; abet, aigrette, ailette, alette, Annette, applet, asset, backset, baguette, banquette, barbette, barquette, barrette, beget, beset, bimbette, blanquette, boneset, brevet, briquette, brochette, brunette, burette, burnet, cadet, cassette, cermet, charrette, chouette, Claudette, Colette, coquette, cornet, corselette, corvette, couchette, coupette, courgette, croquette, crossette, curette, curvet, cuvette, dancette, dead set, deep-set, dinette, diskette, dragnet, drift net, duet, egret, fanjet, fishnet, fléchette, fleurette, florette, fly net, forget, fossette, fourchette, frisette, fumette, fustet, gazette, gearset, genet, georgette, gill net, godet, grisette, Hamlet, hair net, handset, hard-set, headset, ink-jet, inlet, inset, Jeannette, jet set, kismet, labret, languet, laundrette, layette, life net, lockset, lorgnette, love set, lunette, maquette, mindset, mofette, moonset, moquette, motet, mouchette, musette, navette, noisette, nonet, nymphet, octet, offset, omelet, onset, outlet, outset, paillette, palmette, paupiette, pipette, piquet, planchette, poussette, preset, propjet, quartet, quintet, raclette, ramjet, regret, reset, revet, roomette, roquette, rosette, roulette, scramjet, septet, sestet, sextet, smart set, soubrette, stage set, sublet, subset, sunset, tacet, tea set, tercet, thickset, Tibet, toilette, tonette, twinset, typeset, upset, vedette, vignette; aiguillette, alphabet, ambulette, amulet, anchoret, anisette, avocet, balconet, bandelet, banneret, baronet, basinet, bassinet, bayonet, beaverette, bobbinet, briolette, burgonet, calumet, canzonet, caponette, carcanet, cassolette, castanet, cellaret, chansonette, chemisette, cigarette, clarinet, collaret, consolette, coronet, corselet, coverlet, crêpe suzette, crystal set, dragonet, en brochette, epaulet, epithet, estafette, Ethernet, etiquette, extranet, falconet, featurette, flageolet, flannelette, floweret, guillemet, heavyset, hic jacet, imaret, Internet, intranet, jaconet, Juliet, jumbo jet, kitchenette, landaulet, lanneret, launderette, lavaret, leatherette, luncheonette, maisonette, majorette, mantelet, marmoset, marquisette, martinet, medalet, midinette, mignonette, minaret, minuet, miquelet, misbeget, netiquette, novelette, olivette, oubliette, parapet, paraquet, pianette, pillaret, pirouette, quadruplet, quintuplet, quodlibet, ricochet, rigolet, rivulet, rondelet, safety net, satinet, scilicet, sermonette, serviette, silhouette, sobriquet, somerset, soviet, space cadet, spinneret, statuette, stockinette, suffragette, swimmeret, tabinet, taboret, teacher's pet, tête-a-tête, tourniquet, towelette, trebuchet, tricolette, triple threat, turbojet, underlet, usherette, vinaigrette, wagonette, winterset; analphabet, bachelorette, marionette, microcassette, minicassette, mosquito net, photo-offset, Russian roulette, snowy egret, videlicet; audiocassette, videocassette.

**-etch,** etch, fetch, fletch, ketch, kvetch, letch, retch, sketch, stretch, vetch, wretch; backstretch, homestretch, outstretch.

**-ete.** See **-eat.**

**-eth.** See **-eath.**

**-ette.** See **-et.**

**-eu.** See **-ew.**

**-euce.** See **-use.**

**-eud.** See **-ude.**

**-eur.** See **-er.**

**-euth.** See **-ooth.**

**-eve.** See **-eave.**

**-ew,** blew, blue, boo, brew, chew, chou, clew, clue, coo, coup, crew, cru, cue, dew, do, doux, drew, due, ewe, few, flew, flu, flue, fou, glue, gnu, goo, grew, hew, hue, Hugh, Jew, knew, Lew, lieu, loo, Lou, mew, moo, moue, mu, new, nu, ooh, pew, phew, pooh, pugh, queue, roux, rue, screw, shoe, shoo, shrew, Sioux, skew, slew, slough, slue, smew, sou, spew, sprue, stew, strew, sue, Sue, thew, threw, through, to, too, true, two, view, whew, who, woo, yew, you, zoo; accrue, adieu, ado, ague, ahchoo, Ainu, Andrew, anew, Anjou, argue, askew, babu, bamboo, Bantu, battue, bayou, bedew, bestrew, bijou, boo-boo, boohoo, boubou, brand-new, break-through, burgoo, cachou, can-do, canoe, cashew, choo-choo, construe, coo-boo, corkscrew, couru, coypu, cuckoo, curfew, curlew, debut, doo-doo, drive-through, ecru, écu, emu, endue, ensue, eschew, fichu, floor-through, fon-due, froufrou, fugu, genu, goo-goo, ground crew, gumshoe, guru, gym shoe, hairdo, hereto, Hindu, home-brew, hoodoo, hoopoe, horseshoe, how-to, igloo, imbrue, imbue, imu, into, IQ, issue, juju, karroo, kazoo, kerchoo, kudu, kung fu, kuru, lean-to, lulu, make-do, Manchu, me-too, menu, mildew, milieu, miscue, misdo, muumuu, nephew, old shoe, one-two, onto, outdo, perdu, Peru, poilu, pooh-pooh, preview, purlieu, pursue, purview, ragout, renew, review, revue, rough-hew, run-through, see-through, set-to, shampoo, Shih Tzu, sinew, skidoo, sky-blue, snafu, snowshoe, soft-shoe, span-new, subdue, surtout, susu, taboo, tap shoe, tat-too, thank you, thereto, thumbscrew, tissue, to-do, toe shoe, too-too, tree shrew, true-blue, tutu, un-do, undue, unscrew, un-true, vatu, vendue, venue, virtu, virtue, voodoo, wahoo, walk-through, whereto, who's who, with-drew, world view, wu shu, yahoo, yoo-hoo, zebu, Zulu; acajou, amadou, avenue, babassu, baby blue, bally-hoo, barbecue, billet-doux, bird's-eye view, black-and-blue, Brunswick stew, buckaroo, bugaboo, bunraku, callaloo, caribou, catechu, clerihew, cockapoo, cockatoo, curlicue, déjà vu, derring-do, detinue, feverfew, follow-through, gardyloo, hitherto, honeydew, hoochinoo, how-de-do, impromptu, ingénue, interview, IOU, Irish stew, jabiru, jackeroo, jujitsu, kangaroo, kinkajou, loup-garou, Manitou, marabou, microbrew, midnight blue, misconstrue, ormolu, overdo, overdue, overshoe, overview, parvenu, pas de deux, passe-partout, pay-per-view, PDQ, peekaboo, peer review, petting zoo, point of view, potoroo, rendezvous, residue, retinue, revenue, running shoe, seppuku, sneak preview, succès fou, sudoku, switcheroo, talking-to, teledu, tennis shoe, thereunto, thirty-two, Timbuktu, tinamou, toodle-oo, trou-de-loup, twenty-two, vindaloo, wallaroo, Waterloo, well-to-do, whoop-de-do, witches' brew, wooden shoe, Xanadu; didgeridoo, how-do-you-do, hullabaloo, Kalamazoo, merci beaucoup, merry-andrew, mulligan stew, out of the blue, pirarucu, Wandering Jew; cock-a-doodle-doo; mirabile dictu, twenty-three skidoo.

**-ewd.** See **-ude.**

**-ews.** See **-ooze** and **-use.**

**-ewt.** See **-ute.**

**-ex,** ex, flex, grex, hex, lex, rex, Rex, sex, specs, vex; AMEX, annex, apex, auspex, carex, caudex, cimex, codex, complex, connex, convex, cortex, culex, desex, duplex, fair sex, FedEx, funplex, ibex, ilex, index, Kleenex, latex, mirex, murex, narthex, perplex, pollex, Pyrex, reflex, Rx, safe sex, same-sex, scolex, silex, simplex, spandex, telex, Tex-Mex, triplex, unsex, vertex, vortex; antapex, card index, circumflex, cross-index, gentle sex, googolplex, haruspex, heat index, megaplex, multiplex,

PBX, pontifex, price index, retroflex, Rolodex, second sex, spinifex, subindex, thumb index, unisex, weaker sex; neocortex, videotex, wind chill index; body mass index, misery index, Oedipus complex, single-lens reflex.

Also: **-eck** + **-s** (as in *pecks,* etc.)

**-exed.** See **-ext.**

**-ext,** next, sexed, sext, text; context, plaintext, pretext, subtext, urtext; hypertext, undersexed; videotext.

Also: **-ex** + **-ed** (as in *vexed,* etc.)

**-ey** (-ā). See **-ay.**

**-ey** (-ē). See **-ee.**

**-eyed.** See **-ade.**

**-eys.** See **-aze.**

**-ez,** fez, says; Juarez, malaise, Suez; Marseillaise.

**-i** (-ē). See **-ee.**

**-i** (-ī). See **-y.**

**-ib,** bib, bibb, crib, dib, drib, fib, gib, glib, jib, lib, nib, rib, sib, squib; ad-lib, Carib, corncrib, false rib, gay lib, midrib, prime-rib, rad-lib, sahib; memsahib, women's lib.

**-ibe,** bribe, gibe, jibe, scribe, tribe, vibe; ascribe, conscribe, describe, escribe, imbibe, inscribe, prescribe, proscribe, subscribe, transcribe; circumscribe, diatribe, superscribe.

**-ic.** See **-ick.**

**-ice,** bice, Brice, dice, gneiss, ice, lice, lyse, mice, nice, price, rice, slice, spice, splice, syce, thrice, trice, twice, vice, vise; advice, allspice, brown rice, concise, deice, device, dry ice, entice, floor price, fried rice, list price, make nice, no dice, off-price, on ice, pack ice, precise, shelf ice, suffice, wild rice; asking price, beggars-lice, break the ice, comma splice, dirty rice, edelweiss, imprecise, market price, merchandise, on thin ice, overnice, overprice, paradise, sacrifice, Spanish rice, sticker price; self-sacrifice.

**-iced.** See **-ist.**

**-ich.** See **-itch.**

**-ick,** brick, chic, chick, click, creek, crick, dick, Dick, flick, hick, kick, KWIC, lick, mick, nick, Nick, pic, pick, prick, quick, rick, shtick, sic, sick, slick, snick, stich, stick, strick, thick, tic, tick, trick, Vic, wick, wrick; airsick, baldric, beatnik, boychick, bootlick, breadstick, broomstick, carsick, caustic, chick flick, chopstick, cowlick, dabchick, deer tick, derrick, dipstick, distich, dog tick, drop kick, drumstick, finick, fish stick, fossick, free kick, frog kick, gimmick, goal kick, goldbrick, handpick, hat trick, hayrick, heartsick, homesick, ice pick, joss stick, joystick, killick, lipstick, lopstick, lovesick, maffick, mahlstick, matchstick, medic, muzhik, niblick, night stick, nitpick, nonstick, nudnik, odd trick, oil slick, Old Nick, peacenik, pickwick, pinprick, placekick, rollick, rubric, salt lick, seasick, self-stick, shashlik, sidekick, slapstick, sputnik, toothpick, triptych, uptick, yardstick; acoustic, arsenic, artistic, bailiwick, Benedick, biopic, bishopric, Bolshevik, candlestick, candlewick, catholic, cherry-pick, chivalric, choleric, do the trick, double-click, double-quick, fiddlestick, fingerpick, flutter kick, gemütlich, hemistich, heretic, limerick, lunatic, maverick, Menshevik, pogo stick, point-and-click, politic, politick, Reykjavik, rhetoric, scissors kick, swizzle stick, turmeric, walking stick, waterpick; archbishopric, arithmetic, cataleptic, composing stick, impolitic, penalty kick; body politic.

**-icked.** See **-ict.**

**-icks.** See **-ix.**

**-ict,** Pict, strict; addict, afflict, astrict, conflict, constrict, convict, delict, depict, district, edict, evict, inflict, predict, relict, restrict, verdict; benedict, Benedict, contradict, derelict, interdict.

Also: **-ick** + **-ed** (as in *picked*, etc.)

**-id,** id, bid, chid, Cid, did, fid, gid, grid, hid, id, kid, lid, mid, quid, rid, skid, slid, squid; acrid, algid, amid, aphid, bifid, bovid, canid, David, druid, El Cid, Enid, eyelid, fervid, fetid, forbid, frigid, gelid, grandkid, gravid, Hasid, hybrid, kid-vid, limpid, lipid, lurid, Madrid, maggid, morbid, nonskid, orchid, outbid, outdid, Ovid, pavid, putrid, rabid, rancid, rigid, schoolkid, timid, torpid, trifid, turgid, undid, viscid, whiz kid; annelid, aramid, arachnid, bicuspid, Captain Kidd, giant squid, insipid, intrepid, katydid, overbid, overdid, pyramid, serranid, underbid; caryatid.

**-ide,** bide, bride, chide, Clyde, glide, guide, hide, I'd, nide, pied, pride, ride, side, slide, snide, stride, tide, wide; abide, allied, aside, astride, backside, backslide, bed-side, beside, bestride, be-tide, blindside, blue-eyed, broadside, bromide, bug-eyed, Burnside, car-bide, chloride, cockeyed, collide, confide, courtside, cowhide, cross-eyed, curb-side, decide, deride, divide, dockside, doe-eyed, down-side, downslide, dry-eyed, ebb tide, elide, field guide, flip side, flood tide, fluo-ride, foreside, four-eyed, free ride, freeze-dried, glass-eyed, graveside, green-eyed, hang glide, hawk-eyed, hayride, high tide, hillside, horsehide, inside, ironside, joyride, kingside, lakeside, land-slide, low tide, misguide, moon-eyed, mudslide, neap tide, nearside, night-side, noontide, offside, one-eyed, onside, outride, outside, oxide, pale-eyed, pie-eyed, poolside, pop-eyed, preside, provide, queenside, rawhide, red tide, reside, ringside, riptide, roadside, seaside, self-pride, sharp-eyed, shipside, shoreside, Shrovetide, sloe-eyed, snowslide, springtide, squint-eyed, stateside, statewide, storewide, sub-side, sulfide, sun-dried, tie-dyed, tongue-tied, topside, trackside, trailside, upside, vat-dyed, wall-eyed, war bride, wayside, wide-eyed, wild-eyed, worldwide, Yuletide; aldehyde, almond-eyed, alongside, bleary-eyed, bonafide, chicken-fried, Christmastide, citified, citywide, classified, coincide, countrified, countryside, countrywide, cut-and-dried, cyanide, deicide, demand-side, dewy-eyed, dignified, dioxide, double-eyed, eagle-eyed, Eastertide, ecocide, eventide, far and wide, feticide, fireside, fratricide, freedom ride, fungicide, genocide, germicide, glassy-eyed, goggle-eyed, harborside, herbicide, homicide, honeyguide, iodide, matricide, misty-eyed, monoxide, mountainside, nationwide, Naugahyde, on the side, open-eyed, override, parricide, patricide, peroxide, pesticide, qualified, rarefied, regicide, riverside, satisfied, set-aside, side by side, silverside, spermicide, starry-eyed, subdivide, suicide, supply-side, underside, waterside, Whitsuntide, wintertide; diversified, fit to be tied, formaldehyde, hydrochloride, infanticide, insecticide, Jekyll and Hyde, nucleotide, preoccupied, rodenticide, self-satisfied, thalidomide, tyrannicide, unqualified, unsatisfied; carbon dioxide, carbon monoxide, overqualified.

Also: **-ie** + **-d** (as in *lied*, etc.)

Also: **-igh** + **-ed** (as in *sighed*, etc.)

Also: **-y** + **-ed** (as in *cried*, etc.)

**-ides,** ides; besides, burnsides.

Also: **-ide** + **-s** (as in *tides, hides*, etc.)

**-idge.** See **-age** (-ĭj).

**-idst,** bidst, chidst, didst, hidst, midst, ridst; amidst, forbidst.

**-ie** (-ē). See **-ee.**

**-ie** (-ī). See **-y.**

**-iece.** See **-ease.**

**-ied.** See **-ide.**

**-ief,** beef, brief, chief, fief, feoff, grief, leaf, lief, reef, sheaf, thief; bay leaf, belief, chipped beef, debrief, drop leaf, endleaf, enfeoff, fig leaf, flyleaf, gold leaf, in brief, in chief, kerchief, looseleaf, massif, motif, naïf, O'Keeffe, red leaf, relief, sherif, shinleaf, sneak thief, sweetleaf; bas-relief, cloverleaf, come to grief, disbelief, firechief, handkerchief, high relief, interleaf, leitmotif, misbelief, neckerchief, overleaf, Tenerife, unbelief, waterleaf, water leaf; apéritif, barrier reef, comic relief; commander in chief, editor in chief.

**-iege,** liege, siege; besiege, prestige.

**-ield,** field, shield, weald, wield, yield; afield, airfield, backfield, brownfield, canfield, coal field, cornfield, downfield, dress shield, force field, four-wheeled, goldfield, grainfield, Greenfield, hayfield, heat shield, ice field, infield, left field, midfield, minefield, misfield, oil field, outfield, right field, snowfield, Springfield, subfield, upfield, well-heeled, windshield; battlefield, broken-field, center field, chesterfield, Chesterfield, colorfield, current yield, depth of field, killing field, landing field, open field, playing field, play the field, potter's field, sustained yield, track and field.

Also: **-eal** + **-ed** (as in *healed*, etc.)

Also: **-eel** + **-ed** (as in *peeled*, etc.)

**-ien.** See **-ean.**

**-iend** (-ēnd), fiend; archfiend, dope fiend.

Also: **-ean** + **-ed** (as in *cleaned*, etc.)

Also: **-een** + **-ed** (as in *careened*, etc.)

**-iend** (-end). See **-end.**

**-ier** (-ēr). See **-eer.**

**-ier** (-īər). See **-ire.**

**-ierce,** Bierce, fierce, pierce, tierce; transpierce.

**-iest.** See **-east.**

**-ieu.** See **-ew.**

**-ieve.** See **-eave.**

**-iew.** See **-ew.**

**-ieze.** See **-ease.**

**-if,** biff, cliff, diff, glyph, griff, if, jiff, miff, riff, Riff, skiff, sniff, spiff, stiff, tiff, whiff;

Cardiff, Joseph, mastiff, midriff, pecksniff, plaintiff, pontiff, Radcliffe, serif, sheriff, tariff, what-if; bindle stiff, bullmastiff, handkerchief, hieroglyph, hippogriff, neckerchief, petroglyph, sans serif.

**-ife,** fife, knife, life, rife, strife, wife; alewife, a-life, bread knife, broadwife, child wife, farmwife, fish knife, fishwife, folklife, good life, half-life, housewife, jackknife, loosestrife, love life, lowlife, midlife, midwife, nightlife, penknife, pro-life, real-life, shelf life, steak knife, still life, true-life, wildlife; afterlife, bowie knife, butcher knife, butter knife, carving knife, change of life, Duncan Phyfe, fact of life, nurse-midwife, palette knife, paring knife, pocketknife, public life, putty knife, right-to-life, slice-of-life, staff of life, tree of life, trophy wife, wheel of life; larger-than-life, Swiss army knife; utility knife.

**-iff.** See **-if.**

**-iffed.** See **-ift.**

**-ift,** drift, gift, grift, lift, miffed, rift, shift, shrift, sift, swift, thrift; adrift, airlift, blueshift, boatlift, chairlift, day shift, dead lift, downshift, eyelift, face-lift, festschrift, forklift, frameshift, gearshift, makeshift, night shift, redshift, shoplift, short shrift, ski lift, snowdrift, spendthrift, spindrift, split shift, stick shift, swing shift, uplift, upshift; chimney swift, glacial drift, graveyard shift, lobster shift, T-bar lift.

Also: **-iff** + **-ed** (as in *whiffed*, etc.)

**-ig,** big, brig, cig, dig, fig, gig, grig, jig, pig, prig, rig, sprig, swig, trig, twig, Whig, wig, zig; bigwig, brillig, bush pig, buzzwig, cat rig, earwig, fishgig, fright wig, pfennig, renege, shindig, square rig, zaftig, Zelig; caprifig, guinea pig, infra dig, jury-rig, moldy fig, periwig, thimblerig, whirligig, WYSIWYG; fore-and-aft rig, potbellied pig, thingamajig.

**-igh.** See **-y.**
**-ighed.** See **-ide.**
**-ighs.** See **-ize.**
**-ight.** See **-ite.**
**-ign.** See **-ine.**
**-igned.** See **-ind.**
**-igue.** See **-eague.**
**-ike,** bike, dike, haik, hike, like, mike, Mike, pike, psych, shrike, spike, strike, trike, tyke; air strike, alike, called strike, dirt bike, dislike, first strike, garpike, handspike, hitchhike, Klondike, rent strike, shunpike, tenstrike, trail bike, turnpike, unlike, Vandyke; body mike, down the pike, hunger strike, lookalike, marlinspike, minibike, motorbike, mountain bike, open mike, soundalike, thunderstrike, wildcat strike; exercise bike, preemptive strike.
**-il.** See **-ill.**
**-ilch,** filch, milch, pilch, zilch.
**-ild** (-ild), build, gild, guild; ill-willed, rebuild, regild, strong-willed, trade guild, unchilled, unskilled, untilled, weak-willed; unfulfilled.
Also: **-ill** + **-ed** (as in *killed, skilled,* etc.)
**-ild** (-īld), aisled, child, mild, wild, Wilde; brainchild, godchild, grandchild, hog-wild, love child, man-child, schoolchild, self-styled, stepchild; flower child, foster child, inner child, latchkey child, love child, poster child.
Also: **-ile** + **-ed** (as in *filed,* etc.)
Also: **-yle** + **-ed** (as in *styled,* etc.)
**-ile** (-īl), aisle, bile, chyle, dial, faille, file, guile, heil, I'll, isle, lisle, mile, Nile, pile, rile, smile, spile, stile, style, tile, vial, vile, Weill, while, wile; abseil, agile, anile, argyle, awhile, beguile, compile, condyle, cross-file, decile, defile, docile, ductile, edile, enisle, ensile, erewhile, erstwhile, exile, Fair Isle, febrile, fictile, field trial, fissile, fragile, freestyle, futile, gentile, hairstyle, high style, hostile, labile, lifestyle, meanwhile, mistrial, mobile, motile, nail file, nubile,

old style, on file, pantile, penile, pensile, pretrial, profile, puerile, quartile, redial, reptile, retrial, revile, sandpile, senile, servile, sessile, stabile, stockpile, sundial, tactile, tensile, textile, time trial, turnstile, typestyle, utile, virile, woodpile, worthwhile; Anglophile, chamomile, cinephile, contractile, crocodile, diastyle, discophile, domicile, epistyle, erectile, extensile, Francophile, hypostyle, infantile, interfile, juvenile, low-profile, mercantile, oenophile, percentile, peristyle, prehensile, projectile, puerile, rank and file, reconcile, retractile, single file, Slavophile, statute mile, technophile, versatile; aileurophile, audiophile, bibliophile, circular file, family style, Germanophile, Indian file, once in a while, vertical file, videophile.

**-ile** (-ēl). See **-eal.**

**-ile** (-il). See **-ill.**

**-iled.** See **-ild.**

**-ilk,** bilk, ilk, milch, milk, silk; corn silk, ice milk, raw silk, skim milk, spun silk; buttermilk, chocolate milk, malted milk.

**-ill,** bill, Bill, brill, chill, dill, drill, fill, frill, gill, grill, grille, hill, ill, jill, Jill, kill, krill, mil, mill, nil, Phil, pill, quill, rill, shill, shrill, sill, skill, spill, squill, still, swill, thill, thrill, 'til, till, trill, twill, 'twill, vill, will, Will; anthill, backfill, bluegill, broadbill, Brazil, cahill, Churchill, crossbill, distill, doorsill, downhill, duckbill, dullsville, dunghill, foothill, free will, fulfill, gin mill, goodwill, gristmill, groundsill, handbill, hawksbill, hornbill, ill will, instill, landfill, mandrill, mixed grill, molehill, mudsill, no-till, pep pill, playbill, quadrille, refill, roadkill, sawmill, self-will, Seville, showbill, sidehill, sigil, spadille, spoonbill, stabile, stamp mill, standstill, stock-still, T-bill, treadmill, until, uphill, vaudeville, waxbill, waybill, wind chill, windmill; bar-and-grill, bitter pill, chlorophyll, codicil, coffee mill, daffodil, diet pill, domicile, double bill, escadrille, espadrille, fiberfill, fire drill, fit the bill, foreign bill, game of skill, if you will, imbecile, living will, Louisville, over-fill, overkill, pepper mill, poison pill, powder mill, puppy mill, razorbill, su-gar pill, versatile, volatile, water mill, whippoorwill, windowsill, winterkill, Yggdrasil; Buffalo Bill, Capitol Hill, ivory-bill, over-the-hill, run-of-the-mill.

**-ille** (-ēl). See **-eal.**

**-ille** (-il). See **-ill.**

**-illed.** See **-ild.**

**-ilt,** built, gilt, guilt, hilt, jilt, kilt, lilt, milt, quilt, silt, spilt, stilt, tilt, wilt; atilt, bloodguilt, full tilt, rebuilt, well-built; crazy quilt, custom-built, jerry-built, patchwork quilt, to the hilt, Vanderbilt.

**-ilth,** filth, spilth, tilth.

**-im,** brim, dim, glim, grim, Grimm, gym, him, hymn, Jim, Kim, limb, limn, nim, prim, rim, scrim, shim, skim, slim, swim, Tim, trim, vim, whim; bedim, forelimb, megrim, passim, paynim, prelim, Purim, snap brim; acronym, allonym, antonym, cherubim, cryptonym, eponym, Hasidim, homo-nym, interim, junglegym, metonym, paradigm, pseudonym, retronym, seraphim, synonym, toponym; ad interim, heteronym.

**-imb** (-im). See **-im.**

**-imb** (-īm). See **-ime.**

**-ime,** chime, chyme, climb, clime, crime, cyme, dime, grime, I'm, lime, mime, prime, rhyme, rime, slime, thyme, time; airtime, be-grime, bedtime, begrime, big time, birdlime, buy time, chowtime, comp time, runch time, daytime, downtime, drive time, enzyme, eye rhyme, face time, flextime, full-time, halftime, hate crime, in time, Key lime, lead time, lifetime, longtime, lunchtime, make time, mark time, mealtime, meantime, mistime, nighttime, noontime, old-time, one-time, on-time, part-time, pastime, peacetime, playtime, post time, prime time, quicklime, ragtime, real time, showtime, sight rhyme, small-time, sometime, space-time, springtime, straight time, sublime, subprime, teatime, two-time, war crime, wartime; access time, anticrime, anytime, borrowed time, Christmastime, computer crime, dinnertime, double prime, double time, Father Time, Guggenheim, just-in-time, Kaffir lime, maritime, overtime, pantomime, paradigm, running time, soda lime, standard time, summertime, suppertime, travel time, vowel rhyme, wintertime; nickel-and-dime, nursery rhyme, quality time, white-collar crime.

**-imes,** at times, betimes, daytimes, ofttimes, sometimes, wind chimes; oftentimes.

Also: **-ime** + **-s** (as in *crimes,* etc.)

Also: **-yme** + **-s** (as in *rhymes,* etc.)

**-imp,** blimp, chimp, crimp, gimp, guimpe, imp, limp, pimp, primp, scrimp, shrimp, simp, skimp, wimp; com-symp.

**-impse,** glimpse; foreglimpse.

Also: **-imp** + **-s** (as in *skimps,* etc.)

**-in,** been, bin, chin, din, djinn, fin, Finn, gin, grin, in, inn, jinn, kin, pin, shin, sin, skin, spin, thin, tin, twin, whin, win, wynn; add-in, agin, akin, backspin, bearskin, begin, Berlin, blow-in, bluefin, bodkin, bowfin, buskin, break-in, Brooklyn, buckskin, built-in, calfskin, call-in, capeskin, carbine, catkin, chagrin, chaplain, check-in, clothespin, coonskin, Corinne, crankpin, deerskin, doeskin, dolphin, drive-in, duckpin, dustbin, fibrin, florin, goatskin, griffin, hairpin, has-been, hatpin, headpin, herein, kidskin, kingpin, lambkin, lambskin, lead-in, linchpin, live-in, lived-in, love-in, margin, moleskin, munchkin, napkin, ninepin, no-win, phone-in, pigskin, pinyin, pippin, plug-in, plugged-in, pushpin, rosin, run-in, sealskin, sharkskin, sheepskin, shoo-in, shut-in, sidespin, sit-in, sleep-in, sloe gin, snakeskin, stand-in, stickpin, swim fin, tail fin, tailspin, tannin, teach-in, tenpin, therein, tie-in, tiepin, topspin, trade-in, turned-in, walk-in, wear thin, wherein, wineskin, win-win, within, write-in; alkaline, almandine, aniline, aquiline, aspirin, atropine, baldachin, bobby pin, botulin, calamine, chamberlain, chinquapin, chromatin, cotter pin, cotton gin, coumarin, crinoline, crystalline, deadly sin, discipline, endorphin, ephedrine, feminine, gelatin, genuine, globulin, glycerin, grimalkin, harlequin, heparin, heroin, heroine, illumine, imagine, insulin, Jacobin, javelin, jessamine, kaolin, keratin, lambrequin, lanolin, larrikin, lecithin, Lohengrin, loony bin, lying-in, mandarin, mandolin, mannequin, margarine, masculine, melanin, Mickey Finn, moccasin, mortal sin, motor inn, next of kin, niacin, onionskin, paladin, paper-thin, paraffin, peregrine, porcelain, ramekin, rolling pin, saccharine, safety pin, sibylline, sovereign, terrapin, thiamine, thick and thin, violin, vitamin, Zeppelin; adrenaline, Alexandrine, belaying pin, elephantine, hemoglobin, incarnadine, pectoral fin.

**-inc.** See **-ink.**

**-ince,** blintz, chintz, mince, prince, quince, rinse, since, wince; convince, crown prince, evince, province; merchant prince.

Also: **-int** + **-s** (as in *prints,* etc.)

**-inch,** chinch, cinch, clinch, finch, flinch, grinch, inch, lynch, pinch, squinch, winch; bullfinch, chaffinch, goldfinch; inch by inch.

**-inct,** tinct; distinct, extinct, instinct, precinct, succinct; indistinct.
Also: **-ink** + **-ed** (as in *winked,* etc.)

**-ind** (-īnd), bind, blind, find, grind, hind, kind, mind, rind, wind; behind, drip grind, half-blind, in-kind, mankind, nightblind, purblind, remind, rewind, sand-blind, snow-blind, spellbind, stone-blind, streamlined, unkind, unwind, word-blind; ax to grind, color-blind, double bind, double-blind, frame of mind, gavelkind, gravel-blind, humankind, in a bind, mastermind, miniblind, nevermind, nonaligned, overwind, peace of mind, single-blind, undersigned, well-defined, window blind, womankind; one of a kind, presence of mind, venetian blind.
Also: **-ign** + **-ed** (as in *signed,* etc.)
Also: **-ine** + **-ed** (as in *dined,* etc.)

**-ind** (-ind), Ind, wind; abscind, backwind, crosswind, downwind, exscind, rescind, tailwind, thick-skinned, thin-skinned, upwind, whirlwind, woodwind; Amerind, bag of wind, in the wind, second wind, solar wind, tamarind, wunderkind; undisciplined.
Also: **-in** + **-ed** (as in *grinned,* etc.)

**-ine** (-īn), bine, brine, chine, cline, dine, dyne, fine, kine, line, mine, nine, pine, Rhine, shine, shrine, sign, sine, spine, spline, stein, swine, syne, thine, tine, trine, twine, vine, whine, wine; A-line, airline, align, alpine, assign, baseline, beeline, benign, bloodline, blush wine, bovine, bowline, breadline, buntline, bustline, byline, calcine, canine, caprine, carbine, carmine, clothesline, cloud nine, coastline, combine, condign, confine, consign, cosign, cosine, dateline, deadline, decline, define, design, divine, dragline, Einstein, end line, enshrine, ensign, entwine, equine, fault line, feline, flatline, foul line, Fräulein, front line, goal line, gold mine, grapevine, guideline, hairline, hard line, headline, hemline, hircine, Holstein, hotline, ice wine, incline, indign, in-line, jawline, jug wine, landline, land mine, lead line, lifeline, lupine, mainline, main line, malign, midline, moonshine, neckline, offline, old-line, online, opine, outline, outshine, ovine, peace sign, pipeline, piscine, pitch pine, plotline, plumbline, plus sign, pontine, porcine, pound sign, punchline, quinine, railline, rapine, recline, redline, red wine, refine, reline, repine, resign, Rhine wine, ridgeline, roofline, Sabine, saline, Scotch pine, scrub pine, shoreline, sideline, sight line, skyline, streamline, strip mine, strychnine, sunshine, supine, syncline, taurine, time line, times sign, towline, tramline, trephine, trunk line, turbine, vulpine, waistline, white wine, woodbine, yard line; Adeline, aerodyne, alkaline, androgyne, anodyne, Apennine, aquiline, Argentine, asinine, auld lang syne, borderline, bottom line, brigantine, Byzantine, calamine, calcimine, Caroline, centerline, clementine, Clementine, columbine, concubine, conga line, contour line, coralline, countersign, credit line, crystalline, cytokine, dessert wine, disincline, dollar sign, down-the-line, draw the line, eglantine, endocrine, equal sign, etamine, finish line, Florentine, Frankenstein, genuine, interline, intertwine, iodine, leonine, Liechtenstein, minus sign, monkeyshine, muscadine, on the line, opaline, palatine, party line, passerine, picket line, porcupine, realign, redefine, riverine, saccharine, saturnine, serpentine, sibylline, sounding line, sparkling wine, storyline, superfine, table wine, timberline, toe the line, transalpine, turnverein, turpentine, underline, undermine, uterine, valentine, waterline, worry line; assembly line, Capitoline, count palatine, elephantine, firing line, fortified wine, graphic design, heterodyne, incarnadine, poverty line, receiving line, top-of-the-line.

**-ine** (-ēn). See **-ean.**

**-ine** (-in). See **-in.**

**-ined.** See **-ind.**

**-ing,** bing, bling, bring, cling, ding, fling, king, Ming, ping, ring, sing, sling, spring, sting, string, swing, Synge, thing, wing, wring, zing; bedspring, Beijing, bitewing, bowstring, bullring, drawstring, earring, earthling, evening, farthing, first-string, forewing, full swing, G-string, growth ring, hamstring, handspring, heartstring, hind wing, hireling, hot spring, lacewing, lapwing, left-wing, mainspring, offspring, O-ring, plaything, redwing, right-wing, shoestring, showring, something, starveling, stripling, sure thing, unsling, unstring, upswing, waxwing, wellspring, wing-ding; à la king, anything, apron string, atheling, chitterling, cosmic string, delta wing, ding-a-ling, everything, Highland fling, innerspring, on the wing, opening, second-string, signet ring, superstring, teething ring, underling, underwing, wedding ring; buffalo wing.

Also: participles in **-ing** and gerunds (as *clamoring*, etc.)

**-inge,** binge, cringe, dinge, fringe, hinge, Inge, singe, springe, swinge, tinge, twinge; challenge, impinge, infringe, orange, scavenge, syringe, unhinge.

**-ingue.** See **-ang.**

**-ink,** blink, brink, chink, clink, dink, drink, fink, ink, kink, link, mink, pink, plink, prink, rink, shrink, sink, skink, slink, stink, sync, think, wink, zinc; chain-link, cross-link, cuff link, downlink, dry sink, groupthink, heat sink, hoodwink, hotlink, lip-sync, mixed drink, preshrink, ratfink, red ink, rethink, soft drink, uplink; bobolink, coral pink, countersink, doublethink, Humperdinck, hyperlink, interlink, in the pink, kitchen sink, Maeterlinck, missing link, on the blink, out-of-sync, rinky-dink, roller rink, shocking pink, tiddlywink; India ink; invisible ink.

**-inked.** See **-inct.**

**-inks.** See **-inx.**

**-inned.** See **-ind.**

**-inse.** See **-ince.**

**-int,** dint, flint, glint, Gynt, hint, lint, mint, print, quint, splint, sprint, squint, stint, tint; asquint, blueprint, footprint, forint, gunflint, handprint, hoofprint, horsemint, imprint, large print, misprint, newsprint, offprint, preprint, reprint, skinflint, spearmint, thumbprint, voiceprint; aquatint, fingerprint, mezzotint, peppermint; Septuagint.

**-inth,** plinth; absinthe, Corinth, helminth; hyacinth, labyrinth, terebinth.

**-ints.** See **-ince.**

**-inx,** jinx, links, lynx, minx, sphinx; golf links, high jinks, larynx, methinks, salpinx; forty winks, tiddlywinks.

Also: **-ink** + **-s** (as in *thinks,* etc.)

**-ip,** blip, chip, clip, dip, drip, flip, grip, grippe, gyp, hip, kip, lip, nip, pip, quip, rip, scrip, ship, sip, skip, slip, snip, strip, tip, trip, whip, yip, zip; airship, airstrip, backflip, blue chip, bullwhip, call slip, catnip, cleft lip, clerkship, corn chip, courtship, cowslip, deanship, death grip, drag strip, equip, felt-tip, field trip, filmstrip, flagship, foul tip, friendship, guilt trip, half-slip, handgrip, hardship, harelip, horsewhip, judgeship, jump ship, key grip, kingship, kinship, landslip, lightship, lordship, nonslip, outstrip, pink slip, queenship, road trip, rose hip, round-trip, sales slip, sheep-dip, sideslip, spaceship, starship, steamship, township, transship, unzip, V-chip, wardship, warship, wing tip; airmanship, authorship, battleship, biochip, brinkmanship, censorship, chairmanship, comic strip, coverstrip, dealership, draftsmanship, ego trip, externship, fellowship, filter tip, fingertip, gamesmanship, horsemanship, internship, ladyship, landing strip, leadership, marksmanship, membership, microchip, mother ship, ownership, paper clip, partnership, penmanship, pistol grip, pistol-whip, pleasure trip, power strip, readership, ridership, rocket ship, rumble strip, salesmanship, scholarship, showmanship, skinny-dip, sponsorship, sportsmanship, statesmanship, stewardship, swordsmanship, trusteeship, underlip, weatherstrip, workmanship; apprenticeship, assistantship, championship, chancellorship, citizenship, companionship, containership, dictatorship, factory ship, Freudian slip, goodfellowship, governorship, guardianship, median strip, musicianship, one-upmanship, outdoorsmanship, partisanship, postnasal drip, potato chip, professorship, protectorship, receivership, rejection slip, relationship, stiff upper lip, survivorship.

**-ipe,** gripe, hype, pipe, ripe, slype, snipe, stipe, stripe, swipe, tripe, type, wipe, yipe; airpipe, bagpipe, blood type, blowpipe, cold type, drainpipe, half-ripe, half-pipe, hornpipe, mistype, pinstripe, pitch pipe, sideswipe, standpipe, steampipe, stovepipe, subtype, tailpipe, tintype, touch-type, unripe, windpipe; allotype, archetype, candy stripe, collotype, corncob pipe, display type, Dutchman's-pipe, ecotype, ferrotype, foundry type, genotype, guttersnipe, Linotype, monotype,

Monotype, overripe, phenotype, prototype, serotype, stenotype, Teletype, tuning pipe, underripe; daguerrotype, electrotype, honeycomb tripe, Indian pipe, movable type, stereotype.

**-ipse,** thrips; cow chips, eclipse, ellipse, midships; amidships, fish and chips; apocalypse, buffalo chips, lunar eclipse, solar eclipse, total eclipse.

Also: **-ip** + **-s** (as in *lips,* etc.)

**-ipt,** crypt, script; conscript, decrypt, encrypt, playscript, postscript, subscript, tight-lipped, transcript, typescript; filter-tipped, manuscript, nondescript, shooting script, superscript, swivel-hipped.

Also: **-ip** + **-ped** (as in *dripped,* etc.)

**-ique.** See **-eak.**

**-ir.** See **-er.**

**-irch.** See **-urch.**

**-ird.** See **-urd.**

**-ire** (-īər), brier, buyer, choir, dire, fire, flyer, friar, gyre, hire, ire, liar, lyre, mire, plier, prior, pyre, quire, shire, sire, spire, squire, tire, Tyre, wire; acquire, admire, afire, aspire, attire, backfire, balefire, barbed wire, bemire, blow-dryer, bonfire, brushfire, campfire, cease-fire, conspire, crossfire, dehire, desire, drumfire, empire, enquire, entire, esquire, expire, flat tire, for hire, foxfire, grandsire, Greek fire, greenbrier, groundfire, gunfire, haywire, hellfire, highflier, high wire, hot-wire, inquire, inspire, live wire, misfire, newswire, perspire, pismire, quagmire, require, respire, retire, rewire, sapphire, satire, snow tire, spare tire, spitfire, surefire, suspire, sweetbrier, transpire, tripwire, umpire, vampire, wildfire; ball of fire, balloon tire, chicken wire, line of fire, rapid fire, razor wire, set on fire, underwire.

Also: **-y** + **-er** (as in *crier, modifier,* etc.)

See also **-ier.**

**-irge.** See **-erge.**

**-irk.** See **-urk.**

**-irl.** See **-url.**

**-irm,** berm, firm, germ, herm, perm, scherm, sperm, squirm, term, worm; affirm, bloodworm, bookworm, confirm, deworm, earthworm, flatworm, full-term, glowworm, grubworm, heartworm, hookworm, inchworm, infirm, long-term, lugworm, midterm, pinworm, ringworm, roundworm, short-term, silkworm, tapeworm, tubeworm, wheat germ; disaffirm, ectoderm, endosperm, endotherm, gymnosperm, inkhorn term, isotherm, mesoderm, pachyderm, reaffirm; angiosperm, echinoderm.

**-irp.** See **-urp.**

**-irr.** See **-er.**

**-irred.** See **-urd.**

**-irst.** See **-urst.**

**-irt.** See **-ert.**

**-irth,** berth, birth, dearth, earth, firth, girth, mirth, Perth, worth; childbirth, give birth, rare earth, rebirth, scorched-earth, self-worth, stillbirth, unearth; afterbirth, down-to-earth, fuller's earth, mother earth, pennyworth, two cents' worth, virgin birth, wrongful birth; salt of the earth.

**-is** (-iz), biz, fizz, frizz, his, is, Liz, Ms., phiz, quiz, schiz, 'tis, viz, whiz, wiz; Cadiz, gee whiz, hafiz, show biz; agribiz.

**-is** (-is). See **-iss.**

**-ise** (-īs). See **-ice.**

**-ise** (-īz). See **-ize.**

**-ish,** dish, fiche, fish, flysch, Gish, knish, pish, squish, swish, whish, wish; anguish, blowfish, bluefish, catfish, clownfish, codfish, cold fish, crayfish, death wish, deep-dish, dogfish, flatfish, fly-fish, game fish, garfish, goldfish, knish, lumpfish, lungfish, monkfish, rockfish, sailfish, shellfish, side dish, sport fish, starfish, sunfish, swordfish, tilefish, trash fish, weakfish, whitefish; angelfish, chafing dish, cuttlefish, damselfish, devilfish, flying fish, gibberish, jellyfish, kittenish, lanternfish, licorice, microfiche, parrot fish, petri dish, pilot fish, puffer fish, silverfish, zebra fish; gefilte fish, im-

poverish, satellite dish, tropical fish.
Also: words with **-ish** as suffix (as *childish, sluggish*, etc.)

**-isk,** bisque, brisk, disc, disk, fisc, frisk, risk, whisk; hard disk, lutefisk, slipped disk, sun disk; assigned risk, asterisk, basilisk, compact disc, credit risk, floppy disk, laser disk, obelisk, odalisque, optic disk, ruptured disk, tamarisk; videodisk.

**-ism,** chrism, chrisom, ism, prism, schism; abysm, ageism, autism, Babism, baptism, Buddhism, Chartism, cubism, deism, dwarfism, faddism, Fascism, Grecism, Jainism, Mahdism, Marxism, monism, mutism, Nazism, nudism, psellism, purism, racism, sadism, sexism, snobbism, sophism, Sufism, Taoism, technism, theism, tourism, tropism, truism, Whiggism, Yogism; absinthism, actinism, acrotism, activism, alarmism, albinism, algorism, altruism, amorphism, anarchism, aneurysm, Anglicism, animism, aphorism, archaism, asterism, atavism, atheism, atomism, Atticism, barbarism, Biblicism, Bolshevism, botulism, Brahminism, Briticism, Britishism, brutalism, Byronism, cabalism, Caesarism, Calvinism, carnalism, careerism, cataclysm, catechism, Celticism, centralism, chauvinism, classicism, cocainism, Cockneyism, Communism, cretinism, criticism, cronyism, cynicism, dadaism, daltonism, dandyism, Darwinism, demonism, despotism, dimorphism, ditheism, dogmatism, dowdyism, Druidism, dualism, dynamism, egoism, egotism, elitism, embolism, erethism, ergotism, escapism, euphemism, euphonism, euphuism, exorcism, extremism, fatalism, feminism, fetishism, feudalism, fogyism, foreignism, formalism, formulism, Gallicism, galvanism, gentilism, Germanism, giantism, gigantism, globalism, gnosticism, Gothicism, gradualism, grundyism, Hasidism, heathenism, Hebraism, hedonism, Hellenism, helotism, herbalism, Hermetism, heroism, Hinduism, humanism, humorism, hypnotism, idealism, Jansenism, jingoism, journalism, Judaism, laconism, Lamaism, Lamarckism, lambdacism, Latinism, legalism, Leninism, localism, Lollardism, loyalism, lyricism, magnetism, mannerism, martialism, masochism, mechanism, Menshevism, mentalism, mephitism, mesmerism, Methodism, me-tooism, Mithraism, modernism, monadism, monarchism, Maoism, moralism, Mormonism, morphinism, Moslemism, mysticism, narcissism, narcotism, nativism, Naziism, nepotism, nihilism, occultism, onanism, optimism, organism, ostracism, pacifism, paganism, pantheism, paroxysm, Parseeism, pauperism, pessimism, pietism, plagiarism, Platonism, pluralism, pointillism, populism, pragmatism, prognathism, prosaism, pugilism, pyrrhonism, Quakerism, quietism, quixotism, Rabbinism, racialism, realism, regalism, rheumatism, Romanism, rowdyism, royalism, ruralism, satanism, Saxonism, schematism, scientism, Semitism, Shakerism, shamanism, Shintoism, sigmatism, Sinicism, skepticism, socialism, solecism, solipsism, Southernism, specialism, speciesism, spiritism, spoonerism, Stalinism, stoicism, suffragism, syllogism, symbolism, synchronism, syncretism, synergism, tantalism, terrorism, toadyism, tokenism, Toryism, totemism, traumatism, tribalism, tritheism, ultraism, unionism, urbanism, vandalism, verbalism, vocalism, volcanism, voodooism, vulgarism, vulpinism, welfarism, witticism, Yankeeism, Yiddishism, Zionism; absenteeism, absolutism, achromatism, aestheticism, Africanism, agnosticism, alcoholism, alienism, allotropism, amateurism, Anabaptism, anabolism, anachronism, Anglicanism, animalism, antagonism, Arianism, asceticism, astigmatism, athleticism, autochthon-ism, automatism, behav-iorism, bilingualism, bimetallism, Byzantinism, cannibalism, capitalism, catabolism, Catholicism, charlatanism, clericalism, collectivism, commercial-ism, communalism, Con-fucianism, conservatism, consumerism, creationism, democratism, determinism, diabolism, dilletantism, eclecticism, ecotourism, egocentrism, empiricism, eroticism, evangelism, expansionism, expression-ism, externalism, factional-ism, fanaticism, favoritism, federalism, functionalism, generalism, Hibernicism, Hispanicism, historicism, hooliganism, hyperbolism, idealism, idiotism, illusion-ism, Impressionism, in-fantilism, initialism, invalidism, isochronism, isomerism, isomorphism, isotropism, Jacobinism, Jacobitism, Jesuitism, katabolism, laconicism, legitimism, lesbianism, liberalism, libertinism, lit-eralism, Lutheranism, mal-apropism, medievalism, mercantilism, messianism, metabolism, metachro-nism, militarism, mini-malism, moderatism, monasticism, monetarism, monotheism, mutualism, narcoticism, nationalism, naturalism, negativism, neofascism, neologism, neo-Nazism, nicotinism, noctambulism, nominal-ism, nonconformism, objectivism, obscurantism, obstructionism, officialism, opportunism, parallelism, parasitism, paternalism, patriotism, pedagogism, perfectionism, Pharisaism, Philistinism, philosophism, photorealism, plagiarism, plebianism, polymerism, polymorphism, polyphonism, polytheism, positivism, postmodernism, presenteeism, primitivism, probabilism, progressivism, protectionism, Protestantism, provincialism, Puritanism, radicalism, rationalism, recidivism, reductionism, regionalism, relativism, revisionism, ritualism, romanticism, ruffianism, Sadduceeism, scholasticism, secessionism, sectionalism, secularism, sensualism, separatism, Shavianism, somnambulism, somniloquism, structuralism, subjectivism, surrealism, sycophantism, syndicalism, theosophism, Uncle Tomism, universalism, ventriloquism, vigilantism, Wesleyanism; abolitionism, agrarianism, Americanism, anthropomorphism, anti-Semitism, bicameralism, Bohemianism, Cartesianism, colloquialism, colonialism, conceptualism, conventionalism, cosmopolitism, equestrianism, evolutionism, exhibitionism, existentialism, fundamentalism, heliotropism, hermaphroditism, heteromorphism, Hibernianism, histrionicism, imperialism, incendiarism, indeterminism, indifferentism, industrialism, isolationism, Manicheanism, materialism, medievalism, microorganism, millennialism, Mohammedanism, neoclassicism, neo-Darwinism, Neoplatonism, Occidentalism, Orientalism, parochialism, phenomenalism, photojournalism, Post-Impressionism, professionalism, proverbialism, pseudoclassicism, reconstructionism, Republicanism, Rosicrucianism, sacerdotalism, sadomasochism, sectarianism, sensationalism, sentimentalism, Spencerianism, spiritualism, theatricalism, Tractarianism, traditionalism, transmigrationism, Utopianism, vernacularism; agriculturalism, antinomianism, antiquarianism, ceremonialism, Congregationalism, constitutionalism, cosmospolitanism, experimentalism, individualism, intellectualism, internationalism, presbyterianism, preternaturalism, proletarianism, supernaturalism, Unitarianism, vegetarianism; Aristotelianism, humanitarianism, utilitarianism; antidisestablishmentarianism.

**-isp,** crisp, lisp, wisp; will-o'-the-wisp.

**-iss,** biss, bliss, bris, Chris, cuisse, dis, hiss, kiss, miss, priss, sis, Swiss, this; abyss, air kiss, amice, amiss, auspice, caddis, can't miss, cilice, coppice, cornice, crevice, dehisce, dermis, dismiss, French kiss, hospice, jaundice, justice, koumiss, lattice, mortise, near miss, prentice, pumice, remiss, service, solstice, statice, status, surplice, whatsis; ambergris, apprentice, armistice, artifice, avarice, Beatrice, benefice, cannabis, catharsis, chrysalis, cirrhosis, clematis, cockatrice, cowardice, dentrifice, dotted swiss, edifice, emphasis, fortalice, genesis, hit-and-miss, hit-or-miss, interstice, junior miss, licorice, nemesis, orifice, precipice, prejudice, reminisce, synthesis, verdigris; acropolis, amaryllis, anabasis, analysis, antithesis, anuresis, catalysis, dieresis, hypothesis, metropolis, necropolis, paralysis, parenthesis, rigor mortis; metamorphosis; abiogenesis.

**-ist** (-ist), cist, cyst, fist, gist, grist, hist, list, mist, schist, tryst, twist, whist, wist, wrist; ageist, A-list, artist, assist, backlist, Baptist, blacklist, Buddhist, centrist, chartist, checklist, chemist, consist, Cubist, cueist, cyclist, dean's list, deist, delist, dentist, desist, druggist, duelist, enlist, entwist, exist, faddist, Fascist, flautist, florist, flutist, harpist, hit list, hymnist, insist, jurist, leftist, linguist, lutist, lyrist, Marxist, metrist, monist, nudist, palmist, persist, playlist, protist, psalmist, purist, racist, resist, rightist, sacrist, sadist, sexist, short list, short-list, simplist, sophist, statist, stylist, subsist, Taoist, theist, Thomist, tourist, Trappist, tropist, typist, untwist, waitlist, white list, wish list; activist, agonist, alarmist, alchemist, algebrist, Alpinist, altruist, amethyst, amorist, analyst, anarchist, animist, annalist, aorist, aphorist, Arabist, archivist, armorist, atheist, atomist, balloonist, banjoist, biblicist, bicyclist, bigamist, Bolshevist, botanist, cabalist, Calvinist, canoeist, cartoonist, casuist, catalyst, catechist, centralist, chauvinist, choralist, citharist, classicist, coexist, colloquist, colonist, colorist, Communist, conformist, copyist, Calvinist, cymbalist, Darwinist, diarist, dogmatist, Donatist, dramatist, dualist, duelist, egoist, egotist, elegist, essayist, ethicist, Eucharist, eulogist, euphuist, exorcist, extremist, fabulist, factionist, fatalist, feminist, fetishist, feudalist, fictionist, finalist, folklorist, formalist, futurist, guitarist, Hebraist, hedonist, Hellenist, herbalist, hobbyist, homilist, humanist, humorist, hypnotist, intertwist, Jansenist, journalist, Judaist, lampoonist, Latinist, legalist, Leninist, librettist, liturgist, lobbyist, loyalist, lyricist, machinist, mannerist, Maoist, martialist, masochist, mechanist, medalist, mesmerist, Methodist, Mithraist, modernist, monarchist, moralist, motorist, naturist, neofascist, nepotist, nihilist, novelist, occultist, oculist, ophthalmist, optimist, organist, pacifist, pantheist, papalist, pessimist, pharmacist, physicist, pianist, pietist, Platonist, pluralist, pointillist, populist, portraitist, pragmatist, preexist, publicist, pugilist, pyrrhonist, realist, re-enlist, reformist, repealist, reservist, rhapsodist, Romanist, royalist, ruralist, Satanist, satirist, scientist, sciolist, Shamanist, Shintoist, Socialist, solecist, soloist, specialist, Stalinist, strategist, suffragist, symbolist, syncretist, Talmudist, terrorist, theorist, therapist, trombonist, Trotskyist, unionist, Vedantist, violist, vocalist, Zionist, zitherist; absolutist, accompanist, aerialist, agronomist, algebraist, alienist, Anabaptist, anatomist, antagonist, anthologist, apiarist, apologist, automatist, autonomist, aviarist, behaviorist, bimetallist, biologist, capitalist, chiropodist, chronologist, clarinetist, clericalist, collectivist, commercialist, communalist, concessionist, contortionist, determinist, diplomatist, dramaturgist, economist, empiricist, enamelist, equilibrist, ethnologist, Evangelist, exclusionist, expansionist, expressionist, extortionist, Federalist, geologist, geometrist, horologist, hygienist, hyperbolist, idealist, illusionist, impressionist, legitimist, liberalist, literalist, lycanthropist, manicurist, meliorist, metallurgist, militarist, minimalist, misanthropist, misogamist, misogynist, monogamist, monologist, monopolist, monotheist, nationalist, naturalist, necrologist, negationist, negativist, neologist, neuropathist, noctambulist, Nominalist, nonconformist, nutritionist, objectivist, obscurantist, obstructionist, ocularist, opportunist, optometrist, parachutist, pathologist, perfectionist, philanthropist, philatelist, philologist, philogynist, phrenologist, plagiarist, polemicist, polygamist, pomologist, positivist, propagandist, protagonist, protectionist, psychiatrist, psychologist, psychopathist, rationalist, recidivist, religionist, revisionist, revivalist, ritualist, romanticist, salvationist, secessionist, secularist, seismologist, sensualist, separatist, soliloquist, somnambulist, somniloquist, spectroscopist, symbologist, syndicalist, synonymist, tautologist, taxidermist, taxonomist, technologist, telepathist, telephonist, thaumaturgist, theologist, theosophist, therapeutist, tobacconist, traditionist, ventriloquist, violinist, zoologist; abolitionist, agriculturist, anthropologist, anthropomorphist, archaeologist, automobilist, caricaturist, coalitionist, conceptionalist, conceptualist, constitutionist, deconstructionist, demonologist, dermatologist, Egyptologist, elocutionist, emigrationist, encyclopedist, entomologist, etymologist, evolutionist, federationist, floriculturist, genealogist, gynecologist, horticulturist, imperialist, industrialist, inspirationist, instrumentalist, insurrectionist, materialist, medievalist, melodramatist, millennialist, mineralogist, miniaturist, monometallist, neo-Darwinist, Occidentalist, ophthalmologist, oppositionist, Orientalist, ornithologist, osteopathist, pharmacologist, phenomenalist, physiologist, postimpressionist, preferentialist, prohibitionist, psychoanalyst, psychotherapist, radiologist, revolutionist, sacerdotalist, sensationalist, sentimentalist, sociologist, spiritualist, toxicologist, traditionalist, transcendentalist, universalist, violoncellist, vivisectionist; arboriculturist, bacteriologist, ceremonialist, Congregationalist, constitutionalist, controversialist, conversationalist, educationalist, experimentalist, individualist, institutionalist, internationalist, meteorologist, physiotherapist, segregationalist, supernaturalist.

Also: **-iss** + **-ed** (as in *missed*, etc.)

**-ist** (-īst), Christ, feist, heist; Zeitgeist; Antichrist, poltergeist.

Also: **-ice** + **-ed** (as in *sliced*, etc.)

**-it,** bit, bitt, Brit, chit, fit, flit, grit, hit, it, kit, knit, lit, mitt, nit, pit, Pitt, quit, sit, skit, slit, smit, snit, spit, split, sprit, tit, twit, whit, wit, writ, zit; acquit, admit, armpit, base hit, befit, bowsprit, bush tit, close-knit, cockpit, commit, cool it, culprit, dimwit, emit, gaslit, half-wit, hard-hit, hobbit, house-sit, legit, lit crit, mess kit, misfit, moonlit, mosh pit, nitwit, obit, omit, outfit, outwit, peewit, permit, pet-sit, pinch-hit, press kit, pulpit, refit, remit, respite, rough it, sandpit, Sanskrit, snakebit, snake pit, starlit, stock split, submit, sunlit, switch-hit, tar pit, tidbit, tight-knit, tomtit, to wit, transmit, turnspit, twilit, two-bit, unfit, with it; apposite, baby-sit, benefit, bit by bit, cable-knit, candlelit, counterfeit, definite, double-knit, exquisite, favorite, firelit, hissy fit, holy writ, hypocrite, infield hit, infinite, intermit, intromit, Jesuit, manumit, megahit, mother wit, opposite, out of it, perquisite, preterite, pretermit, requisite, retrofit, step on it; banana split, bully pulpit, cost-benefit, death benefit, extra-base hit, fringe benefit, indefinite, lickety-split, overcommit, prerequisite, sacrifice hit; jack-in-the-pulpit.

**-itch,** bitch, ditch, fitch, flitch, glitch, hitch, itch, kitsch, niche, pitch, quitch, rich, snitch, stitch, switch, twitch, which, witch; backstitch, bewitch, catch stitch, chain stitch, clove hitch, cross-stitch, eldritch, enrich, half hitch, handstitch, hemstitch, kulich, last-ditch, lock stitch, low pitch, ostrich, sandwich, slip stitch, topstitch, unhitch, wild pitch; bait-and-switch, cable-stitch, concert pitch, czarevitch, fever pitch, machine-stitch, perfect pitch, rolling hitch, running stitch, saddle stitch, toggle switch; seven-year itch.

**-ite** (-īt), bight, bite, blight,

bright, byte, cite, dight, Dwight, fight, flight, fright, height, hight, kite, knight, krait, light, lite, might, mite, night, plight, quite, right, rite, sight, site, sleight, slight, smite, spite, sprite, tight, trite, white, wight, wright, write; affright, airtight, alight, all right, all-night, aright, attrite, backbite, backlight, bauxite, bedight, benight, birthright, black light, bobwhite, bombsight, box kite, bullfight, calcite, campsite, catfight, cockfight, contrite, cordite, daylight, deadlight, delight, dendrite, despite, dogfight, downright, dunnite, dust mite, excite, eyesight, fanlight, ferrite, finite, fistfight, flashlight, fleabite, floodlight, fluorite, footlight, foresight, forthright, fortnight, frostbite, gaslight, ghostwrite, goodnight, graphite, green light, gunfight, halite, handwrite, headlight, highlight, hindsight, Hittite, hoplite, ignite, incite, indict, indite, infight, in-flight, insight, invite, jacklight, jadeite, klieg light, lamplight, lignite, limelight, Lucite, Luddite, marmite, midnight, millwright, miswrite, moonlight, New Right, nightlight, nitrite, off-site, off-white, on-site, outright, outsight, partite, penlight, perlite, playwright, polite, prizefight, pyrite, quartzite, recite, red light, requite, rewrite, samite, searchlight, Semite, Shiite, shipwright, sidelight, sit tight, skintight, skylight, skywrite, snakebite, snow-white, somite, sound bite, spaceflight, spotlight, stage fright, starlight, stoplight, streetlight, sulfite, sunlight, taillight, termite, tonight, top-flight, torchlight, twilight, twi-night, typewrite, unite, upright, uptight, wainwright, Website, weeknight, wheelwright, white flight, white night; acolyte, aconite, anchorite, anthracite, apartheid, appetite, azurite, Bakelite, bipartite, black-and-white, blatherskite, Brooklynite, bryophyte, calamite, Canaanite, candlelight,

Carmelite, catamite, cellulite, cenobite, chestnut blight, copyright, disunite, disinvite, divine right, dolomite, dynamite, eremite, erudite, expedite, extradite, Fahrenheit, featherlight, fight-or-flight, firefight, firelight, fly-by-night, Gesundheit, gigabyte, hellgrammite, Hepplewhite, impolite, inner light, Jacobite, Jerseyite, kilobyte, laborite, leading light, leukocyte, lewisite, lily-white, line of sight, lymphocyte, magnetite, malachite, marcasite, martensite, megabyte, Mennonite, Moabite, Mr. Right, Muscovite, neophyte, oocyte, out-of-sight, overbite, overnight, oversight, overwrite, parasite, patent right, phagocyte, pilot light, plebiscite, proselyte, recondite, reunite, running light, satellite, see the light, socialite, sodalite, speed of light, stalactite, stalagmite, sybarite, terabyte, traffic light, transvestite, trilobite, tripartite, troglodyte, ultralight, underwrite, urbanite, vulcanite, water sprite, watertight, weathertight, wolframite, Yemenite; alexandrite, anti-Semite, electrolyte, gemütlichkeit, hermaphrodite, heteroclite, Israelite, metabolite, meteorite, multipartite, New Jerseyite, potato blight, property right, suburbanite, theodolite, Turkish delight; Pre-Raphaelite, riparian right.

**-ite** (-it). See **-it.**

**-ites** (-its). See **-itz.**

**-ith,** fifth, frith, kith, myth, pith, smith, Smith, with, withe; blacksmith, Edith, forthwith, goldsmith, gunsmith, herewith, locksmith, songsmith, therewith, tinsmith, tunesmith, wherewith, wordsmith, zenith; acrolith, Arrowsmith, batholith, coppersmith, eolith, Granny Smith, megalith, metalsmith, monolith, neolith, otolith, silversmith.

**-ithe,** blithe, lithe, scythe, tithe, withe, writhe.

**-itz,** blitz, ditz, fritz, Fritz, glitz, grits, its, it's, quits, ritz, spitz, spritz; Auschwitz, kibitz; slivovitz.

Also: **-it** + **-s** (as in *bits,* etc.)

Also: **-ite** + **-s** (as in *favorites,* etc.)

**-ive** (-īv), chive, Clive, dive, drive, five, gyve, hive, I've, jive, live, rive, shive, shrive, skive, strive, thrive, wive; alive, archive, arrive, back dive, beehive, connive, contrive, crash-dive, deprive, derive, disk drive, endive, hard drive, high five, line drive, nosedive, ogive, revive, skin-dive, skydive, survive, swan dive, take five, test-drive; eat alive, forty-five, four-wheel drive, overdrive, power dive, scuba-dive.

**-ive** (-iv), give, live, sheave, shiv, sieve, spiv; active, captive, costive, cursive, dative, fictive, forgive, furtive, massive, misgive, missive, motive, native, outlive, passive, pensive, plaintive, relive, restive, sportive, suasive, votive; ablative, abortive, abrasive, absorptive, abstersive, abstractive, abusive, adaptive, additive, adductive, adhesive, adjective, adjunctive, adoptive, affective, afflictive, aggressive, allusive, amative, arrestive, aspersive, assertive, assuasive, assumptive, attentive, attractive, causative, coercive, cognitive, cohesive, collective, collusive, combative, combustive, compulsive, conative, conceptive, concessive, concussive, conclusive, concoctive, conducive, conductive, conflictive, congestive, conjunctive, connective, constrictive, constructive, consultive, consumptive, contractive, convulsive, corrective, corrosive, corruptive, creative, curative, deceptive, decisive, deductive, defective, defensive, delusive, depictive, depressive, derisive, descriptive, destructive, detective, detractive, diffusive, digestive, digressive, directive, discursive, disjunctive, disruptive, dissuasive, distinctive, distractive, divertive, divisive, divulsive, effective, effusive, elective, elusive, emissive, emotive, emulsive, evasive, excessive, exclusive, excursive, exhaustive, expansive, expensive, expletive, explosive, expressive, expulsive, extensive, extortive, extractive, extrusive, fixative, formative, fugitive, genitive, gerundive, hortative, illusive, impassive, impressive, impulsive, inactive, incentive, incisive, inclusive, incursive, inductive, infective, inflective, infusive, ingestive, inscriptive, instinctive, instructive, intensive, intrusive, invective, inventive, laudative, laxative, lenitive, locative, lucrative, narrative, negative, nutritive, objective, obstructive, obtrusive, offensive, olfactive, oppressive, optative, partitive, perceptive, percussive, perfective, permissive, perspective, persuasive, pervasive, positive, possessive, preclusive, precursive, predictive, pre-emptive, prescriptive, presumptive, preventive, primitive, privative, productive, progressive, projective, propulsive, proscriptive, prospective, protective, protractive, protrusive, punitive, purgative, purposive, putative, reactive, receptive, recessive, redemptive, reductive, reflective, reflexive, regressive, relative, remissive, repressive, repulsive, respective, responsive, restrictive, resumptive, retentive, retractive, revulsive, secretive, sedative, seductive, selective, sensitive, siccative, subjective, subjunctive, submissive, substantive, subtractive, subversive, successive, suggestive, suppressive, talkative, tentative, transgressive, transitive, transmissive, vibrative, vindictive, vocative; abrogative, accusative, acquisitive, admonitive, adumbrative, affirmative, alternative, appellative, attributive, augmentative, calculative, circumscriptive, circumventive, coextensive, combinative, comparative, compensative, competitive, compositive, comprehensive, connotative, consecutive, conservative, contemplative, contributive, conversative, corporative, correlative, counteractive, cumulative, declarative, decorative, dedicative, definitive, demonstrative, denotative, deprecative, derivative, diminutive, disputative, distributive, educative, evocative, excitative, exclamative, execrative, executive, exhibitive, exhortative, expectative, explicative, explorative, expositive, figurative, generative, germinative, hesitative, illustrative, imitative, imperative, imperceptive, inattentive, incohesive, inconclusive, indecisive, indicative, indistinctive, ineffective, inexhaustive, inexpansive, inexpensive, inexpressive, infinitive, informative, innovative, inoffensive, inquisitive, insensitive, integrative, intransitive, introductive, introspective, intuitive, irrespective, irresponsive, irritative, iterative, judicative, legislative, locomotive, medicative, meditative, nominative, operative, palliative, pejorative, preparative, prerogative, preservative, preventative, procreative, prohibitive, provocative, putrefactive, qualitative, quantitative, radiative, rarefactive, recitative, reconstructive, recreative, reformative, regulative, remonstrative, repetitive, reprehensive, reprobative, reproductive, restorative, retributive, retroactive, retrogressive, retrospective, ruminative, speculative, stupefactive, superlative, suppurative, underactive, vegetative, vindicative; accumulative, administrative, agglutinative, alleviative, alliterative, appreciative, argumentative, assimilative, associative, authoritative, coagulative, commemorative, commiserative, communicative, confederative, cooperative, corroborative, deliberative, depreciative, discriminative, exonerative, expostulative, imaginative, initiative, inoperative, interpretative, interrogative, investigative, irradiative, manipulative, photosensitive, postoperative, recuperative, reiterative, remunerative, representative, retaliative, significative, subordinative, undemonstrative, vituperative; incommunicative, neoconservative, philoprogenitive.

**-ive** (-ēv). See **–eave.**

**-ix,** fix, mix, nix, pyx, six, Styx; admix, affix, commix, deep-six, helix, infix, matrix, onyx, prefix, premix, prix fixe, prolix, quick fix, suffix, trail mix, transfix, unfix; cicatrix, crucifix, dirty tricks, eighty-six, fiddlesticks, intermix, politics; double helix, executrix; archaeopteryx, geopolitics.

Also: **-ick** + **-s** (as in *bricks, sticks,* etc.)

**-ixed.** See **-ixt.**

**-ixt,** twixt; betwixt.

Also: **-ix** + **-ed** (as in *mixed,* etc.)

**-iz.** See **-is.**

**-ize,** guise, prize, rise, size, wise; advise, apprise, arise, assize, baptize, bite-size, capsize, chastise, clockwise, comprise, crosswise, demise, despise, devise, disguise, door prize, downsize, earthrise, edgewise, excise, franchise, Grecize, high-rise, incise, king-size, leastwise, lengthwise, lifesize, likewise, low-rise, man-size, midsize, misprize, moonrise, outsize, pint-size, quantize, queensize, remise, reprise, revise, rightsize, slantwise, streetwise, stylize, suffice, sunrise, surmise, surprise, twin-size, unwise, upsize; advertise, aggrandize, agonize, alkalize, amortize, analyze, Anglicize, anodize, anywise, aphorize, Arabize, atomize, authorize, Balkanize, barbarize, bastardize, booby prize, bowdlerize, brutalize, burglarize, canalize, canonize, capsulize, caramelize, carbonize, catalyze, catechize, cauterize, centralize, circumcise, civilize, classicize, colonize, colorize, compromise, concertize, concretize, creolize, criticize, crystallize, customize, demonize, deputize, digitize, disfranchise, dogmatize, dramatize, empathize, emphasize, energize, enfranchise, enterprise, equalize, eulogize, euphemize, euthanize, exercise, exorcise, fantasize, feminize, fertilize, feudalize, finalize, focalize, formalize, fossilize, fractionize, fraternize, Gallicize, galvanize, Germanize, glamorize, globalize, glutinize, gormandize, gourmandize, harmonize, Hellenize, humanize, hybridize, hypnotize, idolize, immunize, improvise, ionize, itemize, jazzercize, jeopardize, Judaize, laicize, Latinize, legalize, lionize, liquidize, localize, magnetize, marbleize, martyrize, maximize, mechanize, memorize, mercerize, merchandise, mesmerize, metallize, methodize, minimize, mobilize, modernize, moisturize, monetize, moralize, motorize, mythicize, narcotize, nasalize, neutralize, Nobel prize, normalize, notarize, novelize, optimize, organize, ostracize, otherwise, oversize, oxidize, palletize, paralyze, pasteurize, patronize, pauperize, penalize, penny-wise, plagiarize, plasticize, pluralize, pocket-size, polarize, polemize, pressurize, privatize, publicize, pulverize, racialize, randomize, rationalize, realize, recognize, rhapsodize, robotize, Romanize, rubberize, ruralize, sanitize, satirize, scandalize, schematize, scrutinize, sensitize, sermonize, signalize, simonize, slenderize, socialize, sodomize, solemnize, specialize, stabilize, Stalinize, standardize, sterilize, stigmatize, strategize, subsidize, summarize, supervise, symbolize, sympathize, symphonize, synchronize, syncretize, synthesize, systemize, tantalize, televise, temporize, tenderize, terrorize, texturize, theorize, totalize, tranquilize, traumatize, tyrannize, unionize, urbanize, utilize, vandalize, vaporize, verbalize, victimize, vitalize, vocalize, vulcanize, vulgarize, weatherize, weather-wise, Westernize, winterize, womanize, worldly-wise; accessorize, acclimatize, actualize, aestheticize, Africanize, allegorize, alphabetize, anatomize, anesthetize, annualize, antagonize, anthologize, anticlockwise, apologize, apostatize, apostrophize, Arabicize, bureaucratize, cannibalize, capitalize, caramelize, categorize, catheterize, catholicize, characterize, Christianize, collectivize, commercialize, commoditize, communalize, computerize, contrariwise, cosmeticize, counterclockwise, criminalize, cross-fertilize, decentralize, decolonize, de-emphasize, defeminize, deformalize, deglamorize, dehumanize, demagnetize, demobilize, democratize, demoralize, deodorize, depersonalize, depolarize, desalinize, desensitize, destabilize, detribalize, devitalize, digitalize, disenfranchise, disorganize, economize, emblematize, epitomize, eroticize, euthanatize, evangelize, extemporize, externalize, familiarize, fanaticize, federalize, fictionalize, floor exercise, free enterprise, generalize, Hispanicize, historicize, homogenize, hospitalize, hydrogenize, hypothesize, idealize, immobilize, immortalize, infantilize, initialize, internalize, italicize, legitimize, liberalize, lobotomize, macadamize, marginalize, metabolize, metastasize, militarize, mineralize, monopolize, mythologize, nationalize, naturalize, oxygenize, parenthesize, personalize, philosophize, plagiarize, politicize, popularize, prioritize, proselytize, Pulitzer prize, radicalize, rationalize, regularize, reorganize, revitalize, ritualize, romanticize, secularize, sexualize, singularize, soliloquize, suburbanize, systematize, temporalize, theologize, theosophize, traditionalize, transistorize, trivialize, ventriloquize, visualize; Americanize, anathematize, apotheosize, colonialize, compartmentalize, conceptualize, consolation prize, contextualize, decriminalize, delegitimize, demilitarize, denaturalize, departmentalize, etymologize, Europeanize, familiarize, industrialize, legitimatize, materialize, memorialize, miniaturize, particularize, private enterprise, professionalize, psychoanalyze, republicanize, revolutionize, sensationalize, sentimentalize, spiritualize, underutilize, universalize; constitutionalize, editorialize, individualize, institutionalize, intellectualize, internationalize.

Also: **-y** + **-s** (as in *testifies,* etc.)

Also: **-eye** + **-s** (as in *eyes,* etc.)

Also: **-igh** + **-s** (as in *sighs,* etc.)

**-o** (-ō). See **-ow.**

**-o** (-o͞o). See **-oo.**

**-oach,** broach, brooch, coach, loach, loche, poach, roach; abroach, approach, caroche, cockroach, day coach, encroach, night coach, reproach, slowcoach, stagecoach; motor coach, self-reproach.

**-oad** (-ôd). See **-aud.**

**-oad** (-ōd). See **-ode.**

**-oaf,** goaf, loaf, oaf; meatloaf, witloof; autotroph, sugarloaf.

**-oak.** See **-oke.**

**-oaks.** See **-oax.**

**-oal.** See **-ole.**

**-oaled.** See **-old.**

**-oam.** See **-ome.**

**-oan.** See **-one.**

**-oap.** See **-ope.**

**-oar.** See **-ore.**
**-oard.** See **-ord.**
**-oared.** See **-ord.**
**-oast.** See **-ost.**
**-oat.** See **-ote.**
**-oath.** See **-oth.**
**-oax,** coax, hoax.
Also: **-oak** + **-s** (as in *cloaks,* etc.)
Also: **-oke** + **-s** (as in *jokes,* etc.)
**-ob,** blob, bob, Bob, cob, Cobb, fob, glob, gob, hob, job, knob, lob, mob, nob, rob, slob, snob, sob, squab, swab, throb; corncob, day job, doorknob, heartthrob, hobnob, kabob, macabre, McJob, nabob, nawab, snow job; shish kebab, thingumbob; thingamabob.
**-obe,** daube, globe, Job, lobe, probe, robe, strobe; bathrobe, conglobe, disrobe, earlobe, enrobe, lap robe, microbe, unrobe, wardrobe; Anglophobe, claustrophobe, Francophobe, frontal lobe, Gallophobe, homophobe, Russophobe, Slavophobe, technophobe, xenophobe; ailurophobe, bibliophobe, computerphobe.
**-ock,** Bach, bloc, Bloch, block, bock, brock, chock, clock, cock, croc, crock, doc, dock, floc, flock, frock, grok, hock, jock, Jock, knock, loch, lock, lough, Mach, moc, mock, nock, pock, roc, rock, shlock, shock, smock, sock, stock, wok, yock; ad hoc, air lock, alt-rock, amok, armlock, ball cock, Balzac, bangkok, Bangkok, bedrock, bitstock, burdock, crew sock, deadlock, defrock, dreadlock, dry dock, duroc, Dvorak, earlock, en bloc, epoch, fetlock, flintlock, folk-rock, forelock, gamecock, gemsbok, gridlock, gunlock, half cock, Hancock, hard rock, havelock, haycock, headlock, heart block, hemlock, in stock, jazz-rock, kapok, kneesock, livestock, matchlock, nostoc, oarlock, o'clock, padlock, peacock, petcock, picklock, post doc, post hoc, punk rock, rhebok, roadblock, rootstock, Rorschach, shamrock, Sheetrock, shell shock, Sherlock, shock jock, Shy-

lock, smock frock, spatchcock, springbok, steenbok, stopcock, sunblock, ticktock, time clock, unfrock, unlock, warlock, wedlock, wheel lock, whipstock, windsock, woodblock, woodcock, wristlock; acid rock, aftershock, alarm clock, alpenstock, antiknock, antilock, Antioch, building block, butcher block, chockablock, chopping block, cinder block, common stock, country rock, cuckoo clock, culture shock, firelock, floating dock, future shock, glitter rock, hammerlock, hollyhock, interlock, Jabberwock, laughingstock, Little Rock, manioc, mantlerock, monadnock, Offenbach, out of stock, penny stock, poppycock, preferred stock, rolling stock, septic shock, shuttlecock, spatterdock, starting block, sticker shock, stumbling block, summer stock, turkey cock, weathercock, writer's block; around-the-clock, atomic clock, grandfather clock, insulin shock.

**-ocked.** See **-oct.**

**-ocks.** See **-ox.**

**-oct,** concoct, decoct, entr'acte; half-cocked, landlocked, shell-shocked.
Also: **-ock** + **-ed** (as in *flocked*, etc.)

**-od,** bod, clod, cod, god, hod, mod, nod, od, odd, plod, pod, prod, quad, quod, rod, scrod, shod, sod, squad, tod, trod, wad; aubade, ballade, bipod, black cod, Cape Cod, couvade, croustade, death squad, dryshod, ephod, estrade, facade, fantad, fly rod, glissade, hot-rod, jihad, lingcod, Nimrod, noyade, peasecod, pomade, push rod, ramrod, roughshod, roulade, saccade, seedpod, slipshod, sun god, synod, tightwad, torsade, tripod, unshod, untrod, vice squad; Aaron's rod, accolade, act of God, arthropod, bigarade, carbonnade, cattle prod, chiffonade, decapod, defilade, demigod, diplopod, dowsing rod, eisteddfod, enfilade, escalade, esplanade, flying squad, fusillade, gastropod, goldenrod, hexapod, isopod, lightning rod, lycopod, man of God, monkeypod, monopod, octopod, piston rod, promenade, pseudopod, rémoulade, rhizopod, son of God, spinning rod, tapenade, tetrapod; brachiopod, cephalopod, divining rod, firing squad, leveling rod, rodomontade, Scheherazade, Upanishad.

**-ode,** bode, code, goad, load, lode, mode, node, ode, road, rode, Spode, strode, toad, woad; abode, anode, bar code, boatload, busload, byroad, carload, caseload, cathode, church mode, commode, corrode, crossroad, decode, diode, download, dress code, dynode, encode, epode, erode, explode, forebode, freeload, front-load, geode, high road, horned toad, implode, inroad, lymph node, Morse code, no-load, offload, outmode, payload, planeload, postcode, post road, railroad, reload, sarod, side road, source code, spring-load, square-toed, trainload, truckload, two-toed, unload, upload, zip code; à la mode, antipode, carbo-load, discommode, electrode, episode, frontage road, front-end load, hit the road, microcode, mother lode, Nesselrode, object code, overload, palinode, penal code, pigeon-toed, service road, trematode, wagonload; area code, genetic code, rule of the road.

Also: **-ow** + **-ed** (as in *towed,* etc.)

**-odge,** dodge, hodge, lodge, podge, stodge; dislodge, garage, hodgepodge, massage, swaraj.

**-oe** (-ō). See **-ow.**

**-oe** (-o͞o). See **-ew.**

**-oes** (-ōz). See **-ose.**

**-oes** (-uz). See **-uzz.**

**-off,** cough, doff, off, prof, scoff, shroff, soph, toff, trough; Bake-Off, blastoff, brush-off, castoff, checkoff, Chekhov, cookoff, cutoff, die-off, drop-off, face-off, falloff, far-off, goof-off, hand-off, hands-off, jump-off, Khrushchev, kickoff, kiss-off, layoff, liftoff, one-off, payoff, pick-off, play-off, rip-off, runoff, sawed-off, sell-off, send-off, setoff, show-off, shutoff, sign-off, spin-off, standoff, takeoff, tipoff, trade-off, turnoff, write-off; better-off, cooling-off, damping-off, Gorbachev, Molotov, Nabokov, philosophe, whooping cough; beef Stroganoff. See also **-aff.**

**-offed.** See **-oft.**

**-oft,** croft, loft, oft, soft; aloft, hayloft; choir loft, semisoft, supersoft, ultrasoft, undercroft.

Also: **-off** + **-ed** (as in *doffed*, etc.)

Also: **-ough** + **-ed** (as in *coughed*, etc.)

**-og,** blog, bog, clog, cog, dog, flog, fog, frog, Gog, grog, hog, jog, log, nog, Prague, quag, slog, smog, tog; agog, backlog, befog, bird dog, bird-dog, bulldog, bullfrog, corn dog, defog, eclogue, eggnog, footslog, groundhog, guide dog, gulag, hangdog, hedgehog, hot dog, hot-dog, ice fog, incog, lap dog, leapfrog, Magog, photog, prologue, pye-dog, quahog, road hog, sandhog, sheepdog, sled dog, top dog, tree frog, unclog, warthog, watchdog, Weblog, whole hog, wood frog, Yule log; analog, analogue, apologue, catalog, chili dog, decalogue, demagogue, dialogue, dog-eat-dog, epilogue, firedog, golliwogg, homologue, monologue, mystagogue, pedagogue, pettifog, pollywog, prairie dog, synagogue, Tagalog, travelogue, underdog, waterlog, yellow dog; ideologue.

**-ogue** (-ōg), bogue, brogue, drogue, rogue, vogue; pirogue, prorogue; disembogue.

**-ogue** (-og). See **-og.**

**-oice,** choice, Joyce, voice; devoice, invoice, pro-choice, rejoice, Rolls Royce, unvoice; dealer's choice, fielder's choice, Hobson's choice; multiple-choice.

**-oiced.** See **-oist.**

**-oid,** droid, Floyd, Freud, Lloyd, void; android, avoid,

chancroid, colloid, crinoid, deltoid, dendroid, devoid, factoid, fibroid, fungoid, mastoid, ovoid, spheroid, steroid, tabloid, thyroid, typhoid; adenoid, alkaloid, aneroid, anthropoid, asteroid, celluloid, flavonoid, hemorrhoid, hominoid, humanoid, Mongoloid, null and void, paranoid, Polaroid, rheumatoid, trapezoid, unemployed; meteoroid, paraboloid.
Also: **-oy** + **-ed** (as in *enjoyed*, etc.)

**-oil,** boil, broil, coil, foil, Hoyle, moil, oil, roil, soil, spoil, toil, voile; airfoil, charbroil, cinquefoil, coal oil, corn oil, despoil, embroil, fish oil, free-soil, fuel oil, gargoyle, gumboil, hard-boil, langue d'oïl, milfoil, night soil, palm oil, parboil, potboil, recoil, shale oil, snake oil, subsoil, tinfoil, topsoil, trefoil, turmoil, uncoil; baby oil, castor oil, counterfoil, hydrofoil, linseed oil, olive oil, peanut oil, quatrefoil, salad oil, soybean oil; canola oil, cottonseed oil, essential oil, mineral oil, safflower oil, vegetable oil.

**-oin,** coin, groin, join, loin, quoin; adjoin, benzoin, Burgoyne, conjoin, Des Moines, disjoin, eloign, enjoin, essoin, purloin, rejoin, sainfoin, short loin, sirloin, subjoin; talapoin, tenderloin.

**-oint,** joint, point; anoint, appoint, aroint, ball joint, ballpoint, bluepoint, break point, butt joint, cashpoint, checkpoint, chokepoint, clip joint, conjoint, dew point, disjoint, drypoint, end point, fixed-point, flash point, game point, grade point, gunpoint, gyp joint, hip joint, ice point, juke joint, knifepoint, lap joint, match point, midpoint, penpoint, pinpoint, pourpoint, price point, set point, spearpoint, standpoint, viewpoint, West Point; basis point, boiling point, breaking point, brownie point, case in point, counterpoint, disappoint, floating point, focal point, freezing point, melting point, miter joint, needlepoint, out of joint, petit point, point-to-point, pressure point, rabbet joint, selling point, silverpoint, sticking point, talking point, to the point, turning point, vantage point, vowel point; critical point, decimal point, percentage point, vanishing point.

**-oise,** noise, poise; turquoise, white noise; counterpoise, equipoise, Illinois, Iroquois; avoirdupois.

Also: **-oy** + **-s** (as in *toys,* etc.)

**-oist,** foist, hoist, joist, moist, voiced; unvoiced.

Also: **-oice** + **-ed** (as in *voiced,* etc.)

**-oit,** coit, doit, moit, quoit; adroit, Beloit, dacoit, Detroit, exploit, introit; maladroit, Massasoit.

**-oke,** bloke, broke, coak, choke, cloak, coke, Coke, croak, folk, hoke, joke, oak, oke, poke, roke, roque, sloke, smoke, soak, soke, spoke, stoke, stroke, toke, toque, woke, yoke, yolk; awoke, backstroke, baroque, bespoke, breaststroke, brush stroke, chain-smoke, convoke, cowpoke, downstroke, evoke, ground stroke, hair stroke, heatstroke, housebroke, in-joke, invoke, jamoke, keystroke, kinfolk, live oak, menfolk, outstroke, pin oak, presoak, provoke, red oak, revoke, scrub oak, sidestroke, slowpoke, stonebroke, sunchoke, sunstroke, townsfolk, tradesfolk, unyoke, upstroke, white oak; artichoke, counterstroke, equivoque, gentlefolk, masterstroke, ministroke, mourning cloak, okeydoke, poison oak, running joke, Roanoke, thunderstroke, womenfolk; pig in a poke, practical joke, secondhand smoke.

**-okes.** See **-oax.**

**-ol** (-ol), col, doll, loll, moll, Sol; Algol, ALGOL, atoll, gun moll; aerosol, alcohol, baby doll, capitol, entresol, folderol, girasol, parasol, protocol, vitriol.

**-ol** (-ōl). See **-ole.**

**-old,** bold, cold, fold, gold, hold, mold, mould, old, scold, sold, told, wold; age-old, all told, behold, billfold, black gold, blindfold, bread mold, choke hold, cuckold, enfold, eyefold, fanfold, fool's gold, foothold, foretold, freehold, gatefold, handhold, head cold, household, ice-cold, kobold, leaf mold, leasehold, old gold, on hold, pinfold, retold, roothold, scaffold, sheepfold, slime mold, stone-cold, stronghold, take hold, threshold, toehold, twice-told, twofold, unfold, unmold, untold, uphold, white gold, withhold; centerfold, common cold, copyhold, fingerhold, liquid gold, manifold, marigold, overbold, stranglehold; as good as gold, blow hot and cold, out in the cold.

Also: **-oal** + **-ed** (as in *foaled*, etc.)

Also: **-ole** + **-ed** (as in *paroled*, etc.)

Also: **-oll** + **-ed** (as in *rolled*, etc.)

**-ole,** bole, boll, bowl, coal, cole, dole, droll, foal, goal, hole, Joel, knoll, kohl, mole, pole, poll, prole, role, roll, scroll, shoal, skoal, sole, soul, stole, stroll, thole, tole, toll, troll, vole, whole; air hole, armhole, atoll, bankroll, beanpole, bedroll, black hole, blowhole, bricole, bunghole, cajole, charcoal, condole, console, control, Creole, dipole, drum roll, egg roll, enroll, extol, field goal, fishbowl, flagpole, foxhole, frijol, half sole, heart-whole, hellhole, insole, keyhole, knothole, leaf roll, logroll, loophole, manhole, Maypole, Nicole, North Pole, parole, patrol, payroll, peephole, pinhole, pistole, porthole, pothole, punch bowl, resole, ridgepole, rissole, sinkhole, ski pole, South Pole, spring roll, tadpole, thumbhole, washbowl, wormhole; aerosol, amphibole, Anatole, aureole, banderole, barcarole, barber pole, barrel roll, buttonhole, cabriole, camisole, capriole, caracole, carmagnole, casserole, cubbyhole, dariole, decontrol, Dover sole, escarole, exit poll, farandole, finger hole, fishing pole, fumarole, girandole, girasole, gloriole, glory hole, honor roll, innersole, jelly roll, kaiser roll, lemon sole, muster roll, on a roll, on the whole, oriole, ozone hole, petiole, pigeonhole, protocol, rabbit hole, remote control, rigmarole, rock-'n'-roll, Seminole, Super Bowl, swimming hole, totem pole, vacuole, water hole; ace in the hole, cholesterol, fillet of sole, magnetic pole, profiterole, telephone pole.

**-oled.** See **-old.**

**-olk.** See **-oke.**

**-oll** (-ol). See **-ol.**

**-oll** (-ōl). See **-ole.**

**-olled.** See **-old.**

**-olt,** bolt, colt, dolt, holt, jolt, molt, poult, volt; deadbolt, eyebolt, revolt, spring bolt, unbolt; megavolt, thunderbolt, toggle bolt.

**-olve,** solve; absolve, convolve, devolve, dissolve, evolve, involve, resolve, revolve.

**-om** (-om), bomb, bombe, dom, from, glom, mom, prom, rhomb, ROM, Tom; A-bomb, aplomb, car bomb, coulomb, dive-bomb, dotcom, EPROM, H-bomb, mail bomb, phenom, pogrom, pompom, sitcom, smoke bomb, therefrom, time bomb, tom-tom, wigwam, wherefrom; atom bomb, carpet-bomb, CD-ROM, cherry bomb, cluster bomb, diatom, firebomb, intercom, letter bomb, neutron bomb, soccer mom, supermom, telecom, Uncle Tom; atomic bomb, hydrogen bomb.

**-om** (-o͞om). See **-oom.**

**-omb** (-om). See **-om.**

**-omb** (-ōm). See **-ome.**

**-omb** (-o͞om). See **-oom.**

**-ome** (-ōm), chrome, comb, dome, foam, gloam, gnome, holm, home, loam, mome, nome, Nome, ohm, pome, roam, Rome, tome; adult home, airdrome, at-home, beachcomb, biome, cockscomb, coulomb, down-home, genome, group home, hot comb, Jerome, rest home, rhizome, salt dome, sea foam, shalom, syndrome; aerodrome, astrodome, catacomb, chromosome, currycomb, double-dome, Down syndrome, fine-tooth comb, foster home, gastronome, harvest home, hecatomb, hippodrome, honeycomb, leisure home, metronome, mobile home, monochrome, motordrome, motor home, nursing home, palindrome, plastic foam, pleasure dome, polychrome, ribosome, second home, stay-at-home, Styrofoam; funeral home.

**-ome** (-um). See **-um.**

**-omp,** chomp, clomp, comp, pomp, romp, stomp, swamp, tromp, trompe, whomp; workers' comp.

**-once** (-ons), nonce, sconce; ensconce, response.

**-once** (-uns). See **-unce.**

**-onch.** See **-onk.**

**-ond,** blond, blonde, bond, fond, frond, pond, sonde, wand, yond; abscond, ash-blond, beau monde, beyond, despond, fishpond, haut monde, junk bond, millpond, respond; bearer bond, correspond, demimonde, Eurobond, overfond, savings bond, solar pond, vagabond; slough of despond, strawberry blond.

Also: **-on** + **-ed** (as in *donned*, etc.)

**-one** (-ōn), blown, bone, clone, cone, crone, drone, flown, groan, grown, hone, Joan, known, loan, lone, moan, mohn, mown, own, phone, pone, prone, roan, Rhone, scone, sewn, shone, shown, sown, stone, throne, thrown, tone, zone; agon, aitchbone, alone, atone, backbone, Bayonne, bemoan, birthstone, bloodstone, breastbone, bridge loan, brimstone, brownstone, call loan, calzone, capstone, car phone, cellphone, cheekbone, chinbone, clingstone, cogon, cologne, Cologne, condone, copestone, corn pone, curbstone, cyclone, daimon, debone, depone, dethrone, dial tone, disown, earphone, earth tone, end zone, enthrone, fieldstone, flagstone, flavone, flyblown, footstone, freestone, free zone, full-blown, gallstone, gemstone, gravestone, grindstone, hailstone, half tone, halftone, handblown, headphone, headstone, hearthstone, high-flown, hipbone, homegrown, hormone, housephone, ingrown, intone, jawbone, ketone, keystone, limestone, lodestone, milestone, millstone, moonstone, nose cone, outgrown, ozone, pay phone, pinecone, postpone, propone, rezone, rhinestone, ring tone, sandstone, shinbone, Shoshone, smart phone, snow cone, soapstone, strike zone, T-bone, tailbone, thighbone, time zone, toadstone, tombstone, touchstone, touchtone, trombone, two-tone, unknown, unsewn, unthrown, war zone, well-known, whalebone, wheel-thrown, whetstone, windblown, wishbone, wristbone; acetone, allophone, altar stone, Anglophone, anklebone, baritone, buffer zone, cannon bone, chaperone, cherrystone, cicerone, cobblestone, collarbone, comfort zone, cornerstone, cortisone, curling stone, cuttlebone, epigone, firestone, Francophone, frigid zone, funny bone, gramaphone, growth hormone, herringbone, homophone, ice-cream cone, ironstone, kidney stone, knucklebone, marrowbone, megaphone, methadone, microphone, mobile phone, minestrone, monotone, neutral zone, overblown, overgrown, overthrown, overtone, pheremone, provolone, quarter tone, saxophone, semitone, silicone, sousaphone, speakerphone, stand-alone, stepping-stone, telephone, torrid zone, traffic cone, twilight zone, undertone, vibraphone, xylophone; accident-prone, bred-in-the-bone, eau de cologne, enterprise zone, foundation zone, progesterone, Rosetta stone, temperate zone, testosterone, videophone.

**-one** (-on). See **-on.**

**-one** (-un). See **-un.**

**-ong** (-ong), bong, dong, flong, gong, long, prong, song, strong, thong, throng, tong, Tong, wrong; agelong, along, art song, barong, belong, biltong, birdsong, chaise longue, daylong, dingdong, diphthong, dugong, erelong, fight song, folk song, furlong, headlong, headstrong, Hong Kong, King Kong, lifelong, livelong, mah-jongg, nightlong, oblong, oolong, part-song, Ping-Pong, plainsong, prolong, sarong, sidelong, singsong, so long, souchong, swan song, theme song, torch song; all along, before long, billabong, cradlesong, drinking song, evensong, overlong, passalong, scuppernong, sing-along, siren song, tagalong, take-along.

**-ong** (-ung). See **-ung.**

**-ongue.** See **-ung.**

**-onk** (-ongk), bonk, bronc, clonk, conch, conk, honk, plonk, tonk, wonk, zonk; honky-tonk.

**-onk** (-unk). See **-unk.**

**-onned.** See **-ond.**

**-onse.** See **-once.**

**-ont** (-ont), font, want; haplont, Piedmont, Vermont; creodont, Hellespont, symbiont.

**-ont** (-unt). See **-unt.**

**-oo.** See **-ew.**

**-ood** (-o͝od), could, good, hood, should, stood, wood, would; basswood, bentwood, boxwood, boyhood, brushwood, childhood, cordwood, deadwood, do-good, dogwood, driftwood, falsehood, feel-good, for good, fruitwood, girlhood, godhood, greenwood, groundwood, gumwood, hardwood, knighthood, make good, manhood, matchwood, monkshood, no-good, pinewood, plywood, priesthood, pulpwood, redwood, rosewood, sainthood, selfhood, softwood, statehood, Talmud, teakwood, wifehood, wildwood, withstood, wormwood; adulthood, babyhood, bachelorhood, brotherhood, buttonhood, cottonwood, fatherhood, firewood, hardihood, Hollywood, knock on wood, likelihood, livelihood, maidenhood, motherhood, nationhood, neighborhood, orangewood, parenthood, personhood, Robin Hood, sandalwood, servanthood, sisterhood, tulipwood, understood, widowhood, womanhood; misunderstood, second childhood.

**-ood** (-ōōd). See **-ude.**

**-oof,** goof, hoof, kloof, poof, pouf, proof, roof, spoof, woof; aloof, behoof, bombproof, childproof, crushproof, disproof, flameproof, foolproof, germproof, heat proof, hip roof, leakproof, lightproof, moonroof, mothproof, pickproof, rainproof, reproof, rustproof, shadoof, shellproof, shockproof, soundproof, stainproof, sunroof, Tartuffe, windproof, witloof; bulletproof, burglarproof, fireproof, gable roof, hit the roof, ovenproof, shatterproof, tamperproof, through the roof, warp and woof, waterproof, weatherproof; burden of proof, idiotproof, opéra bouffe.

**-ook** (-ŏŏk), book, brook, cook, crook, hook, look, nook, rook, schnook, shook, snook, took; bankbook, betook, black book, blue book, boat hook, caoutchouc, casebook, checkbook, Chinook, closed book, codebook, cookbook, daybook, dough hook, dream book, e-book, fake book, fishhook, forsook, guidebook, handbook, hornbook, hymnbook, jokebook, logbook, matchbook, mistook, nainsook, new look, notebook, outlook, partook, passbook, phone book, phrase book, playbook, pothook, prayer book, precook, promptbook, psalmbook, retook, schoolbook, scrapbook, sketchbook, skyhook, songbook, sourcebook, stylebook, textbook, trade book, unhook, white book, wordbook, workbook, yearbook; buttonhook, comic book, copybook, crochet hook, donnybrook, double-book, inglenook, off the hook, overbook, overlook, overtook, picture book, pocketbook, pressure-cook, pruning hook, reference book, service book, statute book, storybook, tenterhook, undertook; audiobook, coloring book, commonplace book, gobbledegook, telephone book.

**-ook** (-ook). See **-uke.**

**-ool,** boule, buhl, cool, drool, fool, ghoul, joule, pool, pul, rule, school, spool, stool, tool, tulle, who'll, you'll, yule; air-cool, ampule, arghool, barstool, befool, B-school, capsule, carpool, cesspool, damfool, day school, edge tool, faldstool, ferrule, ferule, flake tool, footstool, gag rule, gene pool, grade school, ground rule, high school, home rule, homeschool, misrule, night school, old school, prep school, preschool, retool, self-rule, stepstool, toadstool, tomfool, trade school, uncool, whirlpool; April fool, boarding school, charter school, ducking stool, grammar school, Istanbul, Liverpool, machine tool, magnet school, middle school, normal school, numbers pool, overrule, power tool, private school, public school, reform school, summer school, Sunday school, wading pool; finishing school, junior high school, nursery school, primary school, senior high school. See also **-ule.**

**-oom,** bloom, boom, broom, brougham, brume, doom, flume, fume, gloom, groom, loom, neume, plume, rheum, room, spoom, spume, tomb, vroom, whom, womb, zoom; abloom, assume, backroom, ballroom, barroom, bathroom, bedroom, boardroom, bridegroom, broadloom, chatroom, checkroom, classroom, cloakroom, coatroom, consume, costume, courtroom, darkroom, entomb, exhume, Fiume, front room, game room, great room, greenroom, grillroom, guest room, handloom, headroom, heirloom, homeroom, illume, jib boom, ka-boom, Khartoum, legroom, legume, lunchroom, mailroom, men's room, mushroom, newsroom, perfume, playroom, poolroom, pressroom, presume, pump room, push broom, rec room, relume, restroom, resume, salesroom, schoolroom, Scotch broom, showroom, sickroom, simoom, stateroom, stockroom, storeroom, subsume, taproom, tearoom, war room, washroom, weight room, whisk broom, workroom; anteroom, baby boom, banquet room, birthing room, boiler room, changing room, city room, common room, crack of doom, cutting room, dining room, drawing room, dressing room, elbowroom, family room, gloom and doom, hecatomb, Jacquard loom, ladies' room, living room, locker room, nom de plume, powder room, power-loom, reading room, reassume, rumpus room, sitting room, smoke-filled room, sonic boom, standing room, straw mushroom, waiting room, wiggle room, women's room.

**-oon,** boon, Boone, coon, croon, dune, goon, hewn, June, loon, lune, moon, noon, poon, prune, rune, soon, spoon, strewn, swoon, toon, tune; aswoon, attune, baboon, balloon, bassoon, bestrewn, blue moon, bridoon, buffoon, cardoon, cartoon, cocoon, commune, dahoon, doubloon, dragoon, festoon, fine-tune, forenoon, full moon, gaboon, gadroon, galloon, gombroon, half-moon, harpoon, high noon, immune, impugn, jejune, lagoon, lampoon, lardoon, maroon, monsoon, Neptune, new moon, oppugn, patroon, platoon, poltroon, pontoon, puccoon, quadroon, raccoon, Rangoon, ratoon, rockoon, rough-hewn, saloon, shalloon, soupspoon, spittoon, spontoon, teaspoon, tribune, triune, tycoon, typhoon, Walloon; afternoon, Brigadoon, Cameroon, coffee spoon, dessertspoon, greasy spoon, harvest moon, honeymoon, importune, macaroon, octoroon, opportune, pantaloon, perilune, picaroon, picayune, rigadoon, silver spoon, tablespoon, trial balloon; autoimmune, man in the moon, measuring spoon, midafternoon, runcible spoon, sounding balloon.

**-ooned.** See **-ound.**

**-oop,** bloop, coop, coupe, croup, droop, drupe, dupe, goop, group, hoop, jupe, loop, loupe, poop, roup, scoop, scroop, sloop, snoop, soup, stoop, stoup, stupe, supe, swoop, troop, troupe, whoop; age group, blood group, closed loop, duck soup, in-group, newsgroup, out-group, pea soup, peer group, playgroup, recoup, regroup, subgroup, toe loop, war whoop, youth group; alley-oop, bird's-nest soup, chicken coop, control group, eggdrop soup, feedback loop, focus group, Guadeloupe, Hula-Hoop, interest group, loop-the-loop, nincompoop, open loop, paratroop, party poop, pressure group, support group; alphabet soup, encounter group.

**-oor** (-o͝or), Boer, boor, brewer, dour, lure, moor, Moor, poor, Ruhr, sewer, spoor, sure, tour, Ur, your, you're; abjure, adjure, allure, amour, assure, brochure, ceinture, cocksure, contour, couture, detour, dirt-poor, endure, ensure, grandeur, hachure, insure, inure, land-poor, manure, mature, parure, perdure, tambour, tandoor, unsure, velour, velure; amateur, blackamoor, carrefour, carte du jour, coinsure, commissure, confiture, connoisseur, curvature, cynosure, embouchure, garniture, haute couture, immature, Kohinoor, ligature, overture, paramour, plat du jour, premature, reassure, signature, soup de jour, tablature, temperature, troubadour; affaire d'amour, caricature, divestiture, entablature, entrepreneur, investiture, judicature, literature, miniature, musculature, nomenclature, temperature; primogeniture. See also **-ure.**

**-oor** (-ôr). See **-ore.**

**-oors.** See **-ours.**

**-oose** (-o͞os), Bruce, cruse, deuce, douce, goose, juice, loose, luce, moose, mousse, noose, puce, schuss, sluice, spruce, truce, use, Zeus; abduce, abstruse, abuse, adduce, bull moose, burnoose, caboose, ceruse, charmeuse, chartreuse, conduce, couscous, deduce, diffuse, disuse, educe, excuse, fair use, footloose, induce, misuse, mixed use, mongoose, obtuse, papoose, produce, profuse, recluse, reduce, seduce, snow goose, soukous, Toulouse, traduce, transduce, vamoose; calaboose, charlotte russe, fast and loose, introduce, mass-produce, Mother Goose, multiuse, overuse, reproduce, Syracuse; Canada goose, hypotenuse.

**-oose** (-o͞oz). See **-ooze.**

**-oosed.** See **-oost.**

**-oost,** boost, deuced, Proust, roost; langouste.

Also: **-uce** + **-ed** (as in *reduced*, etc.)

Also: **-oose** + **-ed** (as in *loosed*, etc.)

**-oot** (-o͞ot). See **-ute.**

**-oot** (-o͝ot), foot, put, root, soot; afoot, barefoot, Big Foot, bigfoot, Blackfoot, claw foot, coltsfoot, crow's-foot, cube root, flatfoot, forefoot, hotfoot, input, kaput, on foot, output, shot put, snakeroot, splayfoot, square root, taproot, throughput, trench foot, uproot; arrowroot, athlete's foot, bitterroot, gingerroot, hand and foot, pussyfoot, tenderfoot, underfoot.

**-ooth** (-ōōth), booth, couth, ruth, Ruth, sleuth, sooth, tooth, truth, youth; bucktooth, dogtooth, Duluth, eyetooth, forsooth, half-truth, hound's tooth, in truth, milk tooth, phone booth, sweet tooth, tollbooth, uncouth, untruth, vermouth; baby tooth, polling booth, sabertooth, snaggletooth, voting booth, wisdom tooth.

**-oothe** (-ōōth̸), smooth, soothe.

**-oove.** See **-ove.**

**-ooze.** See **-use.**

**-op,** bop, chop, clop, cop, crop, drop, flop, fop, glop, hop, knop, lop, mop, op, plop, pop, prop, shop, slop, sop, stop, strop, swap, top, whop; Aesop, airdrop, atop, backdrop, backstop, bakeshop, barhop bebop, bellhop, big top, blacktop, bookshop, carhop, cash crop, chop-chop, chop shop, clip-clop, clop-clop, closed shop, coin-op, cooktop, co-op, cough drop, desktop, dewdrop, doorstop, doo-wop, dry mop, dust mop, eavesdrop, estop, flattop, flipflop, flip-top, f-stop, full stop, gumdrop, hardtop, head shop, high-top, hilltop, hip-hop, hockshop, housetop, laptop, mail drop, maintop, milksop, name-drop, nonstop, one-stop, outcrop, palmtop, pawnshop, pit stop, pop-top, post-op, pro shop, ragtop, raindrop, rest stop, ridgetop, ripstop, rollmop, rooftop, sharecrop, shortstop, snowdrop, stonecrop, sweatshop, sweetshop, sweetsop, tank top, teardrop, tea shop, thrift shop, tiptop, treetop, truck stop, wineshop, workshop; aftercrop, agitprop, barbershop, beauty shop, belly flop, body shop, bucket shop, carrot-top, channel-hop, coffee shop, countertop, curly top, double-stop, drag-and-drop, gigaflop, glottal stop, lollipop, Malaprop, mom-and-pop, mountaintop, open shop, overstop, photo op, rent-a-cop, riding crop, soda pop, soursop, table-hop, tabletop, techno-pop, traffic cop, turboprop, union shop, whistle-stop, window-shop.

**-ope,** cope, dope, grope, hope, lope, mope, nope, ope, pope, rope, scope, slope, soap, stope, taupe, tope, trope; aslope, boltrope, elope, footrope, jump rope, pyrope, skip rope, soft soap, tightrope, towrope, upslope, white hope; allotrope, antelope, antipope, apocope, arthroscope, biotope, bunny slope, calliope, cantaloupe, chronoscope, endoscope, envelope, fluoroscope, forlorn hope, gyroscope, horoscope, interlope, isotope, kinescope, lycanthrope, microscope, misanthrope, otoscope, periscope, seismoscope, spectroscope, stethoscope, telescope; heliotrope, kaleidoscope, laparoscope, opthalmoscope, slippery slope, stereoscope.

**-opped.** See **-opt.**

**-opt,** Copt, opt; adopt, close-cropped, co-opt, flat-topped, well-chopped; carrot-topped.

Also: **-op** + **-ed** (as in *hopped*, etc.)

**-or** (-ôr), for, nor, or, Thor, tor, war; abhor, and/or, bailor, centaur, condor, décor, Dior, done for, furor, lessor, memoir, mentor, phosphor, psywar, raptor, Realtor, sensor, stentor, stressor, temblor, tensor, therefor, vendor; archosaur, brachiosaur, brontosaur, corridor, cuspidor, dinosaur, Ecuador, either-or, guarantor, hadrosaur, humidor, Labrador, man-of-war, matador, metaphor, meteor, Minotaur, parador, picador, predator, pterosaur, reservoir, Salvador, stegosaur, troubadour, tug-of-war, uncalled-for, warrantor; ambassador, conquistador, conquistador, esprit de corps, ichthyosaur, mixed metaphor, toreador, tyrannosaur. See also **-ore.**

**-or,** bailor, candor, captor, condor, donor, flexor, furor, junior, lector, mentor, phosphor, rancor, raptor, Realtor, rhetor, sector, seignior, senior, sensor, stertor, stressor, temblor, tensor, turgor, vendor; ancestor, auditor, bachelor, chancellor, conqueror, corridor, creditor, counselor, devisor, editor, elector, emperor, governor, guarantor, janitor, metaphor, meteor, monitor, orator, predator, senator, servitor, visitor, warrantor, warrior; ambassador, competitor, compositor, conservator, conspirator, contributor, depositor, executor, inheritor, inquisitor, legislator, mixed metaphor, progenitor, proprietor, solicitor. See also **-ore.**

**-or** (-ōr). See **-ore.**

**-orb,** forb, orb, sorb; absorb, adsorb, resorb.

**-orce.** See **-orse.**

**-orch,** porch, scorch, torch; blowtorch, sun porch.

**-ord,** board, chord, cord, fjord, ford, Ford, gourd, hoard, horde, lord, sward, sword, toward, ward; abhorred, aboard, accord, afford, award, backboard, baseboard, bedboard, billboard, blackboard, breadboard, broadsword, call-board, cardboard, chalkboard, cheeseboard, chessboard, clapboard, clipboard, concord, corkboard, dartboard, dashboard, discord, draft board, drain board, fjord, floorboard, footboard, freeboard, greensward, hardboard, headboard, inboard, keyboard, kickboard, landlord, lapboard, leeboard, moldboard, nerve cord, on-board, outboard, pasteboard, pressboard, punchboard, rearward, record, reward, rip cord, sailboard, scoreboard, seaboard, shipboard, sideboard, signboard, skateboard, slumlord, snowboard, springboard, starboard, surfboard, switchboard, tilt board, untoward, wakeboard, wallboard, warlord, washboard, whipcord, whiteboard, word-hoard; aboveboard, bottle gourd, bungee cord, centerboard, checkerboard, circuit board, clavichord, cloak-and-sword, cutting board, diving board, drawing board, emery board, fiberboard, fingerboard, flutterboard, harpsichord, leader board, mortarboard, motherboard, overboard, overlord, paddleboard, paperboard, plasterboard, room and board, running board, sandwich board, shuffleboard, smorgasbord, sounding board, spinal cord, storyboard, tape-record, teeterboard; emery board, across-the-board, bulletin board, extension cord, ironing board, misericord, particleboard.

Also: **-oar** + **-ed** (as in *roared*, etc.)

Also: **-ore** + **-ed** (as in *scored*, etc.)

**-ore** (-ôr) or (-ōr), boar, Boer, bore, chore, core, corps, door, floor, fore, four, frore, gore, hoar, lore, more, oar, o'er, ore, pore, pour, roar, score, shore, snore, soar, sore, store, swore, tore, whore, wore, yore, your; adore, afore, ashore, backdoor, bedsore, before, bookstore, box score, chain store, claymore, cold sore, deplore, dime store, downpour, drugstore, Dutch door, encore, explore, eyesore, folklore, footsore, forbore, forswore, fourscore, French door, full-bore, galore, ground floor, hardcore, heartsore, ignore, implore, indoor, inshore, in-store, lakeshore, line score, next-door, offshore, onshore, outdoor, outpour, rapport, raw score, restore, seashore, señor, signor, smoothbore, soft-core, sophomore, therefore, trapdoor, uproar, wherefore, wild boar; albacore, alongshore, anymore, Apgar score, Baltimore, battledore, cankersore, carnivore, commodore, door-to-door, endospore, evermore, forest floor, furthermore, general store, hackamore, hellebore, herbivore, heretofore, madrepore, mirador, nevermore, omnivore, open-door, package store, petit four, pinafore, pompadour, saddle sore, sagamore, semaphore, Singapore, sophomore, stevedore, superstore, sycamore, to die for, troubadour, two-by-four, underscore; convenience store, department store, forevermore, hereinbefore, insectivore, revolving door. See also **-or.**

**-ored.** See **-ord.**

**-orf,** corf, dwarf, morph, Orff, wharf; allomorph, ectomorph, endomorph, lagomorph, mesomorph, perimorph.

**-orge,** forge, George, gorge; disgorge, engorge, regorge.

**-ork,** cork, Cork, dork, fork, pork, quark, stork, torque, York; bulwark, New York, pitchfork, salt pork, uncork, white stork.

**-orld,** burled, whorled, world; dream world, First World, Fourth World, free world, New World, Old World, old-world, real world, Third World; afterworld, brave new world, netherworld, other world, Second World, underworld; man of the world, out of this world.

Also: **-url** + **-ed** (as in *curled*, etc.)

**-orm,** corm, dorm, form, norm, storm, swarm, warm; art form, aswarm, barnstorm, brainstorm, by-form, conform, deform, dust storm, free-form, hailstorm, ice storm, inform, landform, life form, lukewarm, misform, perform, platform, preform, rainstorm, reform, sandstorm, snowstorm, transform, waveform, windstorm; chloroform, cruciform, firestorm, letterform, misinform, multiform, outperform, perfect storm, racing form, thunderstorm, uniform, vermiform; combining form, cuneiform, electric storm, iodoform.

**-orn,** born, borne, bourn, corn, horn, lorn, morn, mourn, porn, scorn, shorn, sworn, thorn, torn, warn, worn; acorn, adorn, airborne, bighorn, blackthorn, blue corn, buckthorn, bullhorn, careworn, first-born, flint corn, foghorn, footworn, forewarn, forlorn, forsworn, freeborn, French horn, greenhorn, hawthorn, highborn, inborn, inkhorn, last-born, Leghorn, Longhorn, lovelorn, lowborn, newborn, outworn, popcorn, pronghorn, reborn, saxhorn, sea-born, seaborne, shoehorn, shopworn, Shorthorn, skyborne, soilborne, spaceborne, staghorn, stillborn, stinkhorn, suborn, sweet corn, tick-borne, timeworn, tinhorn, toilworn, tricorn, trueborn, twice-born, unborn, unworn, wellborn, well-worn, wind-borne; alpenhorn, barleycorn, candy corn, Capricorn, city-born, English horn, flügelhorn, firethorn, foreign-born, hunting horn, Matterhorn, nativeborn, peppercorn, powder horn, saddle horn, unicorn, waterborne, weatherworn, winterbourne, yestermorn.

**-orp,** dorp, gorp, thorp, warp; time warp; octothorpe.

**-orse,** coarse, corse, course, dorse, force, gorse, hoarse, horse, morse, Morse, Norse, source, torse; clotheshorse, cockhorse, concourse, crash course, dark horse, dead horse, discourse, divorce, endorse, enforce, golf course, gut course, midcourse, of course, Old Norse, packhorse, perforce, post horse, racehorse, recourse, remorse, resource, sawhorse, seahorse, stringcourse, trial horse, unhorse, warhorse, workhorse; charley horse, firehorse, hobbyhorse, intercourse, iron horse, minicourse, pommel horse, quarter horse, reinforce, rocking horse, saddle horse, stalking-horse, telecourse, tour de force, Trojan horse, vaulting horse, watercourse; collision course, matter of course, obstacle course, par for the course.

**-orst.** See **-urst.**

**-ort,** bort, court, fort, forte, mort, ort, port, quart, short, skort, snort, sort, sport, swart, thwart, tort, torte, wart, wort; abort, airport, assort, athwart, backcourt, bellwort, birthwort, bistort, blood sport, carport, cavort, cohort, colewort, comport, consort, contort, deport, disport, distort, downcourt, escort, exhort, export, extort, fall short, figwort, food court, forecourt, free port, frontcourt, glasswort, gosport, home port, import, jetport, law court, leadwort, milkwort, moot court, Newport, passport, presort, purport, ragwort, rapport, report, resort, retort, seaport, Shreveport, spaceport, spoilsport, support, transport; bladderwort, child support, circuit court, contact sport, davenport, district court, feverwort, heliport, lifesupport, liverwort, misreport, nonsupport, pennywort, price support, prince consort, queen consort, Saint-John's-wort, selfreport, self-support, spiderwort, Supreme Court, teleport, traffic court, treaty port, worry-wart.

**-orth,** forth, fourth, north, swarth; henceforth, thenceforth.

**-orts,** orts, quartz, shorts, sports; boxer shorts, motorsports, out of sorts, undershorts, walking shorts.

Also: **-ort** + **-s** (as in *forts,* etc.)

Also: **-ourt** + **-s** (as in *courts,* etc.)

**-ose** (-ōs), close, dose, gross; arkose, callose, carnose, cirrose, cosmos, crinose, cymose, dextrose, engross, erose, floccose, fructose, globose, glucose, jocose, lactose, maltose, morose, osmose, pathos, pilose, plumose, ramose, ribose, sucrose, verbose, viscose; acerose, adios, adipose, ankylose, annulose, bellicose, calvados, cellulose, comatose, diagnose, foliose, fruticose, galactose, grandiose, granulose, lachrymose, lacunose, megadose, otiose, overdose, racemose, ramulose, tuberose, varicose, verrucose; inter vivos, metamorphose.

**-ose** (-ōz), chose, close, clothes, cloze, doze, froze, gloze, hose, nose, pose, prose, rose, Rose, those; Ambrose, arose, bedclothes, bluenose, brownnose, bulldoze, compose, depose, disclose, dispose, enclose, expose, foreclose, hard-nose, hooknose, impose, inclose, musk rose, nightclothes, oppose, plain clothes, playclothes, primrose, propose, pug nose, repose, rockrose, suppose, tea rose, transpose, tuberose, unclose, unfroze, uprose, wild rose; cabbage rose, China rose, compass rose, counterpose, damask rose, decompose, discompose, evening clothes, indispose, interpose, juxtapose, pantyhose, pettitoes, predispose, presuppose, Roman nose, swaddling clothes, tuberose, twinkletoes, underclothes; evening primrose, metamorphose, overexpose, superimpose, underexpose.
  Also: **-o** + **-s** (as in *punctilios,* etc.)
  Also: **-o** + **-es** (as in *goes,* etc.)
  Also: **-oe** + **-s** (as in *toes,* etc.)
  Also: **-ot** + **-s** (as in *depots,* etc.)
  Also: **-ow** + **-s** (as in *glows,* etc.)

**-osh.** See **-ash.**

**-osk,** bosk, mosque; kiosk.

**-osque.** See **-osk.**

**-oss,** boss, cos, cross, crosse, dross, floss, fosse, gloss, hoss, joss, loss, moss, os, Ross, sauce, toss; across, backcross, brown sauce, bugloss, club moss, cosmos, cream sauce, crisscross, duck sauce, emboss, Eros, Greek cross, hard sauce, hot sauce, lacrosse, lip gloss, pathos, peat moss, pit boss, ringtoss, soy sauce, stop-loss, straw boss, top cross, trail boss, uncross, white sauce; albatross, applesauce, autocross, blanket toss, butter sauce, Celtic cross, chili sauce, cocktail sauce, cyclo-cross, dental floss, double-cross, Irish moss, isogloss, Latin cross, Maltese cross, Mornay sauce, motocross, pitch-and-toss, reindeer moss, reredos, semigloss, Spanish moss, tartar sauce, Thanatos; profit and loss, Worcestershire sauce.

**-ost** (-ôst) or (-ost), cost, frost, lost, wast; accost, exhaust, glasnost, hoarfrost, Jack Frost; holocaust, Pentecost, permafrost, tempest-tossed.

Also: **-oss** + **-ed** (as in *crossed*, etc.)

**-ost** (-ōst), boast, coast, ghost, grossed, host, most, oast, post, prost, roast, toast; almost, at most, bedpost, compost, crown roast, doorpost, endmost, engrossed, foremost, French toast, gatepost, goalpost, Gold Coast, guidepost, headmost, hindmost, impost, inmost, king post, lamppost, milepost, Milquetoast, outmost, outpost, pot roast, provost, queen post, rearmost, rib roast, riposte, seacoast, signpost, topmost, utmost; aftermost, bottommost, coast-to-coast, command post, easternmost, finger post, furthermost, hindermost, hitching post, Holy Ghost, innermost, listening post, lowermost, Melba toast, nethermost, northernmost, outermost, parcel post, southernmost, staging post, trading post, undermost, uppermost, uttermost, westernmost, whipping post.

**-ot,** blot, bot, chott, clot, cot, dot, Dot, ghat, got, grot, hot, jot, knot, lot, lotte, motte, not, phot, plot, pot, rot, scot, Scot, shot, slot, snot, sot, spot, squat, stot, swat, tot, trot, watt, what, wot, yacht; allot, a lot, ascot, bank shot, begot, besot, big shot, black spot, blind spot, bloodshot, bowshot, boycott, buckshot, cachepot, cannot, capot, cheap shot, chip shot, cocotte, complot, crackpot, Crockpot, culotte, despot, dicot, dogtrot, drop shot, dry rot, dunk shot, earshot, ergot, eyespot, feedlot, fleshpot, forgot, foxtrot, fusspot, fylfot, garotte, gavotte, gluepot, grapeshot, gunshot, have-not, hotchpot, hot pot, hotshot, inkblot, inkpot, jackpot, job lot, jump shot, kumquat, leaf spot, long shot, loquat, love knot, mascot, moon shot, mug shot, nightspot, odd lot, one-shot, plumcot, pot-shot, red-hot, repot, robot, root rot, sandlot, sexpot, shallot, slap shot, slingshot, slipknot, snapshot, soft spot, somewhat, square knot, stinkpot, stockpot, subplot, sunspot, sweet spot, teapot, topknot, tosspot, unknot, upshot, wainscot, warm spot, whatnot, white-hot, wood-lot, wood shot; apricot, beauty spot, bergamot, booster shot, burning ghat, cachalot, Camelot, caveat, chamber pot, coffeepot, counterplot, diddley-squat, eschalot, flowerpot, foul shot, gallipot, gigawatt, granny knot, guillemot, hit the spot, honeypot, Hot-tentot, Huguenot, kilo-watt, Lancelot, lobster pot, megawatt, melilot, melting pot, microdot, monkeypot, monocot, monoglot, mis-begot, ocelot, on the spot, overshot, parking lot, pass-ing shot, patriot, Penob-scot, pepper pot, peridot, piping hot, polka dot, polyglot, sans-culotte, scat-tershot, talipot, tie the rot, tommyrot, touch-me-not, turkey trot, unbegot, undershot, Wyandotte; expansion slot, forget-me-not, Gordian knot, hit the jackpot, penalty shot.

See also **-ought.**

**-otch,** blotch, botch, crotch, notch, scotch, Scotch, splotch, swatch, watch; bird-watch, deathwatch, debauch, dogwatch, hop-scotch, hotchpotch, night watch, Sasquatch, stopwatch, topnotch, wrist-watch; butterscotch, morning watch.

**-ote,** bloat, boat, Choate, coat, cote, dote, float, gloat, goat, groat, moat, mote, note, oat, quote, rote, shoat, smote, sproat, stoat, throat, tote, vote, wrote; afloat, banknote, blue note, capote, carcoat, catboat, compote, connote, coyote, cutthroat, deep throat, demote, denote, devote, diptote, dovecote, dreamboat, eighth note, emote, endnote, flatboat, footnote, frock coat, gemot, grace note, greatcoat, gunboat, half note, headnote, houseboat, housecoat, iceboat, keelboat, keynote, lab coat, lifeboat, longboat, manbote, misquote, old goat, one-note, outvote, peacoat, promote, raincoat, redcoat, remote, rewrote, rowboat, sailboat, sauceboat, scapegoat, seed coat, shape note, sheepcote, showboat, sore throat, speedboat, steamboat, straw vote, strep throat, surcoat, swan boat, tailcoat, topcoat, towboat, trench coat, tugboat, turncoat, U-boat, unquote, whaleboat, whole note, zygote; anecdote, antidote, asymptote, billygoat, casting vote, creosote, dead man's float, duffle coat, entrecôte, ferryboat, flying boat, lepidote, locomote, matelote, morning coat, motorboat, mountain goat, nanny goat, overcoat, paddleboat, papillote, pardalote, passing note, petticoat, pilot boat, powerboat, PT boat, quarter note, redingote, riverboat, sixteenth note, sticky note, sugarcoat, symbiote, table d'hôte, undercoat, yellowthroat; Angora goat, torpedo boat, treasury note; promissory note, witenagemot.

**-oth** (-ôth), broth, cloth, froth, Goth, moth, sloth, swath, Thoth, troth, wroth; betroth, breechcloth, broadcloth, cerecloth, cheesecloth, clothes moth, dishcloth, drop cloth, facecloth, grass cloth, ground cloth, ground sloth, haircloth, hawk moth, hellbroth, loincloth, oilcloth, presscloth, sackcloth, sailcloth, Scotch broth, silk moth, sphinx moth, sponge cloth, wash cloth, whole cloth; Ashtaroth, behemoth, gypsy moth, leopard moth, luna moth, Ostrogoth, saddlecloth, tablecloth, terry cloth, three-toed sloth, tiger moth, two-toed sloth, Visigoth.

**-oth** (-ōth), both, growth, loath, oath, quoth, sloth, troth, wroth; ingrowth, old growth, outgrowth; overgrowth, second growth, undergrowth.

**-othe** (-ōth̸), clothe, loath, loathe; betroth, unclothe.

**-ou** (-ou). See **-ow.**

**-ou** (-yo͞o). See **-ew.**

**-oubt.** See **-out.**

**-ouch** (-ouch), couch, crouch, grouch, ouch, pouch, slouch, vouch; avouch; cheek pouch, debouch; casting couch, scaramouch.

**-ouch** (-uch). See **-utch.**

**-ouche** (-o͞osh), bouche, douche, louche, ruche, whoosh; barouche, capuche, cartouche, debouch, farouche, kurus, tarboosh; amuse-bouche, croquembouche, scaramouch.

**-oud,** cloud, crowd, loud, proud, shroud, stroud; aloud, avowed, becloud, enshroud, highbrowed, house-proud, out loud, o'ercloud, rain cloud, unbowed; beetle-browed, funnel cloud, mushroom cloud, overcloud, overcrowd, thundercloud, well-endowed.

Also: **-ow** + **-ed** (as in *plowed*, etc.)

**-ough** (-ôf). See **-off.**

**-ough** (-ou) or (-ō). See **-ow.** or **-ow.**

**-ough** (-o͞o). See **-ew.**

**-ough** (-uf). See **-uff.**

**-oughed.** See **-oft.**

**-ought,** aught, bought, brought, caught, fought, fraught, ghat, naught, nought, ought, sought, taught, taut, thought, wrought; besought, Connaught, distraught, dreadnought, forethought, free thought, handwrought, hard-fought, methought, onslaught, self-taught, store-bought; aeronaut, aforethought, afterthought, aquanaut, Argonaut, astronaut, cosmonaut, juggernaut, overbought, overwrought, second thought.

See also **-ot.**

**-oul** (-oul). See **-owl.**

**-oul** (-ōl). See **-ole.**

**-ould.** See **-ood.**

**-oun.** See **-own.**

**-ounce,** bounce, flounce, frounce, jounce, ounce, pounce, trounce; announce, denounce, enounce, pronounce, renounce; dead-cat bounce, fluid ounce, mispronounce.

Also: **-ount** + **-s** (as in *counts,* etc.)

**-ound** (-ound), bound, found, ground, hound, mound, pound, round, sound, wound; abound, aground, all-round, around, astound, background, bloodhound, boozehound, brassbound, campground, casebound, chowhound, clothbound, compound, confound, coonhound, deerhound, deskbound, dumbfound, earthbound, eastbound, expound, fairground, fishpound, fogbound, footpound, foreground, foxhound, go-round, greyhound, hardbound, hellhound, hidebound, high ground, homebound, home ground, horehound, housebound, icebound, impound, inbound, lose ground, newfound, newshound, northbound, outbound, playground, potbound, profound, propound, rebound, redound, renowned, resound, rockbound, rock hound, snowbound, softbound, southbound, spellbound, stone-ground, stormbound, strikebound, surround, unbound, unfound, unsound, well-found, westbound, wolfhound, year-round; aboveground, Afghan hound, all-around, basset hound, battleground, belowground, breeding ground, common ground, dumping-ground, go-around, honor-bound, hunting ground, in the round, ironbound, middle ground, musclebound, outward-bound, paperbound, perfect-bound, pleasure ground, proving ground, runaround, spiral-bound, staging ground, stamping ground, turnaround, ultrasound, underground, weather-bound, workaround, wraparound; burial ground, burial mound, Irish wolfhound, merry-go-round, Russian wolfhound.

Also: **-own** + **-ed** (as in *clowned*, etc.)

**-ound** (-o͞ond), wound.

Also: **-oon** + **-ed** (as in *swooned*, etc.)

Also: **-une** + **-ed** (as in *tuned*, etc.)

**-ount,** count, fount, mount; account, amount, blood count, discount, dismount, fast-count, head count, high-count, low-count, miscount, recount, remount, surmount, viscount; bank account, bank discount, body count, catamount, cash account, charge account, deep discount, joint account, no-account, paramount, photo-mount, tantamount, trade discount, undercount, wrap account; checking account, expense account, savings account.

**-ounts.** See **-ounce.**

**-oup.** See **-oop.**

**-our,** bower, cower, dour, dower, flour, flower, gaur, glower, hour, lour, lower, our, power, scour, shower, sour, tower; air power, air shower, bellflower, bell tower, black power, brainpower, coneflower, cornflower, deflower, devour, embower, empower, half hour, high-power, horsepower, man-hour, manpower, mayflower, moonflower, off-hour, pasqueflower, rush hour, safflower, sea power, state flower, sunflower, wallflower, watchtower, wildflower, willpower, windflower, wind power, world power; Adenauer, buying power, candlepower, cauliflower, control tower, cooling tower, credit hour, cuckooflower, disempower, Eiffel Tower, Eisenhower, firepower, fire tower, flower power, gillyflower, happy hour, hydropower, minitower, motive power, overpower, passionflower, person-hour, police power, quarter hour, solar power, staying power, superpower, sweet-and-sour, thundershower, trumpet flower, veto power, waterpower, water tower, whisky sour, womanpower; balance of power, eleventh hour.

Also: **-ow** + **-er** (as in *plower,* etc.)

**-ourge.** See **-erge.**

**-ourn** (-ôrn). See **-orn.**

**-ourn** (-ûrn). See **-urn.**

**-ours** (-ourz), ours; small hours, war powers, wee hours; after-hours, bankers' hours, book of hours, Central Powers, Forty Hours, hearts and flowers, little hours, office hours.

Also: **-our** + **-s** (as in *devours,* etc.)

Also: **-ower** + **-s** (as in *flowers,* etc.)

**-ours** (-o͝orz), yours.

Also: **-oor** + **-s** (as in *boors,* etc.)

Also: **-our** + **-s** (as in *amours,* etc.)

Also: **-ure** + **-s** (as in *lures,* etc.)

**-ourse.** See **-orse.**

**-ourt.** See **-ort.**

**-ourth.** See **-orth.**

**-ous.** See **-us.**

**-ouse,** bouse, blouse, chiaus, chouse, douse, gauss, grouse, house, louse, mouse, scouse, souse, spouse, Strauss; alehouse, almshouse, art house, backhouse, bathhouse, Bauhaus, birdhouse, black grouse, blockhouse, boathouse, booklouse, brewhouse, bughouse, bunkhouse, cathouse, chart house, chophouse, clubhouse, coach house, courthouse, crab louse, crackhouse, deckhouse, degauss, delouse, doghouse, dollhouse, dormouse, espouse, farmhouse, field house, field mouse, flophouse, full house, fun house, gatehouse, great house, greenhouse, guardhouse, guesthouse, hash house, henhouse, hothouse, icehouse, in-house, jailhouse, joss house, lighthouse, lobscouse, long house, madhouse, nut house, outhouse, penthouse, plant louse, playhouse, poorhouse, post house, ranch house, roadhouse, roughhouse, roundhouse, row house, ruffed grouse, safe house, schoolhouse, smokehouse, statehouse, steakhouse, storehouse, teahouse, titmouse, tollhouse, town house, tree house, warehouse, wheelhouse, White House, whorehouse, wood louse, workhouse; acid house, barrelhouse, bawdyhouse, boardinghouse, cat and mouse, chapter house, charnel house, Charterhouse, clearinghouse, coffeehouse, counting house, country house, custom house, firehouse, Fledermaus, flittermouse, halfway house, house-to-house, lower house, manor house, meadow mouse, meetinghouse, Mickey Mouse, middy blouse, open house, opera house, overblouse, packinghouse, pilothouse, pleasure house, porterhouse, powerhouse, rooming house, slaughterhouse, station house, sugarhouse, summerhouse, treasure house, upper house; apartment house, bring down the house, man of the house, settlement house.

**-oust,** doused, Faust, joust, oust, roust, soused, spoused; deloused.

**-out,** bout, clout, doubt, drought, flout, gout, grout, knout, kraut, lout, out, pout, rout, route, scout, shout, snout, spout, sprout, stout, tout, trout; ablaut, about, all-out, bailout, blackout, blissed-out, blowout, bombed-out, boy scout, breakout, brook trout, brownout, brown trout, bugout, bull trout, burned-out, burnout, buyout, call-out, cash-out, checkout, cleanout, closeout, comb-out, cookout, cop-out, cross-out, cub scout, cutout, devout, dim-out, downspout, drawn-out, dropout, dryout, dugout, eelpout, en route, fade-out, fallout, far-out, flame-out, flat-out, fold-out, force-out, freak-out, freaked-out, full-out, get-out, Girl Scout, gross-out, groundout, handout, hangout, hideout, holdout, ice-out, knockout, layout, lights out, lockout, lookout, mahout, outshout, payout, phaseout, pig-out, printout, pullout, rainout, rainspout, readout, redoubt, redout, rollout, rubout, runout, sea trout, sellout, shakeout, shoot-out, shutout, sickout, sold-out, spaced-out, spin-out, stakeout, standout, straight-out, stressed-out, strikeout, strung-out, takeout, tear-out, throughout, time-out, trade route, try-out, turnout, umlaut, walk-out, washed-out, washout, way-out, whacked-out, whiteout, wideout, wigged-out, wiped-out, wipeout, without, workout, worn-out; all get-out, Brussels sprout, carryout, coming-out, down-and-out, eagle scout, falling-out, gadabout, golden trout, hereabout, in-and-out, infield out, inside out, knockabout, layabout, long-drawn-out, odd man out, out-and-out, rainbow trout, roundabout, roustabout, runabout, rural route, salmon trout, sauerkraut, speckled trout, talent scout, thereabout, turnabout, walkabout, waterspout, well-thought-out, whereabout; day in day out, first-in first-out, knock-down-drag-out, last-in first-out, photo layout, up and about.

**-outh** (-outh), drouth, mouth, south; bad-mouth, Deep South, goalmouth, loudmouth, New South, poor mouth, trench mouth; blabbermouth, cottonmouth, flannel-mouth, foot-in-mouth, hand-to-mouth, horse's mouth, motor-mouth, mouth-to-mouth, word-of-mouth.

**-outh** (-o͞oth). See **-ooth.**

**-ove** (-uv), dove, glove, love, of, shove; above, foxglove, free love, hereof, in love, kid-glove, ringdove, rock dove, self-love, thereof, tough love, truelove, unglove, whereof, white-glove; baseball glove, boxing glove, courtly love, hand and glove, ladylove, mourning dove, puppy love, turtledove, unheard-of, well-thought-of; hereinabove, labor of love, platonic love, tunnel of love.

**-ove** (-ōv), clove, cove, dove, drove, Fauve, grove, hove, Jove, mauve, rove, shrove, stove, strove, throve, trove, wove; alcove, camp stove, cookstove, mangrove, woodstove; borogrove, interwove, treasure-trove.

**-ove** (-o͞ov), groove, move, prove, who've, you've; approve, behoove, commove, disprove, false move, improve, remove, reprove; disapprove, microgroove.

**-ow** (-ou), bough, bow, brow, chow, ciao, cow, dhow, Dow, frau, hao, how, Lao, mow, now, ow, plow, pow, prau, prow, row, scow, slough, sough, sow, Tao, tau, thou, vow, wow; allow, and how, avow, bow-wow, cash cow, chow chow, chow-chow, endow, enow, eyebrow, gangplow, hausfrau, haymow, highbrow, hoosegow, Jungfrau, know-how, kowtow, landau, lowbrow, luau, Mau Mau, mau-mau, meow, Moldau, Moscow, nohow, powwow, Salchow, sea cow, snowplow, somehow; anyhow, cat's meow, disallow, disavow, here and now, middlebrow, sacred cow, solemn vow, unibrow; Oberammergau.

**-ow** (-ō), beau, blow, bow, bro, crow, do, doe, dough, eau, Flo, floe, flow, foe, fro, frow, glow, go, grow, hoe, Jo, joe, Joe, know, lo, low, mot, mow, no, Nō, O, oh, owe, Po, pro, rho, roe, row, schmo, sew, show, sloe, slow, snow, so, sow, stow,

Stowe, strow, though, throe, throw, toe, tow, trow, whoa, woe, yo, Zoe; aglow, ago, airflow, air show, although, argot, backflow, backhoe, bandeau, banjo, bateau, below, bestow, big toe, bon mot, Bordeaux, bravo, bubo, bureau, cachepot, callow, caló, cash flow, chapeau, chassepot, château, Chi-Rho, cockcrow, cocoa, cornrow, crossbow, dado, Day-Glo, dayglow, deathblow, death row, Defoe, depot, de trop, deco, dido, Dido, duo, elbow, euro, escrow, flambeau, floor show, flyblow, fogbow, forego, foreknow, foreshow, freak show, free throw, Frisco, game show, genro, gigot, gung-ho, hallo, heave-ho, hedgerow, heigh-ho, honcho, hello, ice floe, ice show, inflow, in tow, io, jabot, jambeau, Jane Doe, Jim Crow, Joe Blow, John Doe, kayo, Keogh, KO, light show, longbow, low blow, macho, macro, magot, mahoe, maillot, mallow, manteau, Marlow, marrow, merlot, minnow, Miró, mojo, Monroe, moonglow, morrow, Moscow, mudflow, nightglow, no-go, no-no, no-show, nouveau, oboe, outflow, outgrow, oxbow, peep show, Pernod, Perot, picot, pierrot, Pinot, plateau, poncho, pronto, quarto, quiz show, rainbow, reflow, regrow, repo, reseau, road show, rondeau, rondo, roscoe, rouleau, Rousseau, sabot, scarecrow, serow, sideshow, skid row, ski tow, so-so, sound bow, stone's throw, sunbow, tableau, talk show, tiptoe, tonneau, toro, trade show, trousseau, uh-oh, van Gogh, Velcro, wallow, Watteau, widow, willow, window, winnow, yarrow, yo-yo; ab ovo, afterglow, aikido, albedo, al fresco, allegro, alpenglow, apropos, art deco, art nouveau, audio, barrio, bay window, bibelot, black widow, blow-by-blow, bone marrow, buffalo, Buffalo, bummalo, bungalow, buteo, cachalot, calico, cameo, cembalo, centimo, CEO, cheerio, Cicero, comedo, Cupid's bow, Curaçao, curassow, curio, daimyo, danio, dataflow, Diderot, domino, do-si-do, dynamo, embryo, entrepôt, escargot, Eskimo, fabliau, falsetto, Figaro, folio, fricandeau, furbelow, gazebo, gazpacho, gigolo, golden glow, grass widow, guacharo, hammer throw, hammertoe, haricot, heel-and-toe, hetero, high and low, HMO, horror show, Iago, Idaho, indigo, in escrow, in the know, Jericho, kakapo, latigo, little toe, long-ago, Longfellow, Mario, medico, memento, Mexico, mistletoe, mulatto, Navajo, nuncio, octavo, Ohio, oleo, olio, overflow, overgrow, overthrow, ovolo, paseo, patio, peridot, picaro, piccolo, polio, pomelo, pompano, portico, portmanteau, potato, Prospero, proximo, quid pro quo, radio, ratio, rococo, rodeo, Romeo, rose window, saddlebow, sapsago, Scorpio, sloppy joe, so-and-so, sourdough, status quo, stereo, stiletto, stop-and-go, studio, subito, tae kwon do, tallyho, tangelo, tic-tac-toe, TKO, to-and-fro, tobacco, Tokyo, tomato, torero, torpedo, touch-and-go, touraco, tournedos, tremolo, tuckahoe, tupelo, UFO, ultimo, undergo, undertow, vertigo, video, virago, vireo, volcano, zydeco; Abednego, Acapulco, adagio, arpeggio, bravissimo, centesimo, clock radio, con spirito, continuo, curculio, ex nihilo, fantastico, finocchio, fortissimo, get-up-and-go, hereinbelow, home video, imbroglio, incognito, intaglio, in utero, lentissimo, lothario, magnifico, malapropos, medicine show, mustachio, New Mexico, Ontario, oregano, pistachio, politico, portfolio, presidio, punctilio, pussy willow, scenario, seraglio, simpatico, sound-and-light show, talk radio, tennis elbow; ab initio, archipelago, banderillero, braggadocio, dog and pony show, duodecimo, ex officio, impresario, internuncio, music video, oratorio, pianissimo, Punch-and-Judy show; generalissimo.

**-owd.** See **-oud.**

**-owed** (-ōd). See **-ode.**

**-owed** (-oud). See **-oud.**

**-ower.** See **-our.**

**-owl,** bowel, cowl, foul, fowl, growl, howl, jowl, owl, prowl, scowl, towel, yowl; afoul, barn owl, barred owl, beach towel, befoul, embowel, horned owl, night owl, peafowl, screech owl, tea towel, wildfowl; cheek-by-jowl, disembowel, guinea fowl, jungle fowl, on the prowl, snowy owl, Turkish towel, waterfowl.

**-own** (-oun), brown, Brown, clown, crown, down, drown, frown, gown, noun, town; adown, backdown, boomtown, breakdown, bringdown, button-down, buydown, Capetown, clampdown, closedown, comedown, countdown, count noun, cow town, crackdown, crosstown, cutdown, downtown, drop-down, embrown, facedown, fold-down, Georgetown, ghost town, hands-down, hoedown, hometown, Jamestown, knockdown, laydown, letdown, lockdown, lowdown, markdown, mass noun, meltdown, midtown, new town, nightgown, nutbrown, pat-down, pronoun, pull-down, putdown, renown, rubdown, rundown, scrubdown, shakedown, showdown, shutdown, sit-down, slowdown, small-town, splashdown, stripped-down, sundown, swansdown, takedown, tea gown, teardown, thumbsdown, top-down, touchdown, turndown, uptown; Allentown, broken-down, button-down, Chinatown, common noun, dressing-down, dressing gown, eiderdown, evening gown, hand-me-down, market town, out-of-town, proper noun, shantytown, trickle-down, Triple Crown, tumble-down, up-and-down, upside down, verbal noun, watered-down.

**-own** (-ōn). See **-one.**

**-owned.** See **-ound.**

**-ows** (-ōz). See **-ose.**

**-ows** (-ouz). See **-owse.**

**-owse,** blowse, bouse, browse, dowse, drowse, house, rouse, spouse; arouse, carouse, espouse.

Also: **-ow** + **-s** (as in *cows,* etc.)

**-owth.** See **-oth.**

**-ox,** box, cox, fox, lox, ox, phlox, pox, sox, vox; aurochs, bandbox, black box, boom box, boondocks, Botox, breadbox, call box, cowpox, detox, dreadlocks, farebox, gearbox, gray fox, hard knocks, hatbox, icebox, in-box, jewel box, jukebox, lockbox, lunchbox, mailbox, matchbox, musk ox, outbox, outfox, pillbox, poor box, postbox, press box, red fox, saltbox, sandbox, shoebox, skybox, smallpox, snuffbox, soapbox, soundbox, strongbox, toolbox, voice box, Xerox; Arctic fox, ballot box, batter's box, bobbysocks, catcher's box, chatterbox, chickenpox, equinox, flying fox, music box, orthodox, paradox, sentry box, shadowbox, shadow box, silver fox, tinder box, window box; dialog box, heterodox, jack-in-the-box, Pandora's box, penalty box, unorthodox.

Also: **-ock** + **-s** (as in *knocks,* etc.)

**-oy,** boy, buoy, cloy, coy, goy, hoy, joy, koi, oy, ploy, poi, Roy, soy, toy, troy, Troy; ahoy, alloy, annoy, ball boy, batboy, B-boy, beachboy, bellboy, bell buoy, best boy, Big Boy, bok choy, borzoi, boxboy, boy toy, busboy, callboy, carboy, charpoy, convoy, cowboy, decoy, deploy, destroy, doughboy, drawboy, employ, enjoy, envoy, flyboy, hautboy, highboy, homeboy, houseboy, kill-joy, Leroy, life buoy, McCoy, newsboy, pageboy, playboy, Rob Roy, Saint Croix,

Savoy, schoolboy, sepoy, ship's boy, stockboy, tomboy, viceroy; altar boy, attaboy, breeches buoy, bullyboy, cabin boy, choirboy, copyboy, corduroy, good old boy, glamour boy, hoi polloi, Illinois, Iroquois, mama's boy, misemploy, mooring buoy, office boy, overjoy, paperboy, poster boy, stableboy, teapoy, Tinkertoy, water boy, whipping boy, whistling buoy, wonder boy; drugstore cowboy, hobbledehoy.

**-oyed.** See **-oid.**

**-oys.** See **-oise.**

**-oze.** See **-ose.**

**-ub,** blub, bub, chub, club, cub, drub, dub, flub, grub, hub, nub, pub, rub, schlub, scrub, shrub, slub, snub, stub, sub, tub; backrub, ball club, bathtub, book club, brewpub, fan club, farm club, glee club, golf club, health club, hot tub, hubbub, key club, nightclub, war club, washtub, yacht club; billy club, country club, kennel club, rub-a-dub, service club, supper club, syllabub; Beelzebub.

**-ube,** boob, cube, lube, rube, Rube, tube; boob tube, flashcube, ice cube, jujube, test tube; bouillon cube, inner tube, pastry tube, picture tube, vacuum tube.

**-uce.** See **-oose.**

**-uced.** See **-oost.**

**-uch.** See **-utch.**

**-uck,** buck, chuck, cluck, cruck, duck, guck, luck, muck, pluck, puck, Puck, ruck, schmuck, shuck, snuck, struck, stuck, suck, truck, tuck, yuck, yuk; amok, amuck, awestruck, Canuck, cold duck, dead duck, dumb cluck, dumbstruck, dump truck, eye tuck, fast buck, hand truck, hard luck, lame duck, moonstruck, mukluk, potluck, pressed duck, roebuck, sawbuck, shelduck, stagestruck, starstruck, tow truck, unstuck, upchuck, woodchuck, yuk yuk; chuck-a-luck, eider duck, fire truck, Habakkuk, horror-struck, Lady Luck, ladder truck, muck-a-muck, nip and tuck, panel truck, panic-struck, Peking duck, pickup truck, sitting duck, terror-struck, thunderstruck, tummy tuck, waterbuck, wonderstruck.

**-ucked.** See **-uct.**

**-ucks.** See **-ux.**

**-uct,** duct; abduct, adduct, conduct, construct, deduct, destruct, eruct, induct, instruct, obstruct, product; aqueduct, deconstruct, misconduct, oviduct, reconstruct, safe-conduct, self-destruct, usufruct, viaduct.

Also: **-uck** + **-ed** (as in *tucked*, etc.)

**-ud,** blood, bud, crud, cud, dud, flood, fud, mud, rudd, scud, spud, stud, sud, thud; bad blood, bestud, blueblood, earbud, hotblood, leaf bud, lifeblood, new blood, pureblood, rosebud; flesh and blood, flower bud, in cold blood.

**-ude,** brood, crude, dude, feud, food, Jude, lewd, lude, mood, nude, oud, pood, prude, rood, rude, shrewd, snood, 'tude, who'd, you'd; allude, blood feud, collude, conclude, delude, denude, elude, étude, exclude, extrude, exude, fast food, health food, illude, include, intrude, junk food, obtrude, occlude, plant food, postlude, preclude, prelude, protrude, quaalude, seafood, seclude, transude; altitude, amplitude, aptitude, attitude, certitude, comfort food, consuetude, desuetude, devil's food, finger food, finitude, fortitude, Frankenfood, gratitude, habitude, hebetude, interlude, lassitude, latitude, longitude, magnitude, mansuetude, multitude, Negritude, platitude, plenitude, promptitude, pulchritude, quietude, rectitude, seminude, servitude, solitude, turpitude; beatitude, decrepitude, disquietude, exactitude, inaptitude, incertitude, ineptitude, ingratitude, inquietude, natural food, necessitude, similitude, solicitude, vicissitude, verisimilitude.

Also: **-ew** + **-ed** (as in *brewed*, etc.)
Also: **-oo** + **-ed** (as in *wooed*, etc.)
Also: **-ue** + **-ed** (as in *pursued*, etc.)

**-udge,** budge, drudge, fudge, grudge, judge, nudge, sludge, smudge, trudge; adjudge, begrudge, forejudge, misjudge, prejudge.

**-ue.** See **-ew.**

**-ues.** See **-ooze** and **-use.**

**-uff,** bluff, buff, chough, chuff, cuff, duff, fluff, gruff, guff, huff, luff, muff, 'nuff, puff, rough, ruff, scruff, scuff, slough, snuff, sough, stuff, tough, tuff; breadstuff, cream puff, dyestuff, earmuff, enough, foodstuff, French cuff, green stuff, handcuff, hard stuff, hot stuff, kid stuff, Macduff, rebuff, right stuff, rough stuff; blindman's buff, fisticuff, off-the-cuff, overstuff, powderpuff, up to snuff.

**-ug,** bug, chug, drug, dug, fug, hug, jug, lug, mug, plug, pug, rug, shrug, slug, smug, snug, thug, tug, ugh, vug; bear hug, bedbug, billbug, debug, earplug, goldbug, hard drug, humbug, June bug, lovebug, prayer rug, sea slug, smart drug, spark plug, stinkbug, throw rug, unplug, wall plug; antidrug, chug-a-lug, doodlebug, firebug, fireplug, gateway drug, jitterbug, ladybug, lightening bug, litterbug, mealybug, orphan drug, scatter rug, shutterbug, sulfa drug, superbug, Toby jug, water bug, wonder drug; designer drug, miracle drug, prescription drug.

**-uge,** huge, kludge, luge, rouge, Scrooge, scrouge, stooge; deluge, refuge; calcifuge, centrifuge, febrifuge, subterfuge, vermifuge.

**-uice.** See **-oose.**

**-uise.** See **-ize.**

**-uke,** cuke, duke, fluke, gook, jook, juke, kook, Luke, nuke, puke, snook, spook, suk, uke, zouk; archduke, Baruch, caoutchouc, chibouk, Chinook, grand duke, peruke, rebuke; Heptateuch, Mameluke, Marmaduke, Pentateuch.

**-ul** (-ul), cull, dull, gull, hull, lull, mull, null, scull, skull, stull, trull; annul, mogul, numskull, seagull.

**-ul** (-o͝ol), bull, full, pull, wool, you'll; armful, bagful, bellpull, bowlful, bulbul, capful, carful, chock-full, cupful, dishful, drawerful, earful, eyeful, fistful, forkful, glassful, graceful, gulgul, handful, houseful, jarful, John Bull, jugful, lamb's wool, lapful, leg-pull, mouthful, pailful, panful, pilpul, pit bull, plateful, potful, push-pull, roomful, sackful, shopful, spoonful, steel wool, tankful, trayful, truckful, trunkful, tubful; barrelful, basketful, beautiful, bellyful, bottleful, bountiful, bucketful, candy pull, closetful, cock-and-bull, demand-pull, dutiful, fanciful, Irish bull, ladleful, masterful, merciful, pitiful, platterful, plentiful, pocketful, powerful, shovelful, Sitting Bull, sorrowful, tableful, teaspoonful, thimbleful, tractor pull, wonderful, worshipful; dyed-in-the-wool, tablespoonful.

**-ulch,** culch, gulch, mulch.

**-ule,** fuel, mewl, mule, pule, you'll, yule; ampule, bascule, chondrule, cupule, floccule, gemmule, globule, granule, lobule, module, nodule, papule, pustule, spicule, synfuel, tubule, virgule; fascicule, gallinule, lenticule, majuscule, minuscule, molecule, reticule, ridicule, vestibule; animalcule. See also **-ool.**

**-ulge,** bulge; divulge, effulge, indulge; overindulge.

**-ulk,** bulk, hulk, skulk, sulk.

**-ull.** See **-ul.**

**-ulp,** gulp, pulp, sculp.

**-ulse,** dulse, pulse; appulse, avulse, convulse, divulse, evulse, impulse, repulse.

**-ult,** cult; adult, consult, exult, incult, indult, insult, masscult, midcult, occult, penult, result, tumult; cargo cult, catapult, difficult; antepenult.

**-um,** bum, chum, come, crumb, drum, dumb, from, glum, grum, gum, hum, mum, numb, plum, plumb, rhumb, rum, scrum, scum, slum, some, strum, stum, sum, swum, thrum, thumb, yum; alum, aplomb, bass drum, bay rum, beach plum, become, benumb, dim sum, dumdum, dum-dum, eardrum, green thumb, ho-hum, humdrum, income, in sum, outcome, pablum, pond scum, snare drum, spectrum, steel drum, succumb, sweet gum, therefrom, Tom Thumb, wherefrom, yum-yum; bubblegum, burdensome, cardamom, chewing gum, Christendom, cranium, cumbersome, frolicsome, heathendom, kettledrum, laudanum, martyrdom, maximum, medium, meddlesome, mettlesome, minimum, modicum, odium, opium, optimum, overcome, pabulum, pendulum, platinum, podium, premium, psyllium, quarrelsome, quietsome, radium, rule of thumb, sour gum, speculum, sugarplum, tedium, troublesome, tympanum, vacuum, venturesome, wearisome, worrisome, zero-sum; adventuresome, aluminum, aquarium, chrysanthemum, compendium, continuum, consortium, curriculum, delirium, effluvium, emporium, encomium, exordium, fee-fi-fo-fum, geranium, gymnasium, harmonium, magnesium, millennium, opprobrium, palladium, petroleum, residuum, symposium, viaticum; auditorium, crematorium, equilibrium, moratorium, pandemonium, sanitarium.

**-umb.** See **-um.**

**-ume.** See **-oom.**

**-ump,** bump, chump, clump, crump, dump, drump, flump, frump, grump, Gump, hump, jump, lump, mump, plump, pump, rump, schlump, slump, stump, sump, thrump, thump, trump, ump, whump; air pump, broad jump, heat pump, high jump, long jump, mugwump, no-trump, ski jump, speed bump, sump pump; stomach pump, suction pump, triple jump.

**-un,** bun, chon, done, dun, fun, gun, hon, Hun, none, nun, one, pun, run, shun, son, spun, stun, sun, sunn, ton, tonne, tun, won; A-1, air gun, begun, big gun, blowgun, burp gun, dry run, earned run, end run, finespun, first-run, flashgun, godson, grandson, handgun, hard-won, home run, homespun, long run, milk run, outdone, outgun, outrun, popgun, pressrun, ray gun, redone, rerun, shogun, short run, shotgun, someone, spray gun, stepson, stun gun, top gun, trial run, undone, Watson, well-done, Whitsun, zip gun; Acheron, Albion, anyone, Browning gun, Chesterton, cinnamon, everyone, galleon, Galveston, ganglion, garrison, Gatling gun, gonfalon, halcyon, hired gun, hit-and-run, jettison, jump the gun, kiloton, machine gun, megaton, midnight sun, number one, one-on-one, on the run, orison, overdone, overrun, pellet gun, riot gun, Sally Lunn, simpleton, singleton, skeleton, smoking gun, staple gun, Tommy gun, twenty-one, underdone, unison, venison, water gun; accordion, caparison, comparison, oblivion, phenomenon, son of a gun, submachine gun.

**-unce,** dunce, once.

Also: **-unt** + **-s** (as in *bunts,* etc.)

**-unch,** brunch, bunch, crunch, hunch, lunch, munch, punch, scrunch; box lunch, free lunch, keypunch, milk punch; counterpunch, honeybunch, one-two punch, out to lunch, planter's punch, ploughman's lunch, rabbit punch, sucker-punch.

**-unct,** adjunct, conjunct, defunct, disjunct.

Also: **-unk** + **-ed** (as in *bunked*, etc.)

**-und,** bund, fund; fecund, hedge fund, jocund, obtund, refund, rotund, slush fund, trust fund; cummerbund, moribund, orotund, rubicund, sinking fund, underfund.

Also: **-un** + **-ed** (as in *stunned*, etc.)

**-une.** See **-oon.**

**-uned.** See **-ound.**

**-ung,** bung, clung, dung, flung, hung, lung, rung, slung, sprung, strung, stung, sung, swung, tongue, wrung, young; among, bee-stung, black lung, brown lung, far-flung, forked tongue, geebung, ham-strung, high-strung, low-slung, Shantung, unstrung, unsung; adder's-tongue, Aqua-Lung, double-hung, double-tongue, egg foo yung, iron lung, mother tongue, Niebelung, over-hung, triple-tongue, under-slung.

**-unge,** blunge, grunge, gunge, lunge, plunge, sponge; expunge; muskellunge.

**-unk,** bunk, chunk, clunk, drunk, dunk, flunk, funk, gunk, hunk, junk, lunk, monk, plunk, punk, shrunk, skunk, slunk, spunk, stunk, sunk, thunk, trunk; adunc, chipmunk, debunk, ker-plunk, Podunk, preshrunk, punch-drunk, quidnunc, slam dunk, spelunk; coun-tersunk, cuttyhunk, cyber-punk, splatterpunk, steamer trunk.

**-unked.** See **-unct.**

**-unned.** See **-und.**

**-unt,** blunt, brunt, bunt, front, grunt, hunt, prunt, punt, runt, shunt, stunt, wont; affront, beachfront, break-front, cold front, confront, fall front, fly front, fore-front, home front, job-hunt, lakefront, manhunt, out-front, sea front, shorefront, storefront, up-front, warm front, wave front, witch hunt; battlefront, ocean-front, people's front, river-front, waterfront.

**-unts.** See **-unce.**

**-up,** cup, pup, scup, sup, tup, up, yup; backup, ballup, bang-up, beat-up, blowup, breakup, buildup, built-up, buy-up, call-up, catch-up, change-up, checkup, chin-up, cleanup, close-up, cockup, crack-up, cutup, death cup, dial-up, dried-up, drive-up, dustup, egg-cup, eyecup, faceup, fill-up, flareup, foul-up, frame-up, getup, giddap, grace cup, grown-up, hang-up, heads-up, hiccup, holdup, hookup, hopped-up, hyped-up, jack-up, jam-up, kickup, kingcup, lash-up, lay-up, lead-up, letup, line-up, linkup, lockup, lookup, made-up, makeup, markup, matchup, mix-up, mixed-up, mock-up, mop-up, nip-up, one-up, pasteup, pickup, pileup, pinup, pop-up, prenup, press-up, pull-up, punch-up, push-up, put-up, roundup, run-up, screwup, send-up, setup, shake-up, shape-up, sit-up, slip-up, smash-up, souped-up, speedup, spiffed-up, stand-up, start-up, stepped-up, stickup, stuck-up, sunup, teacup, thumbs-up, tie-up, tossup, touchup, trumped-up, tune-up, wake-up, walk-up, warmup, washed-up, washup, windup, workup, wrap-up, write-up; belly-up, bottom-up, buttercup, buttoned-up, cover-up, follow-up, giddyap, higher-up, loving cup, pick-me-up, runner-up, shoot-'em-up, suction cup, summing-up, up-and-up, wickiup, winding-up; Johnny-jump-up, sunny-side up.

**-upe.** See **-oop.**

**-upt,** abrupt, bankrupt, corrupt, disrupt, erupt, irrupt; interrupt.

Also: **-up** + **-ed** (as in *supped*, etc.)

**-ur.** See **-er.**

**-urb.** See **-erb.**

**-urch,** birch, church, curch, lurch, perch, search, smirch; besmirch, research, strip-search.

**-urd,** bird, curd, fyrd, gird, heard, herd, Kurd, nerd, sherd, surd, third, turd, word; absurd, bean curd, bellbird, blackbird, blue-bird, buzzword, byword, catbird, catchword, code word, cowbird, cowherd, crossword, cussword, engird, foreword, game bird, ghost word, goatherd, good word, guide word, headword, jailbird, jaybird, key word, kingbird, last word, loanword, lovebird, nonce word, oilbird, password, potsherd, railbird, rainbird, redbird, reword, ricebird, seabird, shorebird, snowbird, songbird, state bird, sunbird, swanherd, swearword, swineherd, ungird, unheard, watchword, yardbird; afterword, bowerbird, butcherbird, cedar bird, dickeybird, dirty word, dollarbird, early bird, fighting word, firebird, friarbird, frigate bird, gallows bird, gooney bird, hummingbird, ladybird, lemon curd, lyrebird, mockingbird, ovenbird, overheard, rifle bird, tailorbird, thunderbird, wading bird, water bird, wattlebird, weasel word, weaverbird, whirlybird, word for word.

Also: **-er** + **-ed** (as in *conferred*, etc.)

Also: **-ir** + **-ed** (as in *stirred*, etc.)

Also: **-ur** + **-ed** (as in *occurred*, etc.)

**-ure,** cure, pure, your, you're; ceinture, coiffure, demure, endure, gravure, guipure, immure, impure, inure, ligure, manure, mature, obscure, ordure, perdure, procure, rondure, secure, tenure; aperture, armature, coverture, cubature, curvature, epicure, forfeiture, furniture, garniture, immature, insecure, ligature, manicure, overture, pedicure, portraiture, premature, signature, simon-pure, sinecure, tablature, temperature; caricature, discomfiture, divestiture, entablature, expenditure, investiture, literature, miniature, musculature, nomenclature, temperature; primogeniture.

See also **-oor.**

**-ures.** See **-ours.**

**-urf,** kerf, scurf, serf, surf, turf; enserf, windsurf; Astroturf, body-surf, channel-surf, surf and turf.

**-urge.** See **-erge.**

**-urk,** burke, Burke, chirk, cirque, clerk, dirk, Dirk, irk, jerk, kirk, Kirk, lurk, murk, perk, quirk, shirk, smirk, Turk, work; artwork, beadwork, berserk, bookwork, brainwork, breastwork, brickwork, bridgework, brushwork, canework, casework, classwork, clockwork, coursework, crownwork, cutwork, daywork, dreamwork, Dunkirk, earthwork, fieldwork, file clerk, footwork, framework, fretwork, glasswork, groundwork, grunt work, guesswork, hackwork, handwork, hauberk, homework, housework, knee-jerk, lacework, legwork, lifework, make-work, network, patchwork, piecework, presswork, rework, road work, salesclerk, schoolwork, scrollwork, scutwork, steelwork, stock clerk, stonework, teamwork, town clerk, waxwork, woodwork; bodywork, busywork, city clerk, clean and jerk, crewelwork, dirty work, donkeywork, fancywork, firework, handiwork, ironwork, leatherwork, masterwork, metalwork, needlework, openwork, overwork, paperwork, piece of work, plasterwork, right-to-work, shipping clerk, social work, soda jerk, underwork, wickerwork.

**-url,** birl, burl, churl, curl, earl, furl, girl, hurl, knurl, merle, pearl, purl, skirl, swirl, twirl, whirl, whorl; aswirl, awhirl, ball girl, bat girl, B-girl, call girl, cowgirl, newsgirl, pin curl, playgirl, salesgirl, schoolgirl, seed pearl, shopgirl, showgirl, spit curl, uncurl, unfurl; attagirl, chorus girl, cover girl, cultured pearl, flower girl, Gibson girl, glamour girl, party girl, poster girl, sweater girl, working girl.

**-urled.** See **-orld.**

**-urn,** Berne, burn, churn, durn, earn, erne, fern, hern, kern, learn, quern, spurn, stern, tern, turn, urn, yearn; about-turn, adjourn, astern, attorn, casern, concern, discern, downturn, epergne, eterne, extern, heartburn, intern, inurn, lucerne, Lucerne, nocturn, nocturne, return, Sauternes, secern, sojourn, star turn, steinkern, step turn, sunburn, tree fern, unlearn, upturn, U-turn, windburn; Arctic tern, basket fern, Comintern, overturn, slash-and-burn, subaltern, taciturn, unconcern.

**-urp,** burp, chirp, perp, slurp, stirp, twerp; usurp.

**-urred.** See **-urd.**

**-urse.** See **-erse.**

**-ursed.** See **-urst.**

**-urst,** burst, curst, durst, erst, first, Hearst, thirst, verst, worst, wurst; accursed, at first, athirst, bratwurst cloudburst, feetfirst, headfirst, knackwurst, outburst, starburst, sunburst; liverwurst, wienerwurst.

Also: **-erce** + **-ed** (as in *coerced*, etc.)

Also: **-erse** + **-ed** (as in *dispersed*, etc.)

Also: **-urse** + **-ed** (as in *nursed*, etc.)

**-urve.** See **-erve.**

**-us,** bus, buss, crus, cuss, fuss, Gus, Huss, muss, plus, pus, Russ, suss, thus, truss, us; airbus, cirrus, concuss, cost-plus, discuss, nimbus, nonplus, percuss, Remus, school bus, stratus, surplus; abacus, Angelus, animus, autobus, blunderbuss, Cerberus, cumulus, exodus, harquebus, Hesperus, humerus, impetus, incubus, minibus, minimus, nautilus, nucleus, octopus, Oedipus, omnibus, Pegasus, phosphorous, platypus, Priapus, radius, Romulus, Sirius, stimulus, succubus, syllabus, Tantalus, terminus; caduceus, denarius, esophagus, Homunculus, Leviticus, sarcophagus.

Also: numerous words ending in **-ous** (as *mutinous, perilous,* etc.)

**-use** (-yo͞oz), fuse, fuze, mews, muse, news, use; abuse, accuse, amuse, bemuse, confuse, contuse, diffuse, disuse, effuse, excuse, infuse, misuse, perfuse, recuse, refuse, short

fuse, suffuse, transfuse; disabuse, Syracuse.
Also: **-ew** + **-s** (as in *stews,* etc.)
Also: **-oo** + **-s** (as in *moos,* etc.)
Also: **-ue** + **-s** (as in *cues,* etc.)

**-use** (-o͞os) or (-yo͞os). See **-oose.**

**-use** (-o͞oz), blues, booze, bruise, cruise, Druze, lose, news, ooze, ruse, schmooze, snooze, who's, whose; Chartreuse, contuse, enthuse, peruse.

**-ush** (-ush), blush, brush, crush, flush, gush, hush, lush, mush, plush, rush, shush, slush, smush, squush, thrush, tush; airbrush, bulrush, bum-rush, bum's rush, four flush, gold rush, hairbrush, hot flush, hush-hush, inrush, nailbrush, onrush, paintbrush, sagebrush, scrub brush, shoebrush, song thrush, straight flush, tarbrush, toothbrush, uprush; bottlebrush, pastry brush, royal flush, shaving brush, underbrush, wire brush.

**-ush** (-o͝osh), bush, cush, Cush, mush, push, shush, squoosh, swoosh, tush, whoosh; ambush, costpush, cush-cush, rosebush, spicebush, thornbush; bramblebush, burning bush, Hindu Kush, hobblebush, sugarbush.

**-usk,** brusque, busk, cusk, dusk, husk, musk, rusk, tusk, Usk; cornhusk.

**-uss.** See **-us.**

**-ussed.** See **-ust.**

**-ust,** bust, crust, dost, dust, gust, just, lust, must, rust, thrust, trust, wast; adjust, adust, august, August, beer bust, blind trust, blockbust, bloodlust, brain trust, combust, crop-dust, degust, disgust, distrust, encrust, entrust, gold dust, incrust, in trust, leaf rust, mistrust, moondust, piecrust, robust, sawdust, stardust, unjust, upthrust; angel dust, antitrust, baby bust, bite the dust, boom-and-bust, breach of trust, cosmic dust, counterthrust, dry-as-dust, living trust, public trust, readjust, unit trust, uppercrust, wanderlust.

Also: **-uss** + **-ed** (as in *fussed,* etc.)

**-ut** (-ut), but, butt, crut, cut, glut, gut, hut, jut, mutt, nut, putt, rut, scut, shut, slut, smut, strut, tut, ut, what; abut, beechnut, blind gut, breadnut, buzz cut, catgut, chestnut, clean-cut, clear-cut, cost-cut, crew cut, crosscut, doughnut, earthnut, fine-cut, foregut, groundnut, haircut, hindgut, hognut, jump cut, line cut, lug nut, peanut, pignut, pine nut, precut, price-cut, put-put, rebut, recut, rotgut, rough cut, sackbut, shortcut, somewhat, tut-tut, uncut, walnut, wing nut, woodcut; betel nut, Brazil nut, brilliant cut, butternut, coconut, final cut, halibut, hazelnut, kola nut, litchi nut, Nissen hut, occiput, scuttlebutt, single cut, undercut, uppercut.

**-ut** (-o͝ot). See **-oot.**

**-utch,** clutch, crutch, cutch, Dutch, hutch, much, scutch, smutch, such, touch; nonesuch, retouch, soft touch; common touch, double-clutch, double Dutch, inasmuch, insomuch, Midas touch, overmuch, such and such.

**-ute,** beaut, boot, bruit, brut, brute, bute, butte, chute, cloot, coot, cute, flute, fruit, glute, hoot, jute, loot, lute, moot, mute, newt, root, route, scoot, scute, shoot, sluit, snoot, soot, suit, toot, ut, ute, Ute; acute, Aleut, astute, beetroot, Beirut, birthroot, bloodroot, breadfruit, butut, Canute, catsuit, cheroot, choucroute, clubroot, commute, compute, confute, crapshoot, cube root, deaf-mute, depute, dilute, dispute, elute, en route, flight suit, folkmoot, freeboot, galoot, grapefruit, G suit, gumboot, gym suit, hip boot, hirsute, imbrute, impute, jackboot, jackfruit, jumpsuit, lawsuit, long suit, lounge suit, minute, nasute, offshoot, Paiute, pantsuit, permute, playsuit, pollute, pursuit, reboot, recruit, refute, repute, reroute, salute, Silk Route, ski boot, snakeroot, snowsuit, solute, spacesuit, sport-ute, square root, star fruit, statute, strong suit, sunsuit, sweatsuit, swimsuit, taproot, tracksuit, trade route, transmute, tribute, uproot, volute, wet suit, zoot suit; absolute, arrowroot, attribute, autoroute, bandicoot, bathing suit, birthday suit, bitterroot, bodysuit, boilersuit, bumbershoot, business suit, chukka boot, chute-the-chute, comminute, constitute, contribute, convolute, countersuit, Denver boot, destitute, disrepute, dissolute, evolute, execute, follow suit, gingerroot, hot pursuit, in cahoot, institute, involute, kiwifruit, leisure suit, malamute, marabout, overshoot, parachute, passion fruit, persecute, point-and-shoot, prosecute, prostitute, qiviut, recompute, resolute, restitute, revolute, rural route, subacute, substitute, troubleshoot, undershoot, union suit; electrocute, forbidden fruit, Hardecanute, irresolute, reconstitute, redistribute, telecommute.

**-uth.** See **-ooth.**

**-ux,** crux, dux, flux, lux, luxe, shucks, tux; afflux, aw-shucks, big bucks, conflux, deluxe, efflux, influx, redux, reflux; Benelux, megabucks.

Also: **-uck** + **-s** (as in *plucks,* etc.)

**-uzz,** buzz, 'cause, coz, does, fuzz, 'twas, was; abuzz, because, outdoes, undoes; overdoes.

**-y,** ai, ay, aye, bi, buy, by, bye, chai, cry, die, dry, dye, eye, fie, fly, fry, guy, Guy, heigh, hi, hie, high, I, lie, lye, my, nigh, phi, pi, pie, ply, pry, psi, rye, shy, sigh, sky, Skye, sly, spry, spy, sty, tai, Thai, thigh, thy, tie, try, vie, why, wry, wye; air-dry, ally, anti, apply, assai, awry, aye-aye, Bacchae, Baha'i, banzai, barfly, belie, bigeye, big lie, bird's-eye, black eye, black fly, black tie, blow-dry, blowby, blow fly, blue-sky, bone-dry, bonsai, botfly, bowtie, buckeye, bugeye, bull's-eye, bye-bye, canaille, cat's-eye, chess pie, cock-eye, comply, cow pie, cranefly, cream pie, cross-eye, deadeye, decry, deep-fry, deep-sky, defy, deny, descry, dong quai, drip-dry, drive-by, dry eye, elhi, Eli, espy, fall guy, fisheye, flyby, freeze-dry, French fry, frog-eye, fruit fly, gadfly, GI, glass eye, go-by, goodbye, grisaille, gun-shy, hereby, hi-fi, hogtie, horn fly, horsefly, housefly, imply, jai alai, July, knee-high, lanai, lay-by, magpie, mao-tai, Masai, mayfly, medfly, mince pie, mind's eye, mooneye, mudpie, nearby, necktie, nisi, outcry, outvie, oxeye, pad thai, pan-fry, pigsty, pinkeye, Popeye, pop fly, porkpie, potpie, quasi, rabbi, red-eye, rely, reply, rib eye, rocaille, sandfly, sci-fi, screw eye, semi, serai, shanghai, Shanghai, shoofly, shuteye, Sinai, sky-high, small fry, sockeye, standby, stir-fry, string tie, supply, test-fly, thereby, tie-dye, tongue-tie, twist tie, two-ply, untie, vat dye, Versailles, walleye, well-nigh, whereby, white tie, wild rye, wise guy; abaci, alibi, alkali, alumni, amplify, apple pie, assegai, azo dye, beautify, bolo tie, butterfly, by-and-by, caddis fly, calcify, certify, citify, clarify, classify, codify, college try, cottage pie, counterspy, countrify, crucify, cut-and-dry, cutie-pie, DIY, damnify, damselfly, dandify, deify, densify, dignify, dobsonfly, do-or-die, dragonfly, eagle eye, edify, evil eye, falsify, fancify, firefly, fortify, Frenchify, fructify, Gemini, gentrify, glorify, goggle-eye, goldeneye, gratify, harvest fly, high and dry, hook and eye, horrify, humble pie, hushaby, jollify, junior high, justify, lazuli, lazy eye, lignify, liquefy, Lorelei, lullaby, magnify, misapply, modify, mollify, Mordecai, mortify, Mount Sinai, multi-ply, multiply, mummify, mystify, mythify, nazify, nigrify, nitrify, notify, nuclei, nullify, occupy, old school tie, ossify, overbuy, overlie, pacify, passerby, petrify, preachify, prettify, private eye, prophesy, purify, putrefy, qualify, quantify, ramify, rarefy, ratify, RBI, reapply, rectify, reify, resupply, right to die, runner's high, Russify, salify, samurai, sanctify, satisfy, scarify, senior high, shepherd's pie, shoofly pie, signify, simplify, sine die, Spanish fly, specify, speechify, stratify, stultify, stupefy, superhigh, sweetie pie, terrify, testify, tiger's-eye, tsetse fly, tumble-dry, typify, uglify, ultrahigh, umblepie, underlie, unify, Uruguay, verbify, verify, versify, vilify, vitrify, vivify, weather eye, Windsor tie, yuppify, zombify; acidify, beatify, commodify, cross-multiply, decalcify, decertify, declassify, demystify, detoxify, Dioscuri, disqualify, dissatisfy, diversify, electric eye, electrify, emulsify, exemplify, humidify, identify, indemnify, intensify, Lotophagi, misclassify, money supply, objectify, oversupply, personify, preoccupy, prequalify, reunify, sacrifice fly, saponify, solemnify, solidify, subjectify, syllabify, transmogrify, vox populi, water supply; Aegospotami, anthropophagi, caravanserai, corpus delicti, dehumidify, misidentify, modus vivendi, nolle prosequi, oversimplify; amicus curiae, curriculum vitae, modus operandi.

**-yle.** See **-ile.**

**-yled.** See **-ild.**

**-yme.** See **-ime.**

**-ymn.** See **-im.**

**-ymph,** lymph, nymph.

**-yne.** See **-ine.**

**-ynx.** See **-inx.**

**-yp.** See **-ip.**

**-ype.** See **-ipe.**

**-yph.** See **-iff.**

**-ypse.** See **-ipse.**

**-yre.** See **-ire.**

**-yrrh.** See **-er.**

**-ysm.** See **-ism.**

**-yst.** See **-ist.**

**-yte.** See **-ite.**

**-yth.** See **-ith.**

**-yve.** See **-ive.**

**-yx.** See **-ix.**

# Two-Syllable Rhymes

**-abard.** See **-abbard.**

**-abbard,** clapboard, jabbered, scabbard, slabbered, tabard.

**-abber** (-a-), blabber, clabber, crabber, dabber, drabber, gabber, grabber, jabber, nabber, slabber, stabber, yabber; backstabber, beslabber, land-grabber, rehabber; bafflegabber, bonnyclabber.

**-abber** (-o-). See **-obber.**

**-abbered.** See **-abbard.**

**-abbet.** See **-abit.**

**-abbey.** See **-abby.**

**-abbit.** See **-abit.**

**-abble,** Babel, babble, cabble, dabble, drabble, gabble, grabble, rabble, scabble, scrabble; bedabble, bedrabble, hardscrabble; gibble-gabble, psychobabble, technobabble.

**-abby,** abbey, Abby, blabby, cabby, crabby, flabby, gabby, Gaby, grabby, scabby, shabby, tabby, yabby.

**-abel.** See **-able.**

**-aber.** See **-abor.**

**-abies,** babies, rabies, scabies, tabes.

**-abit,** abbot, babbitt, Babbitt, habit, rabbet, rabbit, Sabbat; cohabit, inhabit, jackrabbit.

**-able,** Abel, able, cable, fable, gable, label, Mabel, sable, stable, table; card table, disable, enable, end table, night table, round table, timetable, turntable, unable, unstable, worktable.

**-abor,** caber, labor, neighbor, saber, tabor, Weber; belabor, big labor, child labor, good-neighbor, slave labor.

**-abra,** sabra; candelabra; abracadabra.

**-aby,** baby, gaby, maybe; blue baby, bush baby, crybaby, grandbaby, tar baby.

**-accy.** See **-acky.**

**-acement.** See **-asement.**
**-acence.** See **-ascence.**
**-acent,** jacent, naissant, nascent; adjacent, complacent, complaisant, connascent, renascent, subjacent; circumjacent, interjacent, superjacent.
**-aceous.** See **-acious.**
**-acet.** See **-asset.**
**-achment.** See **-atchment.**
**-achne.** See **-acne.**
**-acial,** facial, glacial, racial, spatial; abbatial, biracial, palatial, prelatial, subglacial; interfacial, interglacial, interracial, multiracial.
**-acic.** See **-assic.**
**-acid,** acid, flaccid, jassid, placid; Abbasid, antacid.
**-acile.** See **-astle.**
**-acious,** gracious, spacious; audacious, bodacious, bulbaceous, cactaceous, capacious, ceraceous, cetaceous, cretaceous, crustaceous, curvaceous, edacious, fabaceous, fallacious, feracious, flirtatious, fugacious, fumacious, fungaceous, gemmaceous, hellaceous, herbaceous, Horatius, Ignatius, lappaceous, lardaceous, loquacious, marlaceous, mendacious, micaceous, minacious, misgracious, mordacious, palacious, palmaceous, pomaceous, predaceous, procacious, pugnacious, rampacious, rapacious, rosaceous, rutaceous, sagacious, salacious, sebaceous, sequacious, setaceous, tenacious, testaceous, tophaceous, ungracious, veracious, vexatious, vinaceous, vivacious, voracious; acanaceous, acanthaceous, alliaceous, amylaceous, arenaceous, camphoraceous, capillaceous, carbonaceous, contumacious, corallaceous, coriaceous, disputatious, efficacious, erinaceous, execratious, farinaceous, ferulaceous, foliaceous, gallinaceous, incapacious, liliaceous, olivaceous, orchidaceous, ostentatious, perspicacious, pertinacious, resinaceous, saponaceous, violaceous; inefficacious.
**-acis.** See **-asis.**
**-acit.** See **-asset.**

**-acken,** blacken, bracken, flacon, slacken.

**-acker,** backer, clacker, cracker, hacker, lacquer, packer, sacker, slacker, smacker, snacker, stacker, tacker, tracker, whacker, yakker; attacker, backpacker, bushwhacker, carjacker, fast-tracker, Greenbacker, hijacker, kayaker, linebacker, meat packer, nutcracker, racetracker, ransacker, safecracker, skyjacker, wisecracker; firecracker, graham cracker, soda cracker.

**-acket,** bracket, flacket, jacket, packet, placket, racket, tacket; bluejacket, book jacket, flak jacket, life jacket, pea jacket, sports jacket, straitjacket; angle bracket, battle jacket, bomber jacket, dinner jacket, leatherjacket, yellow jacket.

**-ackey.** See **-acky.**

**-ackguard.** See **-aggard.**

**-ackie.** See **-acky.**

**-ackish,** blackish, brackish, knackish, quackish.

**-ackle,** cackle, crackle, grackle, hackle, jackal, mackle, macle, quackle, shackle, Spackle, tackle; debacle, embacle, ramshackle, unshackle; block and tackle, hibernacle, tabernacle.

**-ackney.** See **-acne.**

**-ackpot,** crackpot, jackpot.

**-ackson.** See **-axen.**

**-acky,** ackey, baccy, hackie, Jackie, khaki, knacky, lackey, raki, saki, shacky, tacky, wacky; Iraqi; Nagasaki, ticky-tacky.

**-acle.** See **-ackle.**

**-acne,** acne, hackney; Arachne.

**-acon.** See **-aken.**

**-acquer.** See **-acker.**

**-acre.** See **-aker.**

**-acter.** See **-actor.**

**-actic,** lactic, practic, tactic; apractic, climactic, didactic, emphractic, galactic, phylactic, protactic, stalactic, syntactic; asyntactic, chemotactic, chiropractic, geotactic, hydrotactic, parallactic, paratactic, phonotactic, phototactic, prophylactic; anaphylactic, anticlimactic, autodidactic, extragalactic, heliotactic, intergalactic; morphosyntactic.

**-actice,** cactus, practice; group practice, malpractice; family practice, general practice.

**-actile,** dactyl, tactile, tractile; attractile, contractile, protractile, refractile, retractile; pterodactyl.

**-action,** action, faction, fraction, taction, traction; abstraction, attraction, class action, coaction, compaction, contraction, detraction, diffraction, distraction, exaction, extraction, impaction, inaction, infraction, job action, live-action, olfaction, protraction, reaction, redaction, refraction, retraction, stop-action, subaction, subtraction, transaction; abreaction, benefaction, calefaction, cause of action, chain reaction, common fraction, complex fraction, counteraction, cross-reaction, dark reaction, direct action, interaction, labefaction, liquefaction, malefaction, petrifaction, police action, putrefaction, rarefaction, retroaction, rubefaction, satisfaction, simple fraction, single-action, stupefaction, tumefaction; decimal fraction, dissatisfaction, improper fraction, overreaction, photoreaction, self-satisfaction.

**-active,** active, factive, tractive; abstractive, attractive, coactive; contractive, detractive, diffractive, distractive, enactive, impactive, inactive, olfactive, proactive, protractive, reactive, refractive, retractive, subtractive; bioactive, calefactive, counteractive, cross-reactive, hyperactive, interactive, liquefactive, nonreactive, overactive, petrifactive, photoactive, psychoactive, putrefactive, rarefactive, retroactive, satisfactive, stupefactive, unattractive, vasoactive; radioactive.

**-actly,** abstractly, compactly, exactly; matter-of-factly.

**-actor,** actor, factor, tractor; abstracter, attractor, coactor, cofactor, compactor, contactor, contractor, detractor, distracter, enactor, exactor, extractor, fudge factor, impacter, infractor, olfactor, phylacter, play actor, protractor, reactor, redactor, refractor, retractor, subtracter, transactor; benefactor, chiropractor, common factor, malefactor, multifactor, RH factor, strange attractor, subcontractor, windchill factor.

**-acture,** facture, fracture; compacture, contracture, stress fracture; compound fracture, manufacture, simple fracture.

**-actus.** See **-actice.**

**-actyl.** See **-actile.**

**-acy,** Casey, lacy, Macy, pace, précis, racy, spacey, Tracy.

**-ada,** Dada; airmada, armada, bajada, cicada, fabada, gelada, Grenada, Haggadah, ibada, lambada, Nevada, panada, posada, quebrada, ramada, tostada; autostrada, empanada, enchilada, intifada, yada-yada; aficionada; piña colada; Sierra Nevada, yada-yada-yada.

**-adam,** Adam, madam; macadam.

**-adden,** gladden, madden, sadden; Aladdin.

**-adder,** adder, bladder, gadder, gladder, ladder, madder, padder, sadder; air bladder, fish ladder, gallbladder, puff adder, stepladder, swim bladder; hook and ladder, Jacob's ladder.

**-addie.** See **-addy.**

**-adding.** See **-odding.**

**-addish,** baddish, caddish, faddish, maddish, radish, saddish; horseradish.

**-addle** (-a-), addle, paddle, raddle, saddle, spraddle, staddle, straddle; astraddle, back-paddle, bestraddle, dog paddle, foresaddle, packsaddle, sidesaddle, skedaddle, unsaddle; English saddle, fiddle-faddle, Western saddle.

**-addle** (-o-). See **-oddle.**

**-addock,** haddock, paddock, shaddock. See also **-adic.**

**-addy,** baddie, caddie, caddy, daddy, faddy, haddie, laddie, paddy; crawdaddy, granddaddy, tea caddy;

finnan haddie, sugar daddy.

**-aden,** Aden, laden, maiden; handmaiden, menhaden; heavy-laden, iron maiden, overladen.

**-ader,** aider, blader, braider, fader, grader, nadir, raider, seder, trader, wader; blockader, crusader, Darth Vader, day trader, degrader, dissuader, evader, fair trader, free trader, horse trader, invader, parader, persuader; barricader, corporate raider, gasconader, masquerader, promenader, serenader.

**-adger,** badger, cadger.

**-adi.** See **-ady.**

**-adiant,** gradient, radiant.

**-adic,** Chadic; balladic, Cycladic, dryadic, dyadic, faradic, gonadic, hexadic, maenadic, monadic, nomadic, palladic, sporadic, tetradic, tornadic, triadic, vanadic.

**-adie.** See **-ady.**

**-adient.** See **-adiant.**

**-adish.** See **-addish.**

**-adle,** cradle, dreidel, hadal, ladle; cat's cradle, encradle.

**-adly,** badly, gladly, madly, sadly; comradely.

**-adness,** badness, gladness, madness, sadness.

**-ado** (-ā dō), credo, dado; Alfredo, crusado, gambado, grenado, scalado, stoccado, strappado, tornado; ambuscado, barricado, bastinado, camisado, carbonado, desperado, muscovado, renegado.

**-ado** (-ä dō), bravado, Mikado, passado, pintado, strappado, travado; avocado, bastinado, camisado, Colorado, Coronado, desperado, El Dorado, imbrocado; amontillado; aficionado; incommunicado.

**-ady,** braidy, cedi, glady, lady, qadi, Sadie, shady; bag lady, belady, cascady, chairlady, first lady, landlady, milady, old lady, pink lady, saleslady; cleaning lady, dragon lady, fancy lady, leading lady, painted lady.

**-afer,** chafer, safer, strafer, wafer; cockchafer.

**-affer,** chaffer, gaffer, kafir, laugher, quaffer, sclaffer, staffer, zaffer.

**-affic.** See **-aphic.**

**-affick.** See **-aphic.**

**-affir.** See **-affer.**

**-affle,** baffle, gaffle, haffle, raffle, scraffle, snaffle, yaffle.

**-affled,** baffled, raffled, scaffold, snaffled.

**-affold.** See **-affled.**

**-affy,** baffy, chaffy, daffy, draffy, taffy.

**-after,** after, crafter, dafter, drafter, grafter, hafter, laughter, rafter, wafter; hereafter, ingrafter, sought-after, thereafter; fore-and-after, handicrafter, hereinafter, morning after.

**-afty,** crafty, drafty, grafty; arty-crafty.

**-agar.** See **-agger.**

**-agate.** See **-aggot.**

**-agement,** assuagement, encagement, engagement, enragement, presagement.

**-ageous,** ambagious, contagious, courageous, oragious, outrageous, rampageous, umbrageous; advantageous, noncontagious; disadvantageous.

**-ager,** cager, gauger, major, pager, sager, stager, wager; assuager, drum major, New Ager, presager, teenager.

**-aggard,** blackguard, haggard, laggard, staggard, staggered, swaggered.

**-agger,** bagger, bragger, dagger, flagger, fragger, gagger, jagger, lagger, nagger, ragger, sagger, stagger, swagger, tagger, wagger; brown-bagger, footdragger, sandbagger, wigwagger; agar-agar, bullyragger, carpetbagger, cloak-and-dagger, double dagger.

**-aggered.** See **-aggard.**

**-aggie.** See **-aggy.**

**-aggish,** haggish, naggish, waggish.

**-aggle,** daggle, draggle, gaggle, haggle, raggle, straggle, waggle; bedaggle, bedraggle; raggle-taggle.

**-aggot,** agate, faggot, fagot, maggot.

**-aggy,** Aggie, baggy, braggy, craggy, draggy, faggy, jaggy, Maggie, naggy, quaggy, ragi, saggy, scraggy, shaggy, slaggy, snaggy, waggy.

**-agic,** magic, tragic; pelagic; hemorrhagic; archipelagic.

**-agile,** agile, fragile, vagile.

**-agious.** See **-ageous.**

**-ago** (-ā gō), sago; farrago, galago, imago, lumbago, plumbago, sapsago, Tobago, virago, vorago; San Diego.

**-ago** (-ä gō), Chicago, farrago,

imago, virago; Asiago, Santiago.

**-agon,** dragon, flagon, lagan, wagon; bandwagon, chuck wagon, lunchwagon, pendragon, snapdragon, tea wagon; covered wagon, paddy wagon, patrol wagon, station wagon, Welcome Wagon.

**-agrant,** flagrant, fragrant, vagrant; conflagrant, infragrant.

**-aic,** laic; Alcaic, Altaic, archaic, deltaic, Hebraic, Judaic, Mishnaic, Mithraic, mosaic, Mosaic, Passaic, prosaic, sodaic, spondaic, stanzaic, trochaic, voltaic; algebraic, Alhambraic, Aramaic, faradaic, formulaic, pharisaic, Ptolemaic, tesseraic; paradisaic, photomosaic.

**-aiden.** See **-aden.**

**-aider.** See **-ader.**

**-aidy.** See **-ady.**

**-aighten.** See **-atan.**

**-aigner.** See **-ainer.**

**-ailer,** ailer, alar, bailer, bailor, baler, failer, gaoler, jailer, mailer, malar, nailer, paler, railer, sailor, scalar, scaler, squalor, staler, tailor, trailer, wailer, whaler; assailer, blackmailer, curtailer, derailer, derailleur, detailer, e-mailer, entailer, e-tailer, house trailer, impaler, inhaler, prevailer, regaler, retailer, self-mailer, wassailer, wholesaler.

**-ailie.** See **-alely.**

**-ailiff,** bailiff, caliph.

**-ailing,** ailing, failing, grayling, mailing, paling, railing, sailing, veiling, whaling; boardsailing, plain sailing, prevailing, retailing, unfailing, unveiling; parasailing.

**-ailment,** ailment, bailment; assailment, bewailment, curtailment, derailment, entailment, impalement, regalement.

**-ailor.** See **-ailer.**

**-aily.** See **-alely.**

**-aiment.** See **-ayment.**

**-ainder,** attainder, remainder.

**-ainer,** caner, drainer, feigner, gainer, plainer, planer, saner, stainer, strainer, trainer; abstainer, arraigner, attainer, campaigner, chicaner, complainer, constrainer, container, detainer, distrainor, entrainer, explainer, full gainer, maintainer, no-brainer, obtainer, ordainer, profaner, refrainer, regainer, restrainer, retainer; entertainer.

**-ainful,** baneful, gainful, painful; complainful, disdainful.

**-ainger.** See **-anger.**

**-ainly,** gainly, mainly, plainly, sanely, vainly; germanely, humanely, inanely, insanely, mundanely, profanely, ungainly, urbanely.

**-ainter,** fainter, painter, tainter.

**-aintly,** faintly, quaintly, saintly; unsaintly.

**-ainty,** dainty, fainty, feinty, painty; suzerainty.

**-ainy,** brainy, grainy, rainy, veiny, wany, zany; Eugénie; Allegheny, miscellany.

**-airie.** See **-ary.**

**-airing.** See **-aring.**

**-airish.** See **-arish.**

**-airly.** See **-arely.**

**-airy.** See **-ary.**

**-aisant.** See **-acent.**

**-aiser.** See **-azer.**

**-aissant.** See **-acent.**

**-aisy.** See **-azy.**

**-aiter.** See **-ator.**

**-aitress.** See **-atress.**

**-aiver.** See **-aver.**

**-ajor.** See **-ager.**

**-ake.** See **-ocky.**

**-aken** (-ā-), bacon, Macon, shaken, taken, waken; awaken, forsaken, Jamaican, mistaken, partaken, retaken, unshaken, well-taken; godforsaken, overtaken, reawaken, undertaken, unmistaken.

**-aker,** acre, baker, breaker, faker, fakir, laker, maker, nacre, Quaker, raker, shaker, Shaker, taker, waker; backbreaker, bone shaker, bookmaker, caretaker, carmaker, cheesemaker, chipmaker, clockmaker, dressmaker, earthshaker, filmmaker, God's acre, groundbreaker, grubstaker, handshaker, hatmaker, haymaker, heartbreaker, homemaker, housebreaker, icebreaker, jawbreaker, kingmaker, lawbreaker, lawmaker, mapmaker, matchmaker, moonraker, muckraker, mythmaker, noisemaker, pacemaker, partaker, peacemaker, poll taker, rainmaker, saltshaker, shirtmaker, shoemaker, snowmaker, strikebreaker, tastemaker, tiebreaker, toolmaker, watchmaker, windbreaker, winemaker, wiseacre, world-shaker; automaker, bellyacher, boilermaker, census taker, circuit breaker, coffeemaker, imagemaker, merrymaker, mischief-maker, moneymaker, moviemaker, pepper shaker, troublemaker, undertaker; cabinetmaker, holidaymaker, mover and shaker, policymaker.

**-aki** (-a-). See **-acky.**

**-aki** (-ä-). See **-ocky.**

**-akir.** See **-aker.**

**-alace.** See **-allas.**

**-alad,** ballad, salad; chef's salad, tossed salad, word salad; Caesar salad, Waldorf salad. See also **-alid.**

**-alan.** See **-allon.**

**-alant** (-ā-), assailant, bivalent, covalent, divalent, exhalant, inhalant, surveillant, trivalent; multivalent, univalent.

**-alap.** See **-allop.**

**-alate.** See **-allot.**

**-aldi,** Grimaldi, Vivaldi; Garibaldi.

**-ale.** See **-olly.**

**-alec.** See **-alic.**

**-alely,** bailey, bailie, daily, gaily, grayly, Haley, palely, scaly, shalely, stalely; Disraeli, Israeli, shillelagh, telltalely; triticale, ukelele.

**-alement.** See **-ailment.**

**-alent** (-a-). See **-allant.**

**-alent** (-ā-). See **-alant.**

**-aler.** See **-ailer.**

**-alet.** See **-allot.**

**-aley.** See **-alely.**

**-ali.** See **-olly.**

**-alic,** Alec, Gallic, malic, phallic, salic, thallic; alkalic, cephalic, italic, metallic, oxalic, sialic, smart aleck, tantalic, Uralic, vassalic, vocalic; bimetallic; nonmetallic, postvocalic, prevocalic; brachycephalic, intervocalic; dolichocephalic.

**-alice.** See **-allas.**

**-alid** (-a-), pallid, valid; invalid. See also **-alad.**

**-alid** (-o-). See **-olid.**

**-alin.** See **-allon.**

**-aling.** See **-ailing.**

**-aliph.** See **-ailiff.**

**-allad.** See **-alad.**

**-allant.** See **-alent.**

**-allas,** Alice, balas, callous,

callus, chalice, Dallas, malice, palace, Pallas, phallus, talus, thallous, thallus; digitalis; aurora borealis.

**-allen.** See **-allon.**

**-aller.** See **-allor.**

**-allet.** See **-allot.**

**-allette.** See **-allot.**

**-alley.** See **-ally.**

**-allic.** See **-alic.**

**-allid.** See **-alid.**

**-allment,** appallment, enthrallment, forestallment, installment; disenthrallment.

**-allon,** Alan, Allen, gallon, Lallan, Stalin, talon.

**-allop** (-al-), callop, gallop, galop, jalap, scallop, shallop; bay scallop, escallop, sea scallop.

**-allop** (-ol-). See **-ollop.**

**-allor,** pallor, valor; caballer.

**-allot,** ballot, gallet, mallet, palate, palette, pallet, sallet, shallot, valet; secret ballot.

**-allow** (-al-), aloe, callow, fallow, hallow, mallow, sallow, shallow, tallow; marshmallow, marsh mallow, rose mallow.

**-allow** (-ol-). See **-ollow.**

**-allus.** See **-allas.**

**-ally,** alley, bally, challis, dally, galley, mallee, pally, rally, sally, Sally, tally, valley; back-alley, bialy, blind alley, crevalle, Death Valley, finale, O'Malley, tomalley, trevally; dillydally, hexicali, Mexicali, shilly-shally, teocalli, Tin Pan Alley.

**-almest.** See **-almist.**

**-almist,** calmest, palmist, psalmist; embalmist; Islamist.

**-almon.** See **-ammon.**

**-almy.** See **-ami.**

**-aloe.** See **-allow.**

**-alon.** See **-allon.**

**-alor.** See **-allor.**

**-altar.** See **-alter.**

**-alter,** altar, alter, falter, halter, palter, Psalter, salter, vaulter, Walter; assaulter, defaulter, desalter, drysalter, exalter, Gibraltar, pole-vaulter, unalter.

**-alty,** faulty, malty, salty, vaulty.

**-aly.** See **-alely.**

**-ama,** Brahma, comma, drama, grama, lama, llama, mama, Rama, shama; pajama; closet drama, cosmorama, cyclorama, Dalai Lama, diorama, docudrama, Fujiyama, futurama, georama, melodrama, minidrama, monodrama, music drama, neorama, panorama, photodrama, psychodrama, teledrama, Yokahama.

**-ambeau.** See **-ambo.**

**-amber,** amber, camber, clamber, sambar, timbre.

**-ambit,** ambit, gambit.

**-amble,** amble, bramble, Campbell, gamble, gambol, ramble, scamble, scramble, shamble, wamble; preamble, unscramble.

**-ambo,** ambo, crambo, flambeau, jambeau, sambo.

**-ambol.** See **-amble.**

**-ameful,** blameful, flameful, shameful.

**-amel.** See **-ammel.**

**-amely,** gamely, lamely, namely, tamely.

**-ami,** balmy, mommy, palmy, qualmy, swami, Tommy; gourami, pastrami, salami, tatami, tsunami, umami; origami.

**-amin.** See **-ammon.**

**-amine.** See **-ammon.**

**-amish,** Amish, famish, rammish; affamish, enfamish.

**-amlet,** camlet, hamlet, Hamlet, samlet.

**-ammal.** See **-ammel.**

**-ammar.** See **-ammer.**

**-ammel,** camel, mammal, Tamil, trammel; enamel, entrammel.

**-ammer,** clamber, clamor, crammer, dammar, gammer, glamour, grammar, hammer, jammer, rammer, scammer, shammer, slammer, spammer, stammer, yammer; clawhammer, enamor, flimflammer, jackhammer, programmer, sledgehammer, triphammer, windjammer; katzenjammer, ninnyhammer, yellowhammer.

**-ammish.** See **-amish.**

**-ammon,** Ammon, daman, famine, gamin, gammon, mammon, salmon; backgammon, examine; cross-examine; re-examine.

**-ammy,** chamois, clammy, gammy, Grammy, hammy, jammy, mammy, ramie, Sammy, shammy, tammy, whammy; Miami; double whammy.

**-amois.** See **-ammy.**

**-amon.** See **-ayman.**

**-amor.** See **-ammer.**

**-amos.** See **-amous.**

**-amour.** See **-ammer.**

**-amous,** Amos, famous, ramus, shamus, squamous; biramous, mandamus; ignoramus; Nostradamus.

**-ampas.** See **-ampus.**

**-amper,** camper, champer, clamper, cramper, damper, hamper, pamper, scamper, stamper, tamper, tramper, vamper; happy camper, overpamper.

**-ample,** ample, sample, trample; ensample, example.

**-ampler,** ampler, sampler, trampler.

**-ampus,** campus, grampus, pampas; off-campus; hippocampus.

**-amus.** See **-amous.**

**-ana** (-a-), ana, Anna, canna, Hannah, manna, nana; banana, bandanna, cabana, Chicana, Diana, goanna, Havana, hosanna, lantana, liana, Montana, savannah, Savannah, sultana, Urbana; Africana, damiana, dulciana, Indiana, Juliana, poinciana, Pollyanna, Susquehanna; Americana, Louisiana, Victoriana.

**-ana** (-ä-), ana, anna, bwana, Ghana, kana, thana; Chicana, gymkhana, iguana, liana, nagana, nirvana, piranha, sultana, zenana; Africana, dulciana, hiragana, ikebana, katakana, marijuana, parmigiana, Tatiana, Tijuana; Americana, fata morgana, Victoriana.

**-anate.** See **-anet.**

**-ancer,** answer, cancer, chancer, dancer, glancer, lancer, prancer; advancer, break-dancer, clog dancer, enhancer, entrancer, freelancer, lap dancer, line dancer, lung cancer, merganser, romancer, square dancer, tap dancer; belly dancer, chiromancer, gandy dancer, geomancer, necromancer, taxi dancer.

**-ancet.** See **-ansit.**

**-anchion.** See **-ansion.**

**-anchor.** See **-anker.**

**-anchored.** See **-ankered.**

**-ancor.** See **-anker.**

**-ancy,** chancy, Clancy, dancy, fancy, Nancy; unchancy,

unfancy; belomancy, chiromancy, cleromancy, consonancy, gastromancy, geomancy, gyromancy, hydromancy, lithomancy, militancy, myomancy, necromancy, onomancy, psychomancy, pyromancy, rhabdomancy, stichomancy, sycophancy, termagancy; aleuromancy, anthropomancy, bibliomancy, botanomancy, crystallomancy, oneiromancy, ornithomancy; alectoromancy, alectryomancy.

**-anda,** panda; Amanda, Miranda, red panda, veranda; giant panda, jacaranda, memoranda, propaganda.

**-andal.** See **-andle.**

**-andant,** candent, scandent; demandant.

**-andem.** See **-andom.**

**-ander** (-an-), bander, brander, candor, dander, gander, grander, lander, pander, sander, slander, zander; Auslander, backhander, bystander, commander, demander, dittander, expander, flatlander, germander, glad-hander, grandstander, inlander, Leander, left-hander, Lysander, mainlander, meander, Menander, outlander, philander, pomander, right-hander, soft-lander; Alexander, calamander, coriander, gerrymander, oleander, salamander, single-hander, wing commander.

**-ander** (-on-). See **-onder.**

**-andhi.** See **-andy.**

**-andi.** See **-andy.**

**-andid,** banded, candid, handed, landed, stranded; backhanded, barehanded, forehanded, high-handed, left-handed, offhanded, one-handed, red-handed, right-handed, shorthanded, surehanded, two-handed, uncandid; empty-handed, evenhanded, heavy-handed, openhanded, single-handed, underhanded.

**-andied,** bandied, brandied, candied.

**-anding,** banding, branding, landing, standing; commanding, crash landing, crossbanding, demanding, disbanding, expanding, freestanding, long-standing, outstanding, soft landing, upstanding; belly-landing, mind-expanding, notwithstanding, pancake landing, three-point landing, understanding.

**-andish,** blandish, brandish, grandish, Standish; outlandish.

**-andit,** bandit, pandit; one-armed bandit, technobandit.

**-andle,** candle, dandle, handle, sandal, scandal, vandal; foot-candle, manhandle, mishandle, panhandle.

**-andler,** candler, chandler, dandler, handler; ball handler, panhandler.

**-andom,** fandom, random, tandem; explicandum, memorandum.

**-andor.** See **-ander.**

**-andsome.** See **-ansom.**

**-andstand,** bandstand, grandstand, handstand.

**-andum.** See **-andom.**

**-andy,** Andy, bandy, brandy, candy, dandy, Gandhi, gandy, handy, Mandy, pandy, randy, sandhi, sandy, Sandy, shandy; ear candy, eye candy, hard candy, jim-dandy, nose candy, rock candy, unhandy; apple brandy, cotton candy, handy-dandy, penny candy; modus operandi.

**-aneful.** See **-ainful.**

**-anel.** See **-annel.**

**-anely.** See **-ainly.**

**-aneous,** cutaneous, extraneous, spontaneous; instantaneous, miscellaneous, simultaneous, subcutaneous; contemporaneous, extemporaneous.

**-aner.** See **-ainer.**

**-anet,** gannet, granite, Janet, planet; pomegranate.

**-anger** (-ang ər), banger, clangor, ganger, hangar, hanger, twanger; cliffhanger, coat hanger, haranguer, headbanger, straphanger; paper hanger.

**-anger** (-ān jər), changer, danger, Grainger, granger, manger, ranger, stranger; arranger, bushranger, deranger, endanger, estranger, exchanger, lone ranger, shortchanger; disarranger, forest ranger, interchanger, moneychanger.

**-angle,** angle, bangle, brangle, dangle, jangle, mangle, spangle, strangle, tangle, twangle, wangle, wrangle; bemangle, bespangle, embrangle, entangle, pentangle, quadrangle, rectangle, right angle, straight angle, triangle, untangle, wide-angle; disentangle, interjangle.

**-angled,** newfangled, oldfangled, star-spangled.
Also: **-angle** + **-ed** (as in *tangled,* etc.)

**-ango,** fango, mango, quango, tango; contango, fandango.

**-angor.** See **-anger.**

**-anguer.** See **-anger.**

**-anguish,** anguish, languish.

**-anguor.** See **-anger.**

**-angy,** mangy, rangy.

**-anic,** manic, panic, stannic, tannic; botanic, Brahmanic, Britannic, cyanic, freshmanic, galvanic, Germanic, Hispanic, Koranic, mechanic, melanic, organic, rhodanic, satanic, shamanic, sultanic, tetanic, titanic, tympanic, tyrannic, volcanic, vulcanic; aldermanic, charlatanic, diaphanic, epiphanic, inorganic, lexiphanic, Messianic, oceanic, Ossianic, puritanic, talismanic; ferricyanic, hydrocyanic, Indo-Germanic, megalomanic, Proto-Germanic, transoceanic, valerianic; interoceanic.

**-anics,** annex, panics; humanics, mechanics.

**-anil.** See **-annel.**

**-anion,** banyan, canyon, fanion; companion.

**-anish,** banish, clannish, mannish, planish, Spanish, tannish, vanish; evanish.

**-anite.** See **-anet.**

**-ankard.** See **-ankered.**

**-anker,** anchor, banker, blanker, canker, chancre, clanker, danker, flanker, hanker, rancor, ranker, spanker, tanker; co-anchor, oil tanker.

**-ankered,** anchored, cankered, hankered, tankard.

**-ankle,** ankle, crankle, rankle.

**-ankly,** blankly, dankly, frankly, lankly, rankly.

**-anna.** See **-ana.**

**-annah.** See **-ana.**

**-annal.** See **-annel.**

**-annel,** anil, annal, cannel, channel, flannel, panel, scrannel; clear channel, impanel.

**-anner,** banner, canner, lanner, manner, manor, planner, scanner, spanner, tanner, vanner; CAT scanner, PET scanner, self-tanner, town planner; bedside manner, caravaner, city planner, CT scanner.

**-annet.** See **-anet.**

**-annex.** See **-anics.**

**-annic.** See **-anic.**

**-annie.** See **-anny.**

**-annish.** See **-anish.**

**-annual.** See **-anual.**

**-anny,** Annie, canny, clanny, cranny, Danny, fanny, Fanny, granny, Mannie, nanny; Afghani, uncanny; frangipani, Hindustani, hootenanny.

**-anor.** See **-anner.**

**-anser.** See **-ancer.**

**-ansett.** See **-ansit.**

**-ansion,** mansion, scansion, stanchion; expansion.

**-ansit,** lancet, transit; Narragansett.

**-ansom,** handsome, hansom, ransom, transom; king's ransom, unhandsome.

**-answer.** See **-ancer.**

**-ansy,** pansy, tansy; chimpanzee.

**-anta,** manta, Santa; Atlanta, infanta, maranta, Vedanta; Atalanta.

**-antam,** bantam, phantom.

**-ante.** See **-anty.**

**-anteau.** See **-anto.**

**-antel.** See **-antle.**

**-anter,** antre, banter, canter, cantor, chanter, grantor, panter, plantar, planter, ranter; decanter, descanter, enchanter, implanter, instanter, Levanter, recanter, transplanter, trochanter; covenanter, gallivanter, tam-o'-shanter.

**-anther,** anther, panther; Black Panther, Gray Panther.

**-anti.** See **-anty.**

**-antic,** antic, frantic, mantic; Atlantic, bacchantic, gigantic, pedantic, romantic, semantic, Vedantic; chiromantic, consonantic, corybantic, geomantic, hierophantic, hydromantic, necromantic, North Atlantic, pyromantic, sycophantic, transatlantic, unromantic.

**-antine,** Byzantine, Levantine; adamantine, elephantine.

**-antle,** cantle, mantel, mantle, santal, scantle; atlantal, dismantle, immantle, quadrantal, spirantal; consonantal, covenantal.

**-antler,** antler, mantler, pantler; dismantler.

**-antling,** bantling, mantling, scantling; dismantling.

**-anto,** canto, panto, santo; coranto, portmanteau; Esperanto, palo santo, quo warranto.

**-antom.** See **-antam.**

**-antor.** See **-anter.**

**-antry,** chantry, gantry, pantry.

**-anty,** ante, anti, auntie, canty, chantey, Dante, panty, scanty, shanty, slanty; andante, Ashanti, bacchante, Chianti, ex ante, infante; comandante, dilettante, non obstante, penny ante, vigilante.

**-anual,** annual, manual; biannual, Emmanuel.

**-anuel.** See **-anual.**

**-any** (-ā-). See **-ainy.**

**-any** (-e-). See **-enny.**

**-anyan.** See **-anion.**

**-anyon.** See **-anion.**

**-anza,** stanza; bonanza, nyanza, organza; Sancho Panza; extravaganza.

**-anzee.** See **-ansy.**

**-aoler.** See **-ailer.**

**-apal.** See **-aple.**

**-ape.** See **-appy.**

**-apel.** See **-apple.**

**-apen,** capon; misshapen, unshapen.

**-aper,** aper, caper, draper, gaper, japer, paper, raper, sapor, scraper, shaper, taper, tapir, vapor; bond paper, crepe paper, curlpaper, endpaper, flypaper, graph paper, landscaper, newspaper, notepaper, reshaper, rice paper, sandpaper, skyscraper, term paper, wallpaper, wastepaper, waxed paper, white paper; blotting paper, butcher paper, carbon paper, filter paper, funny paper, litmus paper, tissue paper, toilet paper, tracing paper, writing paper.

**-aphic,** graphic, Sapphic, traffic; digraphic, edaphic, seraphic; autographic, biographic, calligraphic, cartographic, chirographic, chronographic, cosmographic, crytographic, demographic, diagraphic, epigraphic, epitaphic, ethnographic, geographic, hierographic, holographic, homographic, hydrographic, lithographic, monographic, orthographic, pantographic, paragraphic, petrographic, phonographic, photographic, pictographic, polygraphic, pornographic, scenographic, seismographic, stenographic, stratigraphic, stylographic, telegraphic, topographic, typographic, xylographic; bibliographic, choreographic, heliographic, heterographic, iconographic, ideographic, idiographic, lexicographic, physiographic; autobiographic, cinematographic.

**-apid,** rapid, sapid, vapid.

**-apir.** See **-aper.**

**-apist,** papist, rapist; escapist, landscapist.

**-aple,** maple, papal, staple; unstaple; antipapal, sugar maple.

**-apless,** capless, gapless, hapless, napless, sapless, strapless.

**-apling.** See **-appling.**

**-apnel,** grapnel, shrapnel.

**-apon.** See **-apen.**

**-apor.** See **-aper.**

**-apper,** capper, clapper, dapper, flapper, lapper, mapper, napper, rapper, sapper, schnapper, scrapper, slapper, snapper, strapper, tapper, trapper, wrapper, zapper; backslapper, catnapper, didapper, dognapper, dust wrapper, entrapper, fly-sapper, gift-wrapper, kidnapper, knee-slapper, petnapper, red snapper, thigh-slapper; handicapper, understrapper, whippersnapper, wiretapper.

**-appet,** lappet, tappet.

**-appie.** See **-appy.**

**-apple,** apple, chapel, dapple, grapple, scapple, scrapple, thrapple; bad apple, crab apple, love apple, May apple, pineapple; Adam's apple, antechapel, candy apple, custard apple, lady apple.

**-appling,** dappling, grappling, sapling.

**-appy,** chappie, flappy, gappy, happy, knappy, nappy, pappy, sappy, scrappy, snappy, strappy, zappy; grandpappy, serape, slap-happy, unhappy.

**-apter,** apter, captor, chapter, raptor; adapter, recaptor.

**-aptest.** See **-aptist.**

**-aption,** caption; adaption, contraption, recaption.

**-aptist,** aptest, Baptist, raptest; Anabaptist, catabaptist; Southern Baptist.

**-aptor.** See **-apter.**

**-apture,** capture, rapture; enrapture, recapture, screen capture.

**-ara,** Clara, jarrah, Sarah; mascara, Sahara, tantara, tiara; marinara.

**-arab,** arab, Arab, Carib, carob, scarab.

**-arage.** See **-arriage.**

**-araoh.** See **-arrow.**

**-arass.** See **-arras.**

**-arat.** See **-aret.**

**-arbel.** See **-arble.**

**-arber.** See **-arbor.**

**-arbered.** See **-arboard.**

**-arble** (-är-), barbel, garbel, garble, marble; enmarble.

**-arble** (-ôr-), corbeil, corbel, warble.

**-arboard,** barbered, harbored, larboard, starboard.

**-arbor,** arbor, barber, harbor; Bar Harbor, Pearl Harbor.

**-arbored.** See **-arboard.**

**-arcel,** parcel, sarcel, tarsal; metatarsal, part and parcel.

**-archal.** See **-arkle.**

**-archer,** archer, marcher, parcher, starcher; departure.

**-archy,** barky, darky, larky, marquee, snarky, sparky; autarchy, autarky, eparchy, exarchy, heptarchy, malarkey, menarche, pentarchy, tetrarchy; heterarchy, hierarchy, matriarchy, oligarchy, patriarchy.

**-arden** (-är-), Arden, garden, harden, pardon; beer garden, bombardon, caseharden, enharden, rock garden, roof garden; Dolly Varden, kitchen garden, market garden.

**-arden** (-ôr-). See **-ordon.**

**-arder** (-är-), ardor, carder, guarder, harder, larder, yarder; bombarder, Cunarder, green-carder.

**-arder** (-ôr-). See **-order.**

**-ardon.** See **-arden.**

**-ardor.** See **-arder.**

**-ardy,** hardy, lardy, tardy; foolhardy, Lombardy, Picardy.

**-arel.** See **-arrel.**

**-arely,** barely, fairly, rarely, sparely, squarely, yarely; foursquarely, unfairly; debonairly.

**-arent,** arrant, parent; apparent, birth parent, co-parent, godparent, grandparent, houseparent, stepparent, transparent; foster parent, heir apparent.

**-aret,** carat, caret, carrot, claret, garret, karat, parrot.

**-arfish,** garfish, starfish.

**-argent,** argent, sergeant.

**-arger,** charger, larger, sparger; enlarger; supercharger, turbocharger.

**-argo,** Argo, argot, cargo, largo, Margot; botargo, embargo, Wells Fargo; supercargo.

**-argot.** See **-argo.**

**-ari** (-âr-). See **-ary.**

**-ari** (-är-). See **-arry.**

**-arian.** See **-arion.**

**-aric,** baric, carrick, Garrick; agaric, Amharic, barbaric, Dinaric, fumaric, Pindaric, stearic, tartaric; Balearic, cinnabaric, hyperbaric, isobaric. See also **-arrack.**

**-arid,** arid, farad, sparid.

**-aried.** See **-arried.**

**-arier.** See **-arrier.**

**-aring,** airing, bearing, daring, fairing, glaring, pairing, raring, wearing; ball bearing, cheeseparing, childbearing, despairing, livebearing, seafaring, talebearing, timesharing, uncaring, unsparing, wayfaring; overbearing, profit sharing.

**-arion,** Arian, Aryan, carrion, clarion, Marian, Marion, Parian; agrarian, barbarian, Bavarian, Bulgarian, Cesarean, cnidarian, contrarian, fruitarian, grammarian, Hungarian, librarian, ovarian, riparian, rosarian, Rotarian, sectarian, Sumerian, Tocharian, vulgarian; antiquarian, centenarian, doctrinarian, Indo-Aryan, lapidarian, libertarian, millenarian, nonsectarian, postlapsarian, prelapsarian, proletarian, Rastafarian, seminarian, trinitarian, Unitarian, vegetarian; abecedarian, authoritarian, communitarian, disciplinarian, documentarian, egalitarian, humanitarian, nonagenarian, octogenarian, parliamentarian, sexagenarian, totalitarian, utilitarian, veterinarian; establishmentarian, latitudinarian, septuagenarian, valetudinarian.

**-arious,** carious, Darius, scarious, various; Aquarius, bifarious, burglarious, calcareous, contrarious, dinarius, gregarious, hilarious, nefarious, ovarious, precarious, vicarious; multifarious, Sagittarius, temerarious.

**-aris,** Paris, Harris; Polaris; plaster of Paris. See also **-arras.**

**-arish,** barish, bearish, garish, rarish, sparish, squarish; nightmarish; debonairish.

**-arius.** See **-arious.**

**-arken,** darken, hearken.

**-arkish,** darkish, larkish, sparkish.

**-arkle,** darkle, sparkle; exarchal, monarchal, outsparkle; hierarchal, matriarchal, patriarchal.

**-arkling,** darkling, sparkling.

**-arkly,** darkly, sparkly, starkly.

**-arky.** See **-archy.**

**-arler,** gnarler, marler, parlor, snarler.

**-arlet,** carlet, charlotte, Charlotte, harlot, scarlet, starlet, varlet.

**-arley.** See **-arly.**

**-arlic,** garlic, Harlech; pilgarlic.

**-arlie.** See **-arly.**

**-arling,** carling, darling, marling, snarling, sparling, starling.

**-arlor.** See **-arler.**

**-arlot.** See **-arlet.**

**-arly,** barley, Charlie, gnarly, marly, parley, snarly; bizarrely, pearl barley; particularly.

**-armer,** armor, charmer, farmer; dirt farmer, plate armor, snake charmer, truck farmer.

**-arming,** arming, charming, farming; alarming, disarming, Prince Charming.

**-armless,** armless, charmless, harmless.

**-armor.** See **-armer.**

**-army,** army, barmy, smarmy.

**-arnel,** carnal, charnel, darnel.

**-arner,** darner, garner; Silas Marner.

**-arning.** See **-orning.**

**-arnish,** garnish, tarnish, varnish.

**-aro** (-â-), aero, faro, pharoah, taro; bolero, bracero, cruzeiro, dinero, montero, pampero, primero, ranchero, sombrero, torero, vaquero; caballero, pistolero; banderillero, carabinero, embarcadero. See also **-arrow.**

**-arol.** See **-arrel.**

**-aron,** Aaron, baron, barren, Charon, marron, Sharon; robber baron, rose of Sharon.

**-arper,** carper, harper, sharper; cardsharper.

**-arquee.** See **-archy.**

**-arrack,** arrack, barrack, carrack. See also **-aric.**

**-arrant.** See **-arent.**

**-arras,** arras, harass; embarrass. See also **-aris.**

**-arrel** (-ar-), aril, barrel, carol, Carol, carrel, Carroll, parol, parrel; apparel, pork barrel.

**-arrel** (-ôr-). See **-oral.**

**-arret.** See **-aret.**

**-arriage,** carriage, marriage; disparage, miscarriage, mismarriage, mixed marriage; baby carriage, civil marriage, horseless carriage, intermarriage, open marriage, railway carriage, shotgun marriage, undercarriage.

**-arrick.** See **-aric.**

**-arrie.** See **-ary.**

**-arried,** carried, harried, married, parried, tarried, varied; miscarried, remarried, unmarried, unvaried; intermarried.

**-arrier,** barrier, carrier, charier, farrier, harrier, marrier, parrier, tarrier; ballcarrier, mail carrier, sound barrier; aircraft barrier, common carrier, Jersey barrier, letter carrier.

**-arrion.** See **-arion.**

**-arris.** See **-aris.**

**-arron.** See **-aron.**

**-arrot.** See **-aret.**

**-arrow,** arrow, barrow, farrow, harrow, Harrow, marrow, narrow, Pharaoh, sparrow, taro, tarot, yarrow; bone marrow, handbarrow, house sparrow, song sparrow, straight arrow, tree sparrow, wheelbarrow;

straight and narrow. See also **-aro.**

**-arry** (-är-), charry, lari, sari, scarry, sparry, starry, tarry; curare, safari, scalare, shikari, tamari; aracari, calamari, Carbonari, hari-kari, Kalahari, Mata Hari. See also **-orry.**

**-arry** (-ar-), Barry, Carrie, carry, chary, Gary, gharry, harry, Harry, Larry, marry, parry, Shari, tarry; glengarry, miscarry; cash-and-carry, hari-kari, intermarry.

**-arry** (-âr-). See **-ary.**

**-arsal.** See **-arcel.**

**-arshal.** See **-artial.**

**-arsley,** parsley, sparsely.

**-arson,** arson, Carson, parson.

**-artan.** See **-arten.**

**-arte.** See **-arty.**

**-arten,** Barton, carton, hearten, marten, martin, Martin, smarten, Spartan, tartan; dishearten, freemartin, house martin; kindergarten, purple martin.

**-arter,** barter, carter, charter, darter, garter, martyr, starter, tartar; dumb barter, kick starter, nonstarter, self-starter, snail darter, upstarter.

**-artful,** artful, cartful.

**-artial,** marshal, Marshall, martial, partial; court martial, field marshal, grand marshal, immartial, impartial, sky marshal.

**-artin.** See **-arten.**

**-artist,** artist, Chartist, smartest; con artist; body artist, Bonapartist, escape artist, martial artist, trapeze artist, sidewalk artist.

**-artly,** partly, smartly, tartly.

**-arton.** See **-arten.**

**-artridge,** cartridge, partridge.

**-arture.** See **-archer.**

**-arty,** arty, hearty, party, smarty, tarty; Astarte, block party, ex parte, Havarti, hen party, house party, press party, search party, stag party, tea party, third party, war party; arty-farty, cocktail party, garden party, major party, minor party, slumber party, spoiler party, surprise party; commedia dell'arte.

**-artyr.** See **-arter.**

**-arval.** See **-arvel.**

**-arvel,** carvel, larval, marvel.

**-arving,** carving, starving.

**-ary,** aerie, airy, chary, clary, dairy, eyrie, fairy, glairy, glary, hairy, Mary, nary, prairie, scary, vary, wary; canary, contrary, costmary, Hail Mary, hegari, library, nondairy, primary, rosemary, tooth fairy, unchary, unwary, vagary; actuary, adversary, airy-fairy, ancillary, antiquary, apiary, arbitrary, aviary, axillary, bestiary, biliary, Bloody Mary, breviary, budgetary, capillary, cassowary, cautionary, centenary, commentary, commissary, corollary, coronary, culinary, customary, dictionary, dietary, dignitary, dromedary, dysentery, emissary, estuary, February, formulary, fragmentary, functionary, funerary, honorary, Janissary, January, lamasery, lapidary, lectionary, legendary, legionary, literary, luminary, maxillary, mercenary, military, millenary, millinery, missionary, momentary, monastery, monetary, mortuary, necessary, ordinary, ossuary, passionary, pigmentary, planetary, prebendary, presbytery, pulmonary, quaternary, reliquary, salivary, salutary, sanctuary, sanguinary, sanitary, scapulary, secondary, secretary, sedentary, seminary, solitary, stationary, stationery, statuary, sublunary, sumptuary, temporary, tertiary, Tipperary, titulary, topiary, tributary, tumulary, tutelary, unitary, urinary, vestiary, visionary, voluntary, vulnerary; ablutionary, accustomary, additionary, adminculary, apothecary, confectionery, constabulary, contemporary, contributary, deflationary, depositary, disciplinary, discretionary, diversionary, epistolary, exclusionary, extraordinary, fiduciary, hereditary, imaginary, incendiary, inflationary, insanitary, involuntary, itinerary, judiciary, obituary, pecuniary, pituitary, precautionary, preliminary, probationary, proprietary, provisionary, reactionary, residuary, revisionary, subsidiary, tercentenary, ubiquitary, unnecessary, unsanitary, veterinary, vocabulary, voluptuary; accidentiary, beneficiary, eleemosynary, evidentiary, evolutionary, extraordinary, intermediary, interplanetary, paramilitary, penitentiary, quatercentenary, revolutionary, supernumerary. See also **-erry.**

**-aryan.** See **-arion.**

**-asal,** basal, basil, hazel, nasal, phrasal; appraisal, witch hazel.

**-ascal,** mascle, paschal, rascal.

**-ascar.** See **-asker.**

**-ascence,** nascence; complacence, complaisance, obeisance, renascence.

**-ascent.** See **-acent.**

**-asement,** basement, casement, placement; abasement, debasement, defacement, displacement, effacement, embracement, emplacement, encasement, enlacement, erasement, misplacement, outplacement, replacement, retracement, subbasement; bargain-basement, interlacement.

**-aser.** See **-azer.**

**-asey.** See **-acy.**

**-asher,** Asher, basher, clasher, crasher, dasher, flasher, hasher, masher, rasher, slasher, smasher, splasher, thrasher; gatecrasher; atom smasher, haberdasher.

**-ashion.** See **-assion.**

**-ashy** (-a-), ashy, flashy, mashie, mashy, plashy, slashy, splashy, trashy.

**-ashy** (-o-). See **-oshy.**

**-asian.** See **-asion.**

**-asion,** Asian, suasion; abrasion, Caucasian, dissuasion, equation, erasion, Eurasian, evasion, invasion, occasion, persuasion, pervasion; Amerasian, Australasian, dermabrasion, Rabelaisian, tax evasion.

**-asis** (-ā-), basis, crasis, glacis, phasis, stasis; cash basis, oasis; homeostasis.

**-asive,** suasive; abrasive, assuasive, corrasive, dissuasive, evasive, invasive, persuasive, pervasive; noninvasive.

**-asker,** asker, basker, lascar, masker; Madagascar.

**-asket,** basket, casket, flasket, gasket; breadbasket, clothesbasket, handbasket, wastebasket.

**-ason.** See **-asten.**

**-aspar.** See **-asper.**

**-asper,** asper, Caspar, jasper, Jasper.

Also: **-asp** + **-er** (as in *clasper,* etc.)

**-assal.** See **-astle.**

**-assel.** See **-astle.**

**-asses,** molasses.

Also: **-ass** + **-es** (as in *classes,* etc.)

**-asset,** asset, basset, brasset, facet, tacet, tacit.

**-assic,** classic; boracic, Jurassic, potassic, sebacic, thallassic, thoracic, Triassic; neoclassic.

**-assie.** See **-assy.**

**-assion,** ashen, fashion, passion, ration; Circassian, compassion, dispassion, high fashion, impassion, refashion.

**-assive,** massive, passive; impassive.

**-assle.** See **-astle.**

**-assock,** cassock, hassock.

**-assy,** brassie, brassy, chassis, classy, dassie, gassy, glassy, grassy, lassie, massy, sassy; morassy; Malagasy, Tallahassee; Haile Selassie.

**-astard,** bastard, castored, dastard, mastered, plastered.

**-asten** (-ā-), basin, caisson, chasten, hasten, Jason, mason, Mason, sasin; Freemason, Great Basin, stonemason, washbasin.

**-asten** (-a-), fasten; assassin, unfasten.

**-aster** (-ā-), baster, chaster, haster, paster, taster, waster.

**-aster** (-a-), aster, Astor, blaster, caster, castor, faster, gaster, master, pastor, plaster, raster, vaster; bandmaster, brewmaster, broadcaster, cadastre, court plaster, disaster, dockmaster, drill master, grand master, headmaster, newscaster, old master, past master, paymaster, piaster, pilaster, postmaster, remaster, ringmaster, sandblaster, schoolmaster, scoutmaster, shinplaster, shipmaster, sportscaster, spymaster, surf caster, taskmaster, toastmaster, webcaster; alabaster, burgomaster, cablecaster, choirmaster, concertmaster, criticaster, ghetto blaster, harbormaster, medicaster, mustard plaster, oleaster, overmaster, poetaster, quartermaster, stationmaster, sticking plaster, telecaster, weathercaster, Zoroaster.

**-astered.** See **-astard.**

**-astic,** clastic, drastic, mastic, nastic, plastic, spastic; bombastic, dichastic, dynastic, elastic, emplastic, fantastic, gymnastic, monastic, sarcastic, scholastic, stochastic; anaclastic, antiphrastic, chiliastic, holophrastic, inelastic, metaphrastic, onomastic, orgiastic, paraphrastic, periphrastic, pleonastic, protoplastic, pyroclastic, scholiastic, thermoplastic; ecclesiastic, encomiastic, enthusiastic, iconoclastic.

**-asting,** typecasting; everlasting.

Also: **-ast** + **-ing** (as in *fasting,* etc.)

**-astle,** castle, facile, gracile, hassle, Kassel, passel, tassel, vassal, wassail, wrastle; forecastle, Newcastle.

**-astly,** ghastly, lastly, vastly; steadfastly.

**-astor.** See **-aster.**

**-astored.** See **-astard.**

**-asty** (-as-), blasty, nasty, vasty; contrasty; alloplasty, arthroplasty, epinasty, gastroplasty, pederasty, rhinoplasty; angioplasty, blepharoplasty.

**-asty** (-ās-), hasty, pasty, tasty.

**-asy.** See **-assy.**

**-ata** (-ātə), beta, data, eta, strata, theta, zeta; albata, dentata, errata, muleta, peseta, potato, pro rata, tomato; postulata, ultimata, vertebrata; invertebrata.

**-ata** (-ätə), data, kata, strata; balata, cantata, errata, fermata, frittata, pinata, regatta, sonata, toccata; caponata, serenata, terra cotta; inamorata; persona non grata.

**-atal,** datal, fatal, natal, ratel, shtetl, statal; nonfatal, postnatal, prenatal; antenatal, neonatal, perinatal.

**-atan,** Satan, straighten, straiten.

**-atant.** See **-atent.**

**-atcher,** catcher, matcher, patcher, scratcher, snatcher, stature, thatcher; back scratcher, detacher, dispatcher, dogcatcher, eye-catcher, flycatcher, head-scratcher, ratcatcher; body snatcher, train dispatcher.

**-atchet,** hatchet, latchet, ratchet.

**-atchman,** Scotchman, watchman.

**-atchment,** catchment, hatchment, ratchment; attachment, detachment, dispatchment.

**-ateau,** bateau, château, plateau. See also **-ato** (-ä-).

**-atent,** blatant, latent, natant, patent, statent.

**-ater** (-ô-), daughter, slaughter, tauter, water; backwater, bathwater, bilge water, black water, branch water, breakwater, cold-water, cutwater, dead water, deepwater, dishwater, first water, floodwater, forequarter, freshwater, goddaughter, granddaughter, groundwater, headwater, high-water, hindquarter, hot water, ice water, jerkwater, low water, manslaughter, rainwater, rose water, saltwater, seawater, springwater, stepdaughter, still water, tap water, tidewater, tread water, wastewater, white-water; bottled water, firewater, holy water, mineral water, quinine water, seltzer water, soda water, sparkling water, toilet water, underwater, vichy water.

**-ater** (-ā-). See **-ator.**

**-ather** (-a*th*-), blather, Cather, gather, lather, Mather, rather, slather; forgather.

**-ather** (-o*th*-). See **-other.**

**-athos,** Athos, bathos, pathos.

**-ati** (-ä-), basmati, chapati, coati, gelati, karate, metate, Scarlatti; digerati, glitterati, literati.

**-atial.** See **-acial.**

**-atian.** See **-ation.**

**-atic,** attic, Attic, phatic, static, vatic; agnatic, aquatic, astatic, asthmatic, chromatic, climatic, Dalmatic, dogmatic, dramatic, ecbatic, ecstatic, emphatic, erratic, eustatic, fanatic, hepatic, judgmatic, lymphatic, magmatic, phlegmatic, piratic, pneumatic, pragmatic, prismatic, prostatic, quadratic, rheumatic, schematic, schismatic, sciatic, Socratic, somatic, stigmatic, thematic, traumatic; achromatic, acrobatic, Adriatic, aerostatic, aplanatic, aromatic, Asiatic, astigmatic, autocratic, automatic, bureaucratic, charismatic, cinematic, democratic, dichromatic, diplomatic, eleatic, emblematic, enigmatic, Hanseatic, hieratic, Hippocratic, hydrostatic, mathematic, metastatic, morganatic, numismatic, operatic, pancreatic, photostatic, plutocratic, problematic, programmatic, symptomatic, systematic, technocratic, theocratic, thermostatic; anagrammatic, aristocratic, asymptomatic, axiomatic, diagrammatic, electrostatic, epigrammatic, homeostatic, idiocratic, idiomatic, melodramatic, meritocratic, monochromatic, overdramatic, paradigmatic, physiocratic, psychosomatic, undiplomatic; idiosyncratic.

**-atim,** verbatim; literatim, seriatim. See also **-atum.**

**-atin,** gratin, Latin, matin, patin, platen, satin, statin; Manhattan, Powhatan. See also **-atten.**

**-ation,** Asian, Haitian, nation, ration, station, Thracian; ablation, aeration, Alsatian, carnation, castration, causation, cessation, cetacean, citation, Claymation, collation, conflation, C ration, creation, cremation, crenation, Croatian, crustacean, Dalmatian, damnation, deflation, dictation, dilation, donation, duration, elation, equation, filtration, fixation, flirtation, flotation, formation, foundation, frustration, gas station, gestation, gradation, gyration, hortation, hydration, inflation, K ration, lactation, laudation, lavation, legation, libation, location, migration, mutation, narration, negation, notation, nugation, oblation, oration, ovation, plantation, predation, privation, probation, prostration, pulsation, quotation, relation, rogation, rotation, salvation, sedation, sensation, serration, space station, stagflation, stagnation, starvation, striation, substation, summation, tarnation, taxation, temptation, translation, truncation, vacation, venation, vexation, vibration, vocation, way station, workstation; abdication, aberration, abjuration, abnegation, abrogation, acceptation, acclamation, accusation, activation, actuation, adaptation, adjuration, admiration, adoration, adulation, adumbration, aerostation, affectation, affirmation, aggravation, aggregation, agitation, allegation, allocation, alteration, altercation, alternation, Amerasian, amputation, angulation, animation, annexation, annotation, appellation, application, approbation, arbitration, arrogation, aspiration, assignation, attestation, augmentation, automation, aviation, avocation, bifurcation, blaxploitation, blood relation, calcination, calculation, calibration, cancellation, captivation, carbonation, castigation, celebration, chlorination, circulation, cogitation, collocation, coloration, combination, comfort station, commendation, commutation, compensation, compilation, complication, computation, concentration, condemnation, condensation, confirmation, confiscation, conflagration, conformation, confrontation, confutation, congregation, conjugation, conjuration, connotation, consecration, conservation, consolation, constellation, consternation, constipation, consultation, consummation, contemplation, conversation, convocation, copulation, coronation, corporation, correlation, corrugation, coruscation, crenellation, culmination, cultivation, cumulation, cybernation, debarkation, decimation, declamation, declaration, declination, decoration, dedication, defalcation, defamation, defecation, defloration, deformation, degradation, dehydration, delectation, delegation, demarcation, demonstration, denigration, denotation, denudation, depilation, deportation, depravation, deprecation, depredation, deprivation, deputation, derivation, derogation, desecration, desiccation, designation, desolation, desperation, destination, detestation, detonation, devastation, deviation, dislocation, dispensation, disputation, dissertation, dissipation, distillation, divination, domination, duplication, education, elevation, elongation, emanation, embarkation, embrocation, emendation, emigration, emulation, enervation, equitation, eructation, estimation, estivation, evocation, exaltation, excavation, excitation, exclamation, exculpation, execration, exhalation, exhortation, exhumation, expectation, expiation, expiration, explanation, explication, exploitation, exploration, exportation, expurgation, extirpation, exultation, fabrication, fascination, federation, fenestration, fermentation, fibrillation, figuration, filling station, fire station, flagellation, fluctuation, fluoridation, fomentation, forestation, formulation, fornication, fragmentation, fulmination, fumigation, generation, germination, glaciation, grade inflation, graduation, granulation, gravitation, habitation, heat prostration, hesitation, hibernation, hyphenation, ideation, illustration, imitation, immigration, immolation, implantation, implication, importation, imprecation, impregnation, imputation, incantation, incarnation, incitation, inclination, incrustation, incubation, inculcation, indentation, indication, indignation, infestation, infiltration, inflammation, information, inhalation, innovation, inspiration, installation, instigation, instillation, insulation, integration, intimation, intonation, inundation, invitation, invocation, irrigation, irritation, isolation, iteration, jubilation, laceration, lamentation, lamination, legislation, levitation, liberation, limitation, liquidation, litigation, lubrication, lucubration, maceration, machination, malformation, malversation, mastication, masturbation, maturation, mediation, medication, meditation, melioration, menstruation, mensuration, ministration, mistranslation, mitigation, moderation, modulation, molestation, motivation, mutilation, navigation, nomination, numeration, obfuscation, objurgation, obligation, obscuration, observation, obviation, occupation, operation, orchestration, ordination, oscillation, osculation, ostentation, ovulation, oxidation, pagination, palpitation, penetration, percolation, perforation, permeation, permutation, peroration, perpetration, perspiration, perturbation, pigmentation, pixilation, police station, pollination, population, postulation, power station, predication, preparation, presentation, preservation, proclamation, procreation, procuration, profanation, profligation, prolongation, promulgation, propagation, protestation, provocation, publication, punctuation, radiation, recitation, reclamation, recreation, re-creation, reformation, refutation, registration, regulation, rehydration, relaxation, relocation, remonstration, renovation, reparation, replication, reputation, reservation, resignation, respiration, restoration, retardation, revelation, revocation, ruination, rumination, rustication, salutation, sanitation, saturation, scintillation, segmentation, segregation, separation, sequestration, service station, sexploitation, simulation, situation, speculation, spoliation, stimulation, stipulation, strangulation, stylization, subjugation, sublimation, subornation, suffocation, supplication, suppuration, suspiration, syncopation, syndication, tabulation, termination, titillation, toleration, transformation, transmigration, transplantation, transportation, trepidation, tribulation, triplication, ulceration, undulation, urination, usurpation, vaccination, vacillation, validation, valuation, variation, vegetation, veneration, ventilation, vindication, violation, visitation, vitiation, weather station; abbreviation, abomination, acceleration, accentuation, accommodation, accreditation, acculturation, accumulation, adjudication, administration, adulteration, affiliation, agglomeration, agglutination, alienation, alleviation, alliteration, amalgamation, amelioration, amortization, amplification, anglicization, annihilation, annunciation, anticipation, appreciation, appropriation, approximation, argumentation, articulation, asphyxiation, assassination, asseveration, assimilation, association, atomization, attenuation, authentication, authorization, Balkanization, bastardization, beautification, bowdlerization, brutalization, calcification, calumniation, canonization, capitulation, carbonization, catechization, centralization, certification, civilization, clarification, classification, coagulation, codification, coeducation, cohabitation, collaboration, colonization, colorization, columniation, commemoration, commensuration, commiseration, communication, concatenation, conciliation, confederation, configuration, conglomeration, congratulation, consideration, consolidation, contamination, continuation, cooperation, coordination, corroboration, crystallization, debilitation, decapitation, deceleration, defenestration, defibrillation, deforestation, defragmentation, degeneration, deification, deliberation, delimitation, delineation, demonization, denomination, denunciation, depopulation, depreciation, deregulation, desalination, desegregation, despoliation, determination, devaluation, digitization, dignification, dilapidation, disapprobation, discoloration, discrimination, disfiguration, disinclination, disinformation, disintegration, Disneyfication, dissemination, disseveration, dissimulation, dissociation, documentation, domestication, dramatization, echolocation, edification, effectuation, ejaculation, elaboration, elimination, elucidation, emaciation, emancipation, emasculation, embarkation, enumeration, enunciation, equalization, equilibration, equivocation, eradication, evacuation, evaluation, evaporation, evisceration, exacerbation, exaggeration, examination, exasperation, excoriation, exhilaration, exoneration, expatiation, expectoration, expostulation, expropriation, extenuation, extermination, extrapolation, facilitation, falsification, felicitation, feminization, fertilization, finalization, formalization, fortification, fossilization, galvanization, gentrification, gesticulation, glorification, gratification, habilitation, habituation, hallucination, harmonization, Hellenization, humanization, humiliation, hypothecation, idealization, idolization, illumination, imagination, immoderation, immunization, impersonation, implementation, improvisation, inauguration, incarceration, incineration, incorporation, incrimination, indoctrination, inebriation, infatuation, initiation, inoculation, insemination, insinuation, instrumentation, internalization, interpolation, interpretation, interrogation, intimidation, intoxication, invalidation, investigation, irradiation, itemization, justification, legalization, legitimation, liberalization, magnetization, magnification, manifestation, manipulation, matriculation, maximization, mechanization, melioration, memorization, miscalculation, miscegenation, misinformation, mobilization, modernization, modification, mollification, monetization, moralization, mortification, multiplication, mystification, nasalization, naturalization, negotiation, normalization, notification, novelization, nullification, obliteration, organization, orientation, origination, ornamentation, ossification, oxygenation, pacification, participation, pasteurization, perambulation, peregrination, perpetuation, petrification, polarization, pontification, precipitation, predestination, predomination, prefabrication, premeditation, preoccupation, preregistration, prettification, prevarication, privatization, procrastination, prognostication, proliferation, pronunciation, propitiation, protuberation, purification, qualification, ramification, randomization, ratification, realization, reciprocation, recombination, recommendation, recrimination, rectification, recuperation, redecoration, rededication, reduplication, reforestation, reformulation, refrigeration, regeneration, regimentation, regurgitation, reification, reincarnation, reiteration, rejuvenation, remuneration, renunciation, repatriation, representation, repudiation, resuscitation, retaliation, reverberation, sanctification, scarification, sedimentation, Serbo-Croatian, signification, simplification, socialization, solemnization, solicitation, sophistication, specialization, specification, stabilization, standardization, sterilization, stratification, subordination, supplementation, symbolization, synchronization, systemization, tergiversation, transfiguration, transliteration, triangulation, unification, unionization, urbanization, variegation, verification, versification, victimization, vilification, vituperation, vivification, vocalization, vociferation, vulgarization, westernization; amelioration, beatification, characterization, circumnavigation, commercialization, contraindication, criminalization, cross-examination, decentralization, declassification, decontamination, dehumanization, demonetization, demystification, deterioration, differentiation, disassociation, discontinuation, disorganization, disorientation, disqualification, diversification, electrification, excommunication, exemplification, experimentation, extemporization, generalization, homogenization, hospitalization, hyperventilation, idealization, identification, inconsideration, indemnification, individuation, institutionalization, insubordination, intensification, intermediation, italicization, militarization, misappropriation, miscommunication, misinterpretation, mispronunciation, misrepresentation, nationalization, naturalization, nonproliferation, overcompensation, overpopulation, personification, popularization, predetermination, prestidigitation, ratiocination, rationalization, recapitulation, reconciliation, reconsideration, rehabilitation, reinterpretation, reorganization, revitalization, secularization, solidification, spiritualization, superannuation, supererogation, tintinnabulation, transubstantiation, underestimation, undervaluation, visualization.

**-atius.** See **-acious.**

**-ative,** dative, native, stative; creative, dilative, nonnative; aggregative, cogitative, connotative, contemplative, cumulative, decorative, denotative, designative, emulative, estimative, explicative, facultative, federative, generative, germinative, hesitative, imitative, implicative, innovative, instigative, integrative, irritative, iterative, legislative, meditative, nuncupative, operative, predicative, procreative, propagative, qualitative, quantitative, radiative, regulative, replicative, speculative, terminative, vegetative, violative; administrative, appreciative, associative, authoritative, collaborative, commemorative, communicative, continuative, cooperative, corroborative, degenerative, deliberative, determinative, discriminative, exonerative, illuminative, interpretative, investigative, manipulative, multiplicative, obliterative, premeditative, recuperative, regenerative, remunerative, vituperative.

**-atling.** See **-attling.**

**-atly,** fatly, flatly, patly, rattly.

**-ato** (-ā-), Cato, jato, NATO, Plato; potato, tomato; couch potato, hot potato, plum tomato, sweet potato.

**-ato** (-ä-), dato, pato; annatto, castrato, fugato, gelato, legato, marcato, mulatto, rabato, rubato, sfumato, spiccato, staccato, tomato, vibrato; agitato, animato, arigato, moderato, obbligato, ostinato, pizzicato; inamorato. See also **-otto.**

**-ator** (-ā-), cater, crater, freighter, gaiter, gator, grater, greater, later, mater, pater, satyr, stator, tater, traitor, waiter; cunctator, Decatur, dumbwaiter, equator, first-rater, spectator, testator, theater, third-rater; alligator, alma mater, alternator, applicator, calculator, calibrator, carburetor, commentator, conservator, cultivator, detonator, elevator, escalator, generator, incubator, indicator, numerator, percolator, radiator, respirator, second-rater, separator, simulator, tabulator; accelerator, denominator, incinerator, perambulator, refrigerator.

Also: **-ate** + **-er** or **-or** (as in *hater, cultivator, impersonator, procrastinator,* etc.)

**-atron,** matron, natron, patron, waitron.

**-atten,** baton, batten, fatten, flatten, latten, paten, patten, platen, ratten. See also **-atin.**

**-atter** (-a-), attar, batter, blatter, chatter, clatter, fatter, flatter, hatter, latter, matter, natter, patter, platter, ratter, satyr, scatter, shatter, smatter, spatter, splatter, tatter, yatter; back matter, backscatter, bescatter, bespatter, dark matter, front matter, gray matter, Mad Hatter, standpatter, wildcatter; antimatter, foul matter, pitter-patter, printed matter, subject matter.

**-atter** (-o-). See **-otter.**

**-attern,** pattern, Saturn, slattern.

**-attle** (-a-), battle, brattle, cattle, chattel, prattle, rattle, tattle; death rattle, embattle, pitched battle, Seattle; line of battle, tittle-tattle.

**-attle** (-o-). See **-ottle.**

**-attler,** battler, prattler, rattler, Statler, tattler.

**-attling,** battling, fatling, gatling, rattling, spratling, tattling.

**-atto.** See **-ato.**

**-atty,** batty, bratty, chatty, fatty, gnatty, Hattie, matty, natty, patty, ratty, scatty, tatty; Cincinnati.

**-atum,** datum, stratum; adstratum, erratum, pomatum, substratum, verbatim; literatim, seriatim, ultimatum; desideratum. See also **-atim.**

**-ature** (-ā-), nature; denature; call of nature, force of nature, human nature, legislature, Mother Nature, nomenclature, second nature.

**-ature** (-a-). See **-atcher.**

**-aturn.** See **-attern.**

**-aty,** eighty, Haiti, Katie, matey, platy, praty, slaty, weighty.

**-atyr.** See **-atter.**

**-audal.** See **-awdle.**

**-audit,** audit, plaudit.

**-audy.** See **-awdy.**

**-auger** (-ā-). See **-ager.**

**-augher** (-af-). See **-affer.**

**-aughter** (-af-). See **-after.**

**-aughter** (-ô-). See **-ater.**

**-aughty,** haughty, naughty, zloty.

**-aulic,** aulic; hydraulic; interaulic.

**-aulter.** See **-alter.**

**-aulty.** See **-alty.**

**-aunder,** launder, maunder.

**-aunter,** flaunter, gaunter, haunter, jaunter, saunter, taunter, vaunter.

**-auntie.** See **-anty.**

**-auphin.** See **-often.**

**-aural.** See **-oral.**

**-aurel.** See **-oral.**

**-aurus.** See **-orous.**

**-auseous.** See **-autious.**

**-austral,** austral, claustral, costrel.

**-aution,** caution; incaution, precaution.

**-autious,** cautious, nauseous; incautious, precautious.

**-ava,** brava, clava, fava, guava, java, Java, kava, lava; cassava, ottava; balaclava, lavalava.

**-avage,** lavage, ravage, savage, scavage.

**-avel,** cavil, gavel, gravel, ravel, travail, travel; unravel.

**-avelin,** javelin, ravelin.

**-aveling,** knaveling, shaveling.

**-avely,** bravely, gravely, knavely, slavely, suavely.

**-avement,** lavement, pavement; depravement, engravement, enslavement.

**-aven,** craven, graven, haven, maven, raven, shaven;

clean-shaven, engraven, New Haven, safe haven; riboflavin.

**-aver** (-a-), slaver; cadaver, palaver.

**-aver** (-ā-), braver, craver, favor, flavor, graver, haver, laver, paver, quaver, raver, saver, savor, shaver, slaver, waiver, waver; disfavor, engraver, enslaver, face-saver, flag-waver, lifesaver, screensaver, timesaver; demiquaver, hemiquaver, semiquaver; hemi-demisemiquaver.

**-avern,** cavern, klavern, tavern.

**-avid,** avid, gravid, pavid; impavid.

**-avior,** pavior, savior, Xavier; behavior; misbehavior.

**-avis,** Davis, mavis; rara avis.

**-avish** (-ā-), bravish, knavish, slavish.

**-avish** (-a-), lavish, ravish; en-ravish, MacTavish.

**-avo,** bravo; centavo, octavo.

**-avor.** See **-aver.**

**-avy,** cavy, Davy, gravy, navy, slavey, wavy; peccavi.

**-awdle,** caudal, caudle, dawdle.

**-awdry,** Audrey, bawdry, tawdry.

**-awdy,** bawdy, dawdy, gaudy; cum laude.

**-awful,** awful, lawful, offal; unlawful.

**-awning,** awning, dawning, fawning, spawning, yawn-ing.

**-awny,** brawny, fawny, lawny, Pawnee, scrawny, Shawnee, tawny, yawny; mulli-gatawny.

**-awyer,** foyer, lawyer, sawyer; topsawyer.

**-axen,** flaxen, Jackson, klaxon, Saxon, waxen; Anglo-Saxon.

**-axi.** See **-axy.**

**-axon.** See **-axen.**

**-axy,** flaxy, maxi, taxi, waxy; air taxi, galaxy; ataraxy, Cotopaxi.

**-aybe.** See **-aby.**

**-ayday,** heyday, Mayday, pay-day, playday.

**-ayer,** layer, mayor, payer, prayer; conveyor, cro-cheter, obeyer, purveyor, soothsayer, surveyor.

Also: **-ay** + **-er** (as in *player,* etc.)

**-ayey,** clayey, hayey, wheyey.

**-aylay,** Malay, melee, waylay; ukulele.

**-ayling.** See **-ailing.**

**-ayman,** Bremen, caiman, Damon, drayman, flamen, Haman, layman, Lehman, shaman, stamen; examen, foramen, gravamen, highwayman.

**-ayment,** ament, claimant, clamant, payment, raiment; co-payment, defrayment, displayment, down payment, nonpayment, prepayment, repayment, stop payment; overpayment, underpayment.

**-ayo,** kayo, Mayo.

**-aza,** Gaza, plaza; piazza; calabaza; tabula rasa.

**-azard,** hazard, mazzard; haphazard; biohazard.

**-azel.** See **-asal.**

**-azen.** See **-azon.**

**-azer,** blazer, brazer, gazer, glazer, grazer, hazer, laser, maser, phaser, praiser, razor; appraiser, fundraiser, hair-raiser, hell-raiser, stargazer, trailblazer; crystal-gazer, paraphraser.

**-azier,** brazier, glazier, grazier, rasure; embrasure.

**-azon,** blazon, brazen, glazen, raisin; emblazon; diapason.

**-azy,** crazy, daisy, hazy, lazy, Maisie, mazy; half-crazy, stir-crazy; upsy-daisy.

**-azzle,** basil, dazzle, frazzle, razzle; bedazzle; razzle-dazzle.

**-ea,** kea, Leah, Mia, rhea, rya, via, zea; Althea, buddleia, cattleya, chorea, Crimea, dyspnea, idea, Judea, kaffiyeh, Korea, mantilla, Maria, Medea, obeah, rupiah, sangria, Shi'ah, Sofia, spirea, tortilla; barathea, Caesarea, Cytherea, dahabeah, diarrhea, dulcinea, Eritrea, gonorrhea, hamartia, Latakia, logorrhea, panacea, pizzeria, pyorrhea, ratafia, Santería, seborrhea, sinfonia, Tanzania, trattoria; amenorrhea, Andalucia, Arimathea, bougainvillea, Cassiopeia, cavalleria, echeveria, pharmacopoeia; onomatopoeia.

**-eaboard,** freeboard, keyboard, leeboard, preboard, reboard, seaboard.

**-eacher,** beacher, bleacher, breacher, breecher, creature, feature, leacher, peacher, preacher, reacher, screecher, teacher; beseecher, impeacher, school teacher; double feature, student teacher.

**-eachment,** preachment; impeachment.

**-eachy,** beachy, beechy, leachy, litchi, Nietzsche, peachy, preachy, screechy; caliche, Campeche.

**-eacon,** beacon, deacon, sleeken, weaken; archdeacon, Mohican, subdeacon; Neorican, Puerto Rican.

**-eaden,** deaden, leaden, redden, threaden; Armageddon.

**-eading.** See **-edding.**

**-eadle** (-ē-). See **-eedle.**

**-eadle** (-e-). See **-eddle.**

**-eadlock,** deadlock, headlock, wedlock.

**-eadly,** deadly, medley, redly.

**-eady.** See **-eedy.**

**-eafer.** See **-ephyr.**

**-eager,** eager, leaguer, meager; beleaguer, big-leaguer, bush leaguer, intriguer; Ivy Leaguer, Little Leaguer, major-leaguer, minor-leaguer, overeager.

**-eah.** See **-ea.**

**-eaken.** See **-eacon.**

**-eaker.** See **-aker.**

**-eakly,** bleakly, chicly, meekly, sleekly, treacly, weakly, weekly; biweekly, newsweekly, obliquely, uniquely; semiweekly.

**-ealment,** concealment, congealment, repealment, revealment.

**-ealot.** See **-ellate.**

**-ealous,** Hellas, jealous, trellis, zealous; apellous, entellus, Marcellus, nucellus, ocellus, procellous, vitellus.

**-ealy.** See **-eely.**

**-eamer,** creamer, dreamer, emir, femur, lemur, reamer, schemer, screamer, steamer, streamer, teamer, teemer; blasphemer, daydreamer, redeemer.

**-eamish,** beamish, squeamish.

**-eamster,** deemster, seamster, teamster.

**-ean,** aeon, eon, Ian, lien, paean, peon; Achaean, Aegean, Andean, astrean, Augean, Chaldean, Chilean, Crimean, Judean, Korean, Lethean, nymphean, pampean, plebian, protean; amoebean, amphigean, apogean,

Caribbean, empyrean, European, Galilean, Herculean, Jacobean, Maccabean, Manichaean, Mycenaean, Odyssean, perigean, Sisyphean, Tennessean; adamantean, antipodean, epicurean, Pythagorean, terpsichorean, Thucydidean.

**-eaner,** cleaner, gleaner, greener, keener, leaner, meaner, preener, screener, teener, tweener, weaner, wiener; convener, demeanor, dry cleaner, fourteener, machiner, pipe cleaner, street cleaner; carabiner, misdemeanor, submariner, vacuum cleaner.

**-eaning,** gleaning, greening, keening, meaning; demeaning, dry cleaning, housecleaning, spring-cleaning, well-meaning; double meaning, overweening.

Also: **-ean** + **-ing** (as in *cleaning,* etc.)

Also: **-een** + **-ing** (as in *preening,* etc.)

Also: **-ene** + **-ing** (as in *intervening,* etc.)

Also: **-ine** + **-ing** (as in *machining,* etc.)

**-eanly,** cleanly, keenly, leanly, meanly, queenly; obscenely, pristinely, routinely, serenely, uncleanly.

**-eanor.** See **-eaner.**

**-eany.** See **-eeny.**

**-eapen.** See **-eepen.**

**-eaper.** See **-eeper.**

**-earage.** See **-eerage.**

**-earance,** clearance; adherence, appearance, arrearance, coherence, inherence; disappearance, incoherence, interference, perseverance, reappearance.

**-earful,** cheerful, earful, fearful, sneerful, tearful.

**-earing** (-ēr-), Bering, earring; God-fearing, sheepshearing; cannoneering, domineering, fictioneering, hard-of-hearing, power steering; orienteering; bioengineering, civil engineering, reverse engineering, social engineering.

Also: **-ear** + **-ing** (as in *clearing,* etc.)

Also: **-eer** + **-ing** (as in *engineering,* etc.)

Also: **-ere** + **-ing** (as in *adhering,* etc.)

**-earing** (-âr-). See **-aring.**

**-earish.** See **-arish.**

**-early** (-ēr-). See **-erely.**

**-early** (-ûr-). See **-urly.**

**-earner,** burner, earner, learner, spurner, turner, yearner; back burner, barnburner, front burner, page turner, sojourner, wage earner.

**-earnest,** earnest, Ernest, sternest; internist.

**-earning,** burning, churning, earning, learning, spurning, turning, yearning; concerning, discerning, returning.

**-earsal.** See **-ersal.**

**-earten.** See **-arten.**

**-eartener.** See **-artner.**

**-eartlet.** See **-artlet.**

**-earty.** See **-arty.**

**-eary,** aerie, beery, bleary, cheery, dearie, dreary, eerie, Erie, jeery, leery, peri, query, smeary, sneery, sphery, teary, veery, weary; aweary, Lake Erie, Valkyrie, world-weary; hara-kiri, miserere, whigmaleerie.

**-easant** (-ez-), peasant, pheasant, pleasant, present; unpleasant; omnipresent.

**-easants.** See **-esence.**

**-easel,** Diesel, easel, measle, teasel, weasel.

**-easer** (-ēz-), Caesar, easer, freezer, friezer, geezer, pleaser, seizer, sneezer, squeezer, teaser, tweezer, wheezer; appeaser, brainteaser, crowd-pleaser, misfeasor, stripteaser; Ebenezer.

**-easer** (-ēs-), creaser, fleecer, greaser, leaser, piecer; degreaser, increaser, releaser, two-piecer.

**-easing** (-ēz-), breezing, easing, freezing, pleasing, sneezing, squeezing, teasing, wheezing; appeasing, displeasing, unpleasing.

**-easing** (-ēs-), fleecing; increasing, policing, subleasing, surceasing, unceasing.

**-eason,** reason, season, seizin, treason; high treason, in season, off-season, post season, pure reason, unreason; Age of Reason, open season, out of season, rhymreason.

**-easoned,** reasoned, seasoned, treasoned, weasand; unseasoned.

**-easter,** Dniester, Easter, feaster, keister, leister, quaestor; down-easter, northeaster, southeaster; cotoneaster.

**-easting,** bee-sting, easting, feasting.

**-eastly,** beastly, priestly, Priestly.

**-easure** (-e-), leisure, measure, pleasure, treasure; admeasure, displeasure, dry measure, entreasure, outmeasure, tape measure; countermeasure, liquid measure; made-to-measure.

**-easy** (-ē si), creasy, fleecy, greasy, specie.

**-easy** (-ē zi), breezy, cheesy, easy, freezy, greasy, queasy, sleazy, sneezy, wheezy; pachisi, Parcheesi, speakeasy, uneasy, Zambezi; free and easy.

**-eaten,** beaten, Cretan, cretin, eaten, Eton, heaten, neaten, sweeten, wheaten; browbeaten, moth-eaten, storm-beaten, unbeaten, worm-eaten; overeaten, weather-beaten.

**-eater** (-ē-), beater, bleater, cheater, eater, fetor, greeter, heater, liter, meter, neater, Peter, praetor, rhetor, seater, sheeter, skeeter, sweeter, teeter, treater, tweeter; ammeter, anteater, beefeater, Demeter, competer, defeater, depleter, drumbeater, eggbeater, flowmeter, gas meter, goldbeater, light meter, long meter, Main Streeter, man-eater, ohmmeter, quartz heater, repeater, retreater, saltpeter, smoke-eater, space heater, toadeater, voltmeter, Wall Streeter, worldbeater; altimeter, centiliter, centimeter, deciliter, decimeter, dekaliter, dekameter, fire-eater, honey eater, kilometer, lotus-eater, microliter, milliliter, millimeter, nanometer, overeater, parking meter, postage meter, taximeter, trick-or-treater, water heater, water meter.

**-eater** (-ā-). See **-ator.**

**-eather** (-ē-), breather, either, neither, seether, sheather, teether, wreather.

**-eather** (-e-), blether, feather, heather, leather, nether, tether, weather, wether, whether; all-weather, aweather, bellwether, fair-weather, flight feather, glove leather, pinfeather, sea feather, sea leather, together, wash-leather, white leather; altogether, get-together, hell-for-leather, parrot's feather, patent leather, pebble leather, prince's feather, Russia leather, saddle leather, tar and feather.

**-eathing,** breathing, seething, sheathing, teething, wreathing; air-breathing, bequeathing; fire-breathing.

**-eatly.** See **-etely.**

**-eaty,** gleety, meaty, peaty, sleety, sweetie, sweety, titi, treaty, ziti; entreaty, graffiti, scratchiti, Tahiti; spermaceti.

**-eauty.** See **-ooty.**

**-eaven.** See **-even.**

**-eaver,** beaver, cleaver, fever, griever, heaver, keever, leaver, lever, reaver, reiver, weaver, weever; achiever, believer, conceiver, deceiver, enfever, hay fever, receiver, reliever, retriever, spring fever, transceiver; cantilever, cabin fever, disbeliever, eager beaver, jungle fever, nonbeliever, scarlet fever, true believer, unbeliever, wide receiver, yellow fever; golden retriever, overachiever, superachiever, underachiever.

**-eavy.** See **-evy.**

**-eazy.** See **-easy.**

**-ebble,** djebel, pebble, rebel, treble.

**-ebel.** See **-ebble.**

**-eber.** See **-abor.**

**-eble.** See **-ebble.**

**-ebo,** gazebo, placebo.

**-ebtor.** See **-etter.**

**-ecant,** piquant, precant, secant; cosecant; intersecant.

**-ecca,** Mecca; Rebecca.

**-ecco.** See **-echo.**

**-ecent** (-ē-), decent, puissant, recent; indecent, obeisant.

**-echer.** See **-etcher.**

**-echo,** echo, gecko, secco; art deco, El Greco, re-echo.

**-ecian.** See **-etion.**

**-ecious,** specious; capricious, facetious.

**-ecis.** See **-acy.**

**-ecker,** checker, chequer, decker, pecker, trekker,

wrecker; exchequer, fact-checker, henpecker, housewrecker, Quebecer, spell checker, spot-checker, woodpecker; double-decker, flowerpecker, rubbernecker, triple-decker.

**-eckle,** deckle, freckle, heckle, keckle, Seckel, shekel, speckle; bespeckle; Dr. Jekyll.

**-eckless,** feckless, fleckless, necklace, reckless, speckless.

**-ecko.** See **-echo.**

**-eckon,** beckon, reckon, schnecken, zechin; Aztecan, dead reckon.

**-eco.** See **-echo.**

**-econd,** beckoned, fecund, reckoned, second; split-second; millisecond, nanosecond.

**-ectant,** expectant, humectant, infectant, injectant, protectant; disinfectant.

**-ectar.** See **-ector.**

**-ecter.** See **-ector.**

**-ectful,** neglectful, respectful; disrespectful.

**-ectic,** hectic, pectic; cachectic, cathectic, eclectic, synectic; analectic, anorectic, apoplectic, catalectic, dialectic.

**-ectile,** rectal, sectile; erectile, insectile, projectile; colorectal, dialectal.

**-ection,** flection, lection, section; abjection, advection, affection, bisection, collection, complexion, confection, connection, convection, correction, cross section, C-section, defection, deflection, dejection, detection, direction, dissection, ejection, election, erection, infection, inflection, injection, inspection, midsection, objection, perfection, projection, protection, refection, reflection, rejection, selection, subjection, subsection, trajection, trisection; by-election, circumspection, conic section, disaffection, disconnection, disinfection, fuel injection, genuflection, imperfection, indirection, insurrection, interjection, intersection, introjection, introspection, misdirection, predilection, preselection, recollection, reconnection, redirection, re-election, reinfection, resurrection, retroflexion, retrospection, self-direction, self-protection, self-reflection, self-selection, stage direction, venesection, vivisection; antirejection, equal protection, general election, house of correction, hypercorrection, interconnection.

**-ective,** adjective, advective, affective, collective, connective, convective, corrective, defective, deflective, detective, directive, effective, ejective, elective, erective, infective, inflective, injective, invective, neglective, objective, perfective, perspective, projective, prospective, protective, reflective, rejective, respective, selective, subjective; cost-effective, house detective, imperfective, ineffective, introspective, irrespective, nonobjective, retrospective, self-reflective.

**-ectly,** abjectly, correctly, directly, erectly; circumspectly, incorrectly, indirectly.

**-ector,** flector, hector, Hector, lector, nectar, rector, sector, specter, vector; bisector, collector, connector, convector, corrector, defector, deflector, detector, director, dissector, effector, ejecter, elector, erector, infector, injecter, inspector, neglecter, objector, perfecter, projector, prospector, protector, reflector, selector, subsector; lie detector, smoke detector, stage director.

**-ecture,** lecture; confecture, conjecture, prefecture, projecture; architecture.

**-ecund.** See **-econd.**

**-edal** (-e-). See **-eddle.**

**-edal** (-ē-). See **-eedle.**

**-edden.** See **-eaden.**

**-edding,** bedding, dreading, heading, leading, redding, shedding, shredding, sledding, spreading, threading, wedding; beheading, bobsledding, farmsteading, homesteading, subheading; featherbedding, shotgun wedding.

**-eddle,** heddle, medal, meddle, pedal, peddle, reddle,

treadle; back-pedal, soft-pedal; intermeddle, service medal.

**-eddler,** meddler, medlar, peddler, pedlar, treadler.

**-eddy,** bready, Eddie, eddy, Freddy, heady, leady, ready, steady, teddy, Teddy, thready; already, make-ready, rock steady, unready, unsteady; cable-ready, camera-ready, gingerbready, rough-and-ready.

**-edence,** credence; impedance, precedence; antecedence, intercedence.

**-edent,** credent, needn't, sedent; decedent, precedent, succedent; antecedent, intercedent.

**-edger,** dredger, edger, hedger, ledger, pledger, sledger; alleger, stock ledger.

**-edic,** Vedic; comedic; cyclopedic, orthopedic; encyclopedic.

**-edit,** credit, edit; accredit, discredit, miscredit, noncredit; reedit, copyedit, line of credit.

**-edlar.** See **-eddler.**

**-edo,** credo, Ido, Lido, speedo; aikido, albedo, libido, teredo, toledo, Toledo, torpedo, tuxedo, uredo.

**-eecher.** See **-eacher.**

**-eecy.** See **-easy.**

**-eedful,** deedful, heedful, needful; unheedful.

**-eedle,** beadle, creedal, daedal, needle, tweedle, wheedle; darning needle, knitting kneedle, sewing needle.

**-eedling,** needling, reedling, seedling, tweedling, wheedling.

**-eedy,** beady, greedy, heedy, needy, reedy, seedy, speedy, tweedy, weedy; indeedy.

**-eefy,** beefy, leafy, reefy.

**-eekly.** See **-eakly.**

**-eely,** dele, eely, Ely, freely, Greeley, mealy, peely, really, seely, squealy, steely, stele, wheelie; genteelly, scungilli, surreally, Swahili; campanile, touchy-feely.

**-eeman,** demon, freeman, leman, seaman, semen; eudemon, Philemon; cacodemon, Lacedaemon, merchant seaman.

**-eemly.** See **-emely.**

**-eenly.** See **-eanly.**

**-eeny,** beanie, genie, greeny, meanie, queenie, spleeny, Sweeney, teeny, weenie; Alcmene, Athene, Bellini, bikini, Bikini, Cabrini, Cellini, cremini, crostini, Houdini, linguine, martini, Mycenae, porcini, Puccini, rapini, Rossini, tahini, tankini, wahini, zucchini; capellini, fantoccini, fettuccine, Hippocrene, kundalini, Mussolini, nota bene, rollatini, scaloppine, spaghettini, string bikini, teeny-weeny, Tetrazzini, tortellini.

**-eepen,** cheapen, deepen, steepen.

**-eeper,** beeper, cheaper, cheeper, creeper, deeper, Dnieper, keeper, leaper, peeper, reaper, sleeper, steeper, sweeper, weeper; barkeeper, beekeeper, bookkeeper, doorkeeper, gamekeeper, gatekeeper, goalkeeper, Grim Reaper, groundskeeper, housekeeper, innkeeper, minesweeper, peacekeeper, scorekeeper, shopkeeper, spring peeper, stockkeeper, storekeeper, timekeeper, zookeeper; carpet sweeper, chimney sweeper, honeycreeper, hotelkeeper.

**-eeple.** See **-eople.**

**-eeply,** cheaply, deeply.
Also: **-eep + -ly** (as in *steeply,* etc.)

**-eepsie.** See **-ypsy.**

**-eepy,** cheapie, creepy, seepy, sleepy, tepee, weepy.

**-eerage,** clearage, peerage, pierage, steerage; arrearage.

**-eerful.** See **-earful.**

**-eerly.** See **-erely.**

**-eery.** See **-eary.**

**-eesi.** See **-easy.**

**-eesy.** See **-easy.**

**-eeten.** See **-eaten.**

**-eeter.** See **-eater.**

**-eether.** See **-eather.**

**-eetle,** beetle, betel, fetal; decretal, excretal.

**-eetly.** See **-etely.**

**-eety.** See **-eaty.**

**-eever.** See **-eaver.**

**-eevish,** peevish, thievish.

**-eezer.** See **-easer.**

**-eezing.** See **-easing.**

**-eezy.** See **-easy.**

**-egal,** beagle, eagle, legal, regal; bald eagle, illegal, porbeagle, spread-eagle, vice-regal; extralegal, legal eagle, paralegal.

**-eggar,** beggar, egger, kegger; bootlegger, Heidegger.

**-eggy,** dreggy, eggy, leggy, Peggy; Carnegie.

**-egian.** See **-egion.**

**-egion,** legion, region; collegian, Glaswegian, Norwegian; bioregion, foreign legion.

**-egious.** See **-igious.**

**-egnant,** pregnant, regnant; impregnant, queen regnant.

**-egress,** egress, regress.

**-eifer.** See **-ephyr.**

**-eighbor.** See **-abor.**

**-einty.** See **-ainty.**

**-einy.** See **-ainy.**

**-eisance.** See **-ascence.**

**-eist,** deist, theist; monotheist, polytheist.

**-eisure.** See **-easure.**

**-eiter.** See **-itter.**

**-either** (-ī-). See **-ither.**

**-either** (-ē-). See **-eather.**

**-eiver.** See **-eaver.**

**-ekyll.** See **-eckle.**

**-elate,** helot, pellet, prelate, stellate, zealot; appellate.

**-elder,** elder, gelder, melder, welder.

**-elding,** gelding, melding, welding.

**-eldom,** beldam, seldom.

**-ele.** See **-alely.**

**-elee.** See **-aylay.**

**-elfish,** elfish, pelfish, selfish, shellfish, swellfish; unselfish.

**-elic,** bellic, melic, relic, telic; angelic, nickelic, scalpellic; archangelic, evangelic, infidelic, philatelic, psychedelic.

**-eline,** beeline, feline.

**-elion,** Pelion; anthelion, aphelion, Aurelian, carnelian, chameleon, Mendelian, parhelion; perihelion.

**-elix,** Felix, helix; alpha helix, double helix.

**-ella,** Bella, cella, Ella, fella, stella, Stella; brucella, canella, capella, favella, flagella, flavela, glabella, lamella, Louella, marcella, novella, paella, patella, prunella, quinella, rosella, rubella, shigella, umbrella, vanilla; a capella, Cinderella, citronella, fustanella, Isabella, mortadella, mozzarella, panetella, Pulcinella, salmonella, tarantella, varicella, villanella.

**-ellar.** See **-eller.**

**-ellas.** See **-ealous.**

**-ellen.** See **-elon.**

**-eller,** cellar, dweller, feller, heller, meller, seller, smeller, speller, stellar, teller, yeller; bestseller, bookseller, cave dweller, cliff dweller, dispeller, expeller, foreteller, glabellar, impeller, indweller, lamellar, patellar, propeller, rathskeller, rebeller, repeller, saltcellar; cerebellar, fortune-teller, interstellar, Rockefeller, show-and-teller, storyteller.

**-ellet.** See **-elate.**

**-elli.** See **-elly.**

**-ellish,** hellish, relish; embellish.

**-ello,** bellow, cello, felloe, fellow, hello, Jell-O, mellow, yellow; bargello, bedfellow, bordello, duello, good fellow, hail-fellow, Longfellow, marshmallow, morello, niello, Othello, playfellow, sgabello, yokefellow; brocatello, Donatello, lemon yellow, Monticello, Pirandello, portobello, punchinello, ritornello, saltarello; violoncello.

**-ellous.** See **-ealous.**

**-ellow.** See **-ello.**

**-ellum,** vellum; castellum, flabellum, flagellum, labellum, rostellum, scutellum; antebellum, cerebellum.

**-ellus.** See **-ealous.**

**-elly,** belly, Delhi, deli, felly, jelly, Kelly, Nellie, Shelley, shelly, smelly, telly, wellie; beer belly, cancelli, comb jelly, New Delhi, nice nelly, pork belly, potbelly, rakehelly; Botticelli, casus belli, Delhi belly, Donatelli, nervous Nellie, royal jelly, underbelly, vermicelli; Machiavelli.

**-elon,** Ellen, felon, Helen, melon; castellan, Magellan, muskmelon; watermelon.

**-elop,** develop, envelop; overdevelop; underdevelop.

**-elot.** See **-ellate.**

**-elter,** belter, felter, kelter, melter, pelter, shelter, skelter, smelter, spelter, swelter, welter; bomb shelter, tax shelter; air-raid shelter, helter-skelter.

**-elving,** delving, helving, shelving.

**-eman.** See **-eeman.**

**-ember,** ember, member; cardmember, December, dismember, November, remember, September; charter member, congressmember, councilmember, disremember, misremember.

**-emble,** semble, tremble; assemble, dissemble, resemble; reassemble.

**-embly,** trembly; assembly.

**-emely,** seemly; extremely, supremely, unseemly.

**-emer.** See **-eamer.**

**-emic** (-em-), chemic, demic, hemic; alchemic, endemic, pandemic, polemic, racemic, systemic, totemic; academic, diastemic, epidemic, epistemic, theoremic.

**-emic** (-ē-), emic, femic, hemic, mnemic; anemic, glossemic, glycemic, graphemic, ischemic, morphemic, phonemic, racemic, taxemic, toxemic; epistemic, septicemic; hyperglycemic, hypoglycemic.

**-emish,** blemish, Flemish.

**-emlin,** gremlin, Kremlin.

**-emma,** Emma, gemma; dilemma, maremma.

**-emner.** See **-emor.**

**-emon.** See **-eeman.**

**-emor,** emmer, hemmer, tremor; condemner, contemner.

**-emplar,** Templar; exemplar, Knight Templar.

**-empter,** tempter; attempter, exempter, preemptor.

**-emption,** ademption, coemption, diremption, exemption, pre-emption, redemption.

**-emur.** See **-eamer.**

**-ena.** See **-ina.**

**-enace.** See **-ennis.**

**-enal,** penal, renal, venal; adrenal, machinal; duodenal.

**-enant,** pennant, tenant; joint tenant, lieutenant, subtenant.

**-enate.** See **-ennet.**

**-encer.** See **-enser.**

**-encher,** bencher, blencher, censure, clencher, denture, quencher, trencher, venture, wencher; adventure, backbencher, debenture, indenture, joint venture; bonaventure, misadventure, peradventure.

**-enchman,** Frenchman, henchman.

**-encil,** mensal, pencel, pencil, pensil, pensile, stencil, tensile; blue-pencil, commensal, extensile, grease pencil, lead pencil, prehensile, red-pencil, utensil.

**-enda,** Brenda, Zenda; addenda, agenda, credenda; corrigenda, hacienda.

**-endance.** See **-endence.**

**-endant.** See **-endent.**

**-endence,** tendance; ascendance, attendance, dependence, resplendence, transcendence; condescendence, independence; interdependence.

**-endent,** pendant, pendent, splendent; appendant, ascendant, attendant, contendent, defendant, dependent, descendant, descendent, impendent, intendant, resplendent, transcendent, transplendent; codependent, flight attendant, independent; interdependent, overdependent, superintendent.

**-ender,** bender, blender, fender, gender, lender, mender, render, sender, slender, spender, splendor, tender, vendor; amender, ascender, attender, bartender, contender, defender, descender, emender, engender, extender, fork-tender, goaltender, hellbender, mindbender, offender, pretender, rear-ender, surrender, suspender, transgender, weekender; bitterender, double-ender, elbow-bender, fender-bender, first offender, gender bender, legal tender, moneylender, pastry blender, youth offender.

**-ending,** ending, pending; fence-mending, heartrending, mind-bending, nerve ending, unbending, unending; gender-bending.

Also: **-end** + **-ing** (as in *ascending,* etc.)

**-endor.** See **-ender.**

**-endous,** horrendous, stupendous, tremendous.

**-endum,** addendum, agendum, credendum, pudendum; corrigendum, referendum.

**-enely.** See **-eanly.**

**-enet.** See **-ennet.**

**-engthen,** lengthen, strengthen.

**-enial,** genial, menial, venial; congenial.

**-enic** (-e-), fennec, genic, phrenic, splenic; arsenic, asthenic, Edenic, eugenic, Hellenic, hygienic, irenic, transgenic; allergenic, allogenic, calisthenic, cryogenic, hygienic, mutagenic, neurasthenic, Panhellenic, pathogenic, photogenic, psychogenic, schizophrenic, telegenic; carcinogenic; hallucinogenic, hypoallergenic.

**-enic** (-ē-), scenic, splenic; Hellenic, hygienic, irenic; Panhellenic.

**-enie.** See **-ainy.**

**-enim.** See **-enum.**

**-enin.** See **-enon.**

**-enish,** plenish, Rhenish, wennish; replenish.

**-enna,** henna, senna; antenna, duenna, Gehenna, Ravenna, Siena, sienna, Vienna.

**-ennant.** See **-enant.**

**-ennel,** crenel, fennel, kennel; antennal.

**-enner.** See **-enor.**

**-ennet,** Bennett, genet, jennet, rennet, senate, sennet, sennit, tenet.

**-ennis,** Dennis, menace, tenace, tennis, Venice.

**-enny,** any, benne, Benny, blenny, Denny, fenny, jenny, Jenny, Kenny, Lenny, many, penni, penny, wenny; catchpenny, eelblenny, Kilkenny, pinchpenny, rock blenny, sixpenny, tenpenny, threepenny, truepenny, twopenny; nota bene, spinning jenny.

**-eno,** beano, chino, fino, keno, leno, Pinot, Reno, vino, Zeno; bambino, casino, cioppino, Ladino, Latino, merino, neutrino, pepino, sordino; andantino, Angeleno, cappuccino, concertino, Filipino, maraschino, palomino.

**-enom.** See **-enum.**

**-enon,** Lenin, pennon, rennin, tenon.

**-enor,** penner, tenner, tenor; countertenor, heldentenor.

**-enser,** censer, censor, denser, fencer, spencer, Spencer, Spenser, tensor; commencer, condenser, dispenser, extensor, intenser, sequencer.

**-ensil.** See **-encil.**

**-ensile.** See **-encil.**

**-ension.** See **-ention.**

**-ensive,** pensive, tensive; ascensive, defensive, distensive, expensive, extensive, intensive, offensive, ostensive, protensive, suspensive; apprehensive, coextensive, comprehensive, hypertensive, hypotensive, indefensive, inexpensive, inoffensive, reprehensive; counteroffensive, incomprehensive, labor-intensive.

**-ensor.** See **-enser.**

**-enta,** yenta; magenta, placenta, polenta; impedimenta.

**-ental,** cental, dental, dentil, gentle, lentil, mental, rental; fragmental, judgmental, parental, pigmental, placental, segmental, tridental; accidental, alimental, compartmental, complemental, complimental, continental, departmental, detrimental, elemental, fundamental, governmental, incidental, incremental, instrumental, ligamental, monumental, nonjudgmental, occidental, oriental, ornamental, regimental, rudimental, sacramental, sentimental, supplemental, temperamental, testamental, transcendental; coincidental, developmental, environmental, experimental, impedimental, labiodental, temperamental, transcontinental; intercontinental; interdepartmental.

**-entance,** sentence; repentance; unrepentance.

**-entence.** See **-entance.**

**-enter,** center, enter, mentor, renter, tenter, venter; assenter, commenter, consenter, dead center, dissenter, fermenter, fomenter, frequenter, inventor, lamenter, off-center, precentor, presenter, preventer, re-enter, repenter, tormentor; epicenter, front and center, ornamenter, shopping center; experimenter.

**-entful,** eventful, repentful, resentful; uneventful.

**-ential,** agential, credential, essential, potential, prudential, sciential, sentential, sequential, tangential, torrential; confidential, consequential, deferential, differential, evidential, existential, exponential, inessential, inferential, influential, nonessential, penitential, pestilential, precedential, preferential, presidential, providential, quintessential, referential, residential, reverential, unessential; circumferential, equipotential, experiential, inconsequential.

**-entic,** lentic; argentic, authentic, identic.

**-entil.** See **-ental.**

**-entile,** gentile; percentile.

**-entin,** dentin, Lenten, Trenton; San Quentin.

**-enting,** denting, renting, scenting, tenting, venting; absenting, accenting, assenting, augmenting, cementing, consenting, dissenting, fermenting, fomenting, frequenting, lamenting, presenting, preventing, relenting, resenting, tormenting; circumventing, complimenting, ornamenting, representing, supplementing; misrepresenting.

**-ention,** gentian, mention, pension, tension; abstention, ascension, attention, contention, convention, declension, detention, dimension, dissension, distention, extension, high-tension, indention, intention, invention, pretension, prevention, propension, recension, retention, subvention, suspension, sustention; apprehension, circumvention, comprehension, condescension, contravention, fourth dimension, hypertension, inattention, intervention, reinvention, reprehension, surface tension, third dimension; hyperextension, incomprehension, misapprehension, nonintervention, overextension.

**-entious,** abstentious, contentious, dissentious,

licentious, pretentious, sententious, silentious, tendentious; conscientious, pestilentious, unpretentious.

**-entist,** dentist, prenticed; Adventist, apprenticed, preventist; irredentist.

**-entive,** adventive, assentive, attentive, incentive, inventive, presentive, preventive, retentive; disincentive, inattentive.

**-entle.** See **-ental.**

**-entment,** contentment, presentment, relentment, resentment; discontentment.

**-ento,** cento, lento; memento, pimento; pentimento, Sacramento; divertimento.

**-entor** (-ôr-), centaur, mentor, stentor; succentor.

**-entor** (-ər-). See **-enter.**

**-entous,** apprentice, momentous, portentous; compos mentis, filamentous; non compos mentis; in loco parentis.

**-entric,** centric; acentric, concentric, eccentric; Afrocentric, androcentric, biocentric, egocentric, ethnocentric, Eurocentric, geocentric; anthropocentric, heliocentric.

**-entry,** entry, gentry, sentry; reentry, subentry; alimentary, complementary, complimentary, double entry, elementary, port of entry, rudimentary, testamentary.

**-enture.** See **-encher.**

**-enty,** plenty, scenty, twenty; al dente, aplenty, lisente; cognoscenti, twenty-twenty; Deo Volente; Agua Caliente, dolce far niente.

**-enu,** menu, venue.

**-enum,** denim, frenum, plenum, venom.

**-eny.** See **-ainy.**

**-enza,** cadenza, credenza; influenza.

**-eo,** Cleo, guyot, Leo, Rio, trio; bolillo, caudillo, con brio, radio, stereo; monacillo, tomatillo.

**-eomen.** See **-omen.**

**-eon,** aeon, Creon, eon, Freon Leon, neon, peon, pheon, pleon, prion; nucleon, pantheon; Anacreon.

**-eopard,** jeopard, leopard, peppered, shepherd.

**-eople,** people, pipal, steeple; boat people, Plain People, street people, townspeople, unpeople; chosen people, little people.

**-epee.** See **-eepy.**

**-epherd.** See **-eopard.**

**-ephyr,** deafer, feoffor, heifer, zephyr; hasenpfeffer.

**-epid,** tepid, trepid; intrepid.

**-epper,** leper, pepper, schlepper, stepper; bell pepper, black pepper, green pepper, hot pepper, high-stepper, sweet pepper, white pepper; chili pepper, salt-and-pepper.

**-epsy,** catalepsy, epilepsy, narcolepsy.

**-eptic,** peptic, septic, skeptic; aseptic, dyspeptic, eupeptic; antiseptic, cataleptic, epileptic, narcoleptic.

**-era,** era, gerah, Hera, lira, Vera; chimera, hetaera, lempira, Madeira, mbira; Common Era, Halmahera.

**-erance.** See **-earance.**

**-ercer.** See **-urser.**

**-ercion.** See **-ertion.**

**-erder.** See **-urder.**

**-erdure.** See **-erger.**

**-erely,** cheerly, clearly, dearly, merely, nearly, queerly, sheerly, yearly; austerely, severely, sincerely; cavalierly, insincerely.

**-erence.** See **-earance.**

**-ergeant.** See **-argent.**

**-ergence,** convergence, divergence, emergence, resurgence, submergence.

**-ergent,** turgent, urgent, vergent; abstergent, assurgent, convergent, detergent, divergent, emergent, insurgent, resurgent.

**-erger,** merger, perjure, purger, scourger, splurger, urger, verdure, verger; converger, diverger, emerger, submerger.

**-ergy.** See **-urgy.**

**-eri.** See **-erry.**

**-eric,** cleric, Derek, derrick, Eric, ferric, Herrick, spheric, steric; chimeric, choleric, dineric, enteric, generic, Homeric, hysteric, icteric, mesmeric, numeric, valeric; atmospheric, chromospheric, climacteric, congeneric, esoteric, exoteric, hemispheric, isomeric, isosteric, neoteric, peripheric, phylacteric, stratospheric.

**-eries,** Ceres, dearies, queries, series, wearies.

**-eril,** beryl, Cheryl, feral, ferrule, ferule, Merrill, Meryl, peril, sterile. See also **-erule.**

**-erile.** See **-eril.**

**-erish,** cherish, perish.

**-erit,** ferret, merit; demerit, inherit; disinherit.

**-erjure.** See **-erger.**

**-erker.** See **-irker.**

**-erkin,** firkin, gherkin, jerkin, Perkin.

**-erky,** jerky, murky, perky, quirky, smirky, turkey.

**-erling.** See **-urling.**

**-erly.** See **-urly.**

**-ermal,** dermal, thermal; geothermal, isothermal.

**-erman,** Berman, Burman, ermine, firman, German, Herman, merman, sermon, Sherman, Thurman, vermin; determine, Mount Hermon; predetermine.

**-erment,** ferment; affirmant, averment, conferment, deferment, determent, interment, preferment, referment; disinterment.

**-ermes,** Burmese, Hermes, kermes.

**-ermine.** See **-erman.**

**-ermy,** fermi, germy, Nurmi, squirmy, wormy; diathermy, taxidermy.

**-ernal,** colonel, journal, kernel, sternal, urnal, vernal; cavernal, diurnal, eternal, external, fraternal, hibernal, infernal, internal, maternal, nocturnal, paternal, supernal; co-eternal, sempiternal.

**-ernest.** See **-earnest.**

**-erning.** See **-earning.**

**-ernist.** See **-earnest.**

**-ero** (-ē-), gyro, hero, Nero, zero; ground zero, subzero; antihero, superhero.

**-ero** (-â-). See **-aro.**

**-errand,** errand, gerund.

**-errant,** errant; aberrant, knight-errant.

**-errick.** See **-eric.**

**-errier,** burier, merrier, terrier.

**-erring,** derring, erring, herring.

**-erry,** berry, bury, cherry, Derry, ferry, Jerry, kerry, Kerry, merry, perry, Perry, sherry, skerry, terry, Terry, very, wherry; Bambury, barberry, bayberry, bilberry, Bing cherry, blackberry, blueberry, chokeberry, cloudberry, cranberry, equerry, gooseberry, Juneberry, knobkerrie, mulberry, raspberry, strawberry, wheat berry; beriberi, boysenberry, capillary, cemetery, chinaberry, culinary, elderberry, huckleberry, Janissary, lamasery, lingonberry, loganberry, mesentery, millinery, monastery, Pondicherry, presbytery, stationary, stationery. See also **-ary.**

**-ersal,** bursal, tercel, versal; dispersal, rehearsal, reversal, succursal, transversal; dress rehearsal, universal.

**-ersey,** furzy, jersey, Jersey, kersey; New Jersey.

**-ersian.** See **-ersion.**

**-ersion,** Persian, version; aspersion, aversion, conversion, discursion, dispersion, diversion, eversion, excursion, immersion, incursion, inversion, obversion, perversion, recursion, reversion, submersion, subversion; extroversion, introversion; animadversion, Authorized Version.

**-erson,** person, worsen; chairperson, craftsperson, draftsperson, first person, in person, layperson, night person, nonperson, salesperson, spokesperson, third person; anchorperson, businessperson, multiperson, second person.

**-ertain,** Burton, certain, curtain, Merton; uncertain.

**-erter,** blurter, curter, flirter, hurter, skirter, squirter, stertor; asserter, averter, converter, deserter, diverter, frankfurter, inserter, inverter, perverter, subverter.

**-ertie.** See **-irty.**

**-ertile.** See **-urtle.**

**-ertion,** tertian; assertion, Cistercian, coercion, desertion, exertion, insertion, lacertian; self-assertion.

**-ertive,** furtive; assertive, divertive, exertive, revertive.

**-ertly,** curtly, pertly; alertly, expertly, inertly, invertly, overtly; inexpertly.

**-erule,** ferule, ferrule, spherule. See also **-eril.**

**-ervant,** fervent, servant; bond servant, conservant, maidservant, manservant, observant, recurvant; civil servant, public servant, unobservant.

**-ervent.** See **-ervant.**

**-erver,** fervor, server, swerver; conserver, observer, preserver, reserver, time-server.

**-ervy.** See **-urvy.**

**-ery.** See **-erry.**

**-escence,** essence; candescence, concrescence, excresence, florescence, fluorescence, pubescence, putrescence, quiescence, quintessence, senescence, tumescence, turgescence; acquiescence, adolescence, coalescence, convalescence, deliquescence, detumescence, effervescence, efflorescence, evanescence, incandescence, inflorescence, iridescence, luminescence, obsolescence, opalescence, phosphorescence, recrudescence; preadolescence.

**-escent** (-es-), cessant, crescent, jessant; candescent, canescent, concrescent, decrescent, depressant, excrescent, fluorescent, ignescent, incessant, increscent, liquescent, pearlescent, pubescent, putrescent, quiescent, rubescent, senescent, suppressant, tumescent, turgescent; acquiescent, adolescent, coalescent, convalescent, deliquescent, detumescent, effervescent, efflorescent, evanescent, Fertile Crescent, incandescent, inflorescent, iridescent, luminescent, obsolescent, opalescent, phosphorescent, prepubescent, recrudescent; antidepressant, preadolescent.

**-escience,** nescience, prescience.

**-escue,** fescue, rescue; Montesquieu.

**-esence,** pleasance, presence; omnipresence.

Also: **-easant** + **-s** (as in *peasants,* etc.)

**-esent.** See **-easant.**

**-eshen.** See **-ession.**

**-esher,** flesher, fresher, pressure, thresher, tressure; air pressure, blood pressure, high-pressure, low-pressure, peer pressure, refresher.

**-eshly,** fleshly, freshly; specially; especially.

**-esian.** See **-esion.**

**-esion,** Frisian, lesion; adhesion, artesian, Cartesian, cohesion, Ephesian, etesian, Milesian, Parisian, Silesian, Teresian; Indonesian, Melanesian, Micronesian, Polynesian.

**-esis,** Croesus, rhesus, thesis; centesis, ecesis, kinesis, mimesis, paresis, phronesis, prosthesis, tmesis; anamnesis, anuresis, apheresis, catachresis, diuresis, enuresis, exegesis, kinesthesis; hyperkinesis, Peloponnesus, photokinesis, telekinesis; amniocentesis, aposiopesis.

**-essage,** message, presage; expressage.

**-essal.** See **-estle.**

**-essant.** See **-escent.**

**-essel.** See **-estle.**

**-essence.** See **-escence.**

**-esser.** See **-essor.**

**-essful,** stressful; distressful, successful; unsuccessful.

**-essie.** See **-essy.**

**-essing,** blessing, dressing, guessing, pressing.

Also: **-ess** + **-ing** (as in *depressing,* etc.)

Also: **-esce** + **-ing** (as in *convalescing,* etc.)

**-ession,** cession, freshen, Hessian, session; accession, aggression, bull session, compression, concession, confession, depression, digression, discretion, expression, impression, ingression, jam session, obsession, oppression, possession, precession, procession, profession, progression, recession, regression, repression, secession, succession, suppression, transgression; decompression, dispossession, indiscretion, intercession, prepossession, repossession, retrocession, retrogression, self-expression, self-possession, supersession.

**-essive,** crescive, essive; abessive, adessive, aggressive, caressive, compressive, concessive, degressive, depressive, digressive, excessive, expressive, impressive, ingressive, obsessive, oppressive, possessive, processive, progressive, recessive, regressive, repressive, successive, suppressive, transgressive; inexpressive, retrogressive; manic-depressive, passive-aggressive.

**-essor,** dresser, fresser, guesser, lesser, lessor, presser, stressor; addresser, aggressor, assessor, compressor, confessor, cross-dresser, depressor, duressor, hairdresser, oppressor, possessor, professor, successor, suppressor, transgressor; antecessor, intercessor, predecessor, second-guesser, tongue-depressor, vasopressor, window dresser.

**-essure.** See **-esher.**

**-essy,** Bessie, dressy, Jesse, Jessie, messy, Tessie.

**-esta,** cesta, cuesta, testa, Vesta; Avesta, celesta, fiesta, ingesta, podesta, siesta.

**-estal,** festal, vestal.

**-ester,** Chester, ester, Esther, fester, Hester, jester, Leicester, Lester, Nestor, pester, quaestor, tester, vester, wester, wrester, zester; ancestor, arrester, attester, Chichester, Colchester, contester, digester, Dorchester, Eastchester, investor, Manchester, molester, nor'wester, protester, requester, Rochester, semester, sequester, sou'wester, Sylvester, trimester, Westchester; beta tester, empty nester, polyester.

**-estial,** bestial; celestial, forestial.

**-estic,** gestic; agrestic, amnestic, domestic, majestic; anapestic, catachrestic.

**-estine,** destine; asbestine, clandestine, intestine, predestine.

**-estive,** festive, restive; arrestive, attestive, congestive, digestive, ingestive, suggestive, tempestive; decongestive.

**-estle,** Cecil, decile, nestle, pestle, sessile, trestle, vessel, wrestle.

**-esto,** pesto, presto; manifesto.

**-estral,** estral, kestrel; ancestral, campestral, fenestral, orchestral, semestral, trimestral.

**-esture,** gesture, vesture; divesture, investure.

**-esty,** chesty, cresty, pesty, resty, testy, Westie, zesty.

**-esus.** See **-esis.**

**-etal.** See **-ettle.**

**-etcher,** etcher, fetcher, fletcher, kvetcher, lecher, retcher, sketcher, stretcher.

**-etchy,** kvetchy, sketchy, stretchy, tetchy.

**-ete.** See **-etty.**

**-etely,** fleetly, meetly, neatly, sweetly; completely, concretely, discreetly, discretely, effetely; incompletely, indiscreetly, obsoletely.

**-eter.** See **-eater.**

**-ethel,** bethel, Bethel, Ethel, ethyl, methyl.

**-ether.** See **-eather.**

**-ethyl.** See **-ethel.**

**-etic,** etic, thetic; aesthetic, aphetic, ascetic, athletic, balletic, bathetic, cosmetic, docetic, eidetic, emetic, frenetic, gametic, genetic, hermetic, kinetic, magnetic, mimetic, noetic, Ossetic, paretic, pathetic, phenetic, phonetic, phrenetic, poetic, prophetic, prosthetic, pyretic, splenetic, syncretic, syndetic, synthetic, tonetic, Venetic; alphabetic, analgetic, anesthetic, antithetic, apathetic, arithmetic, copacetic, cybernetic, diabetic, dietetic, diuretic, empathetic, energetic, epenthetic, exegetic, geodetic, homiletic, hypothetic, Masoretic, parenthetic, sympathetic, synesthetic, theoretic; antimagnetic, antipathetic, antipyretic, apologetic, biogenetic, cyanogenetic, geomagnetic, hyperkinetic, pathogenetic, peripatetic, psychokinetic, telekinetic; electromagnetic, general anesthetic, parasympathetic, unapologetic; onomatopoetic.

**-etion** (-ē-), Grecian; accretion, completion, concretion, deletion, depletion, excretion, Phoenician, repletion, secretion, Tahitian; Polynesian.

**-etion** (-e-). See **-ession.**

**-etious.** See **-ecious.**

**-etish.** See **-ettish.**

**-eto,** keto, Tito, veto; bandito, bonito, burrito, coquito, finito, graffito, hornito, magneto, mosquito, Negrito, sgraffito, sofrito; Hirohito, incognito, pocket veto, sanbenito.

**-etor.** See **-etter.**

**-etter,** better, bettor, debtor, fetter, fretter, getter, letter, rhetor, setter, sweater, tetter, wetter, whetter; abettor, bedwetter, begetter, block letter, bonesetter, chain letter, dead letter, fan letter, forgetter, go-getter, jet-setter, newsletter, pacesetter, red-letter, trendsetter, typesetter, unfetter.

**-etti.** See **-etty.**

**-ettish,** fetish, Lettish, pettish, wettish; coquettish.

**-ettle,** fettle, Gretel, kettle, metal, mettle, nettle, petal, settle, shtetl; abettal, base metal, bimetal, death metal, gunmetal, hot metal, speed metal, teakettle, unsettle; heavy metal; Popocatapetl.

**-etto,** ghetto, petto, stretto; cavetto, falsetto, larghetto, libretto, palmetto, stiletto, terzetto, zuchetto; allegretto, amaretto, amoretto, fianchetto, lazaretto, Rigoletto, vaporetto; Tintoretto.

**-ettor.** See **-etter.**

**-etty** (-e-), Betty, fretty, Hetty, jetty, Lettie, netty, petit, petty, sweaty, yeti; cavetti, confetti, libretti, machete, Rossetti, spaghetti; Donizetti, Serengeti, spermaceti.

**-etty** (-i-). See **-itty.**

**-etus,** Cetus, fetus, Thetis, treatise; boletus, coitus, quietus; diabetes.

**-euced.** See **-ucid.**

**-eudal.** See **-oodle.**

**-eudo.** See **-udo.**

**-eum,** geum; lyceum, museum, no-see-um, odeum, per diem, Te Deum; athenaeum, coliseum, Colosseum, hypogeum, mausoleum, wax museum; peritoneum.

**-eura.** See **-ura.**

**-eural.** See **-ural.**

**-euter.** See **-ooter.**

**-eutic,** mutic; maieutic, scorbutic; hermeneutic, pharmaceutic, therapeutic.

**-eutist.** See **-utist.**

**-eval.** See **-evil.**

**-evel,** bevel, devil, kevel, level, Neville, revel; bedevil, daredevil, dishevel, dust devil, go-devil, heat devil, high-level, low-level, sea level, split-level, top-level; entry-level, printer's devil, spirit level, water level.

**-even** (-e-), Devon, Evan, heaven, Kevin, leaven, seven; eleven, replevin, thank heaven.

**-even** (-ē-), even, Stephen, Steven; break-even, uneven; even-steven, odeven.

**-ever** (-e-), clever, ever, lever, never, sever, Trevor; assever, dissever, endeavor, forever, however, whatever, whenever, wherever, whichever, whoever, whomever; cantilever, howsoever, whatsoever, whencesoever, whensoever, wheresoever, whichsoever, whomsoever, whosesoever, whosoever.

**-ever** (-ē-). See **-eaver.**

**-evil** (-ē-), evil, weevil; coeval, medieval, primeval, reprieval, retrieval, upheaval; medieval.

**-evil** (-e-). See **-evel.**

**-evious,** devious, previous.

**-evy,** bevy, Chevy, heavy, levee, levy; replevy, top-heavy.

**-ewal.** See **-uel.**

**-eward,** leeward, sewered, skewered, steward.

**-ewdest.** See **-udist.**

**-ewdish.** See **-udish.**

**-ewdly.** See **-udely.**

**-ewel.** See **-uel.**

**-ewer,** brewer, chewer, doer, ewer, fewer, hewer, sewer, shoer, skewer, spewer, suer, viewer, wooer; canoer, ear sewer, me-tooer, misdoer, pooh-pooher, previewer, pursuer, renewer, reviewer, shampooer, snowshoer, storm sewer, tatooer, wrongdoer; evildoer, interviewer, revenuer.

**-ewish,** blueish, Jewish, newish, shrewish; aguish.

**-ewly.** See **-uly.**

**-ewry.** See **-ury.**

**-ewsy.** See **-oozy.**

**-ewy,** blooey, bluey, buoy, chewy, cooee, Dewey, dewy, flooey, gluey, gooey, hooey, looie, Louie, Louis, phooey, screwy, sooey, viewy; andouille, chop suey, life buoy, mildewy; go kerflooey, ratatouille.

**-exas.** See **-exus.**

**-exer,** flexor, vexer; annexer, indexer, perplexer.

**-exile,** exile, flexile.
**-extant,** extant, sextant.
**-extile,** sextile, textile; bissextile.
**-exus,** lexis, nexus, plexus, Texas; Alexis, orexis; solar plexus.
**-exy,** prexy, sexy; apoplexy.
**-eyance,** abeyance, conveyance, purveyance, surveillance.
**-eyor.** See **-ayer.**
**-eyrie.** See **-ary.**
**-ezi.** See **-easy.**
**-ia.** See **-ea.**
**-iad,** dryad, dyad, naiad, Pleiad, triad; hamadryad, jeremiad.
**-ial,** dial, diel, phial, trial, vial, viol; decrial, denial, espial, mistrial, redial, retrial, sundial, supplial.
**-iam,** Priam, Siam; Omar Khayyam; carpe diem.
**-ian.** See **-ion.**
**-iance,** clients, giants, science; affiance, alliance, appliance, compliance, defiance, reliance, suppliance; mésalliance, misalliance, noncompliance, self-reliance.
**-iant,** client, giant, pliant, riant, scient; affiant, blue giant, compliant, defiant, red giant, reliant; significant, super giant.
**-iants.** See **-iance.**
**-iaper.** See **-iper.**
**-iar.** See **-ier.**
**-iary.** See **-iry.**
**-ias,** bias, dais, pious; bacchius, Elias, Tobias; Ananias, nisi prius.
**-iat.** See **-iet.**
**-ibal.** See **-ible.**
**-ibald.** See **-ibbled.**
**-ibber,** bibber, cribber, dibber, fibber, gibber, glibber, jibber, ribber, squibber; ad-libber, winebibber.
**-ibbet.** See **-ibit.**
**-ibble,** cribble, dibble, dribble, fribble, gribble, kibble, nibble, quibble, scribble, sibyl, Sybil, thribble; ish-kabibble.
**-ibbled,** dibbled, dribbled, kibbled, nibbled, piebald, quibbled, ribald, scribbled.
**-ibbling,** dibbling, dribbling, nibbling, quibbling, scribbling, sibling.
**-ibbly,** dribbly, fribbly, glibly, nibbly, quibbly, scribbly, tribbly.
**-ibbon,** gibbon, ribbon.

**-ibel.** See **-ible.**
**-iber,** briber, fiber, giber, liber, Tiber; ascriber, imbiber, inscriber, prescriber, subscriber, transcriber.
**-ibit,** gibbet, Tibbett, zibet; exhibit, inhibit, prohibit.
**-ible,** Bible, libel, pibal, scribal, tribal.
**-iblet,** driblet, giblet, riblet, triblet.
**-ibling.** See **-ibbling.**
**-ibyl.** See **-ibble.**
**-ica,** mica, Micah, pica, pika, plica, spica; Formica, lorica; balalaika.
**-icar.** See **-icker.**
**-icely.** See **-isely.**
**-icial,** altricial, auspicial, comitial, indicial, initial, judicial, official, solstitial, surficial; artificial, beneficial, interstitial, prejudicial, sacrificial, superficial, unofficial.
**-ician.** See **-ition.**
**-icient,** deficient, efficient, omniscient, proficient, sufficient; coefficient, cost-efficient, fuel-efficient, inefficient, insufficient, self-sufficient.
**-icious,** vicious; ambitious, auspicious, capricious, delicious, factitious, fictitious, flagitious, judicious, lubricious, malicious, Mauritius, nutritious, officious, pernicious, propitious, seditious, suspicious; adventitious, avaricious, expeditious, inauspicious, injudicious, meretricious, repetitious, superstitious, suppositious, surreptitious.
**-icken,** chicken, quicken, sicken, stricken, thicken, wicken; awestricken, grief-stricken, mock chicken, spring chicken; city chicken, conscience-stricken, panic-stricken, prairie chicken, terror-stricken.
**-icker,** bicker, clicker, dicker, flicker, kicker, knicker, licker, liquor, picker, quicker, shicker, sicker, slicker, snicker, thicker, ticker, vicar, wicker; bootlicker, brainpicker, drop-kicker, goldbricker, nitpicker, pigsticker, placekicker, potlicker, ragpicker, stock ticker; bumper sticker, cherry picker, city slicker, cotton picker.

**-icket,** clicket, cricket, picket, piquet, pricket, thicket, ticket, wicket; big-ticket, hot ticket, house cricket, meal ticket, split ticket.

**-ickle,** brickle, chicle, fickle, mickle, nickel, pickle, prickle, sickle, stickle, strickle, tickle, trickle; bicycle, icicle, tricycle, vehicle; pumpernickel.

**-ickly,** prickly, quickly, sickly, slickly, thickly, trickly.

**-ickset,** quickset, thickset.

**-ickshaw,** kickshaw, rickshaw.

**-icky,** dickey, Dicky, hickey, icky, kicky, Mickey, Nicky, picky, quickie, rickey, sickie, sticky, tricky, Vicki; doohickey, gin rickey.

**-icle.** See **-ickle.**

**-icon.** See **-iken.**

**-icter,** lictor, stricter, victor; afflicter, conflicter, constrictor, inflicter, predicter; contradicter; boa constrictor, vasoconstrictor.

**-iction,** diction, fiction, friction; addiction, affliction, confliction, constriction, conviction, depiction, eviction, indiction, infliction, nonfiction, prediction, reliction, restriction, transfixion; benediction, contradiction, crucifixion, dereliction, interdiction, jurisdiction, malediction, metafiction, science fiction, valediction.

**-ictive,** fictive; addictive, afflictive, conflictive, constrictive, inflictive, predictive, restrictive, vindictive; benedictive, contradictive, interdictive, jurisdictive, nonrestrictive.

**-ictor.** See **-icter.**

**-ictualler.** See **-ittler.**

**-icture,** picture, stricture; big picture, depicture.

**-icy,** dicey, icy, pricy, spicy.

**-idal,** bridal, bridle, idle, idol, idyll, seidel, sidle, tidal; ecocidal, fratricidal, fungicidal, genocidal, germicidal, herbicidal, homicidal, intertidal, matricidal, parricidal, patricidal, regicidal, spermicidal, suicidal; infanticidal, insecticidal, tyrannicidal.

**-idden,** bidden, chidden, hidden, midden, ridden, stridden; bedridden, forbidden, hagridden, unbidden;

kitchen midden, overridden.

**-iddle,** diddle, fiddle, griddle, middle, piddle, quiddle, riddle, tiddle, twiddle; bass fiddle, bull fiddle; flumadiddle, second fiddle, taradiddle.

**-iddling,** fiddling, kidling, middling, piddling, riddling, twiddling.

**-iddy,** biddy, giddy, kiddie, middy, midi, skiddy, stiddy.

**-iden,** guidon, Haydn, Leyden, widen; Poseidon.

**-ident,** bident, rident, strident, trident.

**-ider,** cider, eider, glider, guider, hider, rider, slider, spider, strider, stridor, wider; backslider, collider, confider, decider, divider, hang glider, hard cider, insider, joyrider, lowrider, night rider, outrider, outsider, provider, roughrider, Top-Sider; freedom rider, paraglider, supply-sider, water strider.

**-idget,** Bridget, digit, fidget, midget, widget.

**-idgy,** midgy, ridgy.

**-idle.** See **-idal.**

**-idly,** idly, widely.

**-idney,** kidney, Sidney.

**-ido.** See **-edo.**

**-idol.** See **-idal.**

**-idy,** Friday, Heidi, tidy; untidy; bona fide.

**-idyl.** See **-idal.**

**-iefly,** briefly, chiefly.

**-ience.** See **-iance.**

**-ient.** See **-iant.**

**-ients.** See **-iance.**

**-ier,** briar, buyer, drier, dyer, flier, friar, fryer, higher, liar, nigher, plier, prior, pryer, shyer, slyer, spryer, spyer, vier.

Also: **-y** + **-er** (as in *amplifier,* etc.). See also **-ire.**

**-iery.** See **-iry.**

**-iestly.** See **-eastly.**

**-iet,** diet, fiat, piet, quiet, riot, striate; disquiet, race riot.

**-ieval.** See **-evil.**

**-iever.** See **-eaver.**

**-ifer,** cipher, fifer, knifer, lifer, rifer; decipher, pro-lifer; right-to-lifer.

**-iffin,** biffin, griffin, griffon, stiffen.

**-iffle,** piffle, riffle, skiffle, sniffle, whiffle.

**-iffy,** cliffy, iffy, jiffy, miffy, sniffy, spiffy.

**-ific,** glyphic; aurific, deific, horrific, pacific, Pacific, pontific, prolific, salvific, somnific, specific, terrific, unific; beatific, calorific, colorific, conspecific, hieroglyphic, honorific, humorific, scientific, soporific, sudorific, tenebrific.

**-ifle,** Eiffel, eyeful, rifle, stifle, trifle.

**-ifling,** rifling, stifling, trifling.

**-ifter,** drifter, grifter, lifter, shifter, sifter, snifter, swifter; shoplifter, uplifter, weightlifter.

**-iftless,** driftless, shiftless, thriftless.

**-ifty,** drifty, fifty, nifty, rifty, shifty, thrifty; makeshifty; fifty-fifty.

**-igate.** See **-igot.**

**-iggard.** See **-iggered.**

**-igger,** bigger, chigger, digger, figger, jigger, rigger, rigor, snigger, swigger, trigger, twigger, vigor; ditchdigger, gold digger, gravedigger, hair trigger, inrigger, outrigger, rejigger, square-rigger.

**-iggered,** figgered, jiggered, niggard.

**-iggle,** giggle, higgle, jiggle, miggle, niggle, sniggle, squiggle, wiggle, wriggle.

**-igher.** See **-ier.**

**-ighland.** See **-island.**

**-ighly.** See **-ily.**

**-ighness.** See **-inus.**

**-ighten,** brighten, Brighton, chitin, chiton, frighten, heighten, lighten, tighten, titan, Titan, triton, Triton, whiten; enlighten.

**-ightening,** brightening, frightening, lightning, tightening, whitening.

**-ighter,** biter, blighter, brighter, fighter, kiter, lighter, miter, niter, smiter, tighter, titer, triter, writer; all-nighter, backbiter, bullfighter, first-nighter, ghostwriter, gunfighter, highlighter, igniter, inciter, inditer, infighter, inviter, lamplighter, moonlighter, nailbiter, prizefighter, reciter, screenwriter, scriptwriter, skywriter, songwriter, speechwriter, sportswriter, street fighter, typewriter; copywriter, dynamiter, expediter, firefighter, freedom fighter, underwriter.

**-ightful,** frightful, mightful, rightful, spiteful, sprightful; delightful, insightful.

**-ighting.** See **-iting.**

**-ightly,** brightly, knightly, lightly, nightly, rightly, sprightly, tightly, tritely, whitely; contritely, finitely, forthrightly, outrightly, politely, unsightly; impolitely.

**-ightning.** See **-ightening.**

**-ighty,** blighty, flighty, mighty, mitey, nightie, righty, whity; almighty; Aphrodite, aqua vitae, arborvitae, arbor vitae, high and mighty, lignum vitae, the Almighty.

**-igil,** sigil, strigil, vigil.

**-igious,** litigious, prodigious, religious; irreligious, sacrilegious.

**-igit.** See **-idget.**

**-igly.** See **-iggly.**

**-igma,** sigma, stigma; enigma.

**-igment,** figment, pigment.

**-ignant,** benignant, indignant, malignant.

**-igner.** See **-iner.**

**-ignly.** See **-inely.**

**-ignment,** alignment, assignment, confinement, consignment, designment, enshrinement, entwinement, inclinement, refinement, resignment.

**-igor.** See **-igger.**

**-igot,** bigot, frigate, gigot, spigot.

**-iguer.** See **-eager.**

**-iken,** icon, kwaiken, lichen, liken.

**-iking,** biking, diking, hiking, liking, piking, spiking, striking, Viking; disliking.

**-ila.** See **-illa.**

**-ilbert,** filbert, gilbert, Gilbert.

**-ilding.** See **-uilding.**

**-ildish,** childish, mildish, wildish.

**-ildly,** childly, mildly, wildly.

**-ildor.** See **-uilder.**

**-ile.** See **-illy.**

**-ilely.** See **-ily.**

**-ili.** See **-illy.**

**-ilian.** See **-illion.**

**-ilient.** See **-illiant.**

**-ilight,** highlight, skylight, stylite, twilight.

**-ilious,** bilious; punctilious; atrabilious, supercilious.

**-ilken,** milken, silken.

**-ilky,** milky, silky, Wilkie.

**-illa,** Scylla, squilla, villa, Willa; ancilla, Anguilla, Attila, axilla, barilla, bletilla, cabrilla, Camilla, cedilla, chinchilla, flotilla, gorilla, guerrilla, hydrilla, mammilla, manila, Manila, mantilla, maxilla, megillah, montilla, papilla, perilla, Priscilla, scintilla, vanilla, zorilla; camarilla, cascarilla, granadilla, kitembilla, plain-vanilla, sabadilla, sapodilla, sarsaparilla.

**-illage,** grillage, millage, pillage, spillage, stillage, tillage, village; no-tillage, permillage; global village, Greenwich Village.

**-iller,** biller, chiller, driller, filler, griller, killer, miller, pillar, schiller, Schiller, spiller, swiller, thriller, tiller; distiller, painkiller; caterpillar, dusty miller, lady-killer, technothriller.

**-illes.** See **-illies.**

**-illet,** billet, fillet, millet, rillet, skillet, willet; distillate, pearl millet.

**-illful,** skillful, willful; unskillful.

**-illian.** See **-illion.**

**-illiant,** brilliant; resilient.

**-illiard,** billiard, milliard, mill-yard.

**-illie.** See **-illy.**

**-illies,** fillies, gillies, lilies, willies; Achilles, Antilles.

**-illing,** billing, drilling, frilling, gilling, killing, quilling, schilling, shilling, skilling, thrilling, willing; bone-chilling, eye-filling, fulfilling, gristmilling, high milling, low milling, painkilling, spine-chilling, top billing, unwilling; interfilling, lipofilling, mercy killing, self-fulfilling.

Also: **-ill** + **-ing** (as in *filling*, etc.)

**-illion,** billion, jillion, Lillian, million, pillion, trillion, zillion; Brazilian, Castilian, centillion, civilian, cotillion, gazillion, modillion, pavilion, postilion, quadrillion, Quintilian, quintillion, reptilian, vaudevillian, vermilion; crocodilian, Maximilian.

**-illo.** See **-illow.**

**-illow,** billow, pillow, willow; Negrillo, tornillo; armadillo, cigarillo, peccadillo, tamarillo, weeping willow.

**-illy,** billy, Billy, Chile, chili, chilly, dilly, filly, frilly, gillie, grilly, hilly, illy, lily, Lily, Millie, Scilly, shrilly, silly, stilly, Tillie, Willie; bacilli, Caerphilly, daylilly, fusilli, hillbilly; Piccadilly, piccalilli, rockabilly, tiger lily, water lily, willy-nilly; daffy-down-dilly.

**-ilo.** See **-illow.**

**-ilot,** eyelet, islet, pilot, stylet; sky pilot, test pilot.

**-ilter,** filter, jilter, kilter, milter, philter, quilter.

**-ilton,** Hilton, Milton, Stilton, Wilton.

**-ily** (-ī-), dryly, highly, maile, Reilly, Riley, shyly, slyly, smiley, spryly, wily, wryly; ancile, O'Reilly.

**-ily** (-i-). See **-illy.**

**-image,** image, scrimmage; after image, body image, father image, graven image, line of scrimmage, mirror image, spitting image.

**-imate,** climate, primate; acclimate.

**-imber,** limber, timber, timbre; unlimber.

**-imble,** cymbal, fimble, gimbal, Gimbel, nimble, symbol, thimble, timbal, timbale, tymbal, wimble.

**-imbo,** bimbo, himbo, limbo; akimbo.

**-imely,** primely, timely; sublimely, untimely.

**-imen.** See **-imon.**

**-imer.** See **-immer.**

**-imey.** See **-imy.**

**-imic,** gimmick, mimic; bulimic; acronymic, antonymic, cherubimic, eponymic, homonymic, matronymic, metonymic, metronymic, pantomimic, patronymic, synonymic, toponymic.

**-iming,** chiming, climbing, liming, priming, rhyming, timing.

**-imly,** dimly, grimly, primly, slimly, trimly.

**-immer,** brimmer, dimmer, glimmer, grimmer, primer, primmer, shimmer, simmer, skimmer, slimmer, swimmer, trimmer.

**-imming,** brimming, dimming, skimming, slimming, swimming, trimming.

**-immy,** gimme, jimmy, Jimmy, shimmy.

**-imon,** Hyman, Hymen, limen, Lyman, pieman, Simon.

**-imper,** crimper, limper, scrimper, shrimper, simper, whimper.

**-imple,** crimple, dimple, pimple, rimple, simple, wimple.

**-imply,** crimply, dimply, limply, pimply, simply.

**-impy,** crimpy, gimpy, impy, scrimpy, shrimpy, skimpy, wimpy.

**-imsy,** flimsy, mimsy, slimsy, whimsy, Wimsey.

**-imy,** blimey, grimy, limey, limy, rimy, slimy, stymie, thymy.

**-ina** (-ē-), Deena, Gina, kina, Lena, Nina, scena, Tina, vena, vina; arena, Athena, cantina, catena, Christina, coquina, corbina, czarina, dracaena, Edwina, euglena, farina, fontina, galena, Georgina, Helena, hyena, kachina, Katrina, marina, Marina, medina, Medina, Messina, nandina, novena, patina, piscina, platina, Regina, retsina, Rowena, sestina, subpoena, tsarina, verbena; Angelina, Argentina, ballerina, cantilena, Catalina, cavatina, concertina, Filipina, javelina, ocarina, Palestrina, Pasadena, philopena, scarlatina, semolina, signorina, sonatina, Wilhelmina; Herzegovina, Pallas Athena.

**-ina** (-ī-), china, China, Dinah, Heine, Ina, mina, myna; angina, bone china, nandina, piscina, Regina, salina, trichina, vagina; Carolina.

**-inal,** binal, clinal, crinal, final, spinal, trinal, vinyl; acclinal, caninal, equinal, piscinal, synclinal; anticlinal, officinal, quarterfinal, semifinal.

**-inas.** See **-inus.**

**-inca,** Inca, finca, vinca; Katrinka, stotinka.

**-incher,** clincher, flincher, lyncher, pincher; affenpinscher, penny-pincher; Doberman pinscher.

**-inctly,** distinctly, succinctly; indistinctly.

**-incture,** cincture, tincture; encincture.

**-inder,** cinder, flinder, tinder; rescinder.

**-indle,** bindle, brindle, dwindle, kindle, spindle, swindle; enkindle, rekindle.

**-indly,** blindly, kindly; unkindly.

**-indy,** Hindi, Lindy, shindy, windy.

**-inea.** See **-inny.**

**-inear.** See **-innier.**

**-inely,** finely; benignly, caninely, divinely, supinely; saturninely.

**-inement.** See **-ignment.**

**-iner,** diner, finer, liner, miner, minor, piner, shiner, Shriner, signer, whiner; airliner, assigner, baseliner, byliner, consignor, cosigner, definer, designer, diviner, eyeliner, flatliner, freightliner, hardliner, headliner, incliner, jetliner, leaf miner, mainliner, moonshiner, one-liner, pipeliner, recliner, refiner, sideliner, softliner, streamliner, strip miner, topliner; Asia Minor, countersigner, forty-niner, ocean liner, party liner, superliner, Ursa Minor.

**-inet.** See **-innet.**

**-inew.** See **-inue.**

**-iney.** See **-iny.**

**-inful,** sinful, skinful.

**-ingent,** ringent, stringent; astringent, constringent, contingent, impingent, refringent, restringent.

**-inger** (-in-jər), binger, cringer, fringer, ginger, hinger, injure, singer, twinger; infringer, wild ginger.

**-inger** (-ing-ər), bringer, clinger, dinger, flinger, pinger, ringer, singer, slinger, springer, stinger, stringer, swinger, winger, wringer, zinger; dead ringer, folksinger, gunslinger, handwringer, hash-slinger, humdinger, left-winger, mudslinger, right-winger, torch singer; mastersinger, Meistersinger, minnesinger.

**-inger** (-ing gər), finger, linger; forefinger, malinger, ring finger.

**-ingle,** cingle, cringle, dingle, ingle, jingle, mingle, shingle, single, swingle, tingle, tringle; commingle, Kris Kringle, surcingle; intermingle.

**-ingly,** jingly, mingly, shingly, singly, tingly.

**-ingo,** bingo, dingo, gringo, jingo, lingo, pingo; Domingo, flamingo, olingo.

**-ingy** (-ing ē), clingy, dinghy, springy, stingy, stringy, swingy, wingy, zingy.

**-ingy** (-in jē), cringy, dingy, fringy, mingy, stingy, swingy, twingy.

**-ini.** See **-eeny.**

**-inian.** See **-inion.**

**-inic,** clinic, cynic, vinic; aclinic, actinic, albinic, delphinic, fulminic, morphinic, platinic, rabbinic; histaminic, Jacobinic, kaolinic, monoclinic, narcotinic, nicotinic, polygynic.

**-ining,** dining, lining, mining, shining.
Also: **-ine** + **-ing** (as in *pining,* etc.)
Also: **-ign** + **-ing** (as in *signing,* etc.)

**-inion,** minion, minyan, pinion, piñon; Darwinian, dominion, Justinian, opinion, Virginian; Abyssinian, Augustinian, Carolinian, Carthaginian, Palestinian.

**-inish** (-in-), finish, Finnish, thinnish, tinnish; bumpkinish, diminish, refinish.

**-inish** (-ī-), brinish, swinish.

**-inist,** plenist; hygienist, machinist, routinist; magazinist.
Also: **-ean** + **-est** (as in *cleanest,* etc.)
Also: **-een** + **-est** (as in *greenest,* etc.)

**-injure.** See **-inger.**

**-inker,** blinker, clinker, drinker, inker, linker, plinker, prinker, shrinker, sinker, slinker, stinker, thinker, tinker, winker; diesinker, eyewinker, freethinker, headshrinker, hoodwinker, nondrinker.

**-inkle,** crinkle, inkle, kinkle, sprinkle, tinkle, twinkle, winkle, wrinkle; besprinkle; periwinkle.

**-inkling,** inkling, sprinkling, tinkling, twinkling, wrinkling.

**-inky,** blinky, dinkey, dinky, inky, kinky, pinkie, slinky, stinky, zincky; Helsinki.

**-inland,** Finland, inland, Vinland.

**-inly,** inly, thinly; McKinley.

**-inner,** dinner, finner, grinner, inner, pinner, sinner, skinner, spinner, spinor, thinner, tinner, winner; beginner, breadwinner, prizewinner, muleskinner.

**-innet,** ginnet, linnet, minute, spinet.

**-innier,** finnier, linear, skinnier.

**-innish.** See **-inish.**

**-innow,** minnow, winnow.

**-inny,** cine, finny, guinea, Guinea, hinny, mini, Minnie, ninny, pinny, Pliny, shinny, skinny, spinney, squinny, tinny, vinny, whinny, Winnie; ignominy, micromini.

**-ino** (-ī-), dino, lino, rhino, wino; albino.

**-ino** (-ē-). See **-eno.**

**-inor.** See **-iner.**

**-inous.** See **-inus.**

**-inster,** minster, Münster, spinster; Leominster, Westminster.

**-intel,** lintel, pintle, quintal.

**-inter,** dinter, hinter, linter, minter, printer, sinter, splinter, sprinter, squinter, stinter, tinter, winter; imprinter, line printer, midwinter; laser printer, overwinter.

**-into,** pinto, Shinto, spinto.

**-intry,** splintery, vintry, wintry.

**-inty,** Dinty, flinty, glinty, linty, minty, squinty.

**-inue,** sinew; continue, retinue; discontinue.

**-inus,** dryness, finis, highness, linous, Minos, minus, shyness, sinus, slyness, spinous, vinous, wryness; Aquinas, echinus, lupinus, salinous, Your Highness.

**-inute.** See **-innet.**

**-iny** (-ī-), briny, liny, miny, piney, shiny, spiny, tiny, twiny, viny, whiney, winy; sunshiny.

**-iny** (-i-). See **-inny.**

**-inyl.** See **-inal.**

**-io.** See **-eo.**

**-ion,** Bryan, cyan, ion, lion, Mayan, scion, Zion; anion, cation, O'Brien, Orion, sea lion; dandelion.

**-iot.** See **-iet.**

**-ious.** See **-ias.**

**-ipend,** ripened, stipend.

**-iper,** diaper, griper, hyper, piper, riper, sniper, striper, swiper, typer, viper, wiper; bagpiper, pied piper, pit viper, sandpiper; candy striper, windshield wiper.

**-ipher.** See **-ifer.**

**-iple** (-ī-), typal; disciple, ectypal; archetypal, prototypal.

**-iple** (-i-). See **-ipple.**
**-iplet,** liplet, triplet.
**-ipling.** See **-ippling.**
**-ippe.** See **-ippy.**
**-ipper,** chipper, clipper, dipper, flipper, gipper, gypper, kipper, lipper, nipper, pipper, ripper, shipper, sipper, skipper, slipper, snipper, stripper, tipper, tripper, whipper, zipper; Big Dipper, day-tripper, drop shipper, mudskipper, nail-clipper, Yom Kippur; ballet slipper, bodice ripper, double-dipper, ego-tripper, gallinipper, Jack the Ripper, lady's-slipper, Little Dipper, skinny-dipper.
**-ippet,** pipit, sippet, skippet, snippet, tippet, trippet, whippet; insipit.
**-ippi.** See **-ippy.**
**-ipple,** cripple, fipple, gripple, nipple, ripple, stipple, swipple, tipple, triple.
**-ippling,** crippling, Kipling, rippling, stippling, tippling.
**-ippo,** hippo, Lippo.
**-ippy,** bippy, chippy, dippy, drippy, grippy, hippie, hippy, lippy, nippy, slippy, snippy, tippy, trippy, whippy, yippee, yippie, zippy; Xanthippe; Mississippi.
**-ipsy.** See **-ypsy.**
**-iptic.** See **-yptic.**
**-iquant.** See **-ecant.**
**-iquely.** See **-eakly.**
**-iquor.** See **-icker.**
**-ira,** eyra, Ira, IRA, Myra, naira, tayra; Elmira, hegira, Palmyra, tityra.
**-irant,** gyrant, spirant, tyrant; aspirant, conspirant, expirant.
**-irate.** See **-yrate.**
**-irchen,** birchen, urchin.
**-irder.** See **-urder.**
**-irdie.** See **-urdy.**
**-irdle,** curdle, girdle, hurdle; engirdle.
**-irdly,** birdly, curdly, thirdly; absurdly.
**-ireling,** hireling, squireling.
**-irely,** direly; entirely.
**-ireme,** bireme, trireme.
**-iren,** Byron, Chiron, gyron, siren; environ.
**-irgin.** See **-urgeon.**
**-irgy.** See **-urgy.**
**-iric.** See **-yric.**
**-iris.** See **-irus.**
**-irker,** burker, irker, jerker, lurker, shirker, smirker,

worker; caseworker, co-worker, dockworker, farmworker, fieldworker, glassworker, guest worker, mineworker, networker, pieceworker, steelworker, tearjerker, woodworker; autoworker, ironworker, metalworker, migrant worker, social worker, wonder-worker.

**-irler.** See **-urler.**

**-irling.** See **-urling.**

**-irlish,** churlish, girlish.

**-irly.** See **-urly.**

**-irma.** See **-urma.**

**-irmant.** See **-erment.**

**-irmer,** firmer, murmur, squirmer, termer, wormer; affirmer, confirmer, infirmer.

**-irmish,** firmish, skirmish, squirmish, wormish.

**-irmy.** See **-ermy.**

**-iro,** Cairo, giro, gyro, tyro; enviro; autogiro.

**-iron.** See **-iren.**

**-irous.** See **-irus.**

**-irrup,** chirrup, stirrup, syrup.

**-irter.** See **-erter.**

**-irtle.** See **-urtle.**

**-irty,** Bertie, cherty, dirty, flirty, Gertie, QWERTY, shirty, spurty, squirty, thirty.

**-irus,** Cyrus, gyrus, iris, virus; desirous, Osiris, papyrus; arbovirus, hantavirus, rhinovirus, West Nile virus.

**-iry,** briery, diary, fiery, friary, miry, priory, spiry, squiry, wiry; expiry, inquiry.

**-isal,** reprisal, revisal, surprisal; paradisal.

**-iscal,** discal, fiscal.

**-iscount,** discount, miscount.

**-iscuit.** See **-isket.**

**-iscus,** discous, discus, viscous; hibiscus, lemniscus, meniscus.

**-isel.** See **-izzle.**

**-isely,** nicely; concisely, precisely.

**-iser.** See **-isor.**

**-isher,** disher, fisher, fissure, swisher, wisher; ill-wisher, kingfisher, well-wisher.

**-ishy,** fishy, squishy, swishy.

**-isian.** See **-ision.**

**-isic.** See **-ysic.**

**-ision,** Frisian, vision; allision, collision, concision, decision, derision, division, elision, Elysian, envision, excision, incision, misprision, Parisian, precision, prevision, provision, recision, rescission, revision, Tunisian; circumcision, Dionysian, double vision, field of vision, first division, imprecision, indecision, line of vision, long division, Phonevision, short division, split decision, stratovision, subdivision, supervision, television, tunnel vision.

**-isis,** crisis, Isis, phthisis.

**-isive,** decisive, derisive, divisive, incisive; indecisive.

**-isker,** brisker, frisker, risker, whisker; bewhisker.

**-isket,** biscuit, brisket, tisket, trisket, wisket.

**-isky,** frisky, risky, whiskey.

**-island,** highland, island, Thailand; Long Island, Rhode Island; Coney Island, Easter Island, traffic island.

**-isly.** See **-izzly.**

**-ismal,** dismal; abysmal, baptismal; cataclysmal, catechismal, paroxysmal.

**-ison.** See **-izen.**

**-isor,** Dreiser, geyser, Kaiser, miser, riser, sizar, visor, wiser; adviser, appriser, chastiser, deviser, divisor, franchiser, high-riser, incisor, reviser, upriser; advertiser, agonizer, analyzer, appetizer, atomizer, authorizer, colonizer, compromiser, criticizer, customizer, energizer, equalizer, eulogizer, exerciser, fertilizer, fraternizer, galvanizer, harmonizer, humanizer, idolizer, improviser, ionizer, magnetizer, maximizer, mechanizer, memorizer, merchandiser, minimizer, modernizer, moisturizer, moralizer, neutralizer, normalizer, organizer, oxidizer, patronizer, plagiarizer, polarizer, pulverizer, randomizer, scrutinizer, socializer, stabilizer, sterilizer, subsidizer, summarizer, supervisor, sympathizer, synthesizer, tenderizer, totalizer, tranquilizer, vaporizer, verbalizer, victimizer, vitalizer, vocalizer, westernizer, womanizer; alphabetizer, characterizer, popularizer, proselytizer, systematizer, visualizer.

**-isper,** crisper, lisper, whisper.

**-ispy,** crispy, lispy, wispy.

**-issal.** See **-istle.**

**-issant.** See **-ecent.**

**-issile.** See **-istle.**

**-ission.** See **-ition.**

**-issor.** See **-izzer.**

**-issue,** fichu, issue, tissue; joint issue, nonissue, reissue, scar tissue, wedge issue.

**-issure.** See **-isher.**

**-istance,** distance; assistance, consistence, existence, insistence, long-distance, outdistance, persistence, resistance, subsistence; coexistence, equidistance, nonexistence, nonresistance, shouting distance, striking distance; passive resistance, public assistance.

**-istant,** distant; assistant, consistent, existent, insistent, persistent, resistant, subsistent; coexistent, equidistant, inconsistent, nonexistent, nonresistant, preexistent.

**-isten,** christen, glisten, listen.

**-istence.** See **-istance.**

**-istent.** See **-istant.**

**-ister,** bistre, blister, glister, lister, mister, sister, twister; half sister, insister, persister, resister, stepsister, tongue twister, transistor.

**-istic,** cystic, distich, fistic, mystic, tristich; artistic, autistic, ballistic, cladistic, deistic, ekistic, eristic, fascistic, heuristic, holistic, juristic, linguistic, logistic, puristic, sadistic, simplistic, sophistic, statistic, stylistic, theistic, touristic, wholistic; altruistic, anarchistic, animistic, atavistic, atheistic, bolshevistic, cabalistic, casuistic, catechistic, chauvinistic, communistic, dualistic, egoistic, egotistic, euphemistic, euphuistic, fatalistic, formalistic, futuristic, hedonistic, Hellenistic, humanistic, journalistic, masochistic, mechanistic, moralistic, nihilistic, optimistic, pantheistic, pessimistic, pietistic, pluralistic, pugilistic, realistic, socialistic, solecistic, syllogistic, voyeuristic; anachronistic, antagonistic, behavioristic, capitalistic, characteristic, idealistic, impressionistic, militaristic, metalinguistic, monopolistic, monotheistic, naturalistic, opportunistic, paternalistic, polytheistic, psycholinguistic, rationalistic, relativistic, ritualistic, sensualistic; imperialistic, materialistic, sadomasochistic, sociolinguistic, spiritualistic; individualistic.

**-istin.** See **-iston.**

**-istle,** bristle, fissile, gristle, missal, missile, scissel, scissile, thistle, whistle; abyssal, dickcissel, dismissal, epistle, globe thistle, wolf whistle; cacomistle, lady's-thistle.

**-istmas,** Christmas, isthmus, trismus.

**-iston,** Kristen, piston, Tristan; phlogiston, sacristan; amethystine.

**-ita** (-ē-), cheetah, keta, pita, Rita, vita; Akita, Anita, Bonita, casita, excreta, fajita, granita, Granita, Juanita, Lolita, partita; amanita, arboreta, dolce vita, incognita, manzanita, Margarita, Margherita, señorita.

**-itain.** See **-itten.**

**-ital,** title, vital; detrital, entitle, half title, recital, requital, subtitle.

**-itan.** See **-ighten.**

**-itcher,** ditcher, hitcher, itcher, pitcher, richer, snitcher, stitcher, switcher, twitcher.

**-itchy,** bitchy, hitchy, itchy, pitchy, snitchy, twitchy, witchy.

**-ite.** See **-ighty.**

**-iteful.** See **-ightful.**

**-itely.** See **-ightly.**

**-itement,** excitement, incitement, indictment.

**-iten.** See **-ighten.**

**-iter.** See **-ighter.**

**-itey.** See **-ighty.**

**-ither** (-ī-), blither, either, lither, neither, tither, writher.

**-ither** (-i-), blither, dither, hither, slither, thither, whither, wither, zither.

**-ithing,** scything, tithing, writhing.

**-ithy,** pithy, smithy, withy.

**-iti.** See **-eaty.**

**-itial.** See **-icial.**

**-itic,** clitic, critic; arthritic,

bauxitic, bronchitic, dendritic, enclitic, granitic, Hamitic, Levitic, mephitic, proclitic, pruritic, pyritic, rachitic, Semitic; analytic, biolytic, catalytic, cenobitic, diacritic, eremitic, hypocritic, Jesuitic, paralytic, parasitic, sybaritic, syphilitic; anti-Semitic, hermaphroditic, meteoritic; psychoanalytic.

**-iting,** biting, whiting; handwriting.

Also: **-ight** + **-ing** (as in *fighting,* etc.)

Also: **-ite** + **-ing** (as in *uniting,* etc.)

Also: **-ict** + **-ing** (as in *indicting,* etc.)

**-ition,** fission, mission, titian, Titian; addition, admission, ambition, attrition, audition, beautician, clinician, cognition, coition, commission, condition, contrition, dentition, edition, emission, fruition, Galician, ignition, lenition, logician, magician, monition, mortician, munition, musician, nutrition, omission, optician, partition, patrician, perdition, permission, petition, physician, position, punition, remission, rendition, sedition, submission, suspicion, tactician, technician, tradition, transition, transmission, tuition, volition; abolition, acquisition, admonition, air-condition, ammunition, apparition, apposition, coalition, competition, composition, cosmetician, decommission, definition, demolition, deposition, dietitian, disposition, disquisition, ebullition, electrician, erudition, exhibition, expedition, exposition, extradition, first edition, imposition, inanition, inhibition, inquisition, intermission, intromission, intuition, linguistician, malnutrition, manumission, micturition, obstetrician, opposition, parturition, phonetician, politician, precondition, premonition, preposition, prohibition, proposition, recognition, repetition, requisition, rescue mission, rhetorician, statistician, superstition, supposition, trade edition, transposition; academician, arithmetician, decomposition, dental technician, diagnostician, dialectician, family physician, fetal position, general admission, geometrician, high-definition, indisposition, interposition, juxtaposition, lotus position, mathematician, metaphysician, out of commission, pediatrician, pocket edition, predisposition, presupposition, pyrotechnician, redefinition, theoretician.

**-itious.** See **-icious.**

**-itle.** See **-ital.**

**-itness,** fitness, witness; earwitness, eyewitness.

**-iton** (-ī-). See **-ighten.**

**-iton** (-i-). See **-itten.**

**-itsy.** See **-itzy.**

**-ittal.** See **-ittle.**

**-ittance,** pittance, quittance; acquittance, admittance, remittance, transmittance; intermittence.

**-ittee.** See **-itty.**

**-itten,** bitten, Britain, Briton, kitten, Lytton, mitten, smitten, written; dust kitten, flea-bitten, frostbitten, Great Britain, half-written, hard-bitten, rewritten, sex kitten, snakebitten, unwritten, well-written.

**-itter,** bitter, chitter, critter, fitter, flitter, fritter, glitter, hitter, jitter, knitter, litter, pitter, quitter, ritter, sitter, skitter, slitter, spitter, splitter, titter, twitter; acquiter, aglitter, atwitter, bed-sitter, cat litter, committer, embitter, emitter, fence-sitter, gas fitter, hair-splitter, house sitter, no-hitter, outfitter, pet sitter, pinch hitter, pipe fitter, rail-splitter, remitter, sidesplitter, steam fitter, switch-hitter, transmitter; baby-sitter, copyfitter, counterfeiter, heavy hitter.

**-itti.** See **-itty.**

**-ittle,** brittle, it'll, little, skittle, spittle, tittle, victual, whittle; acquittal, belittle, committal, hospital, lickspittle, remittal, transmittal.

**-ittler,** victualler, whittler; belittler.

**-itty,** bitty, city, ditty, flitty, gritty, kitty, Kitty, nitty, pity, pretty, witty; banditti, committee, edge city, self-pity; garden city, itty-bitty, little-bitty, New York City, nitty-gritty, Salt Lake City, subcommittee, Walter Mitty.

**-itual,** ritual; habitual.

**-ity.** See **-itty.**

**-itzy,** bitsy, ditsy, Fritzy, glitzy, Mitzi, ritzy; itsy-bitsy.

**-ival,** rival; archival, archrival, arrival, revival, survival; adjectival, conjunctival, genitival; imperatival, infinitival, nominatival.

**-ivance,** connivance, contrivance, survivance.

**-ivel,** civil, drivel, frivol, shrivel, snivel, swivel; uncivil.

**-iven,** driven, given, riven, scriven, shriven; forgiven.

**-iver** (-iv-), flivver, giver, liver, quiver, river, shiver, sliver; almsgiver, caregiver, chopped liver, deliver, downriver, forgiver, lawgiver, life-giver, upriver.

**-iver** (-ī-), diver, driver, fiver, hiver, Ivor, shriver, skiver, stiver, striver, thriver; arriver, cabdriver, conniver, contriver, deriver, pearl diver, reviver, screwdriver, skin diver, sky diver, slave driver, survivor.

**-ivet,** civet, divot, grivet, pivot, privet, rivet, swivet, trivet.

**-ivid,** livid, vivid.

**-ivil.** See **-ivel.**

**-ivor.** See **-iver.**

**-ivot.** See **-ivet.**

**-ivver.** See **-iver.**

**-ivvy.** See **-ivy.**

**-ivy,** chivvy, civvy, divvy, Livy, privy, skivvy, tivy; tantivy.

**-ixer,** fixer, mixer; elixir.

**-ixie,** Dixie, nixie, pixie, tricksy.

**-ixture,** fixture, mixture; admixture, affixture, commixture, immixture; intermixture.

**-izard.** See **-izzard.**

**-izen** (-ī-), bison, dizen; bedizen, horizon.

**-izen** (-i-), dizen, mizzen, prison, ptisan, risen, wizen; arisen, bedizen, imprison.

**-izier.** See **-izzier.**

**-izzard,** blizzard, gizzard, izzard, lizard, scissored, vizard, wizard.

**-izzer,** quizzer, scissor, whizzer.

**-izzier,** busier, dizzier, frizzier, vizier.
**-izzle,** chisel, drizzle, fizzle, frizzle, grizzle, mizzle, pizzle, sizzle, swizzle.
**-izzly,** drizzly, frizzly, grisly, grizzly, sizzly.
**-izzy,** busy, dizzy, fizzy, frizzy, Lizzie, tizzy; tin lizzie.
**-oa,** boa, Goa, koa, moa, Noah, proa, Shoah, stoa, zoa; aloha, anoa, balboa, feijoa, genoa, Genoa, hydroa, jerboa, keitloa, koloa, leipoa, Samoa; Krakatoa, Metazoa, protozoa, Shenandoah, toheroa.
**-oader,** coder, goader, loader, Oder, odor; breechloader, corroder, decoder, encoder, exploder, foreboder, freeloader, front loader, handloader, malodor, railroader, top loader; autoloader, muzzleloader.
**-oaken.** See **-oken.**
**-oaker.** See **-oker.**
**-oaky.** See **-oky.**
**-oaler.** See **-oller.**
**-oaly.** See **-oly.**
**-oamer.** See **-omer.**
**-oaner.** See **-oner.**
**-oarder.** See **-order.**
**-oarer.** See **-orer.**
**-oarish,** boarish, whorish.
**-oarsely,** coarsely, hoarsely.
**-oary.** See **-ory.**
**-oastal,** coastal, postal.
**-oaster,** boaster, coaster, poster, roaster, toaster, throwster; billposter, fourposter, wallposter; roller coaster.
**-oaten,** croton, moton, oaten; verboten.
**-oater.** See **-otor.**
**-oatswain.** See **-osen.**
**-oaty,** dhoti, floaty, goatee, loti, oaty, roti, throaty, zloty; cenote, chayote, coyote, peyote; Don Quixote.
**-obate,** globate, lobate, probate.
**-obber,** blobber, bobber, clobber, cobber, dobber, jobber, lobber, robber, slobber, sobber, swabber, throbber; beslobber, graverobber, hobnobber, oddjobber, stockjobber, truck jobber.
**-obbin,** bobbin, dobbin, robin, Robin.
**-obble,** bobble, cobble, gobble, hobble, nobble, obol, squabble, wabble, wobble.
**-obbler,** cobbler, gobbler, hob-

bler, knobbler, squabbler, wobbler; gollywobbler, sherry cobbler.

**-obby,** bobby, Bobby, cobby, dobby, hobby, knobby, lobby, mobby, Robbie, slobby, snobby, squabby, swabby.

**-obe,** obi, Gobi, goby, obi, Obie, Toby; adobe, Nairobi.

**-ober,** lobar, prober, sober; disrober, enrober, October.

**-obin.** See **-obbin.**

**-obo,** gobo, hobo, kobo, lobo, oboe; adobo, bonobo.

**-obster,** lobster, mobster.

**-ocal,** focal, local, socle, vocal, yokel; bifocal.

**-occer.** See **-ocker.**

**-ocean.** See **-otion.**

**-ocer,** closer, grocer, grosser; engrosser, greengrocer, jocoser, moroser.

**-ochee.** See **-oky.**

**-ocher.** See **-oker.**

**-ocile.** See **-ostle.**

**-ocious,** atrocious, ferocious, precocious.

**-ocker,** blocker, clocker, cocker, docker, Fokker, hocker, knocker, locker, mocker, rocker, shocker, soccer, socker, stocker; boondocker, folk-rocker, foot locker, hard rocker, punk rocker; appleknocker, beta blocker, Knicker-bocker.

**-ocket,** brocket, crocket, Crockett, docket, hocket, locket, pocket, rocket, socket, sprocket; air pocket, changepocket, dame's rocket, eye socket, patch pocket, pickpocket, skyrocket, vest-pocket; out-of-pocket, retrorocket.

**-ockey.** See **-ocky.**

**-ocky,** blocky, cocky, crocky, flocky, hockey, jockey, kaki, locky, pocky, rocky, sake, Saki, schlocky, stocky; bench jockey, disc jockey, field hockey, ice hockey, Iraqi; jabberwocky, Kawasaki, Nagasaki, sukiyaki, teriyaki.

**-oco,** coco, cocoa, koko, loco, poco; baroco, in loco, ro-coco; barococo, crème de cacao, locofoco, Orinoco; poco a poco.

**-ocoa.** See **-oco.**

**-ocre.** See **-oker.**

**-octer.** See **-octor.**

**-oction,** concoction, decoction.

**-octor,** doctor, proctor; concocter, decocter, herb doctor, spin doctor, witch doctor.

**-ocus,** crocus, focus, hocus, locus; Hohokus, soft focus; autofocus, autumn crocus, hocus-pocus.

**-ocust,** focused, locust.

**-oda,** coda, oda, Rhoda, soda; Baroda, club soda, colpoda, pagoda.

**-odal,** modal, nodal, yodel.

**-odden,** sodden, trodden; downtrodden, untrodden, well-trodden.

**-odder,** dodder, fodder, nodder, odder, plodder, prodder, solder; Cape Codder, hot rodder; cannon fodder.

**-oddess,** bodice, goddess.

**-odding,** codding, nodding, plodding, podding, prodding, wadding.

**-oddle,** coddle, model, noddle, swaddle, toddle, twaddle, waddle; remodel, role model, spokesmodel; mollycoddle, supermodel.

**-oddy.** See **-ody.**

**-odel** (-o-). See **-oddle.**

**-odel** (-ō-). See **-odal.**

**-oder.** See **-oader.**

**-odest,** bodiced, modest, oddest; immodest.

**-odger,** codger, dodger, Dodger, lodger, roger, Roger.

**-odic,** anodic, cathodic, dipodic, iodic, melodic, methodic, monodic, parodic, prosodic, rhapsodic, spasmodic, synodic, threnodic; episodic, periodic.

**-odice.** See **-oddess.**

**-odling,** coddling, codling, godling, modeling, swaddling, toddling, twaddling, waddling.

**-odly,** godly, oddly, twaddly, waddly; ungodly.

**-odo,** dodo; Quasimodo.

**-odor.** See **-oader.**

**-odule,** module, nodule.

**-ody,** body, cloddy, Mahdi, noddy, poddy, Roddy, shoddy, soddy, toddy, waddy, wadi; dogsbody, embody, homebody, hot toddy, mind-body, nobody, somebody, wide-body; antibody, anybody, busybody, disembody, everybody, Irrawaddy, out-of-body, student body, underbody.

**-oeia.** See **-ea.**

**-oem,** phloem, poem, proem; found poem, prose poem, tone poem; jeroboam.

**-oeman.** See **-omen.**

**-oer.** See **-ower.**

**-offal,** offal, waffle; pantofle.

**-offee,** coffee, toffee.

**-offer,** coffer, cougher, doffer, goffer, offer, proffer, scoffer, troffer.

**-offin.** See **-often.**

**-offing,** coughing, doffing, offing, scoffing.

**-often,** coffin, dauphin, often, soften.

**-ofty,** lofty, softy.

**-oga,** toga, yoga; hatha yoga, Saratoga; Ticonderoga.

**-ogan,** brogan, hogan, Hogan, shogun, slogan.

**-oger.** See **-odger.**

**-ogey.** See **-ogie.**

**-oggish,** doggish, froggish, hoggish.

**-oggle,** boggle, coggle, goggle, joggle, toggle; boondoggle, hornswoggle.

**-oggy,** boggy, cloggy, doggy, foggy, froggy, groggy, joggy, quaggy, smoggy, soggy.

**-ogi.** See **-ogie.**

**-ogie,** bogey, bogie, dogie, fogy, hoagie, logy, pogy, stogie, yogi; pierogi.

**-ogle,** bogle, Gogol, ogle.

**-oic,** stoic, Stoic; azoic, benzoic, echoic, heroic; Cenozoic, Eozoic, Mesozoic, mock-heroic, protozoic, unheroic; Paleozoic.

**-oidal,** colloidal, cuboidal, rhomboidal, spheroidal; asteroidal, ellipsoidal, trapezoidal.

**-oider,** broider, voider; avoider, embroider.

**-oily,** coyly, doily, oily, roily.

**-oiner,** coiner, joiner; enjoiner, purloiner.

**-ointer,** jointer, pointer; anointer, appointer.

**-ointment,** ointment; anointment, appointment, disjointment; disappointment.

**-oister,** cloister, foister, hoister, moister, oyster, roister.

**-oiter,** goiter, loiter; exploiter; reconnoiter.

**-okay,** croquet, okay, roquet, Tokay.

**-okel.** See **-ocal.**

**-oken,** broken, oaken, spoken, token, woken; awoken, bespoken, betoken, fair-spoken, foretoken, heartbroken, Hoboken, housebroken, outspoken, plainspoken, short-spoken, soft-spoken, unbroken, unspoken, well-spoken.

**-oker,** broker, choker, cloaker, croaker, joker, ocher, poker, smoker, soaker, stoker, stroker, yoker; chain-smoker, convoker, draw poker, evoker, invoker, pawnbroker, provoker, red ocher, revoker, stockbroker, straight poker, strip poker, stud poker; honest broker, mediocre, power broker, red-hot poker, yellow ocher.

**-okey.** See **-oky.**

**-okum,** hokum, locum, oakum.

**-oky,** choky, croaky, folkie, hokey, jokey, Loki, oaky, poky, smoky, soaky, troche, trochee, yolky; enoki; hoky-poky, karaoke, okey-dokey.

**-ola,** bola, cola, kola, Lola, Nola, stola, tola, Zola; Angola, boffola, canola, crapola, Ebola, gondola, granola, mandola, payola, plugola, scagliola, Victrola, viola; ayatollah, braciola, carambola, Coca-Cola, Española, gladiola, Gorgonzola, Hispaniola, Moviola, Pensacola, roseola, rubeola.

**-olar** (-o-). See **-ollar.**

**-olar** (-ō-). See **-oller.**

**-olden,** golden, olden, Soldan; beholden, embolden.

**-older** (-ōl-), bolder, boulder, colder, folder, holder, molder, moulder, older, polder, scolder, shoulder, smolder; beholder, bondholder, cardholder, cold shoulder, freeholder, handholder, householder, jobholder, landholder, leaseholder, placeholder, pot holder, shareholder, slaveholder, stakeholder, stockholder, upholder; copyholder, office holder, titleholder.

**-older** (-od-). See **-odder.**

**-oleful,** bowlful, doleful, soulful.

**-olely.** See **-oly.**

**-olemn.** See **-olumn.**

**-olen.** See **-olon.**

**-oler** (-o-). See **-ollar.**

**-oler** (-ō-). See **-oller.**

**-olic,** colic, frolic, rollick; bucolic, carbolic, embolic, Mongolic, symbolic, systolic; alcoholic, anabolic, apostolic, catabolic, chocoholic, diabolic, diastolic, diabolic, epistolic, hyperbolic, melancholic, metabolic, parabolic, shopaholic, vitriolic, workaholic.

**-olid,** solid, squalid, stolid; biosolid, semisolid.

**-olish,** polish; abolish, demolish; apple-polish, spit-and-polish.

**-ollar,** choler, collar, dollar, holler, loller, scholar, sollar, squalor; blue-collar, brass-collar, cape collar, choke collar, dog collar, flea collar, half-dollar, horse-collar, new-collar, notched collar, pink-collar, sand dollar, shawl collar, top dollar, white-collar, wing collar; Eton collar, Eurodollar, petrodollar.

**-ollard,** bollard, collard, collared, Lollard, pollard.

**-ollege.** See **-owledge.**

**-ollen.** See **-olon.**

**-oller,** bowler, coaler, doler, dolor, droller, molar, polar, poler, poller, roller, solar, stroller, toller, troller; bankroller, bipolar, cajoler, comptroller, consoler, controller, enroller, extoller, high roller, logroller, patroller, premolar, steamroller.

**-ollick.** See **-olic.**

**-ollie.** See **-olly.**

**-ollins,** Collins, Hollins, Rollins.

**-ollo.** See **-ollow.**

**-ollop,** collop, dollop, lollop, polyp, scallop, trollop, Trollope, wallop; bay scallop, codswallop, escallop, sea scallop.

**-ollow,** follow, hollow, Rollo, swallow, wallow; Apollo, barn swallow, cliff swallow.

**-olly** (-o-), Bali, brolly, collie, Dali, Dollie, dolly, folly, golly, holly, jolly, lolly, Mali, Molly, pali, Pali, polly, Polly, poly, quale, Raleigh, trolley, volley; Diwali, finale, loblolly, qawwali, Somali, Svengali, tamale; melancholy.

**-olly** (-ō-). See **-oly.**

**-olo,** bolo, cholo, kolo, polo, solo; palolo; Marco Polo, paniolo, water polo.

**-olon,** colon, solon, Solon, stolen, stollen, stolon, swollen; eidolon, semicolon.

**-olonel.** See **-ernal.**

**-olor.** See **-uller.**

**-olster,** bolster, holster, pollster; upholster; reupholster.

**-olter,** bolter, boulter, colter, jolter, poulter; molter, revolter.

**-oltish,** coltish, doltish.

**-olumn,** column, solemn; fifth column; spinal column, steering column.

**-olver,** solver; absolver, dissolver, evolver, resolver, revolver.

**-oly** (-ō-), coaly, drolly, goalie, holey, holy, lowly, moly, pollee, shoaly, slowly, solely, wholly; aioli, anole, cannoli, frijole, pignoli, pinole, Stromboli, unholy; guacamole, ravioli, roly-poly.

**-oly** (-o-). See **-olly.**

**-oma,** coma, noma, Roma, soma, stoma, stroma; aboma, aroma, blastoma, diploma, fibroma, glaucoma, lymphoma, Natoma, sarcoma, Tacoma; adenoma, angioma, carcinoma, granuloma, hematoma, la paloma, melanoma, myeloma, Oklahoma.

**-omach,** hummock, stomach.

**-omain,** domain, ptomaine, romaine.

**-oman.** See **-omen.**

**-ombat,** combat, wombat.

**-omber.** See **-omer.**

**-ombie,** Dombey, zombie; Abercrombie.

**-omely.** See **-umbly.**

**-omen,** bowman, foeman, gnomon, nomen, omen, Roman, showman, yeoman; abdomen, agnomen, cognomen, crossbowman, longbowman, praenomen.

**-oment,** foment, loment, moment; bestowment.

**-omer** (-ō-), comber, gomer, homer, Homer, omer, roamer, vomer; beachcomber, Lag b'Omer, misnomer.

**-omer** (-u-). See **-ummer.**

**-omet,** comet, grommet, vomit.

**-omic,** comic, gnomic; anomic, atomic; agronomic, anatomic, astronomic, autonomic, diatomic, economic, ergonomic, gastronomic, metronomic, monatomic, palindromic, subatomic, taxonomic, tragicomic.

**-omit.** See **-omet.**

**-omma.** See **-ama.**

**-ommy.** See **-almy.**

**-omo,** chromo, Como, duomo, homo, pomo, Pomo, promo; major-domo.

**-ompass,** compass, rumpus; encompass.

**-onal,** clonal, tonal, zonal; atonal, bitonal, coronal, hormonal; baritonal, polytonal.

**-onday.** See **-undy.**

**-ondent,** fondant, frondent; despondent, respondent; co-respondent, correspondent.

**-onder,** blonder, bonder, condor, fonder, ponder, squander, wander, yonder; absconder, desponder, responder, transponder; corresponder.

**-one.** See **-ony.**

**-onely.** See **-only.**

**-onent,** sonant; component, deponent, exponent, opponent, proponent.

**-oner,** boner, cloner, donor, droner, groaner, loaner, loner, moaner, owner, phoner, stoner, toner, zoner; atoner, brownstoner, condoner, intoner, landowner, shipowner.

**-onest,** honest, non est, wannest; dishonest.

**-oney** (-ō-). See **-ony.**

**-oney** (-u-). See **-unny.**

**-onger** (-o-), conger, longer, monger, stronger; fearmonger, fishmonger, hatemonger, newsmonger, phrasemonger, warmonger, whoremonger; costermonger, gossipmonger, ironmonger, rumormonger, scandalmonger.

**-onger** (-u-). See **-unger.**

**-onging,** longing, thronging, wronging; belonging, prolonging.

**-ongly,** strongly, wrongly.

**-ongo,** bongo, Congo, drongo, mongo, Mongo.

**-oni.** See **-ony.**

**-onic,** chronic, chthonic, conic, monic, phonic, sonic, tonic; Aaronic, agonic, atonic, bionic, bubonic, Byronic, canonic, carbonic, colonic, cryonic, cyclonic, demonic, draconic, dystonic, euphonic, gnomonic, harmonic, hedonic, iconic, ionic, Ionic, ironic, laconic, masonic, mnemonic, moronic, platonic, sardonic, Slavonic, symphonic, synchronic, tectonic, Teutonic; antiphonic, catatonic, colophonic, diachronic, diaphonic, diatonic, electronic, embryonic, hegemonic, histrionic, homophonic, Housatonic, hydroponic, hypertonic, hypotonic, isotonic, macaronic, monophonic, monotonic, nonionic, nucleonic, philharmonic, polyphonic, quadraphonic, semitonic, Solomonic, supersonic, telephonic, ultrasonic; animatronic, anticyclonic, architectonic, oxymoronic, Napoleonic, Neoplatonic, stereophonic.

**-onion,** bunion, Bunyan, grunion, munnion, onion, ronyon, Runyon, trunnion.

**-onish,** donnish, monish, wannish; admonish, astonish, premonish.

**-onkey.** See **-unky.**

**-only,** lonely, only.

**-onnet,** bonnet, sonnet; bluebonnet, sunbonnet, warbonnet.

**-onnie,** Bonnie, bonny, Connie, johnny, Johnny, Lonny, Ronnie.

**-onor** (-o-), goner, honor, wanner; dishonor, maid of honor, marathoner.

**-onor** (-ō-). See **-oner.**

**-onsil,** consul, tonsil; proconsul, responsal.

**-onsul.** See **-onsil.**

**-ontal.** See **-untle.**

**-onter.** See **-unter.**

**-ontract,** contract, entr'acte.

**-onus,** bonus, clonus, Cronus, Jonas, onus, slowness, tonus; Adonis, colonus.

**-ony,** bony, Coney, cony, crony, drony, phony, pony, stony, Toni, tony, Tony; baloney, bologna, canzone, Marconi, padrone, Shoshone, spumoni, tortoni, Zamboni; abalone, acrimony, alimony, antimony, cannelloni, ceremony, chalcedony, cicerone, colophony, hegemony, macaroni, mascarpone, matrimony, minestrone, one-trick pony, palimony, parsimony, patrimony, pepperoni, provolone, rigatoni, sanctimony, Shetland pony, testimony, zabaglione.

**-ooby,** booby, looby, ruby, Ruby.

**-oocher.** See **-uture.**

**-ooding,** hooding, pudding; black pudding, blood pudding, plum pudding; Christmas pudding, cottage pudding, hasty pudding, Yorkshire pudding.

**-oodle,** boodle, doodle, feudal, noodle, poodle, strudel; caboodle, canoodle, flapdoodle, kyoodle, paludal, toy poodle; dipsy-doodle, timberdoodle, Yankee Doodle.

**-oody** (-o͝o-), goody, hoodie, woody.

**-oody** (-o͞o-), broody, Judy, moody, nudie, Trudy.

**-oody** (-u-). See **-uddy.**

**-ooey.** See **-ewy.**

**-ookie.** See **-ooky.**

**-ookish,** bookish, rookish, spookish.

**-ooky** (-o͝o-), bookie, brookie, cookie, hooky, rookie, rooky.

**-ooky** (-o͞o-), fluky, kooky, spooky; bouzouki, Kabuki.

**-oolie.** See **-uly.**

**-oolish,** coolish, foolish, ghoulish, mulish; pound-foolish, tomfoolish.

**-oolly** (-o͝o-). See **-ully.**

**-oolly** (-o͞o-). See **-uly.**

**-oomer.** See **-umer.**

**-oomy,** bloomy, boomy, doomy, fumy, gloomy, plumy, rheumy, roomy, spumy.

**-ooner.** See **-uner.**

**-oony,** goony, loonie, loony, Moonie, moony, spoony, swoony, Zuni; cartoony.

**-ooper,** blooper, cooper, duper, grouper, hooper, scooper, snooper, stupor, super, trooper, trouper, whooper; mosstrooper, state trooper, storm trooper; party pooper, paratrooper, pooper-scooper; super-duper.

**-oopy,** croupy, droopy, goopy, groupie, Kewpie, loopy, rupee, snoopy, soupy, whoopee.

**-oorish,** boorish, Moorish, poorish.

**-ooser.** See **-oser.**

**-oosy** (-ōōzi). See **-oozy.**

**-oosy** (-ōōsi). See **-uicy.**

**-ooter,** bruiter, cooter, cuter, fruiter, hooter, looter, mooter, neuter, pewter, rooter, router, scooter, shooter, suiter, suitor, tooter, tutor; commuter, computer, confuter, crapshooter, diluter, disputer, freebooter, peashooter, polluter, recruiter, refuter, sharpshooter, straight shooter, trapshooter, two-suiter; coadjutor, executer, instituter, motor scooter, parachuter, persecutor, prosecutor, troubleshooter; microcomputer, minicomputer, telecommuter.

**-oothless.** See **-uthless.**

**-ootie.** See **-ooty.**

**-ooty,** beauty, bootie, booty, cootie, cutie, dhuti, duty, fluty, fruity, hooty, rooty, snooty, sooty, tutti, zooty; agouti, clafouti, Djibouti, off-duty; bathing beauty, double-duty, heavy-duty, tutti-frutti.

**-ooza.** See **-usa.**

**-oozer.** See **-oser.**

**-oozle,** foozle, fusil, ouzel, streusel; bamboozle, occlusal, perusal, recusal, refusal.

**-oozy,** bluesy, boozy, choosy, floozy, newsy, oozy, woozy.

**-opal,** opal, copal, nopal; Adrianople, Constantinople.

**-oper** (-ō-), coper, doper, groper, hoper, loper, moper, roper, sloper, soaper, toper; eloper, soft-soaper; interloper.

**-oper** (-o-). See **-opper.**

**-opey.** See **-opy.**

**-ophy.** Sophie, Sophy, strophe, trophy.

**-opic,** topic, tropic; atopic, ectopic, myopic; arthroscopic, cryoscopic, endoscopic, Ethiopic, fluoroscopic, isotopic, lycanthropic, macroscopic, microscopic, misanthropic, periscopic, philanthropic, presbyopic, spectroscopic, stethoscopic, telescopic; heliotropic, kaleidoscopic, laparoscopic, stereoscopic.

**-ople.** See **-opal.**

**-opper,** bopper, chopper, copper, cropper, dropper, hopper, mopper, popper, proper, shopper, stopper, stropper, swapper, topper, whopper; bebopper, cartopper, clodhopper, cornpopper, eavesdropper, eyedropper, eye-popper, froghopper, grasshopper, heartstopper, hedge-hopper, hip-hopper, improper, jaw-dropper, job-hopper, leafhopper, namedropper, pill popper, planthopper, porkchopper, sharecropper, show-stopper, treehopper, woodchopper; belly flopper, teenybopper, window-shopper.

**-opping,** chopping, copping, sopping, topping, whopping; eye-popping, heartstopping, jaw-dropping, job-hopping, namedropping, outcropping, show-stopping; windowshopping.

Also: **-opp** + **-ing** (as in *shopping*, etc.)

**-opple,** popple, stopple, topple; estoppel.

**-oppy,** choppy, copy, floppy, gloppy, hoppy, kopje, loppy, poppy, sloppy, soppy, stroppy; jalopy, okapi, serape; photocopy.

**-opsy,** dropsy, Topsy; autopsy, biopsy, necropsy.

**-opter,** copter; adopter, chiropter, diopter; helicopter.

**-optic,** Coptic, optic; synoptic; fiberoptic.

**-option,** option; adoption, cooption, stock option.

**-opy** (-ō-), dopey, gopi, Hopi, mopey, ropy, soapy, topee, topi.

**-opy** (-o-). See **-oppy.**

**-ora,** aura, bora, Cora, Dora, flora, Flora, fora, hora, Laura, mora, Nora, ora, sora, Torah; agora, amora, Andorra, angora, aurora, Aurora, bandora, begorra, camorra, fedora, Gomorrah, Marmora, Masorah, menorah, pandora, Pandora, rasbora, rhodora, sabora, senhora, señora, signora; Bora-Bora, cyclospora, grandiflora, Leonora, microflora.

**-orage,** borage, floorage, forage, porridge, shorage, storage.

**-oral,** aural, boral, chloral, choral, coral, floral, horal, laurel, loral, moral, oral, quarrel, sorrel; aboral, amoral, auroral, Balmoral, binaural, brain coral, immoral, mayoral, monaural, peroral, sororal.

**-orax,** borax, storax, thorax.

**-orbel.** See **-arble.**

**-orchard,** orchard, tortured.

**-orcher,** scorcher, torture.

**-order,** boarder, border, forder, hoarder, order, warder; awarder, back order, court order, disorder, gag order, keyboarder, mail-order, recorder, reorder, rewarder, sailboarder, short-order, skateboarder, snowboarder, stop order, suborder, surfboarder, wakeboarder, word order; flight recorder, holy order, in short order, law-and-order, made-to-order, market order, money order, mood disorder, pecking order, standing order, super order, tape recorder; eating disorder, panic disorder.

**-ordon,** cordon, Gordon, Jordan, warden.

**-ordy.** See **-urdy.**

**-ore.** See **-ory.**

**-orehead.** See **-orrid.**

**-oreign,** chlorine, florin, foreign, sporran, warren; cyclosporine, helleborin, Neosporin.

**-orer,** borer, corer, floorer, gorer, horror, porer, pourer, roarer, schnorrer, scorer, snorer; abhorrer, adorer, corn borer, explorer, ignorer, restorer.

**-oresail.** See **-orsel.**

**-orest,** florist, forest, sorest; deforest, folklorist, rainforest.

**-orey.** See **-ory.**

**-organ,** gorgon, Morgan, morgen, organ; hand organ, house organ, mouth organ, pipe organ, sense organ; barrel organ.

**-orger,** bordure, forger, gorger, ordure; disgorger, drop-forger.

**-ori.** See **-ory.**

**-oric,** boric, chloric, choric, Doric, toric, Yorick; amphoric, caloric, euphoric, folkloric, historic, motoric, phosphoric, plethoric, pyloric; allegoric, amphigoric, anaphoric, categoric, hydrochloric, metaphoric, meteoric, paregoric, prehistoric, sophomoric; aleatoric, phantasmagoric.

**-orid.** See **-orrid.**
**-oris,** Boris, Doris, loris, Horace, morris, Morris, Norris, orris; cantoris.
**-orker.** See **-irker.**
**-ormal,** cormel, formal, normal; abnormal, conformal, informal, subnormal; paranormal, semiformal.
**-orman,** corpsman, doorman, floorman, foreman, Mormon, Norman; longshoreman; Anglo-Norman.
**-ormant,** dormant; conformant, informant.
**-ormer,** dormer, former, ormer, stormer, warmer; barnstormer, benchwarmer, brainstormer, conformer, informer, performer, reformer, transformer.
**-ormish.** See **-irmish.**
**-ormy.** See **-ermy.**
**-orner,** corner, horner, mourner, scorner, warner; adorner, suborner; amen corner, cater-corner, kitty-corner.
**-ornet,** cornet, hornet.
**-orney.** See **-ourney.**
**-ornful,** mournful, scornful.
**-orning,** morning, mourning, scorning, warning; aborning, forewarning.
**-orny,** corny, horny, thorny.
**-orough,** borough, burro, burrow, furrow, thorough; pocket borough, rotten borough.
**-orous,** chorus, porous, Taurus, torous, torus; canorous, Centaurus, decorous, imporous, pelorus, phosphorous, pylorus, sonorous, thesaurus; allosaurus, brontosaurus, stegosaurus; ichthyosaurus, tyrannosaurus.
**-orpor,** dorper, scorper, torpor, warper.
**-orpus,** corpus, porpoise; habeas corpus.
**-orrel.** See **-oral.**
**-orrent,** horrent, torrent, warrant; abhorrent, bench warrant, death warrant, search warrant.
**-orrid,** florid, forehead, horrid, torrid.
**-orridge.** See **-orage.**
**-orris.** See **-oris.**
**-orror.** See **-orer.**
**-orrow,** borrow, morrow, sorrow; good morrow, tomorrow.

**-orry** (-o-), quarry, sorry. See also **-arry** and **-ory.**

**-orry** (-û-). See **-urry.**

**-orsel,** dorsal, foresail, morsel.

**-orsen.** See **-erson.**

**-orsion.** See **-ortion.**

**-ortal,** chortle, mortal, portal, quartile; aortal, immortal.

**-orten,** Horton, Morton, Norton, quartan, shorten.

**-orter,** dorter, mortar, porter, quarter, shorter, snorter, sorter, sporter; cavorter, olporteur, contorter, distorter, exporter, extorter, first quarter, forequarter, grand quarter, headquarter, hindquarter, importer, last quarter, reporter, ripsnorter, supporter.

**-ortex,** cortex, vortex.

**-ortion,** portion, torsion; abortion, apportion, consortion, contortion, distortion, extortion, intorsion, proportion, retorsion; disproportion, reapportion.

**-ortive,** sportive, tortive; abortive, contortive, extortive, supportive, transportive.

**-ortle.** See **-ortal.**

**-ortly,** courtly, portly, shortly.

**-ortment,** assortment, comportment, deportment, disportment, transportment.

**-orton.** See **-orten.**

**-ortune,** fortune; importune, misfortune.

**-orture.** See **-orcher.**

**-ortured.** See **-orchard.**

**-orty,** forty, shorty, snorty, sortie, sporty, warty; pianoforte.

**-orum,** foram, forum, jorum, quorum; decorum; ad valorem, indecorum, variorum; sanctum sanctorum, schola cantorum.

**-orus.** See **-orous.**

**-ory,** dory, flory, glory, gory, hoary, lorry, lory, nori, story, Tory, zori; backstory, clerestory, fish story, ghost story, John Dory, Old Glory, satori, short story, sob story, vainglory, war story; allegory, a priori, amatory, amphigory, auditory, bedtime story, cacciatore, category, con amore, cover story, crematory, desultory, dilatory, dormitory, excretory, fumitory, gustatory, horror story, hortatory, hunky-dory, inventory, laudatory, lavatory, mandatory, migratory, minatory, Montessori, morning glory, nugatory, offertory, oratory, peremptory, predatory, prefatory, promissory, promontory, purgatory, repertory, signatory, statutory, territory, transitory, vomitory, yakitori; accusatory, a fortiori, ambulatory, cacciatore, celebratory, circulatory, cock-and-bull story, combinatory, commendatory, compensatory, conciliatory, conservatory, contributory, declamatory, declaratory, defamatory, depilatory, depository, deprecatory, derogatory, exclamatory, explanatory, exploratory, expository, inflammatory, laboratory, memento mori, obfuscatory, obligatory, observatory, preparatory, reformatory, regulatory, repository, respiratory, undulatory; anticipatory, a posteriori, conciliatory, congratulatory, discriminatory, hallucinatory, retaliatory. See also **-orry.**

**-osa,** osa, Xhosa; Formosa, margosa, mimosa, mucosa, samosa, serosa; curiosa, mariposa, virtuosa.

**-osely,** closely, grossly; jocosely, morosely, verbosely.

**-osen,** boatswain, chosen, frozen, hosen.

**-oser** (-o͞ozər), boozer, bruiser, chooser, cruiser, doozer, loser, schmoozer; light cruiser; battle cruiser, cabin cruiser, heavy cruiser. See also **-user.**

**-oser** (-ōsər). See **-ocer.**

**-oset.** See **-osit.**

**-osher,** cosher, josher, nosher, swasher, washer; brainwasher, dishwasher, whitewasher; bottlewasher.

**-oshy,** boshy, sloshy, squashy, swashy, washy; wishy-washy.

**-osier,** crosier, hosier, osier.

**-osion,** plosion; ambrosian, corrosion, erosion, explosion, implosion.

**-osit,** closet, posit; composite, deposit.

**-osive,** plosive; corrosive, erosive, explosive, implosive, purposive.

**-oso.** See **-uso.**

**-ossal.** See **-ostle.**
**-osser.** See **-ocer.**
**-ossil.** See **-ostle.**
**-ossom,** blossom, possum; opossum, play possum.
**-ossum.** See **-ossom.**
**-ossy,** Aussie, bossy, drossy, Flossie, flossy, glossy, mossy, posse, quasi, tossy.
**-ostal,** costal, hostel, hostile; youth hostel; infracostal, intercostal, Pentecostal.
**-oster** (-o-), coster, foster, Gloucester, roster; accoster, impostor; paternoster, Pentecoster.
**-oster** (-ō-). See **-oaster.**
**-ostic,** caustic, gnostic; acrostic, agnostic, prognostic; anacrostic, diagnostic, paracrostic, pentacostic.
**-ostle,** docile, dossal, dossil, fossil, glossal, jostle, throstle, wassail; apostle, colossal.
**-ostler,** hostler, jostler, ostler, wassailer.
**-ostly,** ghostly, mostly.
**-ostril,** costrel, nostril, rostral; colostral.
**-ostrum,** nostrum, rostrum; colostrum.
**-osure,** closure; composure, disclosure, enclosure, exposure, foreclosure, reposure; discomposure; overexposure, underexposure.
**-osy,** cozy, dozy, mosey, nosy, posy, prosy, Rosie, rosy.
**-ota,** bota, lota, quota, rota; biota, Dakota, iota, pelota; Minnesota, North Dakota, South Dakota.
**-otal,** dotal, motile, notal, rotal, scrotal, total; sclerotal, subtotal, sum total, teetotal; anecdotal, antidotal, extradotal, sacerdotal.
**-otcher,** blotcher, botcher, notcher, splotcher, watcher; topnotcher.
**-otchy,** blotchy, boccie, botchy, splotchy; hibachi, huarache, vivace; Liberace, mariachi, Pagliacci.
**-ote.** See **-oaty.**
**-otem,** notum, scrotum, totem; factotum, teetotum.
**-oter.** See **-otor.**
**-other** (-o-), bother, father, fother, pother; church father, forefather, godfather, grandfather, stepfather.
**-other** (-u-), brother, mother, nother, other, smother, tother; another, Big

Brother, blood brother, den mother, each other, earth mother, godmother, grandmother, half brother, house mother, queen mother, soul brother, stepbrother, stepmother.

**-othing,** clothing, loathing.

**-othy,** frothy, mothy.

**-otic,** aquatic, biotic, chaotic, demotic, despotic, erotic, exotic, hypnotic, meiotic, mitotic, narcotic, necrotic, neurotic, osmotic, psychotic, pyrotic, quixotic, robotic, sclerotic, zygotic, zymotic; amniotic, epiglottic, idiotic, patriotic, semiotic, symbiotic; antibiotic, antipsychotic, macrobiotic.

**-otion,** Goshen, groschen, lotion, motion, notion, ocean, potion; commotion, demotion, devotion, emotion, love potion, promotion, remotion, slow motion, stop-motion; Arctic Ocean, locomotion, self-promotion.

**-otive,** motive, votive; connotive, denotive, emotive, promotive; automotive, locomotive.

**-otly,** hotly, motley, squatly.

**-oto,** koto, Oto, photo, roto, toto; De Soto, in toto, Kyoto, Lesotho.

**-otor,** bloater, boater, doter, floater, gloater, motor, noter, oater, quoter, rotor, scoter, toter, voter; emoter, houseboater, iceboater, keynoter, promoter, showboater; locomotor, motorboater, vasomotor.

**-ottage,** cottage, pottage, wattage.

**-ottar.** See **-otter.**

**-otten,** cotton, gotten, Groton, rotten, shotten; begotten, forgotten, guncotton, ill-gotten; misbegotten.

**-otter,** blotter, clotter, cottar, cotter, dotter, hotter, jotter, knotter, ottar, otter, plotter, potter, rotter, spotter, squatter, swatter, totter, trotter; boycotter, complotter, garroter, globetrotter, sea otter.

**-ottish,** hottish, schottische, Scottish, sottish.

**-ottle,** bottle, dottle, glottal, mottle, pottle, throttle, tottle, twattle, wattle; bluebottle, squeeze bottle; Aristotle, epiglottal, vacuum bottle.

**-otto,** blotto, grotto, lotto, motto, otto, Otto, potto, Watteau; ridotto, risotto. See also **-ato** (-ä-).

**-otton.** See **-otten.**

**-otty,** blotty, clotty, dotty, grotty, knotty, Lottie, plotty, potty, snotty, spotty, trotty.

**-ouble,** bubble, double, nubble, rubble, stubble, trouble; redouble, soap bubble; body double, daily double, on the double.

**-oubly.** See **-ubbly.**

**-oubter.** See **-outer.**

**-oucher,** croucher, Goucher, sloucher, voucher.

**-ouder.** See **-owder.**

**-oudy.** See **-owdy.**

**-oughen,** roughen, toughen. See also **-uffin.**

**-ougher** (-o-). See **-offer.**

**-ougher** (-u-). See **-uffer.**

**-oughly.** See **-uffly.**

**-oughty.** See **-outy.**

**-oulder.** See **-older.**

**-oulful.** See **-oleful.**

**-ouncil,** council, counsel, groundsel; King's Counsel, Queen's Counsel; city council, privy council, student council.

**-ounder,** bounder, flounder, founder, grounder, hounder, pounder, rounder, sounder; all-rounder, backgrounder, cofounder, confounder, expounder, propounder, tenpounder, type founder, year-rounder.

**-oundly,** roundly, soundly; profoundly, unsoundly.

**-ounger.** See **-unger.**

**-ountain,** fountain, mountain; catamountain, drinking fountain, soda fountain, water fountain.

**-ounter,** counter, mounter; accounter, bean counter, discounter, encounter, lunch counter, surmounter; checkout counter, Geiger counter; over-the-counter, under-the-counter.

**-ounty,** bounty, county, mounty; viscounty.

**-ouper.** See **-ooper.**

**-ouple,** couple, souple, supple; decouple, quintuple, septuple, sextuple, uncouple.

**-oupy.** See **-oopy.**

**-ourage,** courage; demurrage,

discourage, Dutch courage, encourage.

**-ouri.** See **-ury.**

**-ourish,** currish, flourish, nourish; amateurish.

**-ourist.** See **-urist.**

**-ourly,** hourly, sourly.

**-ourney,** Bernie, Ernie, gurney, journey, tourney; attorney.

**-ournful.** See **-ornful.**

**-ourning.** See **-orning.**

**-ousal,** housel, ousel, spousal, tousle; arousal, carousal, espousal.

**-ousel.** See **-ousal.**

**-ouser,** bowser, browser, dowser, houser, Mauser, mouser, rouser, schnauzer, towser, trouser, wowser; carouser, espouser, warehouser; rabble-rouser.

**-ousin.** See **-ozen.**

**-ousle.** See **-ousal.**

**-ousseau.** See **-uso.**

**-ousy,** blowzy, drowsy, frowzy, lousy, mousy.

**-outer,** clouter, doubter, douter, flouter, outer, pouter, router, scouter, shouter, spouter, stouter, touter; come-outer; in-and-outer, out-and-outer.

**-outhful.** See **-uthful.**

**-outy,** doughty, droughty, gouty, grouty, pouty, snouty.

**-ova,** nova, ova; Jehovah, zelkova; bossa nova, Casanova, supernova, Villanova.

**-oval,** approval, disproval, removal, reproval; disapproval.

**-ovel,** grovel, hovel, novel.

**-ovement,** movement; approvement, improvement.

**-oven** (-ō-), cloven, coven, woven; Beethoven, handwoven; interwoven.

**-oven** (-u-), coven, oven, sloven.

**-over** (-ō-), clover, Dover, drover, over, plover, rover, stover, trover; allover, boilover, breakover, cabover, changeover, comb-over, crossover, flashover, flopover, flyover, handover, hangover, Hanover, holdover, hungover, layover, leftover, look-over, makeover, moreover, once-over, Passover, popover, pullover, pushover, red rover, rollover, rove-over, runover, sail-over, sea rover, slop-over, spillover, stopover, strike-over, sweet clover, switch-over, takeover, turnover, voice-over, walkover, warmed-over, wingover; carry-over, four-leaf clover, going-over, golden plover, half-seas over, lunar rover, maiden over.

**-over** (-u-), cover, glover, hover, lover, plover, shover; bedcover, booklover, dis-cover, dust cover, ground cover, hardcover, recover, slipcover, softcover, un-cover.

**-oward,** coward, cowered, flowered, Howard, pow-ered, showered, towered; high-powered, self-pow-ered; ivory-towered.

**-owboy,** cowboy, ploughboy.

**-owder,** chowder, clowder, crowder, louder, powder, prouder; clam chowder, gunpowder, tooth powder; baking powder, chili pow-der, curry powder, dusting powder.

**-owdy,** cloudy, dowdy, howdy, rowdy; cum laude, pan-dowdy; apple pandowdy, magna cum laude, summa cum laude.

**-owel,** bowel, cowl, dowel, foul, fowl, growl, howl, jowl, owl, prowl, rowel, scowl, towel, trowel, vowel, yowl; avowal, barn owl, barred owl, beach towel, befoul, dish towel, embowel, horned owl, night owl, peafowl, screech owl, tea towel, wildfowl; cheek-by-jowl, disavowal, disembowel, guinea fowl, jungle fowl, semi-vowel, Turkish towel, waterfowl.

**-ower** (-ō-), blower, crower, goer, grower, hoer, knower, lower, mower, ower, rower, sewer, slower, sower, thrower, tower; beachgoer, bestower, churchgoer, flamethrower, filmgoer, glassblower, lawnmower, playgoer, snowblower, snowthrower, vetoer, winegrower; concertgoer, moviegoer, overthrower, partygoer, whistleblower.

**-owered.** See **-oward.**

**-owery,** bowery, cowrie, dowry, floury, flowery,

houri, kauri, lowery, Maori, showery, towery.

**-owing,** blowing, crowing, flowing, glowing, going, growing, knowing, lowing, mowing, owing, rowing, sewing, showing, snowing, sowing, stowing, towing, throwing; churchgoing, foregoing, free-flowing, glassblowing, ingoing, mind-blowing, ongoing, outgoing, seagoing, self-knowing; easygoing, moviegoing, oceangoing, theatergoing, thoroughgoing.

Also: **-ow** + **-ing** (as in *bestowing,* etc.)

Also: **-o** + **-ing** (as in *helloing,* etc.)

**-owledge,** college, knowledge; acknowledge, foreknowledge, self-knowledge.

**-owler.** See **-oller.**

**-owly.** See **-oly.**

**-owman.** See **-omen.**

**-owner.** See **-oner.**

**-ownie.** See **-owny.**

**-owny,** brownie, Brownie, downy, frowny, townie.

**-owry.** See **-owery.**

**-owsy.** See **-ousy.**

**-owy,** blowy, Bowie, Chloe, doughy, glowy, joey, Joey, nowy, showy, snowy, towhee, towy, Zoe.

**-oxen,** coxswain, oxen, tocsin, toxin; digoxin, dioxin; aflatoxin, neurotoxin .

**-oxy,** boxy, Coxey, doxy, foxy, moxie, oxy, proxy; Biloxi, epoxy; orthodoxy, paradoxy; heterodoxy.

**-oyal,** loyal, royal; blood royal, disloyal, prince royal; battle royal, pennyroyal. See also **-oil.**

**-oyalty,** loyalty, royalty; disloyalty, viceroyalty.

**-oyance,** buoyance; annoyance, chatoyance, clairvoyance, flamboyance.

**-oyant,** buoyant, chatoyant, clairvoyant, flamboyant.

**-oyer,** boyar, foyer, oyer, toyer; annoyer, caloyer, destroyer, employer, enjoyer.

**-oyly.** See **-oily.**

**-oyment,** deployment, employment, enjoyment; redeployment, self-employment, unemployment.

**-oyster.** See **-oister.**

**-ozen** (-u-), cousin, cozen, dozen; first cousin; baker's dozen, cater-cousin, country cousin, daily dozen, kissing cousin, second cousin.

**-ozen** (-ō-). See **-osen.**

**-ozzle,** nozzle, schnozzle.

**-uager.** See **-ager.**

**-ual.** See **-uel.**

**-uant,** fluent, suint, truant; affluent, congruent, pursuant.

**-uba,** Cuba, juba, scuba, tuba; Aruba.

**-ubbard.** See **-upboard.**

**-ubber,** blubber, clubber, drubber, dubber, grubber, lubber, rubber, scrubber, slubber, snubber, stubber; foam rubber, landlubber, nightclubber; moneygrubber; india rubber.

**-ubberd.** See **-upboard.**

**-ubbish,** clubbish, cubbish, grubbish, rubbish, tubbish.

**-ubble.** See **-ouble.**

**-ubbly,** bubbly, doubly, knubbly, nubbly, rubbly, stubbly.

**-ubby,** bubby, chubby, clubby, cubby, grubby, hubby, nubby, scrubby, shrubby, snubby, stubby, tubby.

**-ubic,** cubic, pubic; cherubic.

**-ubtle.** See **-uttle.**

**-ubtler.** See **-utler.**

**-uby.** See **-ooby.**

**-ucent,** lucent; abducent, adducent, traducent, translucent.

**-ucid,** deuced, lucid, mucid; pellucid, Seleucid.

**-ucker,** bucker, chucker, chukker, ducker, mucker, pucker, shucker, succor, sucker, trucker, tucker; bloodsucker, goatsucker, sapsucker, seersucker, thumb-sucker; bib and tucker.

**-uckett,** bucket, ducat, tucket; gutbucket, lunch bucket, Nantucket, Pawtucket.

**-uckle,** buccal, buckle, chuckle, huckle, knuckle, muckle, suckle, truckle; Arbuckle, bareknuckle, parbuckle, pinochle, swashbuckle, turnbuckle, unbuckle, white-knuckle; honeysuckle.

**-uckled.** See **-uckold.**

**-uckler,** buckler, chuckler, knuckler; swashbuckler.

**-uckling,** buckling, duckling,

suckling; swashbuckling; ugly duckling.

**-uckold,** cuckold; bareknuckled, whiteknuckled.
Also: **-uckle** + **-d** (as in *buckled,* etc.)

**-ucky,** ducky, lucky, mucky, plucky, sucky, yucky; Kentucky, unlucky.

**-ucre.** See **-uker.**

**-ucter.** See **-uctor.**

**-uction,** fluxion, ruction, suction; abduction, adduction, affluxion, conduction, construction, deduction, defluxion, destruction, eduction, effluxion, induction, instruction, obstruction, production, reduction, seduction, subduction, transduction; deconstruction, introduction, liposuction, mass production, misconstruction, reconstruction, reproduction, self-destruction; overproduction, superinduction.

**-uctive,** adductive, conductive, constructive, deductive, destructive, eductive, inductive, instructive, obstructive, productive, reductive, seductive, traductive; deconstructive, introductive, nonproductive, reconstructive, reproductive, self-destructive, superstructive, unconstructive, uninstructive, unproductive; overproductive.

**-uctor,** ductor; abductor, adductor, conductor, constructor, destructor, eductor, inductor, instructor, obstructer; nonconductor; semiconductor, superconductor.

**-udder,** chuddar, dudder, flooder, mudder, rudder, scudder, shudder, spudder, udder.

**-uddhist.** See **-udist.**

**-uddle,** buddle, cuddle, fuddle, huddle, muddle, puddle, ruddle; befuddle.

**-uddler,** cuddler, huddler, muddler.

**-uddy,** bloody, buddy, cruddy, cuddy, muddy, ruddy, studdy, study; brown study, case study, work-study; buddy-buddy, fuddy-duddy, understudy.

**-udel.** See **-oodle.**

**-udely,** crudely, lewdly, nudely, rudely, shrewdly.

**-udent,** prudent, student; concludent, imprudent, nonstudent, occludent; jurisprudent.

**-udest.** See **-udist.**

**-udgeon,** bludgeon, dudgeon, gudgeon; curmudgeon.

**-udgy,** budgie, pudgy, sludgy, smudgy.

**-udish,** crudish, dudish, lewdish, nudish, prudish, rudish, shrewdish.

**-udist,** Buddhist, crudest, feudist, lewdest, nudist, rudest, shrewdest.

**-udo,** judo, kudo, pseudo, scudo; escudo, testudo.

**-udy.** See **-uddy.**

**-uel,** crewel, cruel, dual, duel, fuel, gruel, jewel, newel; accrual, bejewel, eschewal, pursual, refuel, renewal, reviewal, subdual, synfuel; biofuel, diesel fuel, fossil fuel.

**-uet,** bluet, cruet, suet; intuit.

**-uey.** See **-ewy.**

**-uffel.** See **-uffle.**

**-uffer,** bluffer, buffer, duffer, gruffer, huffer, puffer, rougher, snuffer, stuffer, suffer, tougher; candlesnuffer, stocking stuffer.

**-uffin,** muffin, puffin; English muffin, ragamuffin.

**-uffing,** bluffing, cuffing, huffing, puffing, stuffing.

**-uffle,** buffle, chuffle, duffel, muffle, ruffle, scuffle, shuffle, snuffle, truffle; dust ruffle, kerfuffle, reshuffle.

**-uffly,** bluffly, gruffly, roughly, ruffly, shuffly, snuffly, toughly.

**-uffy,** buffy, chuffy, fluffy, gruffy, huffy, muffy, puffy, scruffy, snuffy, stuffy, toughie.

**-ufty,** mufti, tufty.

**-ugal.** See **-ugle.**

**-ugger,** bugger, chugger, drugger, hugger, lugger, mugger, plugger, rugger, slugger, smugger, snugger, tugger; debugger, hiphugger, treehugger, hugger-mugger, jitter-bugger.

**-uggle,** guggle, juggle, smuggle, snuggle, struggle.

**-uggy,** buggy, druggie, druggy, muggy, puggy, sluggy; beach buggy, dune buggy, swamp buggy; baby buggy.

**-ugle,** Breughel, bugle, frugal, fugal, jugal, kugel; MacDougall; febrifugal.

**-ugly,** smugly, snuggly, snugly, ugly; plugugly.

**-uicy,** goosy, juicy, Lucy, sluicy, sprucy; Debussy, Watusi; acey-deucy, loosey-goosey.

**-uid,** druid, fluid.

**-uilder,** builder, gilder, guilder; bewilder, boatbuilder, homebuilder, shipbuilder, rebuilder; bodybuilder, master builder.

**-uilding,** building, gilding; homebuilding, oil gilding, outbuilding, rebuilding, shipbuilding.

**-uin,** bruin, ruin.

**-uiser.** See **-oser.**

**-uitor.** See **-ooter.**

**-uker,** euchre, fluker, lucre, puker; rebuker.

**-uki.** See **-ooky.**

**-uky.** See **-ooky.**

**-ula,** Beulah, doula, hula, moola; tabbouleh, Talullah; Ashtabula, Boola Boola, hula-hula.

**-ulep.** See **-ulip.**

**-ulgar,** Bulgar, bulgur, vulgar.

**-ulgence,** effulgence, indulgence, refulgence; self-indulgence.

**-ulgent,** fulgent; effulgent, indulgent, refulgent; self-indulgent.

**-ulip,** julep, tulip.

**-ulky,** bulky, hulky, sulky.

**-uller,** color, cruller, culler, duller, guller, luller, sculler; annuller, discolor, medullar, off-color, tricolor; Technicolor, multicolor, watercolor.

**-ullet** (-o͝o-), bullet, pullet; magic bullet, silver bullet.

**-ullet** (-ul-), cullet, gullet, mullet.

**-ulley.** See **-ully.**

**-ullion,** cullion, mullion, scullion; slumgullion.

**-ully** (-o͝o-), bully, fully, muley, pulley, woolly.

**-ully** (-ul-), cully, dully, gully, hully, sully, Tully.

**-ulsion,** pulsion; avulsion, compulsion, convulsion, divulsion, emulsion, evulsion, expulsion, impulsion, propulsion, repulsion, revulsion; jet-propulsion, self-revulsion.

**-ulsive,** compulsive, convulsive, emulsive, expulsive, impulsive, propulsive, repulsive, revulsive.

**-ultry,** sultry; adultery.

**-ulture,** culture, vulture; subculture; agriculture, apiculture, aquaculture, aviculture, counterculture, culture vulture, floriculture, horticulture, pisciculture, viniculture.

**-ulu,** Lulu, Zulu; Honolulu.

**-uly,** coolie, coolly, coulee, Dooley, dooly, duly, Julie, muley, newly, puli, ruly, stoolie, Thule, truly; Bernoulli, guayule, patchouli, tabbouleh, unduly, unruly, yours truly; ultima Thule.

**-uma,** duma, pneuma, puma, struma, Yuma; daruma, mazuma, Satsuma; Montezuma.

**-uman.** See **-umen.**

**-umbent,** accumbent, decumbent, incumbent, procumbent, recumbent.

**-umber,** cumber, Humber, lumbar, lumber, number, slumber, umber; cucumber, encumber, outnumber, prime number, real number, whole number; disencumber.

**-umber.** See **-ummer.**

**-umble,** bumble, crumble, fumble, grumble, humble, jumble, mumble, rumble, scumble, stumble, tumble, umbel.

**-umbly,** comely, dumbly, glumly, grumly, numbly.

**-umbo,** Dumbo, gumbo, jumbo, umbo; mumbo-jumbo.

**-umbrous,** cumbrous, slumbrous; penumbrous.

**-umby.** See **-ummy.**

**-umen,** bloomin', crewman, human, lumen, Newman, numen, rumen, Truman; acumen, albumen, albumin, bitumen, cerumen, ichneumon, illumine, inhuman, subhuman; catechumen, superhuman.

**-umer,** bloomer, boomer, fumer, groomer, humor, roomer, rumor, tumor; consumer, costumer, exhumer, ill-humor, late bloomer, perfumer; baby boomer, gallows humor.

**-umid,** fumid, humid, tumid.

**-umly.** See **-umbly.**

**-ummer,** bummer, comer, drummer, dumber, hummer, mummer, number, plumber, rummer, scummer, slummer, strummer, summer, thrummer; latecomer, midsummer, newcomer.

**-ummit,** grummet, plummet, summit.

**-ummock.** See **-omach.**

**-ummy,** chummy, crumby, crummy, dummy, gummy, lummy, mummy, plummy, rummy, scummy, slummy, thrummy, tummy, yummy.

**-umnal,** autumnal, columnal.

**-umous,** brumous, fumous, grumous, humus, spumous; posthumous.

**-umper,** bumper, dumper, jumper, lumper, plumper, pumper, stumper, thumper, trumper; broad jumper, high jumper, long jumper, show jumper, ski jumper, tub-thumper; Bible-thumper, bungee jumper, jolly jumper, puddlejumper.

**-umpet,** crumpet, strumpet, trumpet.

**-umpish,** chumpish, clumpish, dumpish, frumpish, grumpish, lumpish, plumpish.

**-umpkin,** bumpkin, lumpkin, pumpkin.

**-umple,** crumple, rumple.

**-umption,** gumption; assumption, consumption, presumption, resumption.

**-umptious,** bumptious, scrumptious; presumptuous.

**-umptive,** assumptive, consumptive, presumptive, resumptive.

**-umpus.** See **-ompass.**

**-umus.** See **-umous.**

**-una,** kuna, luna, puna, tuna, Una; Fortuna, induna, kahuna, lacuna, laguna, vicuna.

**-unar.** See **-uner.**

**-uncheon,** bruncheon, luncheon, puncheon, truncheon.

**-unction,** function, junction, unction; adjunction, cofunction, compunction, conjunction, disjunction, dysfunction, expunction, injunction, malfunction, subjunction.

**-unctive,** adjunctive, conjunctive, defunctive, disjunctive, subjunctive.

**-uncture,** juncture, puncture; conjuncture, disjuncture.

**-undance,** abundance, redundance; superabundance.

**-undant,** abundant, redundant; superabundant.

**-unday.** See **-undy.**

**-under,** blunder, dunder, plunder, sunder, thunder, under, wonder; asunder, down under, hereunder, jocunder, refunder, rotunder, thereunder.

**-undle,** bundle, rundle, trundle.

**-undy,** Fundy, Grundy, Monday, sundae, Sunday, undie; Bay of Fundy, jaguarundi, Mrs. Grundy, salmagundi; coatimundi.

**-uner,** crooner, lunar, pruner, schooner, sooner, spooner, swooner, tuner; attuner, communer, harpooner, impugner, lacunar, oppugner; honeymooner, importuner, prairie schooner.

**-unger** (-g-), hunger, monger, younger; fearmonger, fishmonger, hatemonger, newsmonger, phrasemonger, scaremonger, warmonger, whoremonger, wordmonger; costermonger, gossipmonger, ironmonger, rumormonger, scandalmonger.

**-unger** (-j-), blunger, lunger, plunger, sponger; expunger.

**-ungle,** bungle, fungal, jungle.

**-unic,** eunuch, Munich, punic, Punic, runic, tunic.

**-union.** See **-onion.**

**-unkard,** bunkered, drunkard, Dunkard.

**-unker,** bunker, clunker, drunker, dunker, Dunker, flunker, funker, hunker, junker, Junker, lunker, plunker, punker, younker; debunker, mossbunker, slam dunker, spelunker.

**-unky,** chunky, clunky, donkey, flunky, funky, gunky, hunky, junkie, junky, monkey, punkie, punky, skunky, spunky; grease monkey.

**-unnage.** See **-onnage.**

**-unnel,** funnel, gunnel, gunwale, runnel, trunnel, tunnel.

**-unny,** bunny, coney, funny, gunny, honey, money, punny, runny, sonny, sunny, Tunney, tunny; blood money, dumb bunny, dust bunny, front money, hush money, mad money, old money, pin money, play money, prize money, seed money, smart money, unfunny; easy money, even money, funny money, pocket money, spending money.

**-untal.** See **-untle.**

**-unter,** blunter, bunter, grunter, hunter, punter; confronter, fox hunter, headhunter, jobhunter, pothunter, witchhunter; bounty hunter, fortune hunter.

**-untle,** frontal, gruntle; confrontal, disgruntle; contrapuntal.

**-unwale.** See **-unnel.**

**-uoy.** See **-ewy.**

**-upboard,** blubbered, cupboard, Hubbard, rubbered.

**-uper.** See **-ooper.**

**-upil.** See **-uple.**

**-uple,** cupel, duple, pupil, scruple; octuple, quadruple, quintuple, septuple, sextuple.

**-uplet,** drupelet; octuplet, quadruplet, quintuplet, septuplet, sextuplet.

**-upor.** See **-ooper.**

**-upper,** crupper, cupper, scupper, supper, upper; cheerer-upper, fixer-upper, ice-cream supper, pepper-upper, picker-upper, potluck supper, warmer-upper.

**-upple.** See **-ouple.**

**-uppy,** Buppy, guppy, puppy, yuppie; hush puppy, mud puppy, sand puppy; bumblepuppy.

**-ura,** dura, durra, pleura, sura, surah, surra; bravura, caesura, datura, tempura; Angostura; coloratura; appoggiatura.

**-ural,** crural, jural, mural, neural, pleural, plural, puerile, rural, sural, Ural; caesural, subdural; epidural, extramural, intermural, intramural, sinecural.

**-urance,** durance; assurance, endurance, insurance; coinsurance, health insurance, life insurance, reassurance, self-assurance.

**-urban,** bourbon, Durban, turban, turbine, urban; exurban, suburban, wind turbine; interurban.

**-urchin.** See **-irchen.**

**-urder,** birder, girder, herder,

murder; absurder, engirder, sheepherder.

**-urdle.** See **-irdle.**

**-urdly.** See **-irdly.**

**-urdy,** birdie, curdy, sturdy, wordy; hurdy-gurdy.

**-urely,** purely, surely; demurely, maturely, obscurely, securely.

**-urement,** abjurement, allurement, immurement, inurement, obscurement, procurement.

**-urer,** curer, führer, furor, furore, juror, lurer, purer, tourer; abjurer, insurer, nonjuror, procurer, securer.

**-urgate,** expurgate, objurgate.

**-urgence.** See **-ergence.**

**-urgent.** See **-ergent.**

**-urgeon,** burgeon, sturgeon, surgeon, virgin; flight surgeon, tree surgeon.

**-urger.** See **-erger.**

**-urgle,** burgle, gurgle.

**-urgy,** clergy, dirgy, splurgy, surgy; chemurgy, liturgy, theurgy, zymurgy; dramaturgy, metallurgy, thaumaturgy.

**-uric,** mercuric, purpuric, sulfuric, telluric; aciduric, barbituric.

**-urist,** jurist, purist, tourist; coiffurist; manicurist, pedicurist; caricaturist, miniaturist.

**-urker.** See **-irker.**

**-urky.** See **-erky.**

**-urler,** burler, curler, furler, hurler, pearler, purler, skirler, twirler, whirler.

**-urlew,** curlew, purlieu.

**-urling,** curling, furling, hurling, purling, skirling, sterling, swirling, twirling, whirling; uncurling.

**-urlish.** See **-irlish.**

**-urloin,** purloin, sirloin.

**-urly,** burly, churly, curly, early, girlie, hurly, knurly, pearly, Shirley, squirrely, surly, swirly, twirly, whirly; hurly-burly.

**-urma,** Burma, derma, herma, Irma; terra firma.

**-urmese.** See **-ermes.**

**-urmur.** See **-irmer.**

**-urnal.** See **-ernal.**

**-urner.** See **-earner.**

**-urning.** See **-earning.**

**-urnish,** burnish, furnish.

**-uror.** See **-urer.**

**-urper,** burper, chirper; usurper.

**-urrage.** See **-ourage.**

**-urrish.** See **-ourish.**
**-urro.** See **-orough.**
**-urrow.** See **-orough.**
**-urry,** burry, curry, dhurrie, flurry, furry, hurry, scurry, slurry, spurry, surrey, worry; hurry-scurry, in a hurry.
**-ursal.** See **-ersal.**
**-urser,** bursar, cursor, mercer, nurser, purser; disburser, precursor.
**-ursor.** See **-urser.**
**-urtain.** See **-ertain.**
**-urter.** See **-erter.**
**-urtive.** See **-ertive.**
**-urtle,** fertile, hurtle, kirtle, myrtle, Myrtle, turtle, whortle; cross-fertile, exsertile, infertile, self-fertile, wax myrtle.
**-urtly.** See **-ertly.**
**-urvant.** See **-ervant.**
**-urvy,** curvy, nervy, scurvy; topsy-turvy.
**-ury** (-o͝o-), curie, Curie, fleury, fury, Fury, houri, Jewry, jury; de jure, grand jury, Missouri, potpourri, tandoori.
**-ury** (-e-). See **-erry.**
**-usa,** Medusa, Sousa; Arethusa; lollapalooza.
**-usal.** See **-oozle.**
**-uscan,** buskin, dusken, Ruskin, Tuscan; Etruscan, molluscan.
**-uscle.** See **-ustle.**
**-usel.** See **-oozle.**
**-user,** muser, user; abuser, accuser, amuser, diffuser, end user, excuser, infuser; multiuser. See also **-oser.**
**-usher,** blusher, brusher, crusher, flusher, gusher, husher, musher, plusher, rusher, shusher, usher; four-flusher.
**-ushy,** brushy, gushy, lushy, mushy, plushy, rushy, slushy, squushy.
**-usi.** See **-uicy.**
**-usier.** See **-izzier.**
**-usion,** fusion; allusion, Carthusian, collusion, conclusion, confusion, contusion, delusion, diffusion, effusion, elusion, exclusion, extrusion, illusion, inclusion, infusion, intrusion, Malthusian, obtrusion, occlusion, perfusion, preclusion, profusion, protrusion, reclusion, seclusion, suffusion, transfusion; disillusion, interfusion, malocclusion.

**-usive,** abusive, allusive, collusive, conclusive, conducive, contusive, deducive, delusive, diffusive, effusive, elusive, exclusive, extrusive, illusive, inclusive, infusive, intrusive, obtrusive, occlusive, preclusive, reclusive, seclusive; inconclusive, unobtrusive.

**-uskin.** See **-uscan.**

**-usky,** dusky, husky, muskie, musky.

**-uso,** Crusoe, Rousseau, trousseau, whoso; Caruso.

**-ussel.** See **-ustle.**

**-usset,** gusset, russet; decussate.

**-ussia,** Prussia, Russia; Belorussia.

**-ussian.** See **-ussion.**

**-ussion,** Prussian, Russian; concussion, discussion, percussion; Belorussian, repercussion.

**-ussive,** jussive, tussive; concussive, discussive, percussive, succussive; antitussive, repercussive.

**-ussy,** fussy, Gussie, gussy, hussy, mussy, pussy.

**-ustard,** blustered, bustard, clustered, custard, flustered, mustard, mustered.

**-uster,** bluster, buster, cluster, Custer, duster, fluster, juster, luster, muster, thruster, truster; adjuster, blockbuster, brain truster, crop duster, gangbuster, lackluster, star cluster, trustbuster; antitruster, baby buster, broncobuster, feather duster, filibuster, knuckle-duster.

**-ustered.** See **-ustard.**

**-ustic,** fustic, rustic.

**-ustion,** fustian; combustion.

**-ustle,** bustle, hustle, justle, muscle, mussel, rustle, tussle; corpuscle, Jack Russell, outmuscle.

**-ustler,** bustler, hustler, rustler, tussler.

**-ustly,** justly; augustly, robustly, unjustly.

**-usty,** busty, crusty, dusty, fusty, gusty, lusty, musty, rusty, trusty.

**-usy.** See **-izzy.**

**-utal,** brutal, futile, tootle, utile; refutal.

**-uter.** See **-ooter.**

**-utest.** See **-utist.**

**-uthful,** ruthful, truthful, youthful; untruthful.

**-uthless,** ruthless, toothless, truthless.

**-utie.** See **-ooty.**

**-utile.** See **-utal.**

**-ution,** Lucian; ablution, Aleutian, capuchin, Confucian, dilution, locution, pollution, solution, volution; absolution, attribution, comminution, constitution, contribution, convolution, destitution, devolution, diminution, dissolution, distribution, elocution, evolution, execution, institution, involution, Lilliputian, persecution, prosecution, prostitution, resolution, restitution, retribution, revolution, Rosicrucian, substitution; circumlocution, coevolution, electrocution, green revolution, irresolution, joint resolution, reconstitution, redistribution.

**-utist,** chutist, cutest, flutist, lutist; absolutist, parachutist, pharmaceutist, therapeutist.

**-utive,** dilutive, pollutive; absolutive, coadjutive, constitutive, diminutive, persecutive, resolutive, substitutive.

**-utler,** butler, cutler, scuttler, subtler, sutler.

**-utor.** See **-ooter.**

**-uttal.** See **-uttle.**

**-utter,** butter, clutter, cutter, flutter, gutter, mutter, nutter, putter, shutter, splutter, sputter, strutter, stutter, utter; abutter, aflutter, haircutter, leaf-cutter, price-cutter, rebutter, stonecutter, unclutter, woodcutter; apple butter, bread and butter, cookie-cutter, daisy-cutter, paper cutter, peanut butter, surrebutter.

**-uttish,** ruttish, sluttish.

**-uttle,** buttle, cuttle, guttle, scuttle, shuttle, subtle; abuttal, coal scuttle, rebuttal, space shuttle.

**-uttler.** See **-utler.**

**-utton,** button, glutton, mutton; hot-button, push-button, unbutton; bachelor button, belly button, on the button, panic button.

**-utty,** gutty, jutty, nutty, puttee, putty, rutty, slutty, smutty, tutty.

**-uture,** blucher, future, moocher, suture.

**-uty.** See **-ooty.**

**-uxion.** See **-uction.**

**-uyer.** See **-ier.**

**-uzzle,** guzzle, muzzle, nuzzle, puzzle; crossword puzzle, jigsaw puzzle.

**-uzzler,** guzzler, muzzler, nuzzler, puzzler.

**-uzzy,** fuzzy, muzzy, scuzzy; fuzzy-wuzzy.

**-yan.** See **-ion.**

**-yer.** See **-ier.**

**-ylla.** See **-illa.**

**-ylon,** nylon, pylon, trylon.

**-yly.** See **-ily.**

**-ymbal.** See **-imble.**

**-ymbol.** See **-imble.**

**-ymic.** See **-imic.**

**-yming.** See **-iming.**

**-yncher.** See **-incher.**

**-yness.** See **-inus.**

**-ynic.** See **-inic.**

**-ypsy,** gypsy, ipse, tipsy; Poughkeepsie.

**-yptic,** cryptic, diptych, glyptic, styptic, triptych; ecliptic, elliptic; apocalyptic.

**-yra.** See **-ira.**

**-yrant.** See **-irant.**

**-yrate,** gyrate, irate, lyrate; circumgyrate.

**-yric,** lyric, Pyrrhic; butyric, empiric, satiric, satyric, vampiric; panegyric.

**-yron.** See **-iren.**

**-yrtle.** See **-urtle.**

**-yrus.** See **-irus.**

**-ysian.** See **-ision.**

**-ysic,** phthisic, physic; metaphysic.

**-ysmal.** See **-ismal.**

**-yssal.** See **-istle.**

**-ystic.** See **-istic.**

**-ytic.** See **-itic.**

# Three-Syllable Rhymes

**-abia,** labia, Swabia; Arabia; Saudi Arabia.
**-abian,** Fabian, gabion, Swabian; Arabian.
**-abion.** See **-abian.**
**-abular,** fabular, tabular; vocabular.
**-abulate,** tabulate; confabulate.
**-abulous,** fabulous; fantabulous.
**-abulum,** pabulum; incunabulum.
**-aceable,** placeable, traceable; displaceable, effaceable, embraceable, erasable, persuasible, replaceable, retraceable, unplaceable, untraceable; ineffaceable, irreplaceable.
**-acerate,** lacerate, macerate.
**-acery,** tracery; embracery.
**-aciate.** See **-atiate.**
**-acity,** audacity, capacity, fugacity, loquacity, mendacity, opacity, rapacity, sagacity, tenacity, veracity, voracity; efficacity, incapacity, perspicacity, pertinacity.
**-ackery,** daiquiri, flackery, quackery; gimcrackery.
**-actable,** actable, tractable; abstractable, attractable, compactible, contractible, distractible, extractable, intractable, retractable.
**-actible.** See **-actable.**
**-actical,** practical, tactical; didactical, impractical, syntactical.
**-actional,** factional, fractional; redactional, transactional.
**-actory,** factory; olfactory, phylactery, refractory; calefactory, manufactory, satisfactory; unsatisfactory.
**-actual,** actual, factual, tactual; contractual; artifactual, counterfactual.
**-acular,** macular, saccular; oracular, piacular, spectacular, tentacular, vernacular.
**-aculate,** maculate; ejaculate; immaculate.

**-adable,** gradable, tradable, wadable; abradable, degradable, evadable, upgradable; biodegradable, photodegradable.

**-adian,** radian; Acadian, Akkadian, Arcadian, Barbadian, Canadian, circadian, Grenadian, Palladian; French Canadian, Trinidadian.

**-adiant,** gradient, radiant.

**-adium,** radium, stadium; palladium, vanadium.

**-aerial.** See **-arial.**

**-agenous.** See **-aginous.**

**-aggery,** jaggery, staggery, waggery; carpetbaggery.

**-aginal,** paginal, vaginal; imaginal.

**-aginous,** collagenous, farraginous, viraginous; cartilaginous, mucilaginous, oleaginous.

**-agonist,** agonist; antagonist, protagonist; deuteragonist.

**-agonize,** agonize; antagonize.

**-agrancy,** flagrancy, fragrancy, vagrancy.

**-aical,** laical; algebraical, pharasaical; paradisaical.

**-aiety.** See **-aity.**

**-ailable,** bailable, mailable, salable, scalable; assailable, available, resalable, unsalable; unassailable, unavailable.

**-ainable,** stainable, trainable; attainable, constrainable, containable, distrainable, explainable, maintainable, obtainable, restrainable, retainable, retrainable, sustainable; ascertainable, unattainable, unobtainable.

**-ainian.** See **-anian.**

**-aiquiri.** See **-ackery.**

**-airable.** See **-earable.**

**-aity,** deity, gaiety, laity; corporeity, spontaneity, synchroneity; diaphaneity; contemporaneity, extemporaneity.

**-akable,** breakable, shakable; mistakable, nonbreakable, unbreakable, unslakable; unmistakable.

**-akery,** bakery, fakery.

**-alary,** calorie, gallery, salary; rogue's gallery; intercalary, kilocalorie.

**-alea.** See **-alia.**

**-algia,** arthralgia, myalgia, neuralgia, nostalgia; fibromyalgia.

**-alia,** galea, palea; Australia, azalea, realia, regalia;

bacchanalia, coprolalia, echolalia, genitalia, glossolalia, inter alia, marginalia, penetralia.

**-ality** (-a-), aurality, banality, brutality, causality, centrality, duality, egality, extrality, fatality, feudality, finality, formality, frugality, legality, lethality, locality, mentality, modality, molality, morality, mortality, nasality, natality, neutrality, nodality, normality, orality, ovality, plurality, primality, rascality, reality, regality, sodality, tonality, totality, venality, vitality; abnormality, actuality, amorality, animality, atonality, bestiality, bipedality, cardinality, classicality, comicality, commonality, communality, cordiality, corporality, criminality, externality, factuality, fictionality, functionality, generality, geniality, hospitality, ideality, illegality, immorality, immortality, informality, internality, joviality, lexicality, liberality, lineality, literality, logicality, marginality, musicality, mutuality, nationality, notionality, nuptiality, optimality, optionality, parfocality, partiality, personality, physicality, practicality, principality, punctuality, rationality, seasonality, sensuality, sexuality, siege mentality, sociality, subnormality, technicality, temporality, textuality, topicality, triviality, typicality, unreality, verticality, virtuality, whimsicality; asexuality, bisexuality, bunker mentality, collegiality, commerciality, conditionality, congeniality, connubiality, conventionality, conviviality, corporeality, dimensionality, directionality, effectuality, eventuality, exceptionality, grammaticality, illogicality, impartiality, impracticality, instrumentality, intentionality, irrationality, municipality, originality, potentiality, proportionality, provinciality, sentimentality, spirituality, universality; artificiality, confidentiality, homosexuality, immateriality, individuality, intellectuality, superficiality, territoriality, unconventionality, virtual reality.

**-ality** (-o-), jollity, polity, quality; equality, frivolity.

**-allage.** See **-alogy.**

**-allery.** See **-alary.**

**-allium,** allium, gallium, pallium, thallium.

**-alogist,** analogist, decalogist, dialogist, mammalogist; genealogist, mineralogist.

**-alogy** (-a-), analogy, hypallage, mammalogy, tetralogy; genealogy, mineralogy.

**-alogy** (-o-). See **-ology.**

**-alorie.** See **-alary.**

**-alysis,** analysis, catalysis, dialysis, paralysis; cryptanalysis, metanalysis, self-analysis, urinalysis; hemodialysis, psychoanalysis.

**-amable,** blamable, claimable, framable, nameable, tamable; reclaimable, untamable; irreclaimable.

**-amatist,** dramatist, grammatist; epigrammatist, melodramatist.

**-ameable.** See **-amable.**

**-amerous.** See **-amorous.**

**-ameter,** amateur; diameter, heptameter, hexameter, octameter, parameter, pentameter, rotameter, tetrameter.

**-amina,** lamina, stamina.

**-amity,** amity; calamity.

**-ammatist.** See **-amatist.**

**-amorous,** amorous, clamorous, glamorous; pentamerous, tetramerous.

**-ampean.** See **-ampion.**

**-ampion,** campion, champion, pampean, tampion.

**-anacle.** See **-anical.**

**-anary** (-ā-). See **-anery.**

**-anary** (-a-). See **-annery.**

**-anatee.** See **-anity.**

**-andable,** mandible; commandable, demandable, expandable; countermandable, understandable.

**-andible.** See **-andable.**

**-anean.** See **-anian.**

**-aneous,** cutaneous, extraneous, spontaneous; instantaneous, miscellaneous, simultaneous, subcutaneous; contemporaneous, extemporaneous.

**-anery,** granary, chicanery.

**-angible,** frangible, tangible; infrangible, intangible, refrangible.

**-ania,** mania; Albania, Tasmania, titania, Urania; Anglomania, collectanea, dipsomania, egomania, kleptomania, Lithuania, Mauretania, melomania, miscellanea, monomania, nymphomania, Oceania, Pennsylvania, pyromania, Transylvania; balletomania, bibliomania, decalcomania, megalomania.

**-anian,** Albanian, Iranian, Jordanian, Romanian, Ukrainian, Uranian, vulcanian; Lithuanian, Mauretanian, Pennsylvanian, Pomeranian, subterranean.

**-anical,** manacle, panicle; botanical, mechanical, tyrannical; puritanical.

**-anicle.** See **-anical.**

**-anikin.** See **-annikin.**

**-animous,** animus; magnanimous, unanimous; pusillanimous.

**-animus.** See **-animous.**

**-anister,** banister, canister, ganister.

**-anity,** manatee, sanity, vanity; humanity, inanity, insanity, profanity, urbanity; Christianity, inhumanity.

**-anium,** cranium; geranium, titanium, uranium.

**-annable.** See **-annibal.**

**-annary.** See **-annery.**

**-annequin.** See **-annikin.**

**-annery,** cannery, granary, stannary, tannery.

**-annibal,** cannibal, Hannibal, scannable.

**-annical.** See **-anical.**

**-annikin,** cannikin, manikin, mannequin, pannikin.

**-annual,** annual, manual; biannual, Emmanuel; semiannual.

**-annular,** annular, cannular, granular.

**-anthropy,** lycanthropy, misanthropy, philanthropy.

**-anual.** See **-annual.**

**-anuel.** See **-annual.**

**-anular.** See **-annular.**

**-apable,** capable, drapable, shapable; escapable, incapable; inescapable.

**-apery,** apery, drapery, grapery, japery, napery, papery; sandpapery.

**-aphical,** graphical; biographical, cartographical, cosmographical, cryptographical, epigraphical, ethnographical, geographical, orthographical, topographical, typographical; bibliographical, lexicographical; autobiographical.

**-apolis,** Anapolis; Minneapolis; Indianapolis.

**-appily,** happily, scrappily, snappily.

**-appiness,** happiness, sappiness, scrappiness, snappiness.

**-arable,** arable, parable; comparable.

**-arative,** narrative; comparative, declarative, preparative, reparative.

**-arcener,** larcener, parcener.

**-archical,** autarchical, monarchical; hierarchical, oligarchical.

**-area,** area, varia; Bavaria, Bulgaria, filaria, malaria, planaria, Samaria; cineraria, luminaria, miliaria, urticaria.

**-areable.** See **-earable.**

**-arean.** See **-arian.**

**-areous.** See **-arious.**

**-arial,** aerial, areal; glossarial, malarial; actuarial, adversarial; calendarial, commissarial, secretarial.

**-arian,** Aryan, carrion, clarion, Marion; agrarian, Aquarian, barbarian, Bavarian, Bulgarian, cesarean, cnidarian, contrarian, fruitarian, grammarian, Hungarian, librarian, ovarian, riparian, rosarian, sectarian, Tocharian, vulgarian; antiquarian, centenarian, Indo-Aryan, lapidarian, libertarian, millenarian, nonsectarian, prelapsarian, proletarian, Rastafarian, seminarian, trinitarian, unitarian, vegetarian; abecedarian, authoritarian, disciplinarian, egalitarian, humanitarian, nonagenarian, octagenarian, parliamentarian, totalitarian, utilitarian, veterinarian.

**-ariat,** chariot, heriot, lariat, variate; bivariate, salariat; commissariat, multivariate, proletariat, secretariat, univariate.

**-ariate.** See **-ariat.**

**-arily,** merrily, verily; primarily, summarily; arbitrarily, customarily, militarily, momentarily, monetarily, necessarily, ordinarily, secondarily, temporarily, voluntarily; extraordinarily, involuntarily.

**-arion.** See **-arian.**

**-ariot.** See **-ariat.**

**-arious,** carious, various; Aquarius, calcareous, denarius, gregarious, hilarious, malarious, nefarious, precarious, vicarious; multifarious, Sagittarius.

**-arison,** garrison, warison; caparison, comparison.

**-arity,** carroty, charity, clarity, parity, rarity; barbarity, disparity, hilarity, polarity, vulgarity; angularity, bipolarity, capillarity, circularity, granularity, insularity, jocularity, linearity, modularity, muscularity, popularity, regularity, similarity, singularity, solidarity; dissimilarity, familiarity, irregularity, particularity, peculiarity.

**-arium,** barium; aquarium, herbarium, solarium, terrarium, vivarium; honorarium, planetarium, sanitarium.

**-arius.** See **-arious.**

**-arlatan,** charlatan, tarlatan.

**-arrier,** barrier, carrier, farrier, harrier, tarrier, varier; ball-carrier, mail carrier, sound barrier; aircraft carrier, common carrier, letter carrier.

**-arrion.** See **-arian.**

**-arrison.** See **-arison.**

**-arroty.** See **-arity.**

**-arrowy,** arrowy, marrowy, sparrowy.

**-article,** article, particle; alpha particle, beta particle.

**-artisan,** artisan, bartizan, partisan; bipartisan.

**-artizan.** See **-artisan.**

**-ascible.** See **-assable.**

**-asible.** See **-aceable.**

**-assable,** passable, passible; impassable, impassible, irascible, surpassable.

**-assible.** See **-assable.**

**-astrophe,** anastrophe, catatastrophe; ecocatastrophe.

**-atable** (-ā-), datable, ratable, statable; beratable, collatable, debatable, dilatable, inflatable, locatable, relatable, rotatable, translatable;

cultivatable, isolatable, undebatable.

**-atable** (-a-). See **-atible.**

**-atenate,** concatenate, palatinate.

**-ateral,** lateral; bilateral, collateral; equilateral, multilateral, quadrilateral, unilateral.

**-athering,** blathering; ingathering, woolgathering.

**-atiate,** gratiate, satiate; emaciate, expatiate, ingratiate.

**-atible,** combatable, compatible, getatable; incompatible.

**-atica,** Attica; hepatica, sciatica, viatica.

**-atical,** statical; aquatical, fanatical, grammatical, piratical, sabbatical; acrobatical, enigmatical, magistratical, mathematical, problematical, ungrammatical.

**-atify,** gratify, ratify, stratify; beatify.

**-atinate.** See **-atenate.**

**-ational** (-ā-), stational; citational, formational, gestational, gradational, narrational, notational, probational, relational, rotational, sensational, vocational; avocational, computational, confrontational, congregational, conservational, conversational, derivational, educational, generational, gravitational, informational, innovational, inspirational, invitational, motivational, navigational, observational, occupational, operational, recreational, situational, transformational; coeducational, denominational, improvisational, organizational, perorational, representational, speciational.

**-ational** (-a-), national, rational; binational, cross-national, irrational, nonrational, transnational; international, multinational.

**-ationist,** creationist, deflationist, inflationist, salvationist, vacationist; confrontationist, conservationist, conversationist, inspirationist, isolationist, liberationist, preservationist, segregationist, separationist; accommodationist, annihilationist, assimilationist.

**-atitude.** See **-attitude.**

**-atomist,** atomist; anatomist.

**-atricide,** fratricide, matricide, patricide.

**-attering,** battering, flattering, nattering, scattering, smattering; backscattering, bespattering, earth-shattering, unflattering.

**-attery,** battery, cattery, clattery, flattery, mattery, tattery; self-flattery.

**-attitude,** attitude, gratitude, latitude, platitude; beatitude, colatitude, ingratitude.

**-atural,** natural; connatural, unnatural; preternatural, supernatural.

**-aurian.** See **-orian.**

**-auricle.** See **-orical.**

**-avarice.** See **-averous.**

**-averous,** avarice, cadaverous.

**-avery,** bravery, knavery, quavery, savory, slavery, wavery; unsavory.

**-avia,** Batavia, Belgravia, Moldavia, Moravia, Octavia; Scandinavia

**-avian,** avian, Shavian; Batavian, Belgravian, Moravian, subclavian; Scandinavian.

**-avity,** cavity, gravity; concavity, depravity; antigravity, biconcavity, body cavity, supergravity, zero gravity.

**-ayable,** payable, playable, sayable; displayable, unplayable, unsayable.

**-eachable,** bleachable, leachable, reachable, teachable; impeachable, unreachable, unteachable; unimpeachable.

**-eachery.** See **-echery.**

**-eadable** (-ē-), kneadable, pleadable, readable; exceedable, unreadable; machine-readable.

**-eadable** (-e-). See **-edible.**

**-eadily,** headily, readily, steadily; unsteadily.

**-eakable.** See **-akable.**

**-ealable,** healable, peelable, stealable; appealable, concealable, repealable, resealable, revealable.

**-ealize,** creolize, realize; idealize.

**-ealty,** fealty, realty.

**-eanery,** beanery, deanery, greenery, plenary, scenery; machinery.

**-earable,** airable, bearable, pairable, tearable, wearable; declarable, repairable, unbearable, unwearable; irreparable.

**-earean.** See **-erian.**

**-easable.** See **-easible.**

**-easible,** feasible, freezable, squeezable; appeasable, defeasible, infeasible; inappeasable, indefeasible, unappeasable.

**-easoning,** reasoning, seasoning; unreasoning.

**-eatable,** beatable, eatable, heatable, treatable; defeatable, unbeatable.

**-eatery.** See **-etory.**

**-eathery,** feathery, heathery, leathery.

**-eautiful.** See **-utiful.**

**-eavable.** See **-eivable.**

**-ecency,** decency, recency; indecency.

**-echery,** lechery, treachery.

**-ecible.** See **-essible.**

**-ecimal.** See **-esimal.**

**-ectable,** affectable, collectible, connectable, correctable, delectable, detectable, ejectable, electable, erectable, inflectable, injectable, perfectible, projectable, protectable, respectable, selectable.

**-ectary.** See **-ectory.**

**-ectible.** See **-ectable.**

**-ectional,** sectional; affectional, complexional, connectional, convectional, correctional, cross-sectional, directional, inflectional, projectional, reflectional; bidirectional, insurrectional, interjectional, intersectional, vivisectional.

**-ectionist,** perfectionist, protectionist; insurrectionist, resurrectionist, vivisectionist.

**-ectomy,** lumpectomy, mastectomy, vasectomy; appendectomy, hysterectomy, tonsillectomy.

**-ectoral,** pectoral, sectoral; electoral, protectoral.

**-ectorate,** rectorate; directorate, electorate, inspectorate, protectorate.

**-ectory,** nectary, rectory, sectary; directory, refectory, trajectory.

**-ectual,** aspectual, effectual; ineffectual, intellectual.

**-ectural,** conjectural, prefectural; architectural.

**-ecular,** secular, specular; molecular.

**-ecutive,** consecutive, executive; chief executive, nonconsecutive.

**-edator.** See **-editor.**

**-edial,** medial, predial; remedial, stapedial.

**-edian,** median; comedian, tragedian; encyclopedian.

**-edible,** credible, edible, spreadable; incredible, inedible.

**-edical,** medical, pedicle; premedical; biomedical, paramedical.

**-edicate,** dedicate, medicate, predicate.

**-edicle.** See **-edical.**

**-edience,** expedience, obedience; disobedience, inexpedience.

**-edient,** mediant; expedient, ingredient, obedient; disobedient, inexpedient.

**-ediment,** pediment, sediment; impediment.

**-editor,** creditor, editor, predator; coeditor; city editor; copyeditor.

**-edium,** medium, tedium; cypripedium.

**-edulous,** credulous, sedulous; incredulous.

**-eeable,** seeable, skiable; agreeable, foreseeable; disagreeable, unforeseeable.

**-eelable.** See **-ealable.**

**-eenery.** See **-eanery.**

**-eezable.** See **-easible.**

**-eference,** deference, preference, reference; cross-reference.

**-eferent,** deferent, efferent, referent.

**-efferent.** See **-eferent.**

**-eficence,** beneficence, maleficence.

**-eity,** deity; velleity; corporeity, spontaneity, synchroneity; diaphaneity, homogeneity, instantaneity, simultaneity; contemporaneity, extemporaneity, heterogeneity.

**-eivable,** cleavable; achievable, believable, conceivable, deceivable, perceivable, receivable, relievable, retrievable; imperceivable, inconceivable, irretrievable, unbelievable.

**-elanie.** See **-elony.**

**-elible.** See **-ellable.**

**-elical,** helical, pellicle; angelical; evangelical.

**-ellable,** fellable, gelable, sellable, spellable, tellable; compellable, indelible.

**-ellicle.** See **-elical.**
**-elony,** felony, Melanie.
**-emeni.** See **-emony.**
**-emeral,** femoral; ephemeral.
**-emery,** emery, memory; cache memory, flash memory, screen memory.
**-emia,** anemia, Bohemia, bulimia, ischemia, leukemia, toxemia, uremia; academia, anoxemia, bacteremia, hyperemia, septicemia, thalassemia, tularemia; hyperglycemia, hypoglycemia.
**-emical,** chemical; alchemical, endemical, polemical; academical, agrochemical, biochemical, epidemical, petrochemical, photochemical, phytochemical.
**-eminal,** geminal, seminal; trigeminal.
**-eminate,** geminate; effeminate.
**-emini.** See **-emony.**
**-emnity,** endemnity, solemnity.
**-emone.** See **-emony.**
**-emony,** Gemini, lemony, Yemeni; anemone, bigeminy, hegemony.
**-emoral.** See **-emeral.**
**-emory.** See **-emery.**
**-emulous,** emulous, tremulous.
**-enable,** tenable; amenable.
**-enacle.** See **-enical.**
**-enary** (-e-), denary, hennery, plenary, senary, venery; centenary, millenary; bicentenary, bimillenary, quincentenary, tercentenary.
**-enary** (-ē-). See **-eanery.**
**-enator,** senator; progenitor; primogenitor.
**-endable,** bendable, endable, lendable, mendable, spendable, vendible; amendable, appendable, ascendable, commendable, defendable, dependable, emendable, expendable, extendable, unbendable; comprehendable, recommendable, undependable.
**-endancy,** pendency, tendency; ascendancy, dependency, transcendancy; central tendency, independency; interdependency, superintendency.
**-endency.** See **-endancy.**
**-endible.** See **-endable.**
**-enerate,** generate, venerate; degenerate, intenerate, regenerate.

**-enery** (-e-). See **-enary.**

**-enary** (-ē-). See **-eanery.**

**-enia,** taenia, xenia; Armenia, asthenia, Slovenia; catamenia, leukopenia, myasthenia, neurasthenia, psychasthenia, sarracenia, schizophrenia.

**-enian,** Fenian; Armenian, Athenian, Essenian, Hellenian, Slovenian.

**-enical,** cenacle; arsenical, galenical; ecumenical.

**-enison,** benison, Tennyson, venison.

**-enitive,** genitive, lenitive; double genitive, primogenitive.

**-enitor.** See **-enator.**

**-enity,** lenity, seniti; amenity, obscenity, serenity.

**-enium,** rhenium; hymenium, proscenium, ruthenium, selenium.

**-ennery.** See **-enary.**

**-ennial,** biennial, centennial, decennial, millennial, perennial, quadrennial, quinquennial, septennial, triennial, vicennial; bicentennial, bimillennial, premillennial, postmillennial.

**-ensable.** See **-ensible.**

**-ensary.** See **-ensory.**

**-ensible,** sensible; compensable, condensable, defensible, dispensable, distensible, extensible, insensible, ostensible; apprehensible, commonsensible, comprehensible, indefensible, indispensable, reprehensible; incomprehensible.

**-ensional,** tensional; ascensional, attentional, contentional, conventional, declensional, dimensional, extensional, intensional, intentional; one-dimensional, three-dimensional, two-dimensional, unconventional, unintentional.

**-ensity,** density, tensity; extensity, immensity, intensity, propensity.

**-ensory,** sensory; dispensary, suspensory; extrasensory, multisensory.

**-ensual.** See **-entual.**

**-entable,** rentable; fermentable, lamentable, presentable, preventable; documentable, representable.

**-entacle.** See **-entical.**

**-entalist,** mentalist; continentalist, documentalist, fundamentalist, governmentalist, incrementalist, instrumentalist, Orientalist, sentimentalist, transcendentalist; environmentalist, experimentalist.

**-entary,** passementerie; alimentary, complementary, complimentary, documentary, elementary, filamentary, mockumentary, parliamentary, rudimentary, sedimentary, supplementary, testamentary; uncomplimentary; unparliamentary.

**-entative,** tentative; augmentative, frequentative, preventative; argumentative, representative.

**-enterie.** See **-entary.**

**-entiary,** century; penitentiary; plenipotentiary.

**-entical,** denticle, pentacle, tentacle; conventicle, identical.

**-enticle.** See **-entical.**

**-entional.** See **-ensional.**

**-entity,** entity; identity, nonentity.

**-entual,** sensual; accentual, consensual, eventual.

**-entury.** See **-entiary.**

**-enuous,** strenuous, tenuis, tenuous; ingenuous; disingenuous.

**-eolize.** See **-ealize.**

**-eptable.** See **-eptible.**

**-eptacle,** skeptical; conceptacle, receptacle.

**-eptible,** acceptable, perceptible, susceptible; imperceptible, unacceptable.

**-eptical.** See **-eptacle.**

**-ercery.** See **-ursary.**

**-ercible.** See **-ersible.**

**-ereal.** See **-erial.**

**-ereon.** See **-erian.**

**-ereous.** See **-erious.**

**-ereus.** See **-erious.**

**-ergency,** urgency; convergency, detergency, divergency, emergency, insurgency; counterinsurgency.

**-ergery.** See **-urgery.**

**-eria,** feria, Syria; Algeria, Assyria, asteria, bacteria, collyria, criteria, diphtheria, hysteria, Iberia, Illyria, Liberia, Nigeria, progeria, Siberia, wisteria; cafeteria, cryptomeria, sansevieria, washateria.

**-erial,** cereal, ferial, serial; arterial, bacterial, empyreal, ethereal, funereal, imperial, material, sidereal, venereal; immaterial, magisterial, managerial, ministerial, presbyterial, raw material; antibacterial, biomaterial.

**-erian,** Styrian, Syrian, therian; Algerian, Assyrian, Chaucerian, Cimmerian, criterion, eutherian, Faulknerian, Hesperian, Hutterian, Hyperion, Iberian, Illyrian, Liberian, mezereon, Mousterian, Nigerian, Shakespearean, Siberian, Spenserian, valerian, Valerian, Valkyrian; Hanoverian, Luciferian, Presbyterian.

**-erical,** clerical, spherical; chimerical, hysterical, numerical; anticlerical, esoterical.

**-erily.** See **-arily.**

**-erion.** See **-erian.**

**-erior,** anterior, exterior, inferior, interior, posterior, superior, ulterior.

**-eriot.** See **-ariat.**

**-erious,** cereus, serious, Sirius; cinereous, delirious, imperious, mysterious, Tiberius; deleterious.

**-erity,** ferity, ferrety, verity; asperity, austerity, celerity, dexterity, legerity, posterity, prosperity, severity, sincerity, temerity; insincerity; ambidexterity.

**-erium,** cerium, Miriam; bacterium, collyrium, criterium, delirium, deuterium, imperium, meitnerium; magisterium.

**-erius.** See **-erious.**

**-erminal,** germinal, terminal.

**-erminate,** germinate, terminate; exterminate.

**-erminous,** terminus, verminous; coterminous.

**-erminus.** See **-erminous.**

**-ernible.** See **-urnable.**

**-ernity,** eternity, fraternity, maternity, modernity, paternity, quaternity.

**-erpentine.** See **-urpentine.**

**-errety.** See **-erity.**

**-errier,** burier, merrier, terrier.

**-errily.** See **-arily.**

**-ersary.** See **-ursary.**

**-ersable.** See **-ersible.**

**-ersible,** coercible, conversable, dispersible, eversible, immersible, reversible, submersible, traversable; irreversible.

**-ervancy,** fervency; conservancy.

**-ervative,** conservative, preservative; neoconservative, ultraconservative.

**-ervency.** See **-ervancy.**

**-esident,** president, resident; nonresident, vice-president.

**-esimal,** decimal; centesimal, millesimal; duodecimal; infinitesimal.

**-essable.** See **-essible.**

**-essible,** decibel, guessable; accessible, addressable, assessable, compressible, confessable, expressible, impressible, processable, repressible, suppressible; inaccessible, inexpressible, irrepressible.

**-essional,** sessional; accessional, concessional, confessional, congressional, digressional, discretional, obsessional, precessional, processional, professional, recessional; intercessional, nonprofessional, unprofessional.

**-essionist,** expressionist, impressionist, secessionist.

**-estible,** testable; comestible, contestable, detestable, digestible, divestible, harvestable, ingestible, suggestible, untestable; incontestable, indigestible.

**-estrian,** equestrian, pedestrian.

**-estuous,** incestuous, tempestuous.

**-etical,** metical, reticle; aesthetical, anthetical, genetical, heretical, pathetical, phonetical, poetical; alphabetical, arithmetical, cybernetical, exegetical, geodetical, hypothetical, parenthetical, theoretical.

**-etory,** decretory, eatery, secretory, suppletory.

**-etrical,** metrical; obstetrical, symmetrical; assymmetrical, barometrical, diametrical, geometrical, unsymmetrical.

**-ettable,** gettable, settable, wettable; forgettable, regrettable, resettable; unforgettable.

**-eutical.** See **-uticle.**

**-evalence.** See **-evolence.**

**-evelry.** See **-evilry.**

**-eviate,** deviate; abbreviate, alleviate.

**-evilry,** devilry, revelry; daredevilry.
**-evious,** devious, previous.
**-evity,** brevity, levity; longevity.
**-evolence,** benevolence, malevolence, prevalence.
**-ewable.** See **-uable.**
**-exity,** complexity, convexity, perplexity; biconvexity.
**-iable,** appliable, dryable, dyeable, flyable, friable, liable, pliable, viable; compliable, deniable, reliable; certifiable, classifiable, falsifiable, justifiable, liquefiable, modifiable, notifiable, pacifiable, qualifiable, quantifiable, rectifiable, satisfiable, specifiable, undeniable, unifiable, verifiable; diversifiable, identifiable.
**-iacal,** heliacal, maniacal, zodiacal; elegiacal, simoniacal; dipsomaniacal, egomaniacal, hypochondriacal, monomaniacal, nymphomaniacal, paradisiacal, pyromaniacal; bibliomaniacal, megalomaniacal.
**-iary,** briery, diary, fiery, friary, priory.
**-iasis,** diesis, diocese; archdiocese, psoriasis; candidiasis, leishmaniasis; elephantiasis, hypochondriasis.
**-ibable,** bribable; ascribable, describable, subscribable; indescribable.
**-ibia,** Libya, tibia.
**-ibitive,** exhibitive, inhibitive, prohibitive.
**-ibular,** fibular, mandibular, vestibular; infundibular.
**-ibya.** See **-ibia.**
**-icative,** fricative, siccative; affricative, applicative, dessicative, explicative, indicative, predicative, vindicative; multiplicative.
**-iccative.** See **-icative.**
**-icicle,** icicle, bicycle, tricycle.
**-iciency,** deficiency, efficiency, proficiency, sufficiency; inefficiency, insufficiency, self-sufficiency.
**-icinal,** vicinal; medicinal, officinal, vaticinal.
**-icity,** causticity, chronicity, complicity, conicity, cyclicity, duplicity, ethnicity, felicity, lubricity, mendicity, plasticity, publicity, rhythmicity, rusticity, simplicity, spasticity, sphericity, tonic-

ity, toxicity; authenticity, domesticity, eccentricity, elasticity, electricity, historicity, infelicity, multiplicity, specificity, synchronicity; egocentricity, ethnocentricity, inelasticity, periodicity.

**-ickety,** rickety, thickety; pernickety, persnickety.

**-ictional,** dictional, fictional, frictional; nonfictional; jurisdictional.

**-ictory,** victory; benedictory, contradictory, interdictory, valedictory.

**-icula,** auricula, corbicula, curricula, reticula.

**-icular,** spicular; acicular, articular, auricular, canicular, clavicular, curricular, fascicular, follicular, funicular, lenticular, navicular, orbicular, particular, radicular, reticular, testicular, vehicular, ventricular, vermicular, versicular, vesicular; in particular, perpendicular; extracurricular, extravehicular.

**-iculate,** articulate, auriculate, denticulate, geniculate, matriculate, particulate, reticulate, vermiculate; inarticulate.

**-iculous,** folliculous, meticulous, pediculous, ridiculous.

**-iculum,** curriculum, reticulum; diverticulum.

**-icycle.** See **-icicle.**

**-iddity.** See **-idity.**

**-idian,** Gideon, Lydian; ascidian, Dravidian, Euclidean, Floridian, meridian, Numidian, obsidian, Ovidian, quotidian, rachidian; enchiridion, prime meridian; antemeridian.

**-idical,** druidical, juridical; pyramidical.

**-ideum.** See **-idiem.**

**-idiem,** idiom; iridium, perideum, presidium, rubidium; post meridiem; ante meridiem.

**-idiom.** See **-idiem.**

**-idium.** See **-idiem.**

**-idity,** quiddity; acidity, aridity, avidity, cupidity, fluidity, frigidity, humidity, liquidity, lucidity, morbidity, rabidity, rancidity, rapidity, rigidity, solidity, stupidity, timidity, turbidity, turgidity, validity, vap-

idity, viscidity; insolidity, invalidity.
**-idual,** residual; individual.
**-idulous,** stridulous; acidulous.
**-ieria.** See **-eria.**
**-iery.** See **-iary.**
**-ietal,** dietal, hyetal; parietal, societal, varietal.
**-ieter,** dieter, quieter, rioter; proprietor.
**-ietor.** See **-ieter.**
**-iety,** piety; anxiety, dubiety, impiety, nimiety, propriety, satiety, sobriety, society, variety; contrariety, impropriety, inebriety, insobriety, notoriety; café society, garden variety, honor society, secret society.
**-ievable.** See **-eivable.**
**-iferous,** aquiferous, auriferous, calciferous, coniferous, cruciferous, pestiferous, splendiferous, vociferous; acidiferous, carboniferous, odoriferous.
**-ificate,** certificate, pontificate, significate; birth certificate, death certificate, gift certificate, stock certificate.
**-ificent,** magnificent, munificent, omnificent.
**-igamy,** bigamy, digamy; polygamy.
**-igenous.** See **-iginous.**
**-igerant.** See **-igerent.**
**-igerent,** belligerent, refrigerant; cobelligerent.
**-iggery,** piggery, priggery, Whiggery.
**-ighlander.** See **-islander.**
**-iginous,** fuliginous, indigenous, vertiginous.
**-ignable.** See **-inable.**
**-ignancy,** benignancy, indignancy, malignancy.
**-igneous,** igneous, ligneous.
**-ignify,** dignify, lignify, signify.
**-ignity,** dignity; benignity, indignity, malignity.
**-igorous,** rigorous, vigorous.
**-igraphy,** calligraphy, epigraphy, stratigraphy.
**-iguous,** ambiguous, contiguous, exiguous; unambiguous.
**-ilia,** cilia; Anglophilia, Francophilia, hemophilia, juvenilia, necrophilia, notabilia, pedophilia, technophilia; memorabilia.
**-ilead,** chiliad, Gilead, Iliad.
**-iliad.** See **-ilead.**
**-ilias.** See **-ilious.**

**-iliate,** ciliate; filiate; affiliate, conciliate, humiliate.

**-ilica,** silica; basilica.

**-iliency.** See **-illiancy.**

**-ilious,** bilious; punctilious; atrabilious, supercilious; materfamilias, paterfamilias.

**-ilitate,** militate; debilitate, facilitate, habilitate; rehabilitate.

**-ility,** ability, agility, anility, civility, debility, docility, ductility, facility, fertility, fragility, futility, gentility, gracility, hostility, humility, lability, mobility, motility, nobility, scurrility, senility, servility, stability, sterility, tranquility, utility, virility; affability, arability, audibility, bankability, bearability, breathability, capability, changeability, contractility, countability, credibility, culpability, curability, disability, drinkability, drivability, durability, edibility, equability, fallibility, feasibility, flammability, flexibility, formability, frangibility, friability, fungibility, gullibility, imbecility, immobility, inability, incivility, infantility, infertility, instability, juvenility, laudability, legibility, liability, likability, livability, lovability, meltability, miscibility, movability, mutability, notability, packability, plausibility, playability, pliability, portability, possibility, potability, pregnability, printability, probability, quotability, readability, rentability, salability, sensibility, sociability, solubility, solvability, spreadability, suitability, tenability, testability, traceability, trainability, treatability, tenability, usability, versatility, viability, visibility, volatility, washability, wearability, workability; absorbability, acceptability, accessibility, accountability, adaptability, adjustability, admissibility, adoptability, advisability, affordability, agreeability, answerability, applicability, approachability, attainability, availability, believability, collapsibility, combustibility, compatibility, convertibility, corruptibility, deniability, dependability, desirability, digestibility, dispensability, downward mobility, electability, eligibility, excitability, expendability, illegibility, immutability, implausibility, impossibility, improbability, incapability, infallibility, inflexibility, invincibility, invisibility, irrititability, manageability, marketability, measurability, navigability, permeability, practicability, predictability, profitability, public utility, reliability, respectability, responsibility, reusability, reversibility, separability, survivability, susceptibility, sustainability, upward mobility, variability, vulnerability.

**-illable,** billable, fillable, spillable, syllable, tillable; distillable, disyllable, refillable; monosyllable, open syllable, polysyllable.

**-illary.** See **-illery.**

**-illery,** Hillary, pillory; artillery, bacillary, distillery, mamillary; codicillary.

**-illiancy,** brilliancy; resiliency.

**-illory.** See **-illery.**

**-illowy,** billowy, pillowy, willowy.

**-iloquence,** grandiloquence, magniloquence.

**-iloquy,** soliloquy, ventriloquy.

**-imeter,** dimiter, limiter, scimitar, trimeter; altimeter, delimiter, dosimeter, gravimeter, lysimeter, oximeter, perimeter, planimeter; acidimeter, calorimeter, colorimeter, polarimeter, saccharimeter, turbidimeter, velocimeter, viscosimeter.

**-iminal,** criminal, Viminal; subliminal, war criminal.

**-iminate,** criminate; discriminate, eliminate, incriminate.

**-imitar.** See **-imeter.**

**-imiter.** See **-imeter.**

**-imity,** dimity; proximity, sublimity; anonymity, equanimity, magnanimity, pseudonymity, synonymity, unanimity; pusillanimity.

**-imulus,** limulus, stimulus.

**-inable,** minable, signable; assignable, combinable, consignable, declinable, definable, inclinable.

**-inary.** See **-inery.**
**-inative.** See **-initive.**
**-indicate,** indicate, syndicate, vindicate; contraindicate.
**-ineal,** finial, pineal; matrilineal, patrilineal.
**-ineous,** gramineous, sanguineous; consanguineous, ignominious.
**-inery** (-ē-). See **-eanery.**
**-inery** (-ī-), binary, finery, pinery, vinery, winery; refinery.
**-inary.** See **-inery.**
**-ingency,** stringency; astringency, contingency.
**-inial.** See **-ineal.**
**-inian,** Darwinian, Justinian, Sardinian, Virginian; Abyssinian, Argentinian, Augustinian, Carolinian, Carthaginian, Palestinian.
**-inical,** binnacle, clinical, cynical, finical, pinnacle; dominical.
**-inious.** See **-ineous.**
**-inister,** minister, sinister; administer, prime minister.
**-initive,** carminative, combinative, definitive, infinitive.
**-inity,** trinity, Trinity; affinity, bovinity, concinnity, divinity, felinity, infinity, Latinity, salinity, sanguinity, vicinity, virginity; alkalinity, aquilinity, consanguinity, femininity, masculinity.
**-innacle.** See **-inical.**
**-intery,** printery, splintery, wintery.
**-inuous,** sinuous; continuous; discontinuous.
**-iolet,** triolet, violate, violet; inviolate; shrinking violet, ultraviolet.
**-iory.** See **-iary.**
**-ioter.** See **-ieter.**
**-ipotent,** omnipotent, plenipotent, precipitant.
**-ippery,** frippery, slippery.
**-iquitous,** iniquitous, ubiquitous.
**-iquity,** antiquity, iniquity, obliquity, ubiquity.
**-irable,** fireable, wirable; acquirable, desirable; undesirable.
**-iracle.** See **-irical.**
**-irical,** lyrical, miracle, spherical, spiracle; empirical, satirical.
**-irious.** See **-erious.**
**-irium.** See **-erium.**
**-irius.** See **-erious.**
**-isable.** See **-izable.**
**-iscible.** See **-issible.**

**-ishioner.** See **-itioner.**

**-isible,** risible, visible; divisible, invisible; indivisible.

**-isional,** visional; collisional, decisional, divisional, excisional, provisional, transitional.

**-isitor,** visitor; acquisitor, inquisitor.

**-islander,** highlander, islander.

**-isory,** advisory, provisory, revisory; supervisory.

**-issable.** See **-issible.**

**-issible,** kissable, miscible; admissible, dismissable, immiscible, municipal, omissible, permissible, transmissible; impermissible, inadmissible.

**-issioner.** See **-itioner.**

**-istency,** consistency, insistency, persistency; inconsistency.

**-istical,** mystical; deistical, eristical, linguistical, logistical, monistical, sophistical, statistical, theistical; anarchistical, atheistical, casuistical, egoistical, egotistical; antagonistical.

**-istory,** blistery, history, mystery; case history, life history, prehistory; ancient history, ethnohistory, natural history, oral history.

**-itable,** citable, writable; excitable, ignitable, incitable, indictable; copyrightable, extraditable.

**-itany.** See **-ittany.**

**-itchery,** bitchery, stitchery, witchery; bewitchery.

**-iterate,** iterate; alliterate, obliterate, reiterate, transliterate.

**-itiate,** vitiate; initiate, noviate, officiate, propitiate.

**-itical,** critical; Levitical, political; analytical, apolitical, diacritical, eremitical, hypercritical, jesuitical, parasitical, supercritical.

**-itigate,** litigate, mitigate.

**-itional,** additional, conditional, nutritional, positional, traditional, transitional, tuitional, volitional; acquisitional, aparitional, compositional, definitional, inquisitional, intuitional, oppositional, prepositional, propositional, repetitional, suppositional, unconditional.

**-itioner,** missioner; commissioner, conditioner,

parishioner, partitioner, petitioner, practitioner; air conditioner, nurse-practitioner.

**-itionist,** nutritionist, partitionist; abolitionist, coalitionist, exhibitionist, expeditionist, prohibitionist.

**-ittable,** admittable, committable, habitable, hospitable, remittable, transmittable; inhospitable.

**-ittany,** dittany, litany.

**-ittiness,** grittiness, prettiness, wittiness.

**-itual,** ritual; habitual.

**-ituate,** situate; habituate.

**-ivable** (-ī-), drivable; contrivable, deprivable, derivable, revivable, survivable.

**-ivable** (-i-), givable, livable; forgivable; unforgivable.

**-ivalent,** ambivalent, equivalent.

**-ivative,** privative; derivative.

**-ivery,** livery, shivery; carnivory, delivery.

**-ivia,** trivia; Bolivia, Olivia.

**-ivial,** trivial; convivial.

**-ivious,** lascivious, oblivious.

**-ivity,** privity; acclivity, activity, captivity, declivity, festivity, nativity, passivity, proclivity; adaptivity; affectivity, aggressivity, coercivity, cognitivity, collectivity, compulsivity, conductivity, connectivity, creativity, destructivity, emotivity, exclusivity, expressivity, impassivity, impulsivity, inactivity, inclusivity, negativity, objectivity, positivity, primitivity, productivity, progressivity, reactivity, receptivity, reflexivity, relativity, resistivity, retentivity, selectivity, sensitivity, subjectivity, transitivity; hyperactivity, insensitivity; overactivity.

**-ivorous,** carnivorous, frugivorous, granivorous, herbivorous, omnivorous, piscivorous; graminiverous, insectivorous.

**-izable,** sizable; advisable, despisable, devisable, excisable; amortizable, analyzable, criticizable, customizable, dramatizable, exercisable, fertilizable, hypnotizable, inadvisable, localizable, magnetizable, mechanizable, memorizable, organizable, pulverizable, realizable, recognizable, satirizable, vaporizable; rationalizable.

**-oable.** See **-uable.**

**-obbery,** bobbery, jobbery, robbery, slobbery, snobbery.

**-obeah.** See **-obia.**

**-obia,** cobia, obeah, phobia; acrophobia, aerophobia, algophobia, Anglophobia, aquaphobia, claustrophobia, Francophobia, homophobia, hydrophobia, photophobia, technophobia, xenophobia; agoraphobia, ailurophobia, arachnophobia, computerphobia.

**-obular,** globular, lobular.

**-ocative,** locative, vocative; evocative, provocative.

**-ocity.** See **-osity.**

**-ockery,** crockery, mockery, rockery.

**-ocracy,** autocracy, bureaucracy, democracy, hypocrisy, kleptocracy, mobocracy, monocracy, ochlocracy, plantocracy, plutocracy, slavocracy, technocracy, theocracy, timocracy; aristocracy, gerontocracy, gynecocracy, meritocracy, pantisocracy, punditocracy, pure democracy, thalassocracy.

**-ocrisy.** See **-ocracy.**

**-ocular,** jocular, locular, ocular; binocular, monocular.

**-odian,** Rhodian; Cambodian, custodian, Herodian, melodeon; nickelodeon.

**-odical,** codical; methodical, monodical, prosodical, rhapsodical, synodical; episodical, periodical.

**-odify,** codify, modify.

**-odious,** odious; commodious, melodious; incommodious.

**-odity,** oddity; commodity.

**-odular,** modular, nodular.

**-ogamous,** endogamous, exogamous, monogamous; heterogamous.

**-ogamy,** endogamy, exogamy, homogamy, misogamy, monogamy; heterogamy.

**-ogative,** derogative, prerogative; interrogative.

**-ogenous,** androgynous, autogenous, endogenous, erogenous, exogenous, homogenous, monogynous, nitrogenous; heterogenous.

**-ogeny,** progeny; androgyny, autogeny, lysogeny, misogyny, ontogeny, orogeny, phylogeny; embryogeny, epeirogeny, heterogeny.

**-ogical,** logical; illogical; algological, analogical, anthological, astrological, biological, bryological, chronological, cosmological, cryptological, cytological, dendrological, ecological, ethnological, ethological, gemological, geological, graphological, histological, homological, horological, hydrological, limnological, metrological, morphological, mycological, mythological, necrological, neurological, nomological, nosological, oncological, ontological, pathological, pedagogical, pedological, penological, philological, phonological, phrenological, phycological, pomological, psychological, rheological, scatological, seismological, serological, sinological, tautological, technological, theological, topological, tropological, typological, urological, virological, zoological; abiological, anthropological, archaeological, climatological, criminological, demonological, deontological, dermatological, entomological, eschatological, etiological, etymological, genealogical, gerontological, gynecological, iconological, ideological, immunological, malacological, methodological, mineralogical, musicological, numerological, orismological, ornithological, physiological, radiological, semiological, sociological, teleological, terminological; bacteriological, epistemological, phenomenological, phraseological, planetological, selenological, somatological, synecological, teratological, thanatological, toxicological, vulcanological.

**-ogony,** cosmogony, isogony, mahogany, schizogony,

sporogony, theogony; heterogony.

**-ographer,** biographer, cartographer, chorographer, cosmographer, cryptographer, demographer, discographer, ethnographer, geographer, lithographer, mythographer, photographer, pornographer, stenographer, typographer; bibliographer, choreographer, chromatographer, hagiographer, lexicographer, oceanographer, videographer; cinematographer, historiographer.

**-ography,** biography, cartography, chorography, chronography, cosmography, cryptography, demography, discography, ethnography, filmography, geography, holography, lithography, mammography, orthography, phonography, photography, pictography, pornography, reprography, sonography, stenography, tomography, topography, typography, xerography; bibliography, choreography, chromatography, hagiography, iconography, lexicography, oceanography; autobiography, cinematography, historiography.

**-ogynous.** See **-ogenous.**

**-ogyny.** See **-ogeny.**

**-olable,** rollable; consolable, controllable; inconsolable, uncontrollable.

**-olater,** bardolater, idolater; bibliolater, heliolater, Mariolater.

**-olatry,** bardolatry, idolatry, zoolatry; bibliolatry, heliolatry, iconolatry, Mariolatry.

**-oleon.** See **-olian.**

**-olia,** scolia; Mongolia, pignolia; Anatolia, melancholia.

**-olian,** Aeolian, eolian, Aetolian, Mongolian, napoleon, Napoleon, simoleon, Tyrolean; Anatolian.

**-oleum.** See **-olium.**

**-olity.** See **-ality.**

**-olium,** oleum, scholium; linoleum, petroleum, trifolium; tetrazolium.

**-ollable.** See **-olable.**

**-ollity.** See **-ality.**

**-ologist,** anthologist, apologist, biologist, chronologist, cosmologist, cryptologist, cytologist, dendrologist, ecologist, ethnologist, ethologist, garbologist, gemologist, geologist, graphologist, histologist, horologist, mixologist, morphologist, mycologist, mythologist, nephrologist, neurologist, oncologist, ontologist, pathologist, philologist, phonologist, phrenologist, psychologist, seismologist, sexologist, sinologist, technologist, theologist, urologist, virologist, zoologist; anthropologist, archaeologist, audiologist, cardiologist, climatologist, cosmetologist, criminologist, dermatologist, Egyptologist, embryologist, entomologist, etymologist, futurologist, genealogist, gerontologist, gynecologist, hematologist, herpetologist, ichthyologist, ideologist, immunologist, kremlinologist, lexicologist, methodologist, mineralogist, musicologist, numerologist, oceanologist, ophthalmologist, ornithologist, pharmacologist, physiologist, planetologist, primatologist, rheumatologist, scientologist, semiologist, sociologist, thanatologist, toxicologist, urbanologist; bacteriologist, endocrinologist, meteorologist, microbiologist, paleontologist, phenomenologist, Sovietologist; anesthesiologist, epidemiologist, gastroenterologist, otolaryngologist.

**-ologous,** autologous, homologous, tautologous; heterologous.

**-ology,** andrology, anthology, apology, astrology, biology, bryology, cetology, Christology, chronology, cosmology, cryptology, cytology, dendrology, doxology, ecology, enology, ethnology, ethology, garbology, gemology, geology, graphology, haplology, histology, homology, horology, hymnology, limnology, lithology, mixology, morphology, mycology, mythology, necrology, neology, nephrology, neurology, nosology, oncology, ontology, pathology, pedology, penology, petrology, philology, phlebology, phonology, phrenology, phycology, proctology, psychology, scatology, seismology, serology, sexology, sinology, symbology, tautology, technology, tetralogy, theology, topology, typology, urology, virology, zoology; anthropology, archaeology, audiology, cardiology, climatology, cosmetology, criminology, dermatology, Egyptology, entomology, eschatology, etiology, etymology, futurology, genealogy, gerontology, gynecology, hematology, herpetology, ideology, immunology, kremlinology, lexicology, Mariology, martyrology, methodology, mineralogy, musicology, numerology, oceanology, opththalmology, ornithology, pharmacology, phraseology, physiology, primatology, radiology, reflexology, rheumatology, scientology, semiology, sociology, terminology, thanatology, toxicology, urbanology, volcanology; bacteriology, dialectology, endocrinology, epistemology, exobiology, kinesiology, metapsychology, meteorology, microbiology, nanotechnology, neurobiology, paleontology, parapsychology, parasitology, phenomenology, Sovietology; anesthesiology, epidemiology, ethnomusicology, gastroenterology, otolaryngology, sociobiology.

**-oluble,** soluble, voluble; dissoluble, insoluble, resoluble; indissoluble, irresoluble.

**-olvable,** solvable; absolvable, dissolvable, evolvable, insolvable, resolvable; indissolvable, irresolvable.

**-omenal.** See **-ominal.**

**-ometer,** aerometer, barometer, bolometer, ceilometer, chronometer, clinometer, coulometer, cyclometer, durometer, ergometer, fathometer, gasometer, geometer, hectometer, hydrometer, hygrometer, hypsometer, kilometer, manometer, micrometer, monometer, odometer, osmometer, pedometer, photometer, potometer, psychrometer, pycnometer, pyrometer, rheometer, salometer, sclerometer, seismometer, spectrometer, speedometer, spherometer, spirometer, tachometer, thermometer, tonometer, viscometer; actinometer, anemometer, audiometer, densitometer, diffractometer, dilatometer, dynamometer, electrometer, eudiometer, extensometer, galvanometer, goniometer, gradiometer, heliometer, inclinometer, magnetometer, mass spectrometer, nephelometer, olfactometer, penetrometer, piezometer, radiometer, reflectometer, refractometer, respirometer, salinometer, scintillometer, sensitometer, tellurometer, tenderometer, tensiometer, urinometer, variometer; accelerometer, interferometer, intervalometer, potentiometer, sphygmomanometer.

**-ometry,** allometry, astrometry, barometry, biometry, chronometry, coulometry, fluorometry, geometry, isometry, manometry, micrometry, morphometry, optometry, osmometry, photometry, psychometry, psychrometry, pyrometry, seismometry, spectrometry, spirometry, thermometry, tonometry; anemometry, anthropometry, cephalometry, craniometry, densitometry, diffractometry, magnetometry, mass spectrometry, plane geometry, refractometry, sociometry, trigonometry.

**-omical,** comical, domical; anatomical, astronomical, economical, tragicomical.

**-ominal,** nominal; abdominal, cognominal, denominal, phenomenal, predominal, pronominal.

**-ominance.** See **-ominence.**

**-ominant.** See **-ominent.**

**-ominate,** dominate, nominate; abominate, denominate, predominate, renominate.

**-ominence,** dominance, prominence; predominance.

**-ominent,** dominant, prominent; predominant.

**-onachal.** See **-onical.**

**-oneus.** See **-onious.**

**-onial,** baronial, colonial; antimonial, ceremonial, matrimonial, patrimonial, testimonial.

**-onian,** chthonian, Zonian; aeonian, Antonian, Baconian, Bostonian, Charlestonian, chelonian, demonian, Devonian, draconian, Estonian, Etonian, favonian, Galtonian, gorgonian, Gorgonian, Houstonian, Ionian, Jacksonian, Johnsonian, Lincolnian, Miltonian, Newtonian, Oxonian, plutonian, Slavonian, Wilsonian; Amazonian, Apollonian, Babylonian, Caledonian, calypsonian, Chalcedonian, Ciceronian, Edisonian, Emersonian, Hamiltonian, Jeffersonian, Macedonian, Madisonian, Pantagonian, parkinsonian, Tennysonian, Washingtonian.

**-onica,** Monica; harmonica, japonica, Salonika, veronica, Veronica; electronica, glass harmonica, Santa Monica, Thessalonica.

**-onical,** chronicle, conical, monachal, monocle; canonical, demonical, ironical, thrasonical.

**-onicle.** See **-onical.**

**-onika.** See **-onica.**

**-onious,** Antonius, erroneous, euphonious, felonious, harmonious, Petronius, Polonius, Suetonius, symphonious; acrimonious, ceremonious, disharmonious, inharmonious, parsimonious, sanctimonious; unceremonious.

**-onishment,** admonishment, astonishment.

**-onium,** onium; ammonium, carbonium, euphonium, harmonium, hydronium, ionium, meconium, muonium, oogonium, phosphonium, plutonium, polonium, stramonium, sulfonium, syconium, zirconium; archegonium, ascogonium, carpogonium, diazonium, hormogonium, pandemonium, pelargonium, positronium, spermagonium.

**-onius.** See **-onious.**

**-onocle.** See **-onical.**

**-onomist,** agronomist, autonomist, economist, eponymist, ergonomist, gastronomist, synonymist, taxonomist.

**-onomous.** See **-onymous.**

**-onomy,** aeronomy, agronomy, antonymy, astronomy, autonomy, economy, eponymy, gastronomy, homonymy, metonymy, synonymy, tautonomy, taxonomy, toponymy; Deuteronomy, hetereonomy, teleonomy.

**-onymist.** See **-onomist.**

**-onymous,** anonymous, antonymous, autonomous, eponymous, homonymous, paronymous, pseudonymous, synonymous, theonomous; heteronomous, nonautonomous, polyonymous.

**-onymy.** See **-onomy.**

**-ookery,** cookery, crookery, rookery.

**-oolean.** See **-ulean.**

**-oonery.** See **-unary.**

**-opean.** See **-opian.**

**-ophagus,** esophagus, sarcophagus.

**-ophany.** See **-ophony.**

**-ophonous,** cacophonous, homophonous.

**-ophony,** cacophony, colophony, homophony, theophany; heterophony, stereophony.

**-opia,** diplopia, dystopia, myopia, nyctalopia, sinopia, utopia; amblyopia, ametropia, cornucopia, Ethiopia, hyperopia, presbyopia.

**-opian,** cyclopean, dystopian, utopian; cornucopian, Ethiopian.

**-opical,** topical, tropical; anthropical, pantropical, subtropical; microscopical, neotropical, philanthropical, semitropical.

**-opolis,** propolis; acropolis, cosmopolis, metropolis, necropolis; megalopolis.

**-oppery,** coppery, foppery.

**-oppiness,** choppiness, floppiness, sloppiness, soppiness.
**-opulate,** copulate, populate; depopulate, outpopulate, repopulate; overpopulate.
**-orable,** pourable, storable; adorable, deplorable, explorable, ignorable, restorable.
**-oracle.** See **-orical.**
**-orative,** explorative, pejorative, restorative.
**-ordinate,** ordinate; coordinate, subordinate; superordinate.
**-oreal.** See **-orial.**
**-orean.** See **-orian.**
**-oreous.** See **-orious.**
**-oreum.** See **-orium.**
**-oria,** coria, gloria, Gloria, noria, scoria, thoria; aporia, ciboria, dysphoria, emporia, euphoria, haustoria, Peoria, Pretoria, scriptoria, sensoria, triforia, victoria, Victoria; appressoria, auditoria, crematoria, moratoria, ostensoria, sanatoria, sanitoria, sudatoria; phantasmagoria.
**-orial,** boreal, loreal, oriel, oriole; arboreal, armorial, auctorial, authorial, cantorial, censorial, corporeal, cursorial, factorial, fossorial, manorial, marmoreal, memorial, pictorial, praetorial, proctorial, raptorial, rectorial, sartorial, seignorial, sensorial, sponsorial, tonsorial, tutorial, uxorial, vectorial; consistorial, curatorial, dictatorial, directorial, editorial, equatorial, immemorial, incorporeal, janitorial, monitorial, monsignorial, natatorial, piscatorial, preceptorial, professorial, purgatorial, reportorial, senatorial, territorial; ambassadorial, combinatorial, conspiratorial, gladiatorial, gubernatorial, prosecutorial; extraterritorial.
**-orian,** Dorian, saurian, Taurean; aurorean, Azorean, Gregorian, historian, Ivorian, praetorian, stentorian, Victorian; dinosaurian, Ecuadorean, hyperborean, Labradorean, madreporian, Salvadorean, senatorian, Singaporean, terpsichorean; salutatorian, valedictorian.

**-orical,** auricle, coracle, oracle; historical, rhetorical; ahistorical, allegorical, categorical, metaphorical, oratorical.

**-oriel.** See **-orial.**

**-oriole.** See **-orial.**

**-orious,** glorious; arboreous, censorious, inglorious, laborious, notorious, sartorius, uproarious, uxorious, vainglorious, victorious; meritorious.

**-ority,** authority, majority, minority, priority, seniority, sonority, sorority; exteriority, inferiority, interiority, superiority.

**-orium,** bohrium, corium, thorium; castoreum, ciborium, emporium, haustorium, pastorium, scriptorium, sensorium, triforium; appressorium, auditorium, cafetorium, crematorium, in memoriam, moratorium, natatorium, ostensorium, sanatorium, sanitorium, sudatorium.

**-orius.** See **-orious.**

**-ormative,** formative, normative; deformative, informative, performative, reformative, transformative.

**-ormity,** abnormity, conformity, deformity, enormity; nonconformity, uniformity.

**-orrier.** See **-urrier.**

**-ortify,** fortify, mortify.

**-oscopy,** arthroscopy, broncoscopy, colposcopy, cryoscopy, cystoscopy, endoscopy, fetoscopy, fluoroscopy, gastroscopy, microscopy, rhinoscopy, spectroscopy; colonoscopy, hysteroscopy, laparoscopy, laryngoscopy, ophthalmoscopy, retinoscopy, sigmoidoscopy, stereoscopy.

**-osily,** cozily, dozily, nosily, prosily, rosily.

**-osity,** atrocity, callosity, ferocity, gibbosity, gulosity, jocosity, monstrosity, nervosity, nodosity, pilosity, pomposity, porosity, precocity, rugosity, schistosity, spinosity, velocity, verbosity, vinosity, viscosity, zygosity; adiposity, animosity, bellicosity, curiosity, generosity, grandiosity, hideosity, lacrymosity, luminosity, nebulosity, otiosity, preciosity, reciprocity, scrupulosity, sensuosity, sinuosity, strenuosity, tortuosity, tuberosity, varicosity, virtuosity; anfractuosity, impetuosity, religiosity, voluminosity.

**-osophy,** philosophy, theosophy; anthroposophy.

**-otable,** notable, potable, quotable.

**-otany,** botany, cottony; monotony, neoteny; ethnobotany.

**-otary,** coterie, notary, rotary, votary; locomotory, prothonotary.

**-oteny.** See **-otany.**

**-oterie.** See **-otary.**

**-otherly,** brotherly, motherly, southerly.

**-otional,** motional, notional; devotional, emotional, promotional; unemotional.

**-otomy,** autotomy, dichotomy, leukotomy, lithotomy, lobotomy, phlebotomy, rhizotomy, vagotomy; craniotomy, hysterotomy, laparotomy, thoracotomy, tracheotomy; episiotomy, ovariotomy, pallidotomy.

**-otony.** See **-otany.**

**-ottery,** lottery, pottery, tottery.

**-ottony.** See **-otany.**

**-ountable,** countable, mountable; accountable, discountable, surmountable; insurmountable, unaccountable.

**-ourian.** See **-urian.**

**-ourier.** See **-urrier.**

**-outherly.** See **-otherly.**

**-ovable,** movable, provable; approvable, disprovable, immovable, improvable, removable, unprovable.

**-oyable,** deployable, employable, enjoyable; unemployable.

**-oyalty,** loyalty, royalty; disloyalty, viceroyalty.

**-ozily.** See **-osily.**

**-uable,** chewable, doable, suable, viewable; accruable, renewable, reviewable, nonrenewable.

**-ubious,** dubious, rubious.

**-ubrious,** lugubrious, salubrious.

**-ucculent.** See **-uculent.**

**-ucible,** crucible; deducible, educible, inducible, producible, reducible; irreducible, reproducible.

**-uctable,** conductible, constructable, deductible, destructible; indestructible, ineluctable, nondeductible, reconstructible.

**-uctible.** See **-uctable.**

**-uculent,** succulent, truculent.

**-udable,** deludable, excludable, extrudable, includable.

**-udity,** crudity, nudity.

**-uggaree.** See **-uggery.**

**-uggery,** buggery, puggaree, thuggery; humbuggery, skulduggery.

**-uitable.** See **-utable.**

**-uitous,** circuitous, fortuitous, gratuitous.

**-uity,** acuity, annuity, circuity, congruity, fatuity, fortuity, gratuity, tenuity, vacuity; ambiguity, assiduity, conspicuity, contiguity, continuity, exiguity, incongruity, ingenuity, innocuity, perpetuity, perspicuity, promiscuity, superfluity; discontinuity.

**-ulean,** Boolean, Julian; Acheulean, Apulian, cerulean, Herculean.

**-ulian.** See **-ulean.**

**-ulity,** credulity, garrulity, sedulity; incredulity.

**-umanous.** See **-uminous.**

**-umeral,** humeral, humoral, numeral, tumoral; Roman numeral; Arabic numeral.

**-umerous.** See **-umorous.**

**-umerus.** See **-umorous.**

**-uminate,** ruminate; acuminate, illuminate.

**-uminous,** luminous, numinous; albuminous, aluminous, bituminous, leguminous, quadrumanous, voluminous.

**-ummary.** See **-ummery.**

**-ummery,** flummery, mummery, summary, summery.

**-umoral.** See **-umeral.**

**-umorous,** humerus, humorous, numerous, tumorous; innumerous.

**-umulous.** See **-umulus.**

**-umulus,** cumulous, cumulus, tumulus; altocumulus, cirrocumulus, stratocumulus.

**-unary,** unary; buffoonery, festoonery, poltroonery, sublunary; superlunary.

**-unnery,** gunnery, nunnery.

**-uperate,** recuperate, vituperate.

**-urable,** curable, durable; endurable, incurable, insurable, nondurable, perdurable, procurable, securable; unindurable, uninsurable.

**-uralist,** muralist, pluralist, ruralist.

**-urative,** curative, durative; indurative.

**-urean.** See **-urian.**

**-urein.** See **-urian.**

**-ureous.** See **-urious.**

**-urety.** See **-urity.**

**-urgency.** See **-ergency.**

**-urgery,** perjury, surgery.

**-urgical,** surgical; liturgical, nonsurgical, postsurgical, theurgical; chemosurgical, cryosurgical, demiurgical, dramaturgical, metallurgical, microsurgical, neurosurgical.

**-urial,** curial, urial; manurial, mercurial, seigneurial, tenurial; entrepreneurial.

**-urian,** durian, Hurrian, murein; Arthurian, Asturian, centurion, decurion, Etrurian, Ligurian, Manchurian, Missourian, Silurian; epicurean.

**-uriant.** See **-urient.**

**-urient,** prurient; esurient, luxuriant, parturient.

**-urion.** See **-urian.**

**-urious,** curious, furious, spurious; injurious, luxurious, penurious, perjurious, sulfureous, usurious.

**-urity,** purity, surety; futurity, impurity, maturity, obscurity, security; immaturity, insecurity, prematurity; Social Security.

**-urnable,** burnable; discernable, returnable; indiscernable, unreturnable.

**-urpentine,** serpentine, turpentine.

**-urrian.** See **-urian.**

**-urrier,** courier, currier, furrier, hurrier, scurrier, worrier.

**-ursary,** bursary, cursory, mercery, nursery; day nursery; anniversary.

**-ursory.** See **-ursary.**

**-usable,** fusible, usable; abusable, confusable, diffusible, excusable, infusible, protrusible, reusable, transfusible, unusable; inexcusable.

**-uscular,** muscular; corpuscular, crepuscular, majuscular.

**-usible.** See **-usable.**

**-ustable.** See **-ustible.**
**-ustible,** trustable; adjustable, combustible; incombustible.
**-ustrious,** illustrious, industrious.
**-utable,** mutable, scrutable, suitable; commutable, computable, disputable, immutable, imputable, inscrutable, permutable, refutable, transmutable; executable, incommutable, incomputable, indisputable, irrefutable, prosecutable, substitutable.
**-utative,** mutative, putative; commutative, confutative, imputative, transmutative.
**-uteous,** beauteous, duteous, gluteus, luteous.
**-uteus.** See **-uteous.**
**-uticle,** cuticle; cosmeceutical, epicuticle, hermeneutical, nutraceutical, pharmaceutical.
**-utiful,** beautiful, dutiful.
**-utinous,** glutinous, mutinous.
**-utiny,** mutiny, scrutiny.
**-utionist,** devolutionist, elocutionist, evolutionist, revolutionist; redistributionist.
**-uvial,** fluvial, pluvial; alluvial, colluvial, diluvial, eluvial, exuvial; interfluvial.
**-uvian,** alluvion, diluvian, Peruvian, vesuvian, Vesuvian; postdiluvian; antediluvian.
**-uvion.** See **-uvian.**
**-yetal.** See **-ietal.**
**-yllable.** See **-illable.**
**-ymity.** See **-imity.**
**-yndicate.** See **-indicate.**
**-ynical.** See **-inical.**
**-yreal.** See **-erial.**
**-yria.** See **-eria.**
**-yrian.** See **-erian.**
**-yrical.** See **-irical.**
**-yrium.** See **-erium.**
**-ysical,** physical, quizzical; metaphysical.
**-ystery.** See **-istory.**
**-ystical.** See **-istical.**
**-yzable.** See **-izable.**

# Glossary of Poetic Terms

**accent,** the stress or emphasis placed on certain syllables, usually indicated by a mark (´) above the stressed syllable. An unaccented syllable is usually indicated by a short mark (˘) above the syllable. Example:

Hăd wé bŭt wórld ĕnóugh, ănd tíme

**alexandrine** (al′ig zan′drin), a line of verse consisting of six iambic feet. Example:

Ăll clád | ĭn Líncŏln gréen, | wĭth cáps | ŏf réd | ănd blúe |

**alliteration,** the repetition of the same consonant sound or sound group, especially in initial stressed syllables. Example:

The *s*oft *s*weet *s*ound of *S*ylvia's voi*c*e

**amphibrach** (am′fə brak′), a foot consisting of an unaccented syllable followed by an accented and an unaccented syllable. Example (the first three feet are amphibrachs):

Thĕ cláns ăre | ĭmpátĭent | ănd chíde thy̆ | dĕláy

**amphimacer** (am fim′ə sər), a foot consisting of an accented syllable followed by an unaccented syllable and an accented syllable. Example:

Cátch ă stár, | fállĭng fást |

**anapest** (an′ə pest′), a foot consisting of two unaccented syllables followed by one accented syllable. The adjective form is *anapestic.* Example:

Nĕvĕr héar | thĕ swĕet mú|sĭc ŏf spéech |

**assonance,** the use of identical vowel sounds in several words, often as a substitute for rhyme. Example:

Shr*i*nk h*i*s th*i*n essence like a r*i*veled flow'r

**ballad, 1.** a simple narrative poem of popular origin, composed in short stanzas, often of a romantic nature and adapted for singing. **2.** any poem written in such a style.

**ballade** (bə läd′, ba-), a poem consisting (usually) of three stanzas having an identical rhyme scheme, followed by an envoy. The final line of each stanza and the envoy are the same.

**ballad stanza,** a four-line stanza in which the first and third lines are in iambic tetrameter while the second and fourth lines are in iambic trimeter; the second and fourth lines rhyme. In a common variant, the alternate lines rhyme. Example:

They followed from the snowy bank
Those footsteps one by one,
Into the middle of the plank—
And further there was none.

**blank verse,** unrhymed verse in iambic pentameter, usually not in formal stanza units. Example:

Fair seed|time had | my soul, | and I | grew up
Fostered | alike | by beau|ty and | by fear
Much fa|vored in | my birth|place, and | no less
In that | belov|èd Vale | to which | erelong
We were | transplant|ed . . .

**caesura** (si zhŏŏr′ə), the main pause in a line of verse, usually near the middle. Example:

Know then thyself, || presume not God to scan

**cinquain** (sing kān′), a stanza consisting of five lines.

**consonance,** the use of an identical pattern of consonants in different words. Examples:

time – tome – team – tame
fall – fell – fill – full
slow – slew – slay – sly

**closed couplet,** a couplet whose sense is completed within its two lines. Example:

True wit is nature to advantage dress'd
What oft was thought, but ne'er so well express'd

**couplet,** two consecutive lines that rhyme. Example:

Touch her not scornfully;
Think of her mournfully

**dactyl** (dak′til), a foot consisting of one accented syllable followed by two unaccented syllables. The adjective form is *dactylic.* Example:

Cánnŏn tŏ | ríght ŏf thĕm |

**dimeter** (dim′i tər), a line of verse consisting of two feet.

**distich** (dis′tik), a couplet.

**elegy,** a subjective, meditative poem, especially one that expresses grief or sorrow.

**enjambment** (en jam′mənt). See **run-on line.**

**envoy** (en′voi), **1.** a short stanza concluding a poem in certain archaic metrical forms. **2.** a postscript to a poetical composition, sometimes serving as a dedication.

**epic,** a long narrative poem about persons of heroic stature and actions of great significance, and conforming to a rigid organization and form. Examples are the *Iliad* and the *Odyssey* of Homer, Virgil's *Aeneid, Beowulf,* and Milton's *Paradise Lost.*

**epigram,** a short and pithy remark, often in verse.

**feminine ending,** an ending on a word in which the final syllable is unaccented. Examples:

softness, careful, another, fairest

**foot,** the metrical unit in poetry, consisting of one accented syllable and one or more unaccented syllables. The most commonly found feet are the **iamb,** the **anapest,** the **dactyl,** and the **trochee.** The foot is usually marked in scansion by a vertical line. Example:

Ĭ ăm mónǀărch ŏf áll ǀ Ĭ sŭrvéy ǀ

**free verse,** verse that does not adhere to a fixed pattern of meter, rhyme, or other poetic conventions. Example:

The sea is calm tonight.  
The tide is full, the moon lies fair  
Upon the straits; on the French coast the light  
Gleams and is gone; the cliffs of England stand,  
Glimmering and vast, out in the tranquil bay.

**heptameter** (hep tamʹi tər), a line of verse consisting of seven feet.

**heroic couplet,** two consecutive rhyming lines in iambic pentameter. Example:

O thoughtless mortals! Ever blind to fate,  
Too soon dejected, and too soon elate.

**hexameter** (hek samʹi tər), a line of verse consisting of six feet.

**iamb** (ī′am), a foot consisting of one unaccented syllable followed by one accented syllable. The iamb is the most common metrical foot in English verse because it fits the natural pattern of English words. The adjective form is *iambic.* Example:

> The cur|few tolls | the knell | of part|ing day. |

Following is an example of *iambic pentameter:*

> Shall I | compare | thee to | a sum|mer's day?
> Thou art | more love|ly and | more tem|perate:
> Rough winds | do shake | the dar|ling buds | of May,
> And sum|mer's lease | hath all | too short | a date . . .

**internal rhyme,** a rhyme that occurs within a line. Example:

> So *slight* the *light*
> I could not see
> My *fair,* dear *Clair,*
> That it was thee.

**Italian sonnet,** a sonnet written in iambic pentameter with a rhyme scheme of *abba abba cde dde.* There are occasional variants of the rhyme scheme in the last six lines. The first eight lines (the *octave*) usually present a theme or premise; the last six lines (the *sestet*) present the conclusion or resolution. Also called **Petrarchan sonnet** after the 14th-century Italian poet.

**limerick,** a five-line poem using trimeters for the first, second, and fifth lines, and using dimeters for the third and fourth lines. It is usually written in a mixture of amphibrachs and iambs.

**lyric,** a poem with a particularly musical, songlike quality.

**macaronic verse** (mak′ə ron′ik), verse in which two or more languages are interlaced.

**masculine ending,** an ending on a word in which the final syllable is accented. Examples:

resound, avoid, reply, consume

**meter,** the basic rhythmic description of a line in terms of its accented and unaccented syllables. Meter describes the sequence and relationship of all the syllables of a line. Examples of meter are *iambic pentameter* and *dactylic hexameter.*

**monometer** (mə nom′i tər), a line of verse consisting of one foot.

**octave,** the first eight lines of an Italian sonnet.

**octometer** (ok tom′i tər), a line of verse consisting of eight feet.

**ode,** a poem, usually complicated in its metrical and stanzaic form, on a highly serious or particularly important theme.

**onomatopoeia** (on′ə mat′ə pē′ə), the quality of a word that imitates the sound it designates. Examples:

honk, bang, tintinnabulation

**ottava rima** (ō tä′və rē′mə), a stanza written in iambic pentameter with a rhyme scheme of *abababcc.*

**pastoral,** a poem dealing with simple rural life.

**pentameter** (pen tam′i tər), a line of verse consisting of five feet.

**Petrarchan sonnet.** See **Italian sonnet.**

**quatrain** (kwo′trān), a stanza consisting of four lines.

**refrain,** an expression, a line, or a group of lines that is repeated at certain points in a poem, usually at the end of a stanza.

**rhyme,** an identity of certain sounds in different words, usually the last words in two or more lines.

**rhyme royal,** a stanza written in iambic pentameter with a rhyme scheme of *ababbcc.*

**rhyme scheme,** the pattern of rhyme used in a stanza or poem. Rhyme scheme is indicated with letters: *abab, cdcd, abba, cddc,* etc. An example of *ababcc* rhyme scheme is:

I wandered lonely as a cloud *a*
That floats on high o'er vales and hills, *b*
When all at once I saw a crowd, *a*
A host, of golden daffodils; *b*
Beside the lake, beneath the trees, *c*
Fluttering and dancing in the breeze. *c*

**rondeau** (ron′dō), a poem consisting of three stanzas of five, three, and five lines, using only two rhymes throughout. A refrain appears at the end of the second and third stanzas.

**rondel** (ron′dl), a poem consisting (usually) of fourteen lines on two rhymes, of which four are made up of the initial couplet repeated in the middle and at the end (the second line of the couplet sometimes being omitted at the end).

**rondelet** (ron′dl et′), a poem consisting of five lines on two rhymes, the opening word or words being used after the second and fifth lines as an unrhymed refrain.

**run-on line,** a line of verse having a thought that carries over to the next line without a pause. Also called **enjambment.**

**scansion,** the process of indicating the pattern of accented and unaccented syllables in a line of verse.

**septet,** a stanza consisting of seven lines.

**sestet,** a group of six lines, especially those at the end of a sonnet.

**sestina** (se stē′nə), a poem of six six-line stanzas and a three-line envoy, originally without rhyme, in which each stanza repeats the end words of the lines of the first stanza, but in different order. The envoy uses these six end words again, three in the middle of the lines and three at the end.

**Shakespearean sonnet,** a sonnet written in iambic pentameter with a rhyme scheme of *abab cdcd efef gg.* The theme is often presented in the three quatrains, and the poem is concluded with the couplet.

**sight rhyme,** not a rhyme but two or more words which end in identical spelling. Examples:

though, bough, through

**slant rhyme,** an approximate rhyme, usually characterized by assonance or consonance.

**song,** a short and simple poem, usually suitable for setting to music.

**sonnet,** a poem consisting of fourteen lines in iambic pentameter. The most common forms are the **Italian sonnet** and the **Shakespearean sonnet.**

**Spenserian stanza,** a stanza consisting of eight iambic pentameter lines and a final iambic hexameter line, with a rhyme scheme of *ababbcbcc.* The Spenserian stanza is named after the 16th-century English poet, Edmund Spenser.

**spondee** (spon′dē), a foot consisting of two accented syllables. Example:

Spéak sóft, | stánd stíll |

**stanza,** a fixed pattern of lines or rhymes, or both.

**stress.** See **accent.**

**tercet** (tûr′sit), a group of three consecutive lines that rhyme together or relate to an adjacent tercet by rhymes.

**terza rima** (tert′sə rē′mə), a poem in iambic meter consisting of eleven-syllable lines arranged in tercets, the middle line of each tercet rhyming with the first and third lines of the following tercet. Dante's *Divine Comedy* is written in terza rima.

**tetrameter** (te tram′i tər), a line of verse consisting of four feet.

**trimeter** (trim′i tər), a line of verse consisting of three feet.

**triolet** (trē′ə lā′), an eight-line stanza in which line 1 recurs as line 4 and line 7, while line 2 recurs as line 8.

**triplet,** a stanza consisting of three lines.

**trochee** (trō′kē), a foot consisting of one accented syllable followed by one unaccented syllable. The adjective form is *trochaic.* Example:

Whý sŏ | pále ănd | wán fŏnd | lóvĕr

Príthĕe, | whý sŏ | pále?

**vers de société,** (ver də sô syā tā′), a light-spirited and witty poem, usually brief, dealing with some social fashion or foible.

**verse, 1.** one line of a poem. **2.** a group of lines in a poem. **3.** any form in which rhythm is regularized.

**villanelle** (vil′ə nel′), a poem consisting of (usually) five tercets and a final quatrain, using only two rhymes throughout.

**weak rhyme,** rhyme which falls upon the unaccented (or lightly accented) syllables.

# Notes